Technology, Work and Globalization

Series Editors
Leslie P. Willcocks
Department of Management
London School of Economics and Political Science
London, UK

Mary C. Lacity
Sam M. Walton College of Business
University of Arkansas
Fayetteville, AR, USA

The Technology, Work and Globalization series was developed to provide policy makers, workers, managers, academics and students with a deeper understanding of the complex interlinks and influences between technological developments, including information and communication technologies, work organizations and patterns of globalization. The mission of the series is to disseminate rich knowledge based on deep research about relevant issues surrounding the globalization of work that is spawned by technology.

More information about this series at
http://www.palgrave.com/gp/series/14456

François-Xavier de Vaujany
Anouck Adrot
Eva Boxenbaum • Bernard Leca
Editors

Materiality in Institutions

Spaces, Embodiment and Technology
in Management and Organization

palgrave
macmillan

Editors
François-Xavier de Vaujany
Université Paris-Dauphine PSL
Paris, France

Anouck Adrot
Université Paris-Dauphine PSL
Paris, France

Eva Boxenbaum
Department of Organization
Copenhagen Business School
Copenhagen, Denmark

Bernard Leca
ESSEC Business School
Cergy-Pontoise, France

Centre de gestion scientifique (CGS)
MINES ParisTech - PSL University
i3 UMR CNRS
Paris, France

Technology, Work and Globalization
ISBN 978-3-319-97471-2   ISBN 978-3-319-97472-9   (eBook)
https://doi.org/10.1007/978-3-319-97472-9

Library of Congress Control Number: 2018962548

This Palgrave Macmillan imprint is published by the registered company Springer Nature Switzerland AG.
The registered company address is: Gewerbestrasse 11, 6330 Cham, Switzerland

Foreword: Thinking About Materiality and Institutions

The intersection of materiality and institutions represents a profoundly underexamined facet of social life. To begin to understand this intersection, imagine being homeless:

> Among the throngs of commuters packed onto the subway, you are lying on a seat beside the door, a seat barely wide enough for one and a half riders to sit down. *Lying* isn't really the word; you are folded up, fakir style, somehow managing a horizontal position in a space explicitly demanding the vertical. Your knees are shoved up to your face, and your sneaker-clad feet are folded and twisted to fit around the bars at the end. Resting on top of your body is a large, somewhat tattered, overstuffed plastic bag. The people around you can tell very little about you: man or woman, race, age, although perhaps the flexibility needed to maintain this position suggests younger rather than older. They all see the same thing, a body folded impossibly small, a body marked by its position and its effects as a homeless body. (Adapted from Kawash 1998: 319)

Homelessness is not simply a description of a condition whereby one lacks access to ongoing, reliable housing—it is an institution constituted by sets of beliefs, norms, and values that define who is "homeless", attributes we associate with being homeless, rules about how the homeless may occupy and navigate urban spaces, images of what homeless people look like, and fantasies about how they got there. Homelessness as an institution enjoys an important, but somewhat ironic, relationship with the notion of inhabited institutions (Hallett and Ventresca 2006): people inhabit the institution of homelessness, and it inhabits them. Homelessness as an institution does not define homeless people, but it constructs harsh outlines of lives with which homeless people must cope. At the same time, homelessness inhabits people, and not just homeless people. It provides identities and "others" with whom we contrast ourselves—"if only", or "but by the grace of God". Despite influential research that highlighted the discursive construction of identities by homeless people (Snow and Anderson 1987), homelessness as an institution is profoundly material.

To understand the materiality of homelessness as an institution, consider the immensely helpful, conceptual organization of the present volume—the division of the material into artifacts and objects, space and time, digitality and information, and body and embodiment. The identification of dimensions of materiality is an important step in understanding how it infuses institutions and institutional processes, and one that has the potential, both to offer some specificity to intellectual discussions of materiality and to provide a basis for integration across research and writing. Staying with the institution of homelessness, we can see how it is infused with all these different dimensions of materiality, and how by considering them jointly we begin to appreciate the materiality of homelessness as an institution.

The role of artifacts and objects is crucial to constituting homelessness, not only by their lack—the lack of ongoing, reliable housing—but also by their presence. As you lay on the subway train, attempting to rest in a space hostile to repose, you experience only what you experience every day in myriad public locations, the design of which injects physical suffering into your life: ubiquitous park benches with arm rests spaced specifically to make sleeping difficult, and the profoundly more brutal installation of metal "anti homeless" spikes in areas frequented by homeless people (Rosenberger 2014). These material interventions into the lives of homeless people are not coincidental to the institution—they are constitutive of the moral evaluation of homelessness, and the subjugation of people who inhabit that institution.

Space and time are also core to the institution of homelessness, in obvious ways that involve the lack of control over space, as well as rules, laws, and norms that keep people without housing out of public spaces, a public that is defined as excluding the homeless (Deutsche 1998). Less obvious is the temporal quality of homelessness. Homelessness as an institution is defined in opposition to "the public", which is associated with the freedom not only to go home but to treat common spaces in ways that homelessness forbids. Homelessness thus invokes a battle not only over space but over time: "The question that daily confronts every homeless person is what to do with the day, which seems to stretch out infinitely and inexorably before you. … For the homeless, life could be described as endless tedium broken only by periods of physical and emotional suffering" (Snyder 1986: 110).

Although digitality and information may seem less closely connected to the institution of homelessness, they play an important role in constituting homelessness both as a concept and as a local object of action. The institution of homelessness depends on being able to "count" people who are homeless, but this is not trivial, either ontologically or epistemologically. Before counting homeless people, we need to decide what "homelessness" is, and consequently who counts as homeless. At its most restrictive, the concept describes people who are not "buying or paying mortgage or rent on a primary residence and living in it regularly" (Bogard 2001: 107), but Shelter (the advocacy NGO) says "You count as homeless if you are: staying with friends or family; staying in a hostel, night shelter or B&B; squatting (because you have no legal right to stay); at risk of violence or abuse in your home; living in poor conditions that affect your health; living apart from your family because you don't have a place to live together" (Shelter 2018). On top of these definitional challenges comes the epistemological political problem of counting, as illustrated by the wide variation in estimates of the US homeless population. In 1980, a housing-focused NGO estimated there were 2.2 million people lacking shelter; in 1984, the federal government put that number between 250,000 and 350,000; in 1987, the Urban Institute interviewed soup kitchen and shelter users in 178 cities to produce an estimate of 500,000–600,000 people living homeless. These numbers and their heterogeneity are anything but academic; how many people are understood to be homeless profoundly shapes local and global meanings of homelessness, particularly in relation to responsibility and the need for action (Lawrence and Dover 2015).

Finally, there is the body and embodiment. Kawash (1998) argues that the homeless body is not the homeless person. The homeless body is a part of homelessness as an institution—another brutal part through which homelessness is defined in opposition to the public. It represents "a mode of corporeality … through which the public struggles to define and secure itself as distinct and whole" (Kawash 1998: 324). One part of that struggle is the assignment of the marks of homelessness: unlike many domains of marginality, homeless people are not typically identified by skin colour or sex, but rather by "dirty or disheveled clothing, the possession of carts or bags of belongings, and particular activities such as panhandling and scavenging" (Kawash 1998: 324). And, whereas the public body is extensive—enmeshed and welcomed in public spaces, congregating at will, fed and satisfied through networks of commercial and freely available opportunities—the homeless body is constricted, "pressed closer and closer to the bodily boundary marked out by the skin" (Kawash 1998: 331). This constriction occurs in part through the institution's conception of feeding and toileting. Providers of food to homeless people are often known as "soup kitchens", a label not inconsequential to homelessness as an institution: although these places serve a variety of food, the label signals the institution's attitude to feeding homeless people, providing them with a food that is "a texture more than sustenance" (Kawash 1998: 332). The institutional cycle completes itself, since the "less food the body consumes, the less waste it produces" (Kawash 1998: 331–332). Homelessness as an institution has led to the disappearance of public toilets in many large cities, with toilet facilities in coffee shops taking up the slack and further demarcating between the public (consumers) and homeless people.

Homelessness as an institution is in all these ways material, and its materiality is consequential for every person inhabiting that institution, whether homeless or not. It is not unique in this regard, of course, and that is the point. All institutions are similarly material, though each in distinctive ways that shapes both the institution and our experience of it. Without a thorough deconstruction of the materiality of institutions, we are left with an imaginary world made up only of ideas, thoughts, beliefs, and the texts through which those are shared. But our institutions are so much more than that. The academic fascination with the cognitive and discursive dimensions of institutions may represent a pathology more directly traceable to our own working lives, where the written and spoken work prevail, than to the worlds we claim to examine. Many of the institutions that operate in worlds outside of universities may not be cognitive or discursive at their core, even if those remain important dimensions; instead, the material may be the most central, powerful, facet of many institutions—the part of institutions that most people who inhabit them recognize and respect.

The present volume provides not just a step forward in the exploration of materiality and institutions, but a foundation for what could and should become a long wave of research and writing in this area. Exploring the intersection of materiality and institutions is of immediate importance for both theoretical and practical reasons. Theoretically, the study of institutions has reached the point where the dominant frameworks—institutional logics and institutional work—are in danger of stagnation, and thus the whole institutional tradition is in serious need of new intellectual energy. The study of materiality and institutions represents one of the most promising sources of that energy. Integrating materiality into institutional research opens up a wide array of new questions and issues, as illustrated by this volume: understanding the role of materiality in the establishment and maintenance of institutions; how institutions are constituted materially and how materials are constituted in and through institutions; how and why actors work with specific materials in the course of institutional work; and the material bases of institutional logics. Practically, the integration of materiality into institutional studies may be our best opportunity yet to advance the relevance of our research beyond the academic community. As illustrated by the case of homelessness, understanding the intersection of materiality and institutions could provide managers, policy makers, government agents, activists, and citizens with tools for change that go beyond traditional discursive and relational strategies.

So, this is not The Matrix. We live in a material world—one in which every thought, feeling, action, relationship, and especially every institution exists in material form, whether as biophysical bodily processes, sounds and marks, actions of bodies and built forms, or physical structures. Every bit of every life. Every second of every day for every person that is or was is a material second—lived in, among, and as a physical entity. The materiality of social life is not only universal, but profound. To the degree that one can sensibly talk about the possibilities and impossibilities of social life, one is talking about the capacities and limits of the material world. What we can do, know, and be is ultimately determined by those material capacities and limits. But, we don't generally operate at those limits. We operate within the opportunities and constraints that emerge from the interplay and co-constitution of the material and the social. When we talk about the challenges we face in our lives or in our societies, what we mean are the stubborn combinations of physical properties, social networks, personal aims, cultural meanings, and historical imaginations that can only be addressed by exploring and understanding the meeting points of materiality and institutions.

Saïd Business School, University of Oxford   Thomas B. Lawrence
Oxford, UK
June 20, 2018

References

Bogard, C. J. (2001). Advocacy and enumeration: Counting homeless people in a suburban community. *American Behavioral Scientist, 45*(1), 105–120.

Deutsche, R. (1998). *Evictions: Art and spatial politics*. MIT Press.

Hallett, T., & Ventresca, M. J. (2006). Inhabited institutions: Social interactions and organizational forms in Gouldner's "Patterns of industrial bureaucracy." *Theory and Society, 35*(2), 213–236.

Kawash, S. (1998). The homeless body. *Public Culture, 10*(2), 319–339.

Lawrence, T. B., & Dover, G. (2015). Place and institutional work: Creating housing for the hard-to-house. *Administrative Science Quarterly, 60*(3), 371–410.

Rosenberger, R. (2014, June 19). How cities use design to drive homeless people away. *The Atlantic*. https://www.theatlantic.com/business/archive/2014/06/how-cities-use-design-to-drive-homeless-people-away/373067/

Shelter. (2018, April 3). What is homelessness? *Shelter England.* http://england. shelter.org.uk/housing_advice/homelessness/rules/what_is_homelessness

Snow, D. A., & Anderson, L. (1987). Identity work among the homeless: The verbal construction and avowal of personal identities. *American Journal of Sociology, 92*(6), 1336–1371.

Snyder, M. (1986). Life on the streets. In M. E. Hombs & M. Snyder (Eds.), *Homelessness in America: A forced march to nowhere* (pp. 107–118). Washington, DC: Community for Creative Non-violence.

Acknowledgements

This book is based on a selection of thoroughly revised papers presented in the context of the sixth Organizations, Artifacts & Practices (OAP) workshop, held in Lisbon in July 2016. This international event gathered 80 leading management and organization scholars at the Nova School of Business & Economics. For more information about OAP, see http://workshopoap.dauphine.fr.

Contents

List of Figures

List of Tables

1

Introduction: How Can Materiality Inform Institutional Analysis?

François-Xavier de Vaujany, Anouck Adrot, Eva Boxenbaum, and Bernard Leca

Introduction: Materiality in Institutions

In recent years, scholars of organizations and management have embraced the "material turn" in the social sciences (Boxenbaum et al. 2018; Leonardi et al. 2012; Carlile et al. 2013a, b; de Vaujany and Mitev 2013;

F.-X. de Vaujany (✉) • A. Adrot
Université Paris-Dauphine PSL, Paris, France
e-mail: Francois-Xavier.deVAUJANY@dauphine.fr; Anouck.adrot@dauphine.fr

E. Boxenbaum
Department of Organization, Copenhagen Business School,
Copenhagen, Denmark

Centre de gestion scientifique (CGS), MINES ParisTech - PSL University, i3
UMR CNRS, Paris, France
eb.ioa@cbs.dk

B. Leca
ESSEC Business School, Cergy-Pontoise, France
e-mail: bernard.leca@essec.edu

© The Author(s) 2019   1
F.-X. de Vaujany et al. (eds.), *Materiality in Institutions*, Technology, Work and
Globalization, https://doi.org/10.1007/978-3-319-97472-9_1

Robichaud and Cooren 2013). The material turn seeks to investigate and theorize the unique roles that materiality, including bodies, artifacts and technologies, play in social and organizational dynamics, such as their enabling and constraining influences on a variety of organizational phenomena. The attention to materiality is adding a novel and exciting layer of analysis to scholarship in organization and management theory, which—like the social science more broadly—has been dominated by cognitive and verbal perspectives for several decades (Barad 2003; De Vaujany and Mitev 2015). The integration of materiality is helping to shed light on many organizational and managerial phenomena that were previously neglected because our theories and methods were ill-equipped to capture them. In recent years, several branches of organization and management theory have started to engage with the material turn. Some scholarly communities were created around a shared interest in formulating theoretical accounts and developing empirical methods to decipher how materiality interacts with cognition, discourse and/or behavior in organizational dynamics (Carlile et al. 2013b; de Vaujany et al. 2014; Leonardi et al. 2012; de Vaujany and Mitev 2013).

In line with this view, scholars from multiple subdisciplines have highlighted the need for a more profound consideration of materiality within the areas of organizational communication (Castor 2016; Cooren et al. 2012; Vásquez and Plourde 2017), management of information systems (Robey et al. 2013), and management and organization studies (MOS) (Boxenbaum et al. 2018; Carlile et al. 2013a, b; de Vaujany and Mitev 2015). The objective is not only to grasp tangible, yet overlooked, aspects of materiality, but also to increase the empirical richness of scholarly investigation (Faraj and Azad 2012), in particular, to account better for visible dimensions of materiality in its literal sense (Carlile et al. 2013a; Vásquez and Plourde 2017). This turn to studying more tangible objects relates to growing voices from MOS that question discourses as primary analytical objects for research in MOS (Carlile et al. 2013b; Leonardi et al. 2012; Mitev and de Vaujany 2013; Orlikowski 2007). Gestures, pictures, social media, architectures and spaces are as performative as the verbal texts that often surround them. The heuristic journey to materiality has been frustrating so far due to the separation between the material and discursive worlds (Castor 2016; Cooren et al. 2012; Vásquez and

Plourde 2017) and, in our view, due to the challenges related to investigating materiality without a prior discussion of its methodological, epistemological and ontological underpinnings.

The rising interest in materiality within MOS manifests also in conjunction with the fact that institutional theories have previously paid only limited attention to materiality. Institutions represent a dominant topic of study within MOS and have a pervasive impact on a large spectrum of organizational phenomena. They shape the definition of an organization's mission (DiMaggio and Powell 1991), regulate relationships between organizations (DiMaggio and Powell 1983; Suchman 1995) and contribute either positively or negatively to an organization's success (Meyer and Rowan 1977). They also deeply influence the sustainability of an organizational system (Merton 1938), if not its survival, through trust repairing (Bachmann et al. 2015), role definition (Abdelnour et al. 2017) and complex integration mechanisms (Jourdan et al. 2017). Because institutions correspond to a core matter in organizational life, research on institutions has been attracting a significant proportion of analytical attention within the MOS scholarly community.

Past institutional research has emphasized the discursive and ideational views of institutions and institutional dynamics (Boxenbaum et al. 2016, 2018; Jones et al. 2013; Meyer et al. 2018; de Vaujany et al. 2014). As a result, the analysis of how objects and artifacts contribute to institutional dynamics has been neglected. To better integrate the material dimension of institutions, scholars are increasingly turning their interest toward materiality. Examples of research on the material turn in institutional theory include the material dimensions of institutional work (Lawrence et al. 2013), sensemaking (Stigliani and Ravasi 2012), legitimacy (Puyou and Quattrone 2018), and organizational responses to institutional pressure (Raaijmakers et al. 2018). Other examples include the role of space in organizational legitimation (Jones and Massa 2013; Lawrence and Dover 2015; Lawrence et al. 2013; de Vaujany et al. 2014), bodies and institutions (Martí and Fernández 2013; Stowell and Warren 2018), and the role of technology in institutional dynamics (Petrakaki et al. 2016).

Institutional scholars are also calling for an integration of material dimensions (Boxenbaum et al. 2016; de Vaujany et al. 2014; Jones et al. 2013) into institutional scholarship. Accordingly, institutional scholars have begun to incorporate artifacts, bodies, gestures, movements, architecture, and buildings in their methodological procedures (see Boxenbaum et al. 2018). Further integration of materiality into institutional theory is likely to not only renew the theory but also broaden our understanding of materiality within social and organizational settings. For instance, recent research suggests that elaborating an institutional approach to materiality leads scholars to embrace a more historical and temporal view of artifacts and movements, including how actors embody symbolic aspects that resonate with broader institutional dimensions (Arena and Douai, this volume; Carlile et al. 2013a, b; Stowell and Warren 2018; de Vaujany et al. 2014).

In this introduction, we discuss three aspects of the ongoing engagement of institutional research with materiality, which collectively represent the specific approach taken in this book. First, we discuss the way the increasing attention to materiality is structuring how institutional researchers think about the main conceptual components of institutional theory, in particular in relation to the two major substreams of institutional research: institutional logics and institutional work. Second, we consider how this material turn opens new questions related to the deeper conceptual layers of institutional inquiry, that is, questions related to the articulation of ontological, epistemological, methodological and, eventually, theoretical positions in institutional theory. This deeper approach stimulates institutional researchers to address the inherent diversity of materiality. Finally, we introduce an encompassing view of materiality within institutional analysis in the form of a reflexive journey, which points to four prominent aspects of materiality: artifacts and objects, space and time, digitality and information, bodies and embodiment. We then detail how the different chapters of the book exemplify the engagements of institutional research with materiality.

Increasing Attention to Materiality from Institutional Researchers

Institutional scholars have in recent years drawn on materiality to investigate institutional phenomena that deeply influence organizational dynamics. In opening this line of inquiry, many institutionalists have called for an extended investigation of how materiality impacts core theoretical concepts, such as institutional logics and institutional work.

Institutional logics are understood as collective practices and beliefs that root a system wider than an organization and shape the cognition and action of its members at a field level (Friedland and Alford 1991; Ocasio 1997). Institutional logics deeply impact the behavior of organizations and their members (Thornton et al. 2012) by "organizing cognitive frameworks that provide social actors with 'rules of the game' (...) and that operate, often implicitly, as practical guides for action" (Jones et al. 2013, p. 52).

An organization's pattern of development can be deeply influenced by institutional logics combined with local meanings (Binder 2007). More specifically, institutional logics allow groups of actors to question, redefine, refine or legitimate identities, assumptions, practices and so on. By doing so, they frame material, practical and symbolic experiences in a dynamic fashion (Friedland and Alford 1991). Previous research has emphasized that rather than being mere "cultural dopes", actors can use logics as a "tool kit" (Swidler 1986) and employ different logics at different times to achieve certain goals, such as making legitimacy claims. Scholarship has thus increasingly emphasized the importance of exploring how logics are enacted on the ground, assuming that individuals use them in their daily enactments (Thornton et al. 2012).

A traditional method to empirically study institutional logics in organizations is to trace the verbal discourse of organizational members (Reay and Jones 2015). However, some authors have argued that verbal discourse, including rhetoric, is not the predominant expression of institutional logics. On the contrary, institutional logics guide material practices, which can impact "material subsistence, time and space, organization and meaning provided to social reality" (Thornton, Ocasio 1999, p. 804). Therefore, to study how institutional logics permeate everyday practices, scholars have recently begun to acknowledge the need to focus on the material, temporal and spatial dimension of practices and routines as they unfold in the everyday life of organizations (Thornton et al. 2012; Smets et al. 2012).

Institutional theorists are only beginning to take into account the most vivid dimensions of materiality. So far, the material dimension of logics has mostly been conceptualized (and studied) as practices or structures rather than as actual physical artifacts (Friedland and Alford 1991; Jones et al. 2013), which remain "inert and invisible" (Friedland 2012, p. 590). One can infer the need to examine precisely how institutional logics are sustained or changed through material means (Jones et al. 2013).

The increasing interest in materiality also impacts how authors account for institutional work. Institutional work refers to the "purposive action of organizations and individuals aimed at creating, maintaining, and disrupting institutions" (Lawrence and Suddaby 2006, p. 215). This topic has traditionally been studied through the lenses of actors' discursive strategies, social positions and relational strategies and, to a lesser extent, their use of resources (for a review, see Battilana et al. 2009). While authors acknowledge the importance of materiality (Lawrence et al. 2013; Lawrence and Suddaby 2006), only a few studies have so far analyzed how materiality enables institutional work (Blanc and Huault 2014; Jones and Massa 2013; Lanzara and Patriotta 2007; Patriotta et al. 2011).

These works consider the complex interrelations between the forms of institutional work and materiality. Exploring how Frank Lloyd Wright's Unity Temple became a consecrated exemplar of modern architecture, Jones and Massa (2013) show that the material architecture instantiates ideas by making them "real", stimulating actors to engage in subsequent struggles regarding this reality and the ideas it encompasses. Interestingly, Jones and Massa suggest that it might be in materiality that authors should look for elements that may account for the viscosity of institutional work. A paradox of current research on institutional work is that institutional work is presumed, theoretically speaking, to be difficult and most likely to fail (DiMaggio 1988), yet almost all the documented cases are successful accounts of surprisingly skillful actors who shape social constructions through discourse. Recent research on institutional work suggests that the integration of the material dimension reveals that social reality is far less malleable than previously assumed, showing instead that institutional work needs to address material aspects such as space (Dover and Lawrence 2010), architecture (de Vaujany and Vaast 2016; Rowland and Rojas 2006; Jones and Massa 2013) or, at a more mundane level, existing artifacts and how they affect intra-organizational institutional change (Raviola and Norbäck 2013). This research suggests a certain viscosity of materiality that is different from the symbolic or discursive dimensions of institutions (Boxenbaum et al. 2016).

Another aspect of the institutionalist literature is how actors use artifacts in their institutional work to diffuse their institutional project (e.g., Gawer and Phillips 2013; Hargadon et Douglas 2001). In this view, artifacts do not offer resistance to institutional work for change but are mobilized in favor of this institutional work (e.g., Lanzara and Patriotta 2007). Actors shape artifacts into vehicles conveying their institutional project. Eventually, those different uses raise questions regarding the ontology of artifacts, which is a current topic of debate within institutional theory. At the moment, there is not a single privileged approach to materiality in institutional theory, nor is it clear whether different studies of institutional work share a common view of materiality.

As a case in point, Monteiro and Nicolini (2015, p. 63) argue for the importance of including materiality in institutional analyses, suggesting that it will yield "richer explanations [...] that are closer to the reality of social processes". They ground their work in practice theory and explore how material entities take part in institutional work in the context of prizes. They highlight the embeddedness of materiality in institutional processes, such as mimicry, education, and the reconfiguration of normative networks that were previously viewed as largely a-material. Paraphrasing Suddaby (2010, p. 17), Monteiro and Nicolini (2015) argue that the traditional ideal that "institutional work, of course, is conducted by individuals" should be revised and read as "institutional work, of course, is shared between human and materials entities, although how this happens is an issue that needs to be explored empirically on a case-by-case basis" (p. 74). If we consider the traditional definition of institutional work as purposive action, do artifacts then have purposes of their own? This stance, often associated with the social science of technology scholars, exemplifies the diversity of ontological and epistemological questions that are raised in conjunction with the integration of materiality in institutional theory.

To conclude on institutional work, materiality offers a window into how institutions are being maintained and transformed through everyday activities. This process appears to be jointly human and material in nature (Monteiro and Nicolini 2015), embodied (Merleau-Ponty 1945/2003; Stowell and Warren 2018) and central to professional activities and occupational communities (Mäkitalo 2012). More generally, materiality is grounded into numerous performative mediations and instrumentations that potentially lie at the heart of an institutional analysis (Boxenbaum et al. 2016; Lawrence et al. 2013). Many non-neutral, material elements are involved in the maintenance of particular institutions, such as technologies (e.g., algorithms performing and extending regulations) and the enactment of spatial arrangements (e.g., choice of an open space as a location for future activities). Institutional research has explored this topic through historical analysis, ethnographies and auto-ethnographies, eliciting the micro-foundations of institutions (de Vaujany and Vaast 2016; Delacour and Leca 2017). This line of inquiry has resulted in fine-grained taxonomies of legitimacy claims grounded, for instance, in the use of spatial arrangements in institutional work.

The integration of materiality in institutional inquiry facilitates the identification of practices and dynamics that would otherwise have remained overlooked (see e.g., Dacin et al. 2010). However, materiality does not restrict itself to a simple concept, but opens up the question of what materiality *actually* is, which also implies a careful look at all its implications (Carlile et al. 2013b). A reflexive consideration of materiality in institutional studies compels researchers to adopt an exploratory and reflexive posture, which represents a double challenge. First of all, they confront the need to *go deeper* into the concept of materiality, which literally means the need to appropriate the deeper conceptual layers of the material turn. However, the challenge is not only vertical but also horizontal, as scholars also need to make sense of the increasing diversity of institutional studies on materiality. The rationale underlying this book project stems from the consideration of these two challenges and calls for a reflexive journey through materiality in institutions, both vertically and horizontally.

Digging into the Deeper Layers of the Material Turn

How we define materiality matters crucially from the epistemological and ethical perspectives (Carlile et al. 2013a). Knowledge created with respect to materiality builds on scholars' capacity to define and discuss its ontology and specify the methods used in an empirical investigation. How scholars define materiality influences society through decision-making in relation to empowerment, work policies, human resource management, innovation, and so on. From this perspective, materiality is not restricted to an intellectual challenge but also plays a significant role in shaping the future of our societies, either by offering opportunities or by constraining organizations and their stakeholders. In line with this view, international scholars have called for increased reflexivity on materiality (Carlile et al. 2013a; Leonardi 2013). Such reflexivity is all the more important in light of the essential role that institutions play in society.

The introduction of materiality in institutional studies is generating questions about the theoretical status of materiality and the position it occupies—or should occupy—relative to other analytical components, such as verbal discourse (Hardy et al. 2003), and the social positions of actors (Battilana 2006). Materiality prompts scholars to engage with broader theoretical and epistemological issues as they contemplate which approaches to materiality are the most compatible with institutional theory (e.g., Jones et al. 2013; Boxenbaum et al. 2016). Relatedly, institutional scholars are struggling with how to study materiality empirically, given that commonly used research methods are adapted primarily to the analysis of verbal discourse (Höllerer et al. 2018; Jancsary et al. 2016). If materiality is to become fully integrated into institutional theory, then the theoretical formulations of materiality must fit conceptually with the ontological assumptions of institutional theory. Moreover, alignment is needed between the methods that scholars use to study materiality and the epistemological assumptions that underpin such methods. In other words, the introduction of materiality into institutional theory depends on the alignment of deeper layers. This alignment is important to ensure consistency within, and across different streams of research within institutional theory, an important quality indicator of theoretical development (David and Bitektine 2009; Suddaby and Greenwood 2009; Greenwood et al. 2008, 2017).

The achievement of consistency between theory, method, epistemology and ontology is a complicated undertaking. Efforts to align these intertwined dimensions of research can be approached in multiple ways. We conceptualize them as layers, similarly to the multiple levels that compose a building. We further suggest, as indicated with arrows in Fig. 1.1, that efforts to align these layers are not a unidirectional undertaking but one that may work in both directions. Regardless of the direction, researchers need, we argue, to articulate their positions consistently across these layers to justify the pertinence and validity of their methods, and the relevance and salience of their findings for institutional theory development. Such requirements apply not only to the introduction of materiality in institutional theory but also to theory development more broadly, far beyond the specific topic of materiality.

In the sections below, we briefly define and then illustrate the layers in Fig. 1.1. We insist on the importance of establishing solid links between those layers and of aiming for consistency across all the layers. Our treatment of this topic is exploratory and excludes an extensive discussion of different positions that institutional researchers may have on the appropriate content of each layer. The aim of this book is to explore the relationship between layers case by case, and to reflect collectively upon the conceptual foundations of different approaches to the study of materiality in institutional theory.

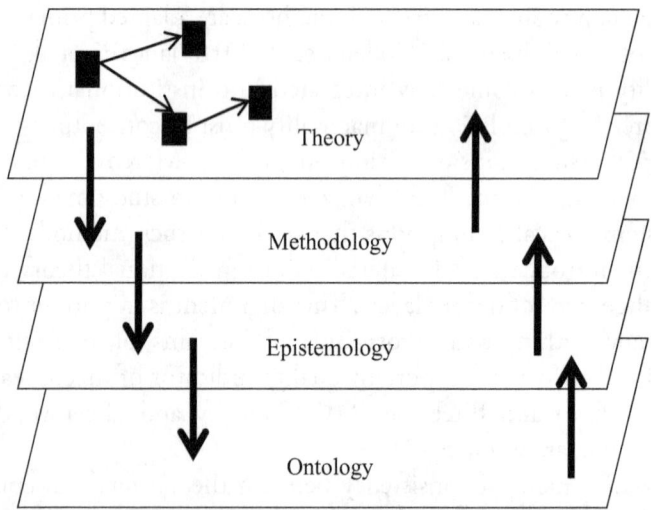

Fig. 1.1 Conceptual layers of theory, methodology, epistemology and ontology

Ontology

Ontology relates to the researcher's assumptions regarding what exists and the nature of the things that exist. Institutional researchers mostly share an ontological position whereby they consider that social structures are social constructions that emerge from interactions among actors and eventually become "taken for granted" (Berger and Luckmann 1967). Yet, within this initial, broadly constructivist approach, substantially different approaches exist (see Edwards 2016 for a more complete discussion). For instance, institutionalists are likely to disagree on the nature of agency. Some will see in it a social construction and the outcome of an institutionalization process, prompting them to engage in a deconstruction of the naturalized notion of individual actorhood (Frank and Meyer 2002). In contrast, others will consider agency to have an ontological reality of its own and explore how actors participate in institutional processes (DiMaggio 1988). Incidentally, discussing what exists, and what its nature is, also implies an agreement on the definitions of the notions used. A potential challenge here is that authors use the same notion to refer to different, sometimes unrelated or even contradictory, social phenomena. For instance, Friedland (2012) points to different definitions of the notion of institutional logics. Contradictory and competing definitions of the same notion are likely to impede theory development, unless authors reflect on the ontology that underpins their chosen definitions. Different ontological positions correspond to different understandings of reality and eventually to different research foci, reflecting a very large spectrum of philosophical streams of work. If scholars are inconsistent in their definition of materiality, in terms of mixing and matching elements from the large spectrum of philosophical perspectives, they might struggle to establish logical ties between their methodology, ontology and the nature of the knowledge created.

Epistemology

Whereas the ontological stance relates to what exists (according to the researcher), epistemology relates to what can be known through research and science, and how it can (best) be known. As such, the epistemological stance sets the boundaries for what can be known through research, respectively, for what cannot be examined through this form of inquiry. In addition, epistemology relates to what sort of knowledge can be achieved through different forms and techniques of scholarly inquiry. For instance, epistemology is at play when researchers claim that the knowledge produced is either objective or subjective, that is, whether it results from an act of interpretation (Morgan and Smircich 1980). Although ontology and epistemology differ from one another, strong connections exist between the assumptions we make about the nature of reality (i.e., our ontological stance) and how we seek to gain valid knowledge about that reality (i.e., our epistemological stance), including the kind of materiality we encounter in our inquiry (i.e., our situated position). In fact, some authors prefer to use the notion of ontogenesis instead of ontology to stress that the existence of things is intertwined with our knowing about them (see e.g., Ingold 2011). Scholars have different convictions about how to best generate knowledge, for instance, through dialogue, observations or introspection.

Methodology

Methodology refers to the design of research and the methods used to analyze data. The methodology is often the only visible indicator of the deeper layers that readers see when browsing through a research paper. Methodology reveals, often implicitly, the ontological and epistemological positions that underpin a research paper. For instance, assumptions about reality (i.e., ontology) will have an impact on the selection of research methods, such as when researchers conceptualize discourse as the source of institutions (as their ontological stance) and consequently undertake discourse analysis to study institutions (Philipps et al. 2004). In the same way, our epistemological assumptions about how to acquire valid knowledge about reality will have an impact on the methodology that we adopt to gain insight into our object of study.

Theory

The upper layer of our framework, depicted in Fig. 1.1, expresses the theory construction itself. It represents the theoretical relationships that we claim between materiality and other conceptual components of institutional theory. It may be our theoretical starting point for inquiry, or it may emerge as the outcome of a research study as its theoretical contribution. In the latter case, the theoretical relationships are fundamentally shaped by the methodological, epistemological and ontological stances that scholars adopt, more or less consciously, in conducting the research study. The validity of the theoretical contributions depends on the internal consistency of the ontological assumptions, epistemological foundations and methodological approaches, as well as on their compatibility with positions previously adopted in, and characteristic of, institutional theory.

The Importance of Attending to Alignment

The purpose of this book is to illuminate the deeper conceptual layers of institutionalist studies of materiality, draw attention to the importance of their internal alignment and discuss the relevance of different stances for institutional theory. This topic has eluded previous theorizing about materiality in institutional theory, yet it is essential for the credibility and the utility of this emerging stream of research. In fact, extant theoretical formulations, methodologies, epistemological stances and ontological assumptions in institutional theory inspire current research on materiality and shape researchers' approach to the nature of reality and to the creation of knowledge about reality. Significant reflexivity is required if the introduction of materiality into institutional theory is to succeed in substantially advancing institutional theoretical development. In addition to the need for reflexivity related to the conceptual layers of institutional studies of materiality, the inherent diversity of materiality is also challenging for institutional researchers.

Diversity, Emerging Topics and Related Challenges

Diversity among institutional studies on materiality is expanding quickly, which represents an additional challenge for scholars, one that calls them back to the essential questions of what materiality is and how to investigate and theorize it. Diversity does not only concern ontological approaches to the materiality, methodology and epistemological stances but also to the different types of materiality investigated. This book covers four interrelated forms of materiality, namely artifacts and objects, digitality and information, space and time, body and embodiment. These types of materiality are all on the rise in institutional inquiry.

The diverse forms of materiality mean that institutional researchers rely on a broad range of empirical phenomena to develop theory, including campuses, factories, clothes, rooms, webcams, records, protocols, robots, physical bodies or yet other material phenomena. As an illustration, Lanzara and Patriotta (2007) analyze how engineering knowledge becomes institutionalized through an unbounded spectrum of artifacts, including cars, assembly lines, textbooks and spaces. Likewise, Marti and Fernandez (2013) analyze segregation through the growing restrictions that applied to Jewish people's use of artifacts, such as telephones, shops, avenues and clothes, during the Holocaust.

Exploring the inner diversity of the material dimension of institutions has two major implications for future institutional studies. First of all, taking into account the various instances of materiality highlights the power it exerts in institutional dynamics. For instance, institutional logics diffuse through a seemingly unlimited set of artifacts, objects, bodies, gestures, spaces and so on. Secondly, an exploratory approach to materiality facilitates cross-level analyses and favors a more holistic understanding of its role in institutional matters (Huault et al. 2015) by not restricting it to one single type of artifact. A more holistic analysis of institutional dynamics also evidences individuals' meaningful role in institutional work and institutional change by drawing attention to the resources that they already have, or can gain access to. This explorative approach is well suited for a deeper investigation of what materiality is and how to approach it in institutional studies. At the same time, it can be conducive to focus explicitly on a particular form of materiality rather than trying to apprehend materiality at large, which is why we divide the book into four types of materiality.

Artifacts and Objects

First of all, *artifacts and objects* have attracted the attention of institutional scholars for more than a decade. Institutionalists use the generic term of "artifact" to signify a large spectrum of objects and articulate different institutional effects of artifacts. For instance, Miettinen and Virkkunen (2005) highlight the role of objectification that artifacts play in institutional disruption. Arguing that routine cannot solely account for changes, they advocate for institutional scholars to consider alternate ontologies to build knowledge about the role of artifacts as epistemic objects in institutional disruption. They raise the ontological question of how to draw the boundaries of an artifact from a methodological perspective. Interestingly, Lanzara and Patriotta (2007) adopt a methodology that is adapted to an ontological conception of artifacts as unbounded, reflecting a long-standing tradition in Actor-Network studies. Such an ontological stance is quite unfamiliar in institutional studies, which favor a more bounded conception of artifacts.

Space and Time

Organizations and collective activities have been conceptualized from multiple ontological stances, including topological (Amaeshi and Amao 2009), spatial (Kornberger and Clegg 2004), cognitive and rhetorical (Orlitzky 2011), as well as temporal (Barley and Tolbert 1997; Giddens 1984; Schatzki 2010). Space and spatial practices are expected to convey and embody institutions and organizations (Lefebvre and Nicholson-Smith 1991). Time represents a primary institutional space in our daily lives (Merleau-Ponty 2003), which manifests increasingly in institutional analysis (Granqvist and Gustafsson 2016; Pittz et al. 2017). Time, temporality and temporal work are intricately related to physical spaces and embodied practices (Czarniawska 2004; Schatzki 2010; Grosz 1995).

Time itself can be seen as a materialization as much as materiality can be seen as a temporal process (de Vaujany et al. 2014). From this perspective, *space and time* correspond to a second major form of materiality that institutional studies investigate. In recent years, the conceptualization of space has become significantly enriched and sophisticated. For instance, through an ethnography of institutional work, Lawrence and Dover (2015) explored the role of spaces as signifiers and analyzed the symbolic resources comprised in spaces. From their perspective, a space does not only contain but also constitutes meaningful objects or bodies. Objects and people help spaces gain boundaries that can become institutionalized. However, as a signifier, space can also convey additional meanings that may contradict boundaries and lend support to competing institutional logics. In line with this view, Souto-Otero and Beneito-Montagut (2013) highlight that digital spaces may embody active users that challenge established institutions.

Time can also be conceptualized as a performed and materialized space in everyday activities and technologies (de Vaujany et al. 2014). Recently, some institutionalists have started to draw on a pragmatist philosophy to conceptualize the role of time in institutionalization processes (Granqvist and Gustafsson 2016; Pitz 2017; Reinecke and Ansari 2015). Granqvist and Gustafsson (2016, p. 1009) stress, for instance, that "research has overlooked how temporality, as a negotiated organizing of time, shapes institutional processes, despite the fact that timing, duration, and tenor of relationships are their foundational elements". Time represents a meaningful set of happenings that require continuous activities, flesh and embodiments, visibilities and invisibilities (Merleau-Ponty, 1945/2013, 1964). Sometimes, time is viewed as the archetype of an institution, giving order and seriality to all our happenings as a kind of meta-event (Merleau-Ponty 2003).

The study of spaces and time can be approached from an unlimited spectrum of ideas, events, processes, bodies, artifacts, events, objects and other data sources. Despite being a source of heuristic richness, space can also be conceptualized as a labyrinthic experience (Bachelard 1938), prompting methodological choices, such as the extent to which space should be considered as a set of boundaries or rather approached as a set of bodies and their production.

Digitality and Information

Orlikowski and Barley (2001) advocated for scholars to further investigate the role of technology in institutions. In the same vein, Pinch (2008) called for thorough investigation of the role of technology and its materiality in institutional matters. Since then, institutional studies have increasingly examined digitality and information as a form of materiality and included these features in their definitions of an artifact. In this book we view digitality as the digital culture, semiosis and practices related to information. In fact, *digital(ity)* is currently emerging as a relevant, but also challenging, topic for scholars interested in artifacts and materiality. While Leonardi (2010) encourages scholars to address challenges relating to the analysis of digital materiality, the inclusion of digitality within materiality may not seem obvious at first sight. In his work on virtual teams, Yakhlef (2009) shows that digital organizations actually rely on the physical existence of material resources, such as railroads, offices, and computers. According to Yakhlef, the virtual and the concrete should be considered intertwined, which raises the question of whether seemingly immaterial artifacts should be primarily considered through their materiality or their virtuality. The question expands beyond the scope of digitality, as materiality comprises practices that are not always tangible (Jones et al. 2013). However, this question prompts a deeper reflection on the ontological relationship between visuality and materiality, both of which are relevant for institutions (see Jones et al. 2017 for a deeper discussion of this topic). Alternatively, some studies rely on the notion of space to approach digitality as a whole (Boisot 2013; Souto-Otero and Beneito-Montagut 2016).

Body and Embodiment

Body and embodiment compose the fourth and last major topic that we identified as relevant for institutional studies on materiality. Bodies are the locus of perceptions and emotions and constitute our pre-reflexive relationship with the world (i.e., our perceptions in, below and beyond words and thought) (see Merleau-Ponty 1945/2013). As Jones (2013,

p. 200) explains, "Human action (…) necessarily involves (material) bodies" and bodies draw their assertion from practices that involve routinized body movements (Reckwitz 2002). In his analysis of nursing care, Reckwitz highlights the importance of the body and the physical embodiment of the sociomaterial realm. For example, nurses carry out their mission through repetitive body movements. They also adapt and make sense of their tasks according to the physical constraints of the patients' health situation and their own physical capabilities.

Although bodies and embodiment have been addressed in studies on practices, routines and sensemaking at work, institutionalists have only recently begun to explore the notions of body and embodiment (see e.g., Stowell and Warren 2018). Part of the reason may be that it is difficult to develop methodologies that take embodiment into consideration in relation to institutional dynamics. Bodies and embodiment have been explored through makeup, physical appearance, clothes and so on—but we are still lacking a conceptual definition of what the body is and which boundaries it has. As an example, Czarniawska (2010) analyzed the place of women in the organizing of cities. She outlined how representations and a certain vocabulary about women progressively became institutionalized in cities. However, she focused her analysis on the spatial representation of female bodies (e.g., location, dimensions) rather than on tangible female bodies. Although scholars recognize the relevance of female embodiment in urban representation, this topic remains to be explored from an epistemological and methodological stance. The section of this book that addresses embodiment aims to encourage researchers to reflect on the body, as a form of materiality, through the multiple layers of theory, methodology, epistemology and ontology.

Horizontal and Vertical Challenges

Institutional studies that approach materiality tend to do so through an analysis of the four major types of materiality that are depicted in Fig. 1.2. Previous research has not clarified how these four types relate to one

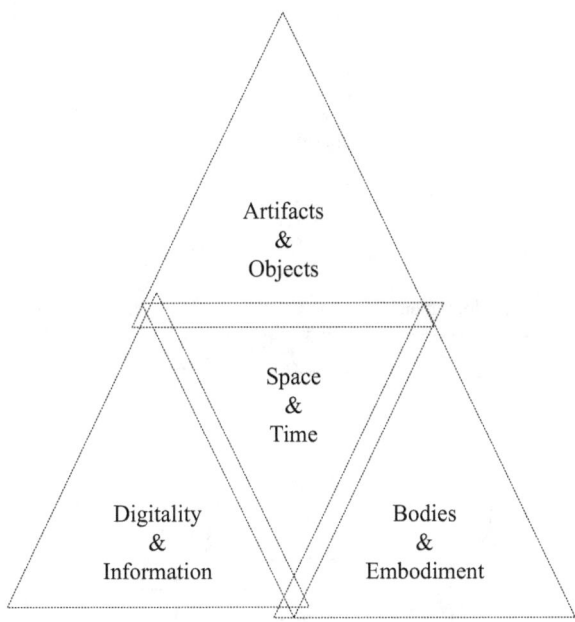

Fig. 1.2 Interrelated topics of materiality in institutions, which are taken into account in this book

another, such as the extent to which they can be clearly distinguished from each other. Figure 1.2 is not exhaustive when it comes to representing different forms of materiality. Rather, it corresponds to the topics primarily investigated in institutional studies, as well as their porosity. It thus does not address the boundaries between them, nor the possibilities that additional forms of materiality may appear (or has already appeared) in institutional research.

Apprehending materiality in institutions confronts researchers with a double challenge. The first challenge pertains to how to theorize materiality and its role in institutional dynamics. To do so, researchers are encouraged to reflect on the consistency between the ontological, epistemological and methodological layers of the material turn. We label this challenge "vertical". The second challenge, which we label "horizontal", refers to the

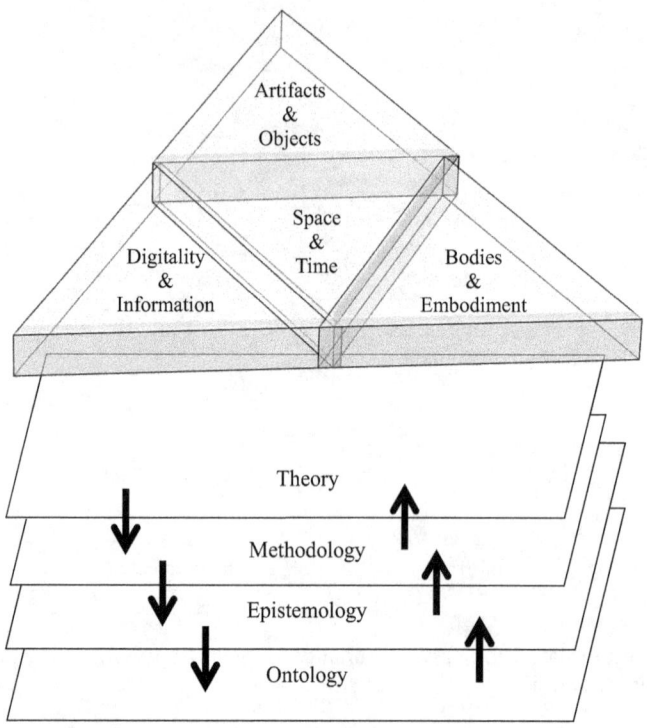

Fig. 1.3 Materiality in institutions: vertical and horizontal challenges

ever-expanding diversity of the empirical expression of materiality taken into consideration in institutional studies. As an always expanding and diversifying landscape, materiality can become particularly difficult to grasp. We believe that building theory on materiality in institutions can be supported if researchers simultaneously address these two interdependent challenges. On the one hand, the inherent diversity of materiality compels researchers to further elaborate consistency between their ontological, epistemological and methodological stances. On the other hand, reflexivity through conceptual layers of materiality encourages an enriched and open consideration of the essence of materiality and its empirical boundaries. Figure 1.3 represents these challenges spatially.

A Reflexive Journey Through Materiality in Institutions: The Structure of the Book and Its Rationale

This book addresses the vertical and horizontal challenges in an original fashion, through an exploratory and reflexive journey. All four forms of materiality are covered in this book. The chapters explore very diverse empirical settings—from hospital infrastructures to the game industry, firefighting organizations, surgery rooms, education and films—to help the reader understand the essential importance of materiality to institutions. The chapters also venture into the "vertical" conceptual layers of materiality to explore different methodological, epistemological and ontological stances. Exploring materiality in its different expressions with reflexive rigor is challenging, but also enriching. The authors engage in an iterative dialogue between two key questions: (i) what is materiality in institutions? and (ii) How can we develop institutionalist knowledge about materiality? To guide the reader through the journey, the book is divided into four parts, each of which corresponds to one form of materiality. Each chapter contributes to the enrichment of knowledge about materiality in institutions by addressing more than one layer of Fig. 1.3.

In the first part of the book labeled "artifacts and objects" (I), Mélodie Cartel and Eva Boxenbaum use bricolage as a theoretical lens to explore the role of materiality and further our understanding of institutional innovation. Institutional studies have previously considered emergence as a key aspect of institutional dynamics (Czarniawska 2009) but have hardly considered the conceptual avenues brought about by materiality and the notion of bricolage. Bricolage is original from an epistemological stance in as much as it can help generate new knowledge about how materiality contributes to institutional change and renewal. Also from an epistemological perspective, Julien Jourdan builds on the metaphor of footprint to examine the role of traces in institutional conformity, thereby providing new insights into the influence of (material) traces on organizational survival. He also discusses the relevance of this notion for the study of materiality in institutional theory, and consider its ontological and epistemological implications. Finally, Bernard Leca, Frédérique

Dejean, Isabelle Huault and Jean-Pascal Gond examine the early stages of the institutionalization of Socially Responsible Investment in France, highlighting the three institutional effects of artifacts: enabling, constraining and entangling practices. Their work further sheds light on the relations between artifacts, discourse and practices in institutional processes.

In the second part entitled "space and time" (II), Lise Arena and Ali Douai investigate the legitimation of business education through a detailed exploration of the Oxford University campus. Relying on historical methodology, they outline the role of materiality in micro and macro institutional changes. Through three historical episodes, they detail how materiality, in particular space and time, contributes to the progressive hybridization of institutional logics. Space can also represent a valuable lens from an epistemological perspective; Anouck Adrot and Marie Bia-Figueiredo focus on space as a valuable intermediary concept to stimulate reflection in action with respect to information flows shaped by the pursuit for legitimacy by a firefighting organization. Finally, François-Xavier de Vaujany, Sara Winterstorm-Varländer and Emmanuelle Vaast's chapter speaks to the issue of legitimacy and highlights the importance of space for organizations that seek to develop or maintain their legitimacy. Through walking practices, institutions invoke space in legitimacy claims. From an ontological perspective, the chapter questions what space is. Going further, this chapter suggests that from an epistemological perspective, additional knowledge can be created on the role of spaces in legitimation. The authors point to diverse observation units, such as practices—including walking, sitting, moving—and speech acts, as enabling legitimation.

In the third part of the book entitled "digitality and information" (III), Fernando Pinto Santos, through the analysis of websites and the materialization of digital discourse, reveals how entrepreneurs manage to handle tensions between the originality of their business and institutional expectations. He thus discusses the ontological status of materiality in a digital environment. Anna-Morgan Thomas, Agostinho Abrunhosa and Ignacio Canales propose a theoretical contribution that tackles the burning issue of incompatibility between institutional logics and identifies a major role played by materiality in the institutional processes resulting from it. While European business schools promote the development of Massive Open Online Courses (MOOCs) in business education, they also confront deep contradictions between the open philosophy underlying MOOCs and a growing production of customized but expensive education programs. They describe digitality and its materiality as anchors of institutional logics rather than a simple mirror of it. From this perspective, they analyze the material outcomes of digital artifacts as an avenue for stimulating scholars' reflexivity on ontology. Catherine Felix, Lise Arena and Bernard Conein propose an innovative methodology that takes into consideration the use of digital artifacts at different levels of practices, including the institutional environment, the organizational level and situated action. Their work gives access to recorded sequences of actions that provide a fine grained analysis of the relation between the setting as a local workspace and the arena as a broader institutional context.

Finally, in the section of the book entitled "bodies and embodiment" (IV), Sine Nørholm Just and Line Kirkegaard explore bodies as an essential dimension of materiality in an army institution. In this chapter, they suggest that a dichotomous approach of materiality and discourse can mislead institutional analysis. Rather, to illuminate the role of materiality in institutions, they propose that scholars take into account both bodies and discourses in their analysis. By doing so, they question the ontology of body and discuss, as a theoretical contribution, its symbolical role in institutionalization. They propose that bodies correspond to an original effort to renew our knowledge on institutions and materiality. The authors offer the concept of plasticity as an intermediary concept to investigate the relationship between bodies and institutions. François-Xavier de Vaujany proposes a Merleau-Pontian view on bodies, space and time in legitimation processes, thereby challenging existing epistemological divides in MOS. He proposes three ontologies drawn on Merleau-Ponty's thinking: the ontology of discourse, the ontology of sculpture and the ontology of bubbles. Based on these ontologies, he provides new theoretical perspectives on legitimation processes and organizing.

In the Steps of a Reflexive Journey

This book encourages readers to join a reflexive journey across the various conceptual layers of materiality in institutions and the diverse expressions of materiality in institutional theory: artifacts and objects, digitality and information, space and time, bodies and embodiment. Sharing an interest in the theoretical, methodological, epistemological and ontological aspects of institutional theory development, the contributors to in the present book provide insights into both the advantages and challenges of integrating materiality into an institutional analysis. Incidentally, the chapters also provide insights into the specificities of studying materiality from an institutional perspective, and offer insights into how institutional analysis can inform our understanding of materiality. Each chapter, in its own fashion, contributes to the reflexive journey that we invite the reader to join.

References

Abdelnour, S., Hasselbladh, H., & Kallinikos, J. (2017). Agency and institutions in organization studies. *Organization Studies, 38*(12), 1775–1792.

Amaeshi, K., & Amao, O. O. (2009). Corporate social responsibility in transnational spaces: Exploring influences of varieties of capitalism on expressions of corporate codes of conduct in Nigeria. *Journal of Business Ethics, 86*(2), 225.

Bachelard, G. (1938). *La formation de l'esprit scientifique*. Paris: Vrin.

Bachmann, R., Gillespie, N., & Priem, R. (2015). Repairing trust in organizations and institutions: Toward a conceptual framework. *Organization Studies, 36*(9), 1123–1142.

Barad, K. (2003). Posthumanist performativity: Toward an understanding of how matter comes to matter. *Signs: Journal of Women in Culture and Society, 28*(3), 801–831.

Barley, S. R., & Tolbert, P. S. (1997). Institutionalization and structuration: Studying the links between action and institution. *Organization Studies, 18*(1), 93–117.

Battilana, J. (2006). Agency and institutions: The enabling role of individuals' social position. *Organization, 13*(5), 653–676.

Battilana, J., Leca, B., & Boxenbaum, E. (2009). 2 how actors change institutions: Towards a theory of institutional entrepreneurship. *Academy of Management Annals, 3*(1), 65–107.

Berger, P., & Luckmann, T. (1967). *The social construction of reality*. New York: Anchor.

Binder, A. (2007). For love and money: Organizations' creative responses to multiple environmental logics. *Theory and Society, 36*(6), 547–571.

Blanc, A., & Huault, I. (2014). Against the digital revolution? Institutional maintenance and artifacts within the French recorded music industry. *Technological Forecasting and Social Change, 83*, 10–23.

Boisot, M. (2013). *Information Space (RLE: Organizations)* (Vol. 2). Abingdon: Routledge.

Boxenbaum, E., Huault, I., & Leca, B. (2016). *Le tournant "materiel" dans la theorie neoinstitutionnaliste*. In F.-X. de Vaujany, A. Hussenot et J.-F. Chanlat (Eds.), *Théories des organisations: Nouveaux tournants (pp. 227–238). Paris: Economica*.

Boxenbaum, E., Jones, C., Meyer, R., & Svejenova, S. (2018). Towards an articulation of the material and visual turn in organization studies. *Organization Studies, 39*(5/6): 597–616.

Carlile, P. R., Nicolini, D., Langley, A., & Tsoukas, H. (2013a). How matter matters: Objects, artifacts and materiality in organization studies: Introducing the third volume of "perspective on organization studies". In P. R. Carlile, D. Nicolini, A. Langley, & H. Tsoukas (Eds.), *How matter matters: Objects, artifacts and materiality in organization studies* (pp. 1–15). Oxford: Oxford University Press.

Carlile, P. R., Nicolini, D., Langley, A., & Tsoukas, H. (2013b). *How matter matters: Objects, artifacts, and materiality in organization studies*. Oxford: Oxford University Press.

Castor, T. (2016). The materiality of discourse: Relational positioning in a fresh water controversy. *Communication Research and Practice, 2*(3), 334–350.

Cooren, F., Fairhurst, G., & Huët, R. (2012). Why matter always matters in (organizational) communication. In P. M. Leonardi, B. A. Nardi, & J. Kallinikos (Eds.), *Materiality and organizing: Social interaction in a technological world* (pp. 296–314). Oxford: Oxford University Press.

Czarniawska, B. (2004). On time, space, and action nets. *Organization, 11*(6), 773–791.

Czarniawska, B. (2009). Emerging institutions: Pyramids or anthills? *Organization Studies, 30*(4), 423–441.

Czarniawska, B. (2010). Women, the city and (dis) organizing. *Culture and Organization, 16*(3), 283–300.

Dacin, M. T., Munir, K., & Tracey, P. (2010). Formal dining at Cambridge colleges: Linking ritual performance and institutional maintenance. *Academy of Management Journal, 53*(6), 1393–1418.

David, R. J., & Bitektine, A. B. (2009). The deinstitutionalization of institutional theory? Exploring divergent agendas in institutional research. In *The SAGE handbook of organizational research methods* (pp. 160–175). Los Angeles: Sage.

de Vaujany, F.-X., & Mitev, N. (2013). *Materiality and space: Organizations, artifacts and practices*. London: Springer.

de Vaujany, F.-X., & Mitev, N. (2015). Introduction au tournant matériel en théories des organisations: Economica.

de Vaujany, F.-X., & Vaast, E. (2016). Matters of visuality in legitimation practices: Dual iconographies in a meeting room. *Organization, 23*(5), 763–790.

de Vaujany, F.-X., Mitev, N., Laniray, P., & Vaast, E. (2014). *Materiality and time: Historical perspectives on organizations, artifacts and practices*. London: Springer.

Delacour, H., & Leca, B. (2017). The paradox of controversial innovation: Insights from the rise of impressionism. *Organization Studies, 38*(5), 597–618.

DiMaggio, P. (1988). Interest and agency in institutional theory. In L. Zucker (Ed.), *Institutional patterns and organizations* (pp. 3–21). Cambridge, MA: Ballinger Publishing Co.

DiMaggio, P. J., & Powell, W. W. (1983). The iron cage revisited: Institutional isomorphism and collective rationality in organizational fields. *American Sociological Review, 48*(2), 147–160.

DiMaggio, P. J., & Powell, W. W. (1991). *The new institutionalism in organizational analysis* (Vol. 17). Chicago: University of Chicago Press.

Dover, G., & Lawrence, T. B. (2010). A gap year for institutional theory: Integrating the study of institutional work and participatory action research. *Journal of Management Inquiry, 19*(4), 305–316.

Edwards, T. J. 2016. Institutional theory: reflections on ontology. In: Mir, R., Willmott, H. and Greenwood, M. eds. Routledge Handbook of Philosophy in Organization Sciences (pp.1–26). Routledge Companions in Business, Management and Accounting. London: Routledge.

Edwards. (Forthcoming).

Faraj, S., & Azad, B. (2012). The materiality of technology: An affordance perspective. In P. M. Leonardi, B. A. Nardi, & J. Kallinikos (Eds.), *Materiality and organizing*. Oxford: Oxford University Press.

Frank, D. J., & Meyer, J. W. (2002). The profusion of individual roles and identities in the postwar period. *Sociological Theory, 20*(1), 86–105.

Friedland, R. (2012). The institutional logics perspective: A new approach to culture, structure, and process. *M@n@gement, 15*(5), 583–595.

Friedland, R., & Alford, R. R. (1991). Bringing society back in: Symbols, practices and institutional contradictions. In W.W. Powell & P. J. DiMaggio (Eds.), *The new institutionalism in organizational analysis (pp. 232–263). Chicago: University of Chicago Press.*

Gawer, A., & Phillips, N. (2013). Institutional work as logics shift: The case of Intel's transformation to platform leader. *Organization Studies, 34*(8), 1035–1071.

Giddens, A. (1984). *The constitutions of society: Outline of the theory of structure.* Berkeley: University of California Press.

Granqvist, N., & Gustafsson, R. (2016). Temporal institutional work. *Academy of Management Journal, 59*(3), 1009–1035.

Greenwood, R., Oliver, C., Sahlin, K., & Suddaby, R. (2008). Introduction. In *SAGE handbook of organizational institutionalism* (pp. 1–46). London: Sage.

Greenwood, R., Oliver, C., Lawrence, T. B., & Meyer, R. E. (2017). Introduction: Into the fourth decade. In *SAGE handbook of organizational institutionalism* (2nd ed., pp. 1–23). London: Sage.

Grosz, E. A. (1995). *Space, time, and perversion: Essays on the politics of bodies.* St Leonards: Allen & Unwin.

Hardy, C., Phillips, N., & Lawrence, T. B. (2003). Resources, knowledge and influence: The organizational effects of interorganizational collaboration. *Journal of Management Studies, 40*(2), 321–347.

Hargadon, A. B., & Douglas, Y. (2001). When innovations meet institutions: Edison and the design of the electric light. *Administrative Science Quarterly, 46*(3), 476–501.

Höllerer, M. A., Daudigeos, T., & Jancsary, D. (2018). Multimodality, meaning, and institutions: Editorial. *Research in the Sociology of Organizations, 54A,* 1–24.

Huault, I., Boxenbaum, E., & Leca, B. (2015). Le tournant "matériel" dans la théorie néo-institutionnaliste. In F.-X. De Vaujany, A. Hussenot, & J.-F. Chanlat (Eds.), *Théories des organisations—Nouveaux tournants* (pp. 227–238). Paris: Economica.

Ingold, T. (2011). *Being alive: Essays on movement, knowledge and description.* London: Taylor & Francis.

Jancsary, D., Höllerer, M. A., & Meyer, R. E. (2016). Critical analysis of visual and multimodal texts. In R. Wodak & M. Meyer (Eds.), *Methods of critical discourse studies* (3rd ed., pp. 180–204). Los Angeles: Sage.

Jones, M. (2013). Untangling sociomateriality. In P. R. Carlile, D. Nicolini, A. Langley, & H. Tsoukas (Eds.), *How matter matters* (Vol. 3, pp. 197–226). Oxford: Oxford University Press.

Jones, C., & Massa, F. G. (2013). From novel practice to consecrated exemplar: Unity Temple as a case of institutional evangelizing. *Organization Studies, 34*(8), 1099–1136.

Jones, C., Boxenbaum, E., & Anthony, C. (2013). The immateriality of material practices in institutional logics. In E. Boenbaum & M. Lounsbury (Eds.), *Institutional logics in action, Part A* (pp. 51–75). Bingley: Emerald Group Publishing Limited.

Jones, C., Meyer, R. E., Jancsary, D., & Höllerer, M. A. (2017). The material and visual basis of institutions. In R. Greenwood, C. Oliver, T. B. Lawrence, & R. E. Meyer (Eds.), *SAGE handbook of organizational institutionalism* (2nd ed., pp. 621–646). London: Sage.

Jourdan, J., Durand, R., & Thornton, P. H. (2017). The price of admission: Organizational deference as strategic behavior. *American Journal of Sociology, 123*(1), 232–275.

Kornberger, M., & Clegg, S. R. (2004). Bringing space back in: Organizing the generative building. *Organization Studies, 25*(7), 1095–1114.

Lanzara, G. F., & Patriotta, G. (2007). The institutionalization of knowledge in an automotive factory: Templates, inscriptions, and the problem of durability. *Organization Studies, 28*(5), 635–660.

Lawrence, T. B., & Dover, G. (2015). Place and institutional work creating housing for the hard-to-house. *Administrative Science Quarterly, 60*(3), 371–410.

Lawrence, T. B., & Suddaby, R. (2006). 1.6 institutions and institutional work. In *The Sage handbook of organization studies* (Vol. 2, pp. 215–254). London: Sage.

Lawrence, T. B., Leca, B., & Zilber, T. B. (2013). Institutional work: Current research, new directions and overlooked issues. *Organization Studies, 34*(8), 1023–1033.

Lefebvre, H., & Nicholson-Smith, D. (1991). *The production of space* (Vol. 142). Oxford: Blackwell.

Leonardi, P. M. (2010). Digital materiality? How artifacts without matter, matter. *First Monday, 15*(6).

Leonardi, P. M. (2013). The emergence of materiality within formal organizations. In P. R. Carlile, D. Nicolini, A. Langley, & H. Tsoukas (Eds.), *How matter matters: Objects, artifacts and materiality in organization studies* (Vol. 3, pp. 142–170). Oxford: Oxford University Press.

Leonardi, P. M., Nardi, B. A., & Kallinikos, J. (2012). *Materiality and organizing: Social interaction in a technological world.* Oxford: Oxford University Press on Demand.

Mäkitalo, Å. (2012). Professional learning and the materiality of social practice. *Journal of Education and Work, 25*(1), 59–78.

Martí, I., & Fernández, P. (2013). The institutional work of oppression and resistance: Learning from the Holocaust. *Organization Studies, 34*(8), 1195–1223.

Merleau-Ponty, M. (1964). *Le visible et l'invisible: suivi de notes de travail* (Vol. 36). Paris: Gallimard.

Merleau-Ponty, M. (2003). *L'institution, la passivité.* Paris: Belin.

Merleau-Ponty, M. (1945/2013). *Phénoménologie de la perception.* France: Gallimard.

Merton, R. K. (1938). Social structure and anomie. *American Sociological Review, 3*(5), 672–682.

Meyer, J. W., & Rowan, B. (1977). Institutionalized organizations: Formal structure as myth and ceremony. *The American Journal of Sociology, 83*(2), 340–363.

Meyer, R., Jancsary, D., Höllerer, M., & Boxenbaum, E. (2018). The role of verbal and visual text in the process of institutionalization. *Academy of Management Review. 43*(3), 1–27.

Miettinen, R., & Virkkunen, J. (2005). Epistemic objects, artifacts and organizational change. *Organization, 12*(3), 437–456.

Monteiro, P., & Nicolini, D. (2015). Recovering materiality in institutional work: Prizes as an assemblage of human and material entities. *Journal of Management Inquiry, 24*(1), 61–81. https://doi.org/10.1177/1056492614546221.

Morgan, G., & Smircich, L. (1980). The case for qualitative research. *Academy of Management Review, 5*(4), 491–500.

Ocasio, W. (1997). Towards an attention-based view of the firm. *Strategic Management Journal, 18*, 187–206.

Orlikowski, W. J. (2007). Sociomaterial practices: Exploring technology at work. *Organization Studies, 28*(9), 1435–1448. https://doi.org/10.1177/0170840607081138.

Orlikowski, W. J., & Barley, S. R. (2001). Technology and institutions: What can research on information technology and research on organizations learn from each other? *MIS Quarterly, 25*(2), 145–165.

Orlitzky, M. (2011). Institutionalized dualism: Statistical significance testing as myth and ceremony. *Journal of Management Control, 22*(1), 47.

Patriotta, G., Gond, J. P., & Schultz, F. (2011). Controversies, orders of worth, and public justifications. *Journal of Management Studies, 48*(8), 1804–1836.

Petrakaki, D., Klecun, E., & Cornford, T. (2016). Changes in healthcare professional work afforded by technology: The introduction of a national electronic patient record in an English hospital. *Organization, 23*(2), 206–226.

Phillips, N., Lawrence, T. B., & Hardy, C. (2004). Discourse and institutions. *Academy of Management Review, 29*(4), 635–652.

Pinch, T. (2008). Technology and institutions: Living in a material world. *Theory and Society, 37*(5), 461–483.

Pittz, T. G., Boje, D. M., Intindola, M. L., & Nicholson, S. (2017). 'COPE'ing with institutional pressures: A reintroduction of pragmatism to the study of organisations. *International Journal of Management Concepts and Philosophy, 10*(2), 113–129.

Puyou, F.-R., & Quattrone, P. (2018). The visual and material dimensions of legitimacy: Accounting and the search for socie-ties. *Organization Studies, 39*, 727–752.

Raaijmakers, A., Vermeulen, P., & Meeus, M. (2018). Children without bruised knees: Responding to material and ideational (mis)alignments. *Organization Studies, 39*, 817–836.

Raviola, E., & Norbäck, M. (2013). Bringing technology and meaning into institutional work: Making news at an Italian business newspaper. *Organization Studies, 34*(8), 1171–1194.

Reckwitz, A. (2002). The status of the "material" in theories of culture: From "social structure" to "artifacts". *Journal for the Theory of Social Behaviour, 32*(2), 195–217.

Reay, T., & Jones, C. (2016). Qualitatively capturing institutional logics. *Strategic Organization, 14*(4), 441–454.

Reinecke, J., & Ansari, S. (2015). When times collide: Temporal brokerage at the intersection of markets and developments. *Academy of Management Journal, 58*(2), 618–648.

Robey, D., Anderson, C., & Raymond, B. (2013). Information technology, materiality, and organizational change: A professional odyssey. *Journal of the Association for Information Systems, 14*(7), 379.

Robichaud, D., & Cooren, F. (Eds.). (2013). *Organization and organizing: Materiality, agency and discourse.* New York: Routledge.

Rowland, N. J., & Rojas, F. (2006). Bringing technology back in: A critique of the institutionalist perspective on museums. *Museum and Society, 4*(2), 84–95.

Schatzki, T. R. (2010). *The timespace of human activity: On performance, society, and history as indeterminate teleological events.* Lanham: Lexington Books.

Smets, M., Morris, T. I. M., & Greenwood, R. (2012). From practice to field: A multilevel model of practice-driven institutional change. *Academy of Management Journal, 55*(4), 877–904.

Souto-Otero, M., & Beneito-Montagut, R. (2013). 'Power on': Googlecracy, privatisation and the standardisation of sources. *Journal of Education Policy, 28*(4), 481–500.

Souto-Otero, M., & Beneito-Montagut, R. (2016). From governing through data to governmentality through data: artifacts, strategies and the digital turn. *European Educational Research Journal, 15*(1), 14–33.

Stigliani, I., & Ravasi, D. (2012). Organizing thoughts and connecting brains: Material practices and the transition from individual to group-level prospective sense-making. *Academy of Management Journal, 55*, 1232–1259.

Stowell, A., & Warren, S. (2018). The institutionalisation of suffering: Embodied inhabitation and the maintenance of health and safety in e-waste recycling. *Organization Studies, 39*, 791–815.

Suchman, M. C. (1995). Managing legitimacy: Strategic and institutional approaches. *Academy of Management Review, 20*(3), 571–610.

Suddaby, R., & Greenwood, R. (2009). Methodological issues in researching institutional change. In D. Buchanan & A. Bryman (Eds.), *The SAGE handbook of organizational research methods* (pp. 177–195). London: Sage.

Swidler, A. (1986). Culture in action: Symbols and strategies. *American Sociological Review, 51*, 273–286.

Thornton, P. H., & Ocasio, W. (1999). Institutional logics and the historical contingency of power in organizations: Executive succession in the higher education publishing industry, 1958–1990. *American Journal of Sociology, 105*(3), 801–843.

Thornton, P. H., Ocasio, W., & Lounsbury, M. (2012). *The institutional logics perspective: A new approach to culture, structure, and process.* Oxford: Oxford University Press on Demand.

Vásquez, C., & Plourde, M. C. (2017). Materiality and organizing. *In The international encyclopedia of organizational communication.* Chichester, UK: John Wiley & Sons.

Yakhlef, A. (2009). We have always been virtual: Writing, institutions, and technology! *Space and Culture, 12*(1), 76–94.

Part I

Artifacts and Objects

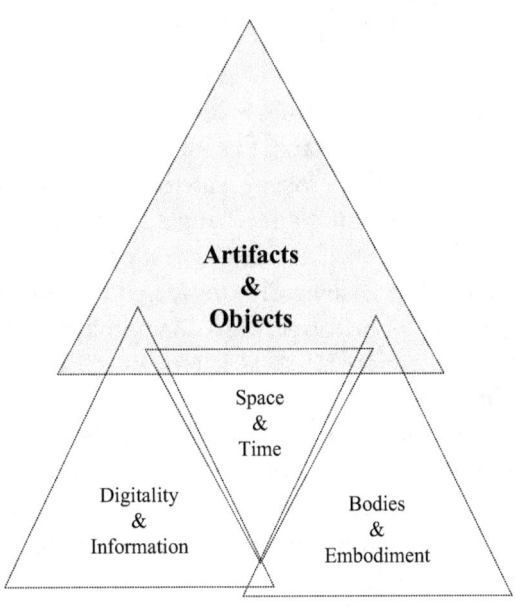

Key Questions

- Which roles do objects, artifacts and technologies play in processes of legitimation?
- How do objects and artifacts afford and constrain the process of legitimation?
- What is the role of materiality and material practices in institutional dynamics?
- How can objects and artifacts be conceptualized ontologically in relation to institutions?
- Through which epistemological stances can objects, artifacts and instruments be studied empirically to better illuminate the material dimension of institutions?

In this first part of the book, we discuss the topic of objects, artifacts and instruments and their relationship with institutional dynamics. In the first chapter, Mélodie Cartel and Eva Boxenbaum use bricolage as a theoretical lens to explore the role of materiality and further our understanding of institutional shifts and changes. Institutional studies have already considered emergence as a key aspect of institutional dynamics (Czarniawska 2009) but have hardly considered the conceptual avenues brought by the notion of bricolage. Such an approach is original from an epistemological stance in as much as it renews scientific approaches to institutions by including materiality.

The second chapter authored by Julien Jourdan builds on the materialization metaphor to examine the role of traces in institutional conformity. More precisely, the chapter elaborates the notion of institutional footprint, and provides two empirical illustrations, including business education and French film industry. The discussion covers the ontology of institutional footprints and its epistemological implications.

In the last chapter, Bernard Leca, Frédérique Dejean, Isabelle Huault and Jean-Pascal Gond examine the early stages of institutionalization of socially responsible investment in France. It highlights three effects of artifacts: enabling, constraining and entangling practices. Figure 1 represents each of the three chapters' engagement with the multiple layers of materiality in institutions.

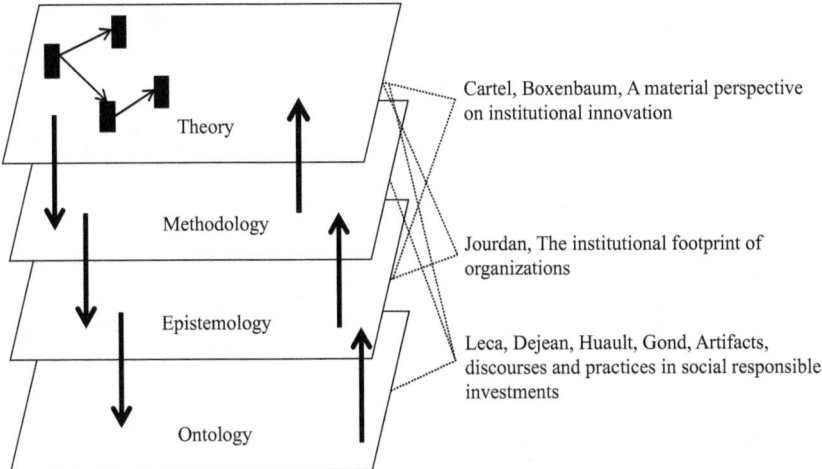

Fig. 1 Reflexive journey on artifacts and objects through the chapters

2

Materiality in Institutional Analysis: A Bricolage Approach

Mélodie Cartel and Eva Boxenbaum

Introduction

In the early stages of institutionalization, innovative ideas become imbued with generic properties that appeal to receiving audiences and that help them spread (Berger and Luckmann 1967; Tolbert and Zucker 1996). Institutional scholars have inquired into this process for decades (Sahlin and Wedlin 2008; Strang and Meyer 1993; Suddaby and Greenwood 2005), a process known as institutional innovation and defined as the introduction

M. Cartel (✉)
UNSW Business School, University of New South Wales,
Sydney, NSW, Australia
e-mail: m.cartel@unsw.edu.au

E. Boxenbaum
Department of Organization, Copenhagen Business School,
Copenhagen, Denmark

Centre de gestion scientifique (CGS), MINES ParisTech - PSL University, i3
UMR CNRS, Paris, France
e-mail: eb.ioa@cbs.dk

© The Author(s) 2019   **37**
F.-X. de Vaujany et al. (eds.), *Materiality in Institutions*, Technology, Work and
Globalization, https://doi.org/10.1007/978-3-319-97472-9_2

and mainstreaming of new ideas. However, they primarily analyzed the cognitive and verbal dimensions of this process, overlooking the role of materiality (Jones et al., 2013). In this chapter, we build on the concept of bricolage to develop a model that articulates how materiality contributes, in combination with cognitive and verbal aspects, to how innovative ideas acquire the generic properties that facilitate their institutionalization.

Some institutionalist studies have recently turned to the concept of bricolage to articulate processes of institutional innovation (Boxenbaum and Rouleau 2011; Carstensen 2011; Cartel et al. 2017; Garud and Karnøe 2003; Højgaard Christiansen and Lounsbury 2013; Leca and Naccache 2006). They draw on the concept of bricolage as formulated by Lévi-Strauss (1962, 1966). Lévi-Strauss used the concept of bricolage to describe a particular way in which actors deviate from established ways of doing. When facing a problem, actors may engage in bricolage, that is, recombine resources at hand in their local environment to come up with a temporary solution (Duymedjian and Rüling 2010). Bricolage may, in solving a problem, produce a prototype that can provide tangible support for innovative ideas (see e.g., Jones and Massa 2013). We draw on this notion of bricolage to articulate a material dimension of institutional innovation that specifies how innovative ideas gain generic properties.

We first break down the concept of bricolage into two core components: crafting and trial. Crafting consists in reshuffling of resources at hand and prototyping a solution. Trial refers to testing the prototype by assessing its ability to solving the problem. We then further elaborate on the recursive relationship between crafting and trial, which captures a material dimension of institutional innovation. We conclude the chapter with a model that articulates how this material dimension interacts with the cognitive and verbal dimensions of institutional innovation.

The chapter contributes to the stream of research on institutional innovation processes with an articulation of the role of materiality. First, it specifies how bricolage enables institutional innovation, elaborating on the dynamic interactions of crafting and trial and explaining how they unfold in consecutive cycles of bricolage that contribute to institutional innovation. Second, the chapter specifies the role of materiality in relation to the cognitive and verbal dimensions of institutional innovation.

The Objectification Process

The process by which innovative ideas become imbued with generic properties is referred to as objectification (Tolbert and Zucker 1996: 181; Zucker 1977). Objectification entails the development of generic categories and a shared meaning of innovative ideas that thereby become decontextualized from their original cradle (Berger and Luckmann 1967). Objectification is integral to the processes of institutional innovation (Zucker 1977). When an innovative idea becomes objectified, it gains a more factual and permanent status[1] (Tolbert and Zucker 1996). Two core activities are central to objectification: theorization and rhetorical strategies.

Theorization refers to the framing of new ideas into conceptual models of cause and effect (Strang and Meyer 1993). Such models present the innovative idea in a rational light, suggesting that the proposed relationship always holds true, regardless of the context (Greenwood et al. 2002; Strang and Meyer 1993). Such models may be more or less complex, ranging from simple causal relations (Cartel et al. 2018; Greenwood et al. 2002) to more elaborate theories (Lounsbury and Crumley 2007; Strang and Meyer 1993). Theorization makes new (and potentially complex) ideas readily understandable to large audiences (Mena and Suddaby 2016; Nigam and Ocasio 2010).

Rhetorical strategies aim at adapting the new idea to a targeted audience, encouraging this audience to engage with it and to adopt it (Suddaby and Greenwood 2005). Rhetorical strategies help imbue innovative ideas with legitimacy (Suchman 1995; Suddaby and Greenwood 2005), reinforcing the effects of theorization. Actors use rhetorical strategies when they use emotionally loaded vocabulary (e.g., values, ethics, tradition, fate) to formulate ideas so that they resonate with the beliefs and values of the targeted audiences (Green 2004; Suddaby and Greenwood 2005; Swidler 1986, 2003). For instance, Currie et al. (2012) show how professional elites use the concept of risk rhetorically to maintain prevailing

---

[1] For more discussion on institutional permanence, please refer to the postface. In the postface, Jones details how the transferability of materiality accounts for its durability, which echoes our point related to the organizational reliance on objectification.

conventions. Rhetorical strategies were also used to promote the spread of the camera (Munir 2005).

Apart from a handful of recent studies (Cartel et al. 2018; Jones and Massa 2013; Nigam and Ocasio 2010), the role of prototypes has been neglected in institutional studies of objectification. Prototypes refer to the material expression of innovative ideas. They offer concrete examples of innovative ideas and evidence that these ideas work (Sahlin and Wedlin 2008). When ideas first get implemented into "the real world", they usually take the form of prototypes. Those early instantiations of innovative ideas draw on readily available resources and "common sense" rather than formal guidelines (Czarniawska and Joerges 1996; Czarniawska and Sevón 2005; Gond and Boxenbaum 2013). This process of making do with 'whatever is at hand' is also known as bricolage.

The Role of Bricolage in Objectification

Lévi-Strauss (1962, 1966) used the concept of bricolage to describe a particular way in which actors engage with the production of novelty. He described the bricoleur as engaging in unplanned and non-dogmatic recombinations of elements at hand, which he opposed to the *ingénieur* (e.g., engineer), who relies on logic and deduction to innovate. Adapting the work of Lévi-Strauss to organizational theory, Duymedjian and Rüling (2010) propose that bricolage and engineering constitute two ideal typical "regimes of action". The former regime is based on trial and learning and does not presuppose any hierarchy between different resources prior to trying them out. In contrast, the latter regime follows a linear and pre-determined path and respects scientific rules and ex ante project planning. Both processes may result in a prototype that could develop into an institutional innovation.

Previous organizational literature points to two elementary activities that are involved in bricolage: crafting and trial. *Crafting* refers to the reshuffling of resources at hand, leading to the material expression of a new idea. *Trial* consists in testing the ability of the prototype to serve the purpose for which it was intended.

Crafting

Bricoleurs select and combine resources from a repertoire that functions as a "toolbox"; an operation otherwise known as crafting. The repertoire includes physical spaces, such as a workshop, a storage unit or even a cupboard (Baker and Nelson 2005; Garud and Karnøe 2003; Meyer 2012), as well as online spaces, such as an organization's intranet where managerial resources are stored (e.g., collective schedules, SAP systems, standardized PowerPoint presentations). The repertoire also includes the bricoleur's own stock of knowledge, skills and processes (Perkmann and Spicer 2014; Rao et al. 2005). Despite its heterogeneity, the repertoire is limited to a finite number of resources, which constrains the panel of possible combinations. Moreover, some resources may be more readily available than others to a bricoleur. Resources may acquire new meanings and status depending on their use. For instance, apparently worthless resources may acquire value when combined with each other to address a problem (Duymedjian and Rüling 2010). Several prototypes may be crafted for the purpose of resolving a given problem and these different prototypes may enter into competition with one another (Zietsma and McKnight 2009). Their relative relevance is assessed through trials.

Trial

Bricoleurs (and their collaborators) assess whether a prototype fits their initial purpose (Baker and Nelson 2005; Garud and Karnøe 2003); an operation otherwise known as trial. Trials do not assess the broader value of the newly crafted prototype but only its ability to solve the targeted problem under the specific conditions that apply to this context.

Some trials are performed directly in the organization or the field and do not involve the creation of specific conditions. Trials that are conducted in the "real world" are referred to as in vivo trials (Muniesa and Callon 2007). Other trials are performed in protected spaces, away from other's scrutiny, sometimes under sophisticated experimental conditions (Bucher and Langley 2016; Canales 2016; Cartel et al. forthcoming; Zietsma and Lawrence 2010), such trials are referred to as laboratory trials (Latour 1987; Latour and Woolgar 1979). In vivo and laboratory trials constitute two opposite ideal types. A potential infinity of trial forms may be constituted from the combination of particularities associated with each of them.

Trials help the bricoleur determine which components of a prototype are most useful, which ones can be suppressed, and which ones should be enhanced (Baker and Nelson 2005). Trials operate as learning opportunities (Baker and Nelson 2005; Duymedjian and Rüling 2010; Garud and Karnøe 2003), enabling bricoleurs to identify the potential weaknesses of a prototype and addressing these weaknesses in a new round of crafting (Baker and Nelson 2005; Garud and Karnøe 2003). Hence, when bricoleurs subject a prototype to trial, they do not conclude that they made a mistake if it does not work; instead, they remove or add a resource and check if it works better. As such, trials proceed crafting, but they may also be conceptualized as a preliminary step for crafting. We propose that recursive relations exist between crafting and trial, which we label "bricolage cycles". In the following section, we articulate how these bricolage cycles facilitate objectification.

Bricolage Cycles

We propose that crafting and trial form cycles of bricolage. Each of these two activities may simultaneously be considered as a determinant and as a consequence of the other. Cycles of bricolage represent a material dimension of objectification. Prototypes can be adapted to different audiences through recursive cycles of crafting and trials to help make an innovative idea understandable and relevant for a broad audience. The appearance of prototypes may be modified through bricolage cycles to appeal better to specific audiences. This is, for instance, the case for innovative commercial products in B to C startups. After a first beta test and before commercialization, the product appearance is often modified to fit preexisting cognitive representations—a process similar to what Hargadon and Douglas (2001) referred to as robust design.

Bricolage cycles can also be mobilized in combination with rhetorical strategies or theorization to legitimize an innovative idea and provide the audience with a visual and tangible representation of the innovative idea (Cartel et al. 2018; Nigam and Ocasio 2010). Trials confirm the validity of an innovative idea by providing evidence that the innovative idea generates certain desirable effects, which demonstrates its pragmatic legitimacy (den Hond and de Bakker 2007). Even though trials are specific to a given context, some measure of pragmatic legitimacy enhances the effects of theorization.

Central to our conceptualization of how bricolage cycles facilitate objectification is: (1) the number of bricolage cycles that the crafted entity endures, (2) the variety of settings in which they occur, and (3) the increasing number of actors engaged in these cycles, either directly or indirectly. A prototype that is continuously subjected to bricolage cycles is likely to be sustained over time, which favors its objectification. If, in addition, a prototype is subjected to cycles of bricolage in many different contexts, then it is more likely to become decontextualized from a specific organizational setting, which facilitates its theorization. And the more audiences that encounter the prototype, the more likely the prototype is to become refined in its theorization and rhetorical form. Audiences may become enrolled in bricolage cycles and partake in shaping and adapting the prototype to new contexts, and they may employ new resources to (re-)craft the prototype and subject it to new trials. We propose that consecutive cycles of bricolage progressively expose an innovative idea, via a malleable prototype, to wider and wider circles of stakeholders, thereby facilitating its objectification.[2]

An example of such iterative cycles of bricolage is the institutionalization of windmills in Denmark as studied by Garud and Karnøe (2003). Windmills were crafted in increasingly institutionalized locations, spanning from workshops to laboratories and collaborative platforms. Over time, increasing numbers of users, both consumers and companies, tried out windmills. The outcomes of these trials encouraged actors to re-craft the windmills into more energy-efficient and user-friendly forms. Many

---

[2] This proposition echoes the importance of time in institutional matters. For additional details about time, please refer to Part II of this book, and in particular Chap. 5, in which Arena and Douai detail the emergence of Saïd Business School through three historical periods.

trials were also mobilized in rhetorical battles and in efforts to theorize windmills, which led to windmills becoming objectified, and eventually to becoming fully institutionalized in Danish energy production.

Objectification as Interaction Between Bricolage Cycles, Rhetorical Strategies and Theorization

This section articulates how bricolage cycles may interact with theorization and rhetorical strategies during the objectification process. We propose, as depicted in Fig. 2.1, that bricolage cycles represent an initial phase of objectification, which is consolidated through theorization and rhetorical strategies.

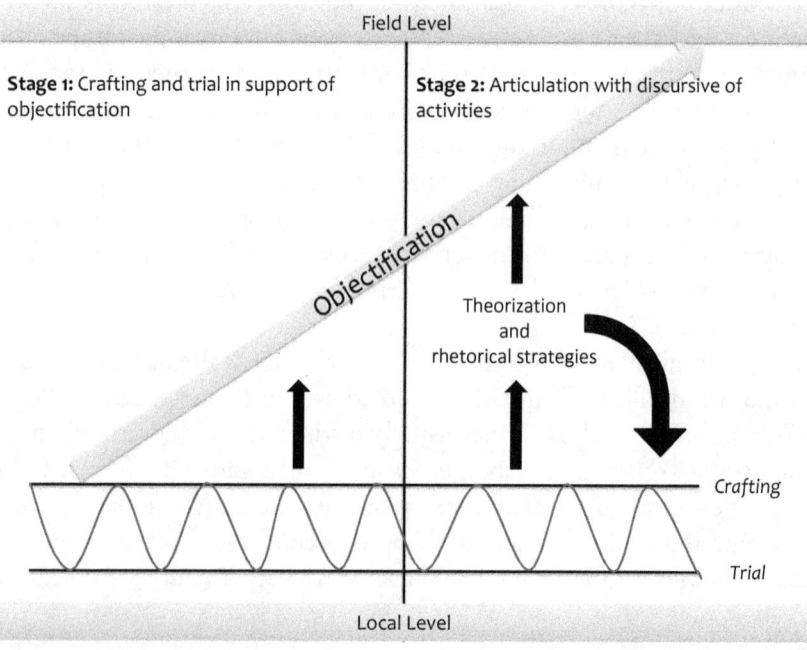

Fig. 2.1 Two stages of objectification

Stage 1: Crafting and Trial Support Objectification

Objectification starts when bricoleurs craft a prototype or an innovative idea and subject it to trial. Empirically, this moment can be quite difficult to trace. Different prototypes may arise spontaneously in the process of problem-solving, generating variations to established practices (Lounsbury and Crumley 2007). At this stage, the prototype may become subject to a pragmatic process, involving local trials and feedback loops (Barnes 1983). Early trials may be organized in a few bounded pilot sites; therefore protecting the prototype from peers' scrutiny and public controversy (Cartel et al. forthcoming; Zietsma and Lawrence 2010). During early trials, a reduced range of actors acquires practical experience with the prototype.

Stage 2: Articulation with Discursive Activities

When a prototype starts to spread outside its original cradle, an increasing number of actors and a diversity of audiences are likely to encounter it, as either opponents or promoters (Akrich et al. 1988a, b). At this stage, cycles of bricolage may be combined with discourses aimed at either undermining or magnifying the prototype. Multiple cycles of bricolage may unfold during this stage and become increasingly formalized and combined with rhetorical strategies. Crafting may become an essential component in rhetorical strategies aiming at persuading audiences of the validity and relevance of an innovative idea. Crafting can help align a prototype with the values and beliefs of a particular community (Déjean et al. 2004; Hargadon and Douglas 2001). The initial prototype may be re-crafted until it resonates with institutionalized understandings and patterns of practice (Gond and Boxenbaum 2013; Hargadon and Douglas 2001), which imbue the prototype with a "robust design" (ibid). As objectification proceeds, crafting may become increasingly infused with intentionality and strategy.

At this stage of objectification, trials aim at publicly demonstrating the efficacy of the prototype and hence at nurturing theorization (Akrich et al. 1988a, b). Such trials may take place in visible locations, such as public sites (Muniesa and Callon 2007). For instance, the prototypes for buildings in reinforced concrete were subjected to multiple trials from 1885 to 1939, trials that were undertaken directly in cities and made as visible and exemplary as possible to fuel expert debates between architects and engineers at the field level (Cartel et al. 2018). Companies and non-profit organizations may also undertake a pilot study or implement an early prototype to verify its problem-solving abilities in a new context (Boxenbaum 2006). The main role of trials at this stage of objectification is to empirically demonstrate the advantages of a given prototype compared to existing alternatives. Such demonstrations are likely to be combined with rhetorical strategies and aimed at theorization. The nature of proofs may also be shaped by ongoing debates at the field level (Tolbert and Zucker 1996).

Theoretical Implications of Integrating Materiality

Our conceptualization of objectification differs in several ways from previous accounts, which describe objectification as a purely discursive process (Tolbert and Zucker 1996). A core difference is that we highlight the material dimension of objectification, which takes the form of cycles of bricolage that are recursive in nature, iterating between crafting and trial. Each episode of crafting leads to a novel combination of resources into a material expression of the innovative idea. Each episode of trial helps establish the prototype's empirical validity and relevance. Through multiple rounds of crafting and trials, that is, cycles of bricolage, the novel idea is shaped into a material form that is increasingly robust and that appeals to ever-wider audiences. Our proposal extends the work of Lanzara and Patriotta (2007), which also articulates institutionalization as a recursive process through which ideas are materialized into the physical world. They emphasize the crafting process and organizational consequences of materialization, to which we add trial as a key component of institutional innovation.

We also propose that the material and discursive dimensions of objec-tification interact and reinforce each other through cycles of bricolage. Figure 2.1 reflects our conceptualization of how materiality, in the form of bricolage cycles, interacts with theorization and rhetorical strategies to objectify an innovative idea. The specific activities involved in crafting and trial differ somewhat depending on whether they occur in the early stage of objectification or the more advanced stage. An important impli-cation of our model is that trials that repeatedly produce unsatisfactory results for all prototypes of an innovative idea may undermine the efforts of theorization and prematurely conclude the objectification process.

A third contribution of our model is that objectification is subject to material constraints. The prototype is crafted from the resources to which bricoleurs have access and which constrain and orient their ability to materialize an innovative idea. These limitations set material boundaries for the form that a prototype can take and shape subsequent efforts of theorization. This process tends to reduce the possible paths that actors can take, leading to situations of path dependence (Garud and Karnøe 2001). Material constraints are evident at the beginning of the objectifi-cation process but may become even more pronounced during the later stage of objectification in as much as bricoleurs are likely to introduce additional constraints on the (re-)crafting as they begin to engage with theorization and rhetorical strategies. The very process of objectification thus imposes some material constraints on the prototype, which shapes the theorizing of an innovative idea.

Finally, our chapter contributes to current reflections about the ontol-ogy of institutions. Institutional theory traditionally conceptualizes insti-tutions as cognitive and discursive in nature. This conceptualization draws on Durkheim's (1982/1895) notion of "social facts", which refers to beliefs, norms and social structures that come to exist independently from the individual and that can exert social control. Accordingly, mate-riality is conceptualized as an *expression* of the cognitive and discursive nature of institutions. In other words, materiality does not exercise inde-pendent agency but only reinforces cognitive and discursive features of institutions. Our conceptualization of objectification extends this onto-logical stance, adding that material artifacts (e.g., prototypes) are crafted in an empirical context composed of actors, resources and locations that shapes which features of cognition and discourse are most likely to become institutionalized. As such, we propose that materiality *shapes*, but does not *determine*, institutional innovation.

Conclusion

We argued in this chapter that prototypes, that is, material expressions of an innovative idea, are essential ingredients for theorization and rhetorical strategies. Not only do they give material shape to an innovative idea, they are also discussed and used as "objective facts" to convince audiences and consolidate collective understandings. The presence of a prototype is thus able to imbue an innovative idea with collective meaning and legitimacy above and beyond what can be accomplished discursively. Essentially, our conceptualization of objectification illuminates the important role that materiality plays in determining whether, and in which form, an innovative idea will be objectified. Materiality, we argue, is therefore essential to accomplishing the early stages of institutional innovation.

References

Akrich, M., Callon, M., & Latour, B. (1988a). A quoi tient le succès des innovations? Premier épisode: L'art de l'intéressement. *Gérer et comprendre. Annales des Mines, 11,* 4–17.

Akrich, M., Callon, M., & Latour, B. (1988b). A quoi tient le succès des innovations? Deuxième épisode: L'art de choisir les bons porte-parole. *Gérer et comprendre. Annales des Mines, 12,* 14–29.

Baker, T., & Nelson, R. (2005). Creating something from nothing: Resource construction through entrepreneurial bricolage. *Administrative Science Quarterly, 50*(3), 329–366.

Barnes, B. (1983). Social life as bootstrapped induction. *Sociology, 17,* 524–545.

Berger, P., & Luckmann, T. (1967). *Social construction of reality.* New York: Anchor Books.

Boxenbaum, E. (2006). Lost in translation? The making of the Danish diversity management. *American Behavioral Scientist, 49*(7), 939–948.

Boxenbaum, E., & Rouleau, L. (2011). New knowledge products as bricolage: Metaphors and scripts in organizational theory. *Academy of Management Review, 36*(2), 272–296.

Bucher, S., & Langley, A. (2016). The interplay of reflective and experimental spaces in interrupting and reorienting routine dynamics. *Organization Science, 27*(3), 594–613.

Canales, R. (2016). From ideals to institutions: Institutional entrepreneurship and the growth of Mexican small business finance. *Organization Science, 27*, 1548–1573.

Carstensen, M. B. (2011). Paradigm man vs. the bricoleur: Bricolage as an alternative vision of agency in ideational change. *European Political Science Review, 3*(1), 147–167.

Cartel, M., Boxenbaum, E., Aggeri, F., & Caneill, J.-Y. (2017). Policymaking as collective bricolage: The role of the electricity sector in the making of the European carbon market. In C. Garsten & A. Sörbom (Eds.), *Power, policy and profit: Corporate engagement in politics and government* (pp. 64–81). Cheltenham: Edward Elgar Publishing.

Cartel, M., Colombero, S., & Boxenbaum, E. (2018). Towards a multimodal model of theorization processes. *Research in the Sociology of organizations, 54A*, 153–182.

Cartel, M., Boxenbaum E., & Aggeri, F. (Forthcoming). Just for fun! How experimental spaces stimulate innovation in institutionalized fields. *Organization Studies,* Online First, January 11, 2018. https://doi.org/10.1177/0170840617736937.

Currie, G., Lockett, A., Finn, R., Martin, G., & Waring, J. (2012). Institutional work to maintain professional power: Recreating the model of medical professionalism. *Organization Studies, 33*(7), 937–962.

Czarniawska, B., & Joerges, B. (1996). Travels of ideas. In B. Czarniawska & G. Sevón (Eds.), *Translating organizational change* (pp. 13–48). Berlin: Walter de Gruyter.

Czarniawska, B., & Sevón, G. (2005). *Global ideas: How ideas, objects and practices travel in a global economy.* Malmö: Liber & Copenhagen Business School Press.

Déjean, F., Gond, J.-P., & Leca, B. (2004). Measuring the unmeasured: An institutional entrepreneur strategy in an emerging industry. *Human Relations, 57*(6), 741–764.

den Hond, F., & de Bakker, F. (2007). Ideologically motivated activism: How activist groups influence corporate social change activities. *Academy of Management Review, 32*(3), 901–924.

Durkheim, E. (1982/1895). What is a social fact? *The rules of sociological method* (pp. 50–59). London: Palgrave.

Duymedjian, R., & Rüling, C.-C. (2010). Towards a foundation of bricolage in organization and management theory. *Organization Studies, 31*(2), 133–151.

Garud, R., & Karnøe, P. (2001). Path creation as a process of mindful deviation. In R. Garud & P. Karnøe (Eds.), *Path dependence and creation* (pp. 1–38). Mahwah: Lawrence Earlbaum Associates.

Garud, R., & Karnøe, P. (2003). Bricolage versus breakthrough: Distributed and embedded agency in technology entrepreneurship. *Research Policy, 32*(2), 277–300.

Gond, J.-P., & Boxenbaum, E. (2013). The glocalization of responsible investment: Contextualization work in France and Québec. *Journal of Business Ethics, 115*(4), 707–721.

Green, S. (2004). A rhetorical theory of diffusion. *Academy of Management Review, 29*(4), 653–669.

Greenwood, R., Suddaby, R., & Hinings, C. R. (2002). Theorizing change: The role of professional associations in the transformation of institutionalized fields. *Academy of Management Journal, 45*(1), 58–80.

Hargadon, A. B., & Douglas, Y. (2001). When innovations meet institutions: Edison and the design of the electric light. *Administrative Science Quarterly, 46*(3), 476–501.

Højgaard Christiansen, L., & Lounsbury, M. (2013). Strange brew: Bridging logics via institutional bricolage and the reconstitution of organizational identity. In M. Lounsbury & E. Boxenbaum (Eds.), *Institutional logics in action, Research in the sociology of organizations* (Vol. 39B, pp. 199–232). Bingley: Emerald.

Jones, C., & Massa, F. G. (2013). From novel practice to consecrated exemplar: Unity Temple as a case of institutional evangelizing. *Organization Studies, 34*(8), 1099–1136.

Jones, C., Boxenbaum, E., & Anthony, C. (2013). The immateriality of material practices in institutional logics. *Institutional logics in action, Research in the sociology of organizations, 39A,* 51–75.

Lanzara, G. F., & Patriotta, G. (2007). The institutionalization of knowledge in an automotive factory: Templates, inscriptions, and the problem of durability. *Organization Studies, 28*(5), 635–660.

Latour, B. (1987). *Science in action: How to follow scientists and engineers through society.* Cambridge, MA: Harvard University Press.

Latour, B., & Woolgar, S. (1979). *Laboratory life: The social construction of scientific facts.* Beverly Hills: Sage.

Leca, B., & Naccache, P. (2006). A critical realist approach to institutional entrepreneurship. *Organization, 13*(5), 627–651.

Lévi-Strauss, C. (1962). *La pensée sauvage.* Paris: Plon.

Lévi-Strauss, C. (1966). *The savage mind.* Chicago: University of Chicago Press.

Lounsbury, M., & Crumley, E. (2007). New practice creation: An institutional perspective on innovation. *Organization Studies, 28*(7), 993–1012.

Mena, S., & Suddaby, R. (2016). Theorization as institutional work: The dynamics of roles and practices. *Human Relations, 69,* 1669–1708.

Meyer, M. (2012). Bricoler, domestiquer et contourner la science: L'essor de la biologie de garage. *Réseaux, 3,* 173–174.

Muniesa, F., & Callon, M. (2007). Economic experiments and the construction of markets. In D. McKenzie, F. Muniesa, & L. Siu (Eds.), *Do economists make markets? On the performativity of economics* (pp. 163–189). Princeton: Princeton University Press.

Munir, K. A. (2005). The social construction of events: A study of institutional change in the photographic field. *Organization Studies, 26*(1), 93–113.

Nigam, A., & Ocasio, W. (2010). Event attention, environmental sensemaking, and change in institutional logics: An inductive analysis of the effects of public attention to Clinton's Health Care Reform initiative. *Organization Science, 21*(4), 823–841.

Perkmann, M., & Spicer, A. (2014). How emerging organizations take form: The role of imprinting and values in organizational bricolage. *Organization Science, 25*(6), 1785–1806.

Rao, H., Monin, P., & Durand, R. (2005). Border crossing: Bricolage and the erosion of categorical boundaries in French gastronomy. *American Sociological Review, 70*(6), 968–991.

Sahlin, K., & Wedlin, L. (2008). Circulating ideas: Imitation, translation and editing. In R. Greenwood, C. Oliver, R. Suddaby, & K. Sahlin (Eds.), *The Sage handbook of organizational institutionalism* (pp. 218–242). Los Angeles: Sage.

Strang, D., & Meyer, J. W. (1993). Institutional conditions for diffusion. *Theory and Society, 22*(4), 487–511.

Suchman, M. C. (1995). Managing legitimacy: Strategic and institutional approaches. *Academy of Management Review, 20,* 571–611.

Suddaby, R., & Greenwood, R. (2005). Rhetorical strategies of legitimacy. *Administrative Science Quarterly, 50*(1), 35–67.

Swidler, A. (1986). Culture in action: Symbols and strategies. *American Sociological Review, 51*(2), 273–286.

Swidler, A. (2003). *Talk of love: How culture matters*. Chicago: Chicago University Press.

Tolbert, P. S., & Zucker, L. G. (1996). The institutionalization of institutional theory. In S. Clegg, C. Hardy, & W. R. Nord (Eds.), *The Sage handbook of organization studies* (pp. 175–190). Thousand Oaks: Sage.

Zietsma, C., & Lawrence, T. B. (2010). Institutional work in the transformation of an organizational field: The interplay of boundary work and practice work. *Administrative Science Quarterly, 55*, 189–221.

Zietsma, C., & McKnight, B. (2009). Building the iron cage: Institutional creation work in the context of competing proto-institutions. In T. B. Lawrence, R. Suddaby, & B. Leca (Eds.), *Institutional work: Actors and agency in institutional studies of organizations* (pp. 143–175). Cambridge, UK: Cambridge University Press.

Zucker, L. (1977). The role of institutionalization in cultural persistence. *American Review of Sociology, 42*(5), 726–743.

3

The Institutional Footprint of Organizations

Introduction

This chapter develops the notion of institutional footprint of organizations and provides an empirical illustration of how footprints vary in depth and availability. I discuss the contribution of this notion for the study of materiality in institutional theory and consider its implications for the understanding of organizations and institutions.

Layers of Organizationally Imprinted Institutions at the Abbey of Fontevraud

To the scholar of organizations, visiting the Royal Abbey of Our Lady of Fontevraud in the French Loire valley can be a disorienting experience. Visitors enter a UNESCO World Heritage site, and discover a vast

J. Jourdan (✉)
Université Paris-Dauphine PSL, Paris, France
e-mail: julien.jourdan@dauphine.fr

© The Author(s) 2019
F.-X. de Vaujany et al. (eds.), *Materiality in Institutions*, Technology, Work and
Globalization, https://doi.org/10.1007/978-3-319-97472-9_3

cultural complex with modern art exhibits, an haute-cuisine restaurant, a convention center, and a luxury boutique hotel. Soon, they realize that, until recently and for more than 150 years, the site served a much less entertaining purpose: the Maison Centrale de Fontevraud was the strictest prison in the country, and one of its largest penitentiary factories—a place packed with 2000 inmates forced to work in complete silence. Yet, as the name of the place suggests, the buildings perpetuate the memory of a much older organization: before the French revolution, *l'Abbaye de Fontevraud* ruled over a powerful monastic order overlooking a hundred priories spread across France, Spain, and England.

Throughout the building complex, from the cellars to the cloister, architectural ornaments, sculptures, Latin inscriptions, and symbols engraved in stone are discreet reminders of the strict rule of life the nuns and monks of Fontevraud observed for centuries. Written in 1101 by the itinerant preacher Robert d'Abrissel, the founder of the abbey, and enforced by a lineage of powerful abbesses, the rule was based upon the rule of St. Benedict, and dictated silence, good work, humble food, and utmost simplicity of life and dress. Inside the church, the recumbent statues of Henry II, Alienor of Aquitaine, Isabelle of Angoulème, and Richard the Lionheart recall the paramount role of religious institutions and the entanglement of religious and secular power in medieval life.

The institutions that once inhabited the buildings of Fontevraud are long gone. Abbeys do not rule the land anymore. The French judicial system abandoned imprisonment with hard labor in 1960. The organizations that forged, reproduced, and actively diffused these institutions did not survive their demise. Along with the abolition of the feudal system, the revolutionaries dissolved the monastic order of Fontevraud in 1789, confiscated all the riches of the abbey, and nationalized the land and all remaining buildings. The state prison closed doors in 1963 and convicts transferred to more modern facilities. The abandoned building complex was repurposed and entirely renovated in recent years. In spite of the many destructions, reconfigurations, and inevitable decay it suffered, the abbey still bears the marks—some very visible, others harder to decipher—of the institutions instantiated by the organizations that operated within its walls.

Organizational Alterations of the Institutional Context

The world as we experience it is shaped and, for a large part, produced by organizations. The objects populating our houses, offices, and streets, the radio we listen to in our cars, the website we visit, the public transport we use to commute, the beds we sleep on at night, the sport activities we engage in, the religious service we attend to: all are thought, designed, and materially produced by organizations. Even what we typically tend to think as nature, such as fields, forests, and rivers, has been for a large part affected and, often, materially shaped by the purposeful actions of human organizations. Organizations are created to make products and services, to serve communities, and at times to build common goods; organizations' *raison d'être*, in other words, is to change the world—to produce material effects on how humans live.

It would be naïve though to see organizations as pure technical entities, assembling labor and capital to make products or deliver services. It is a central tenet of new institutional theory that organizations are pressured to adopt institutionalized rules that function as myths linking formal structures to the attainment of desirable ends (Meyer and Rowan 1977) and are disciplined to act in conformity with institutional expectations (DiMaggio and Powell 1983). Both the issues organizations attend to and the repertoire of solutions they propose to these issues are shaped by institutionalized beliefs, assumptions, and values, encapsulated in institutional logics (Thornton and Ocasio 1999). Not only are the structures and practices of organizations shaped by institutions: organizational outcomes as well are subject to critical external pressures. A wide range of stakeholders (e.g., clients, investors, employees, regulators, activists) constantly scrutinize modern organizations to make sure their production meets institutionalized expectations about what is desirable and proper—withdrawing support and resources if organizations fail to do so (Jourdan 2018).

Consider, for illustration purposes, the (stylized) case of two business schools.[1] School A operates under a dominant market logic, that is, the organization is primarily viewed as a service firm, marketing and providing a line of education programs, thought as products suiting the expectations of clients expecting an education premium in exchange for the fees they pay. Now, compare the output of school A to the curriculum of school B operating under a more traditional professional logic, that is, the organization is primarily viewed as a professional training school, offering business education degrees, assembled and developed by professors based on what they think is best for their students and society at large, based on their professional expertise. Because the functioning of these two organizations is shaped by different institutions, the output (business education) they produce is likely to differ in critical ways, including the type of curriculum offered, the content of the courses, and the way students and faculty are evaluated. While education is in essence immaterial, these organizations' outputs carry very material, second-order, consequences in the world: compared to former students of school B, school A's alumni may, for instance, place greater emphasis on contractual relationships in the workplace, more often put clients first in the way they set up and manage teams, and rank market objectives higher when devising organizational strategies, not to mention the broader effects schooling might have on students' citizenship and political views. As thousands of students graduate each year, the magnitude of the accumulated impact these two schools might have on society is likely to be significant. The differences in schools' outputs may materialize in various forms, including the production of physical artifacts. The schools' campuses and buildings, for instance, may reflect the organizational primacy given to market or, conversely, professional concerns, visible through

---

[1] Other chapters in the book take into consideration business schools and education organizations as a vivid arena of institutional dynamics. In Chap. 5, Arena and Douai analyze the emergence of business education as an alternate institutional logic in Oxford University. In Chap. 7, De Vaujany, Winterstorm, Valander, and Vaast examine how universities rely on campus tours to enhance their legitimacy. Finally, in Chap. 9, Thomas Abrunhosa and Canales present Massive Open Online Courses (MOOCs) as a competing institutional logic to traditional education.

architectural choices and spatial configurations (e.g., library space vs. students' lounge).

Organizational outputs may, in turn, yield long-standing effects, persisting even when the organization that originally created—or commissioned—them left or dissolved. The "NATO palace" in Paris offers a case in point (De Vaujany and Vaast 2013): designed by and for the North Atlantic Treatise Organization in the 1950s, the building was originally conceived as a "cold war fortress" with restricted entry points and series of identical office units, a design that still shapes practices and legitimacy claims at the university that has been occupying the premises for 50 years since the allied military organization deserted them.

With this short essay, my aim is to open a discussion on the implications of a critical, yet largely overlooked, observation: because they instantiate, reproduce, and alter various sets of institutions, or institutional logics, organizations leave what I refer to as an *institutional footprint*, a trail reflecting the institutions that shape organizational purpose, structuring, and functioning. Through the institutional footprint metaphor, I am interested in characterizing the way organizations contribute to model the institutional environment of society—the reverse relationship being well established (e.g., institutional environments affect firms' structure, discourse, and practices through, for instance, isomorphism, decoupling, and diffusion). Much like animals leave different footprints, various organizationally instantiated institutions leave different marks that are imperfect, never exactly twice the same, and hardly predictable; the imprints may vary in depth, availability, and durability with the nature and softness of the institutional terrain, and they are more informative (e.g., of directions) when considered in temporal series.[2] Unlike physical footprints, however, institutional footprints are social in nature; yet, much like the former (e.g., animal footprints can be followed by more or less friendly others), the latter are partly visible to a goal-oriented audience of direct and indirect observers: stakeholders monitor organizations through their institutional footprint.

---

[2] For more discussion about durability, please refer to the postface of the book.

The Notion of Institutional Footprint

Institutions—social structures that have attained a high degree of resilience—present an intriguing feature: individual or organizational actors can hardly single-handedly and purposefully change institutions, yet institutions would cease to exist should actors cease to reproduce them. If organizations, as social actors, routinely reproduce largely taken-for-granted institutions, with some degree of variance, and in doing so, play a role in the continuous maintenance or gradual alteration of institutions, how can we characterize the influence organizations may have on the institutional environment?

A conceptual thought experiment can be used to make progress in accomplishing this task (Tetlock and Belkin 1996). The thought experiment consists in asking, for a given organization A: what would the institutional environment be, absent organization A? Conceptually, the institutional footprint of an organization is whatever difference there is between the actual institutional environment I_A and what the environment would have been in the counterfactual case $I_{\bar{A}}$ in which the organization had not existed. In essence, the institutional footprint is the sum of alterations the organization has created since its inception in the institutional environment available to other actors in society, comprising the outputs (products and services) the organization delivers, and any institutional effect organizations may have through the handling of production "inputs" (e.g., train employees, modify supplier practices, create physical artifacts or premises).

Figure 3.1 offers a tentative visual illustration of the institutional footprint of organization A. Panel (b) represents the institutional context as it is (I_A) and panel (a) the institutional context in the counterfactual case ($I_{\bar{A}}$), absent A, with vertical blocks figuring institutional elements (e.g., practices, norms, beliefs, values, assumptions). The differences across the two panels—that is, the institutional footprint of organization A—are colored in panel (b): some components of the institutional context are added (e.g., A augmented some elements or created new components) while others are subtracted (e.g., A altered or contributed to make components obsolete).

The schematic representation of Fig. 3.1 should not be misinterpreted: organizational-level alterations of the institutional context, if any, are likely to be subtle. Organizations are embedded in dominant institutions and they tend to reproduce without much variation, such that institutional alterations may be limited—for example, when actors face contradictions across institutions (Seo and Creed 2002). Another misconception would be to assume that the institutional footprint of an organization always results from purposeful actions engaged by the organization to alter the institutional landscape, that is, some form of institutional entrepreneurship or work (Battilana et al. 2009). Given the largely taken-for-granted nature of institutions, one may rather expect institutional footprints to be mostly incidental; for example, the unexpected result of organizational decisions viewed by organizational members from a technical angle and regarded, as such, as rational, such as entering a new business area, importing practices from distant fields, experimenting new discourses, producing artifacts.

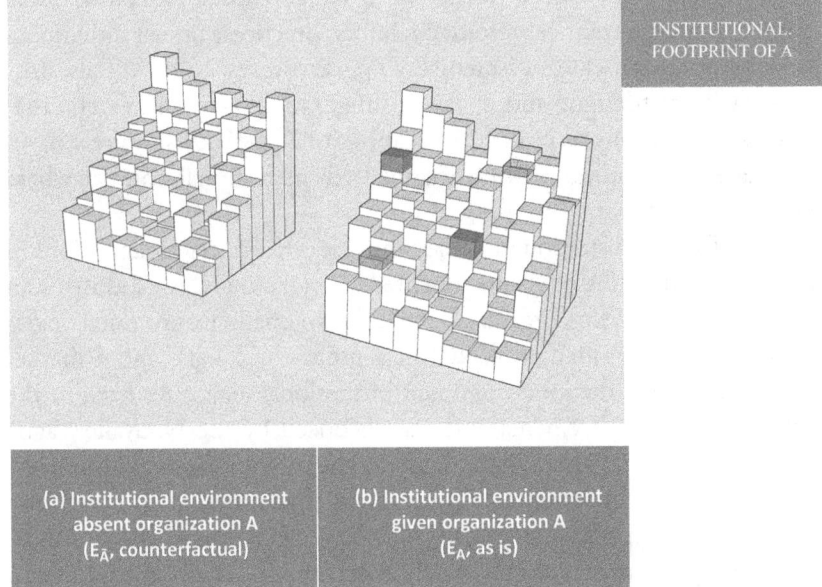

INSTITUTIONAL FOOTPRINT OF A

(a) Institutional environment absent organization A $(E_{\bar{A}}$, counterfactual)

(b) Institutional environment given organization A $(E_A$, as is)

Fig. 3.1 Stylized illustration of organization A's institutional footprint

Also, it is important to keep in mind that the institutional footprint of an organization is not fixed but evolves as the organization operates and makes choices: organizational alterations made to the institutional environment accumulate over time. Yet, given the path-dependent nature of institutional choices, the early life of organizations may strongly determine their future institutional footprints (Marquis and Tilcsik 2013; Stinchcombe 1965).

A Closer Look at Institutional Footprints: An Empirical Illustration

I have defined the institutional footprint of an organization as the sum of (accumulated) alterations the organization has created in the institutional context. While these alterations have both symbolic and material consequences—as illustrated by the business schools' example—they are not readily observable by organizational audiences. Yet, institutional footprints manifest in various ways, for instance through organizational structure and governance, resource choices, practices, ties to individuals and organizations, category membership, discourses, texts, visuals, artifacts, facilities, design, and spatial configurations—to the extent that these manifestations serve as cues organizational audiences can rely upon to situate an organization in a fragmented institutional context where several logics coexist.

Consider, for illustration purposes, the case of producer organizations in the French film industry. As documented in prior studies, the industry can be described as being organized around two main institutional logics (Jourdan 2018; Jourdan et al. 2017): a professional logic and a market logic (Table 3.1). The long-dominant professional logic goes back to the early days of French cinema and was theorized by the Nouvelle Vague movement of the 1950s and 1960s. Under the professional logic, filmmaking is primarily conceived as a form of art that needs to be constantly perfected through craft and cutting-edge professional techniques. Authors are typically granted multiples roles to accomplish their creative vision (e.g., screenwriter and director) and occupy a leading position in production teams (e.g., they enjoy final cut rights). Production organizations largely

Table 3.1 Ideal types of institutional logics in the French film industry (Jourdan 2018)

	Professional logic	Market logic
Societal-level logic	Profession (secondary: Family)	Market
Symbolic analogy	Profession as relational network	Market as allocation mechanism
Economic system	Personal capitalism	Market capitalism
Sources of identity	Film as art and culture Director as artist	Film as asset Producer as manager
Sources of status and legitimacy	Film aesthetics Prestigious awards Box office admissions	Film economics Firm performance Box office profits
Goals	Build art Break even	Build firm reputation Maximize returns
Basis of norms	Membership in guild	Self-interest
Focus of attention	Film historical position	Quality of deal flow
Strategy (of film production)	Build producer's reputation	Hedge risks Predict box office hits
Theory of values	Quality of craft	Mass market demand

rely on subsidy schemes to finance projects. Producers are engaged in status competitions, and compete for peer consecration (Cattani et al. 2014) at professional prize ceremonies (e.g., Césars awards) and film festivals (e.g., Cannes, Venice, Toronto). They also strive for advantageous network positions, affiliating with star actors, directors, and other talents. Their discourses, through media appearances or ceremonial speeches, tend to underline the professional and artistic nature of production activities, and be protective of the boundaries of the industry against perceived threats against its integrity.

By contrast, advocates of the professional logic see filmmaking as an entertainment business that needs to be organized as such. Under the market logic, producers are given larger control over production teams, schedules, and creative content. Marketing and distribution activities are paramount, as it is believed that film audiences are not given but need to be constructed through media exposure—as exemplified by the "take-the-money-and-run" approach of the blockbuster model (Durand and Jourdan 2012). Financing is largely achieved through distribution and broadcasting deals, when money is not provided by market investors. While prizes and accolades are not neglected, they are primarily sought after for their market benefits (e.g., increased media exposure and box office). Production houses' affiliations with brands, through product placement deals, are unproblematic and regarded as an appropriate source of financing and income—much like consumer products. Producer discourses and texts typically include business information, such as box office numbers and deal flows, in addition to creative information.

In a context where various institutional logics coexist,[3] stakeholder audiences use these various observable cues to form an inherently incomplete picture of the institutional footprint of an organization. Of particular importance are cues carried by the actual production output of film production companies: each movie is accompanied by text (e.g., film title, plot synopsis), discourses (e.g., interviews in specialized and mainstream media, reviews), visuals (e.g., film posters, web pages, still pictures, teasers and trailers), audio recordings (e.g., radio interviews, recorded score), and artifacts (e.g., chemical prints, increasingly replaced by digital hard drives, digital video discs (DVDs), promotional leaflets, press dossiers, printed posters, in-theater promotional material, goodies) provide a set of observable traces routinely made available to organizational audiences, including film investors, distributors, exhibitors, talents, film critics, and moviegoers.

Importantly, these observable cues are encoded, such that audiences can only make sense of them—that is, use them to proxy the institutional footprint of an organization—when they possess some knowledge and understanding of institutional codes. The codes may include language, for instance Baumann (2001) shows how film critics in US newspapers gradually incorporated an intellectualizing discourse starting in the 1950s, adopting new vocabulary to describe film as a form of art rather than as an entertainment product. An observer knowing the language of the professional logic of filmmaking may recognize an arthouse film just by reading a plot summary or a short film review. Institutional codes may also be visual: the design of a poster (including colors, fonts, layout, labels) may be sufficient for a knowledgeable audience to distinguish a mainstream movie, developed according to the market logic, from a more artistically

---

[3] In Chap. 9, Thomas, Abrunhosa, and Canales also explore the co-existence of institutional logics and the associated conflicts.

oriented film released by a production house instantiating a professional logic. Likewise, arthouse films may be accompanied by a limited set of artifacts (e.g., DVDs, still pictures, books), with recognizable stylistic traits, whereas mainstream films may be associated with consumer products (e.g., T-shirts, cereals, fast food). Obviously, the features of the film itself provide strong cues, including the title, the name of the actors, and the members of the creative team, but also the plot and the cinematography. These cues are magnified by mediating audiences, including certification bodies (e.g., "Art & Essay" label) and film critics, which help other audiences further interpret and decipher institutional codes (Fig. 3.2).

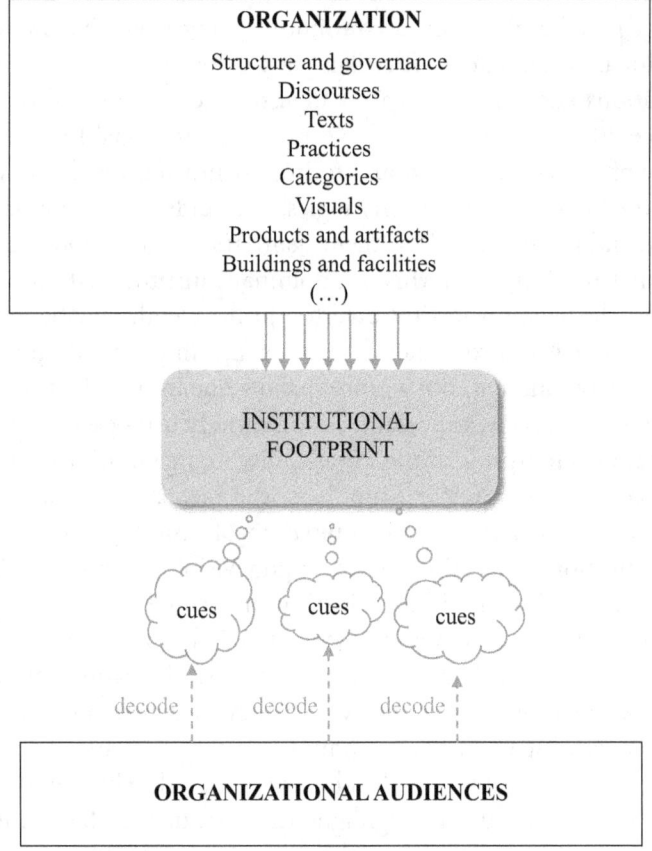

Fig. 3.2 Organizations, institutional footprints, and audiences

The Shape of Institutional Footprints

Institutional footprints vary across organizations. I discuss in what follows two important dimensions. First, the institutional footprints of organizations may vary in depth. As illustrated in Fig. 3.1, an organization that would leave the institutional environment mostly unaffected may barely have any institutional footprint (i.e., I_A and $I_{\bar{A}}$ are identical); this would happen if the organization were to faithfully reproduce existing institutions without much, if any, alteration. Conversely, an organization that would dramatically reshape the local institutional context would have a deep institutional footprint. Thus, an organization's institutional footprint may be placed on a continuum going from shallow to deep. Institutional entrepreneurs (Battilana et al. 2009) and, more generally, organizations successfully engaged in institutional work (Zietsma and Lawrence 2010) can be said to have a deep institutional footprint. This category of actors may contribute to import institutional logics that are new to the field, diffuse minority logics, and undermine dominant ones (Durand and Jourdan 2012). Other organizations—probably more common—that passively conform to a dominant institutional order would have a much shallower institutional footprint. Depth may be relative to the institutional context: small alterations may imprint a deep footprint in a stable environment, but a more shallow one in turbulent contexts.

Another potentially important, if not entirely orthogonal, dimension of institutional footprints is their availability to organizational audiences, such as consumers, investors, suppliers, the media, activists, and other stakeholders. Availability is a combination of visibility and readability. Some institutional footprints may be highly visible, for instance, because the organization is central in the institutional context or has caught the attention of the media. Other institutional footprints may be more discreet, only noticeable by attentive observers. The various dimensions of organizational outputs are likely to be key in that regard. Visual cues (e.g., in advertising or corporate communication) and largely distributed (e.g., products) or visible (e.g., headquarter or flagship building) physical artifacts may contribute to highlight the institutional footprint of an organization, disseminating cues that organizational audiences may use

Table 3.2 Four archetypes of institutional footprints

	High availability	Low availability
Shallow	Gatekeepers	Quiet conformists
Deep	Institutional activists	Covert institutional innovators

to make sense of the institutions instantiated by an organization. Yet, visibility may not be sufficient for making footprints available to audiences; they also need to be readable. Readability has to do with the ability of audiences to decipher the institutional code in which cues are encoded. Physical cues, such as artifacts and buildings for instance, may remain visible for centuries and outlive the institutions that originally led to their creation, yet audiences may not be able to recognize and interpret the codes embedded in the artifacts.

Going back to the example of the Abbey of Fontevraud, numerous monasteries and priories dating back to the Middle Ages can be found across Europe: each monastery was built by a religious order (e.g., Cistercian, Benedict), and their buildings still display cues (e.g., architectural features, building layouts, symbols) meant to signal to medieval observers the institutional logics instantiated by the religious orders that built and inhabited the premises. Whereas these cues made the institutional footprints of the religious orders available to the organizational audiences of the time, they are mostly lost on contemporary audiences—with maybe the exception of a few scholars and religious specialists.[4] Readability may be further reduced when many cues relating to different footprints are juxtaposed. Contemporary visitors of Fontevraud have to sort out intertwined cues related to the religious, penitentiary, and cultural institutions.

Retaining depth and availability as critical dimensions, one may classify the institutional footprints of organizations along four archetypes presented in Table 3.2. I expect most organizations to fall under the "quiet conformist" type: they are passively and inconspicuously reproducing the existing institutional order, thus leaving discreet and shallow

---

[4] Variations in availability—related to heterogeneous diffusion and readability—opens the possibility that perceptions of institutional footprint vary across audiences.

footprints in the institutional context. Organizations acting as "gatekeepers", actively protecting the institutional status quo, have shallow, yet more available, institutional footprints. Organizations forcefully contesting the institutional order, promoting new or minority logics—which we may call "institutional activists"—leave a deeper institutional footprint that is highly available to organizational audiences. Finally, some organizations quietly work to alter the institutional context, acting as "covert institutional innovators": while being deep, their institutional footprint is not much available to organizational audiences.

Evidence from the French film industry suggests that most producer firms are quiet conformists, specialized in either the professional logic or the market logic of filmmaking. For instance, empirical evidence suggests that about two-thirds of production houses specialize in one of the logics available in the industry (Jourdan 2018). These organizations leave a shallow institutional footprint. A subset of organizations, including production houses and professional bodies, is made of active gatekeepers, aggressively protecting the industry from any substantial institutional change. For instance, two producer associations sued Warner Brothers in 2004 when the American major studio set up a local production company to access the French production subsidy scheme—a move, they reasoned, that threatened the professional logic of French filmmaking. Through publicity, the shallow institutional footprint of these gatekeepers is made largely available to organizational audiences. Other organizations play an activist role, including studios that imported market-oriented practices and beliefs from Hollywood, advocating changes in the institutional order—leaving a deep and highly available institutional footprint. Europa Corp, the production company set up by Luc Besson and conspicuously built on a North American template, is exemplary of this archetype: the publicly listed firm makes English-speaking movies for global audiences (e.g., the Taken franchise), shot and distributed under a blockbuster model mostly unknown to French film producers. Finally, organizations—such as specialized investment funds (Jourdan et al. 2017)—have effectively, albeit more quietly, contributed to the rise of market logic in the French film industry, imprinting a deep but discreet institutional footprint.

Institutional Footprints, Availability, and Organizational Survival

I have argued that institutional footprints are by-products of (past) routine organizational activities rather than purposefully produced by organizations and have a path-dependent nature. Does it imply that organizations are passive subjects of established institutional footprints? The previous discussion of the properties of institutional footprints opens some room for organizational agency.

A key observation is that institutional footprints are not directly observable but are partially reconstructed by organizational audiences using available cues. Organizations may have some ability to increase or decrease the availability of their institutional footprint to audiences by affecting the diffusion and readability of cues. Diffusion may be shaped, for instance, by selectively releasing or withholding information that might reveal the institutional footprint of the organization. To some extent, organizations may also be able to influence the readability of cues, for instance, by educating organizational audiences about institutional codes or, on the contrary, obfuscating the cues so that audiences are less likely to decipher them.

This means that organizations may reduce or decrease the potential effects of their institutional footprints on critical outcomes by shaping cues availability. For instance, I have argued in prior work (and found empirical evidence) that firms specialized in an institutional logic have higher chances to survive—more so when the contrast across institutional logics decreases (Jourdan 2018). This is because institutional specialists have an evaluation advantage with stakeholders in fragmented environments, making them better positioned to form and maintain the reciprocal stakeholder relationships they need to survive. If the theory holds, availability may critically moderate this relationship. Institutional specialists may enjoy a greater survival advantage when they make their institutional footprint more available to external audiences (i.e., when they are more gatekeepers than quiet conformists). Conversely, institutional generalists (straddling different institutional logics) may have a lower survival disadvantage when their institutional footprint is not much available to key audiences (i.e., when they are more covert institutional innovators than institutional activists). In other words, depending on their institutional footprint, organizations may be better off making it either more or less available to organizational audiences.

Conclusion

In this brief essay, I introduced the concept of institutional footprint as the sum of alterations an organization creates in the institutional context. In doing so, my intention was to redirect attention to, and characterize, the (typically unintended) effect organizations have on their institutional environment. The argument encompasses, but goes beyond, the idea of organizational activities and relational systems as carriers of institutions (Scott 2001), implicit in most institutional diffusion studies: adopting and shaping practices, like golden parachutes or domestic partner benefits (Briscoe and Safford 2008; Fiss et al. 2012), is one of many ways through which organizations may contribute to alter their institutional environment.[5]

A key assumption is that organizations actually contribute to model their institutional context—that is, institutional footprints have an ontological status. Yet, institutional footprints are not readily observable: rather, organizations as they operate leave cues that organizational audiences can observe and decode to partially reconstruct institutional footprints. Footprints vary across organizations: they can be more or less deep (depending on how much alteration the organization has created) and more or less available to organizational audiences (depending on the diffusion and readability of cues).

Institutional footprints have material properties: organizations affect the material world in various ways—they shape matter and form (Leonardi 2012) in ways that "afford or restrict how and who experiences an environment, shaping interpretation and meaning-making processes" (Boxenbaum et al. 2018, p. 4). As a matter of fact, most of the material

---

[5] Conceptually, failing to adopt (e.g., a practice that gains momentum) could also be a source of institutional alteration.

world we live in is organizationally produced. The notion of institutional footprint emphasizes the deeply institutional nature of that production process. The Abbey of Fontevraud's original design was critically shaped by the religious institutions that governed the functioning of the monastic order at the time of construction. The university building, formerly known as the NATO's palace, would not be the same had the building being ordered by a higher education institution operating under a different institutional logic that NATO. More generally, the material properties, shapes, and forms of products are influenced by the institutions instantiated by their producers. While institutional footprints are not entirely material (e.g., they may also involve alterations in beliefs, values, norms), their non-material parts may carry indirect second-order material effects, as the example of business schools illustrates.

At this stage, a couple of observations are in order. First, the material instantiation of institutional footprints is likely to be stickier than the non-material part; for example, while values and beliefs, for instance, hinge on social reproduction, material objects and buildings remain available until disposed of or destroyed. Materiality, in other words, shapes another property of institutional footprints: their durability. While an organization may experience institutional change, the material cues relating to its institutional footprint stay unchanged for some time, constantly reminding the shadow of the past—which may contribute to slowing down institutional change, or at least temper perceptions of change by external audiences. When Volkswagen (VW), for instance, will have entirely phased out diesel engines, as announced after the 2015 emission scandal and the related decay of the institution supporting this technology, VW-branded diesel cars will remain in circulation for many years.

Second, organizations are often survived by the material and non-material instantiation of their institutional footprints. These bits and pieces of partly realized or failed institutional projects remain available as resources for future projects. Schneiberg (2007), for instance, shows how municipal and cooperative forms of organizations—which developed in the early twentieth century US utility sector as an alternative to the dominant market-oriented and for-profit corporation model—left fragments of institutional projects available to the actors of society as resources to be revived, combined, and redeployed to elaborate new institutional logics.

The case of the Abbey of Fontevraud illustrates how the material remains of past institutions can be interpreted, reinterpreted by organizations to serve as a basis for novel institutional projects. The buildings left by the royal abbey were transformed into a state prison by the Ministry of Justice. The former prison was repurposed into a cultural complex by the cultural organization now in charge. Transitions required symbolic and material adjustments, and also involved compromises. Fontevraud was known as the prison of "one thousand and one windows and doors": the buildings were not meant to serve as a prison. The contemporary cultural center struggles to combine the religious and penitentiary history of the place into a narrative consistent with its recent orientation toward luxury hospitality.

The history of the place suggests a dynamic recursive relationship between the institutional and the material realms: institutional projects turn into material institutional footprints (e.g., buildings) that serve as a resource for new institutional projects when the original institutional project is defeated and so on. Creation and renewal phases are organizationally driven: a religious order turned a meadow into an abbey according to the dominant religious institutions of the twelfth century; when feudal institutions collapsed, the penitentiary administration used the remains of the abbey to perpetuate and adapt the institutional project of imprisonment with hard labor; when the latter institution was abandoned, a state-sponsored cultural organization took over, crafting a new institutional project on the remains of the abbey/prison. No one can tell how long this latest organization and associated institutional project will last, but its institutional footprint will add up another (material) layer to Fontevraud's history.

References

Battilana, J., Leca, B., & Boxenbaum, E. (2009). How actors change institutions: Towards a theory of institutional entrepreneurship. *The Academy of Management Annals, 3*(1), 65–107.

Baumann, S. (2001). Intellectualization and art world development: Film in the United States. *American Sociological Review, 66*(3), 404–426.

Boxenbaum, E., Jones, C., Meyer, R. E., & Svejenova, S. (2018). *Towards an articulation of the material and visual turn in organization studies*. London: Sage.

Briscoe, F., & Safford, S. (2008). The Nixon-in-China effect: Activism, imitation, and the institutionalization of contentious practices. *Administrative Science Quarterly, 53*(3), 460–491.

Cattani, G., Ferriani, S., & Allison, P. D. (2014). Insiders, outsiders, and the struggle for consecration in cultural fields: A core-periphery perspective. *American Sociological Review, 79*(2), 258–281.

De Vaujany, F.-X., & Vaast, E. (2013). If these walls could talk: The mutual construction of organizational space and legitimacy. *Organization Science, 25*(3), 713–731.

DiMaggio, P. J., & Powell, W. W. (1983). The iron cage revisited: Collective rationality and institutional isomorphism in organizational fields. *American Sociological Review, 48*(2), 147–160.

Durand, R., & Jourdan, J. (2012). Jules or Jim: Alternative conformity to minority logics. *Academy of Management Journal, 55*(6), 1295–1315.

Fiss, P. C., Kennedy, M. T., & Davis, G. F. (2012). How golden parachutes unfolded: Diffusion and variation of a controversial practice. *Organization Science, 23*(4), 1077–1099.

Jourdan, J. (2018). Institutional specialization and survival: Theory and evidence from the French film industry. *Strategy Science, 3*(2), 408.

Jourdan, J., Durand, R., & Thornton, P. H. (2017). The price of admission: Organizational deference as strategic behavior. *American Journal of Sociology, 123*(1), 232–275.

Leonardi, P. M. (2012). Materiality, sociomateriality, and socio-technical systems: What do these terms mean? How are they different? Do we need them. In P. M. Leonardi, B. A. Nardi, & J. Kallinikos (Eds.), *Materiality and organizing: Social interaction in a technological world*. Oxford: Oxford University Press.

Marquis, C., & Tilcsik, A. (2013). Imprinting: Toward a multilevel theory. *Academy of Management Annals, 7*(1), 195–245.

Meyer, J. W., & Rowan, B. (1977). Institutionalized organizations: Formal structure as myth and ceremony. *American Journal of Sociology, 83*(2), 340–363.

Schneiberg, M. (2007). What's on the path? Path dependence, organizational diversity and the problem of institutional change in the US economy, 1900–1950. *Socio-Economic Review, 5*(1), 47–80.

Scott, W. R. (2001). *Institutions and organizations*. Thousand Oaks: Sage.

Seo, M. G., & Creed, W. E. (2002). Institutional contradictions, praxis, and institutional change: A dialectical perspective. *Academy of Management Review, 27*(2), 222–247.

Stinchcombe, A. L. (1965). Social structure and organizations. In J. G. March (Ed.), *Handbook of organizations* (pp. 142–193). Chicago: Rand McNally.

Tetlock, P., & Belkin, A. (1996). *Counterfactual thought experiments in world politics: Logical, methodological, and psychological perspectives*. Princeton: Princeton University Press.

Thornton, P. H., & Ocasio, W. (1999). Institutional logics and the historical contingency of power in organizations: Executive succession in the higher education publishing industry, 1958–1990. *American Journal of Sociology, 105*(3), 801–843.

Zietsma, C., & Lawrence, T. B. (2010). Institutional work in the transformation of an organizational field: The interplay of boundary work and practice work. *Administrative Science Quarterly, 55*(2), 189–221.

4

The Role of Artifacts in Institutionalization Process: Insights from the Development of Socially Responsible Investment in France

Bernard Leca, Frédérique Déjean, Isabelle Huault, and Jean Pascal Gond

Introduction

As institutional researchers pay increasing attention to artifacts, they face two challenges. The first one is to elaborate an analysis of artifacts consistent with the tenets of institutional theory. This is challenging

---

An initial version of this paper was presented at the European Group of Organizational Studies in 2006.

B. Leca (✉)
ESSEC Business School, Cergy-Pontoise, France
e-mail: bernard.leca@essec.edu

F. Déjean • I. Huault
Université Paris-Dauphine PSL, Paris, France
e-mail: frederique.dejean@dauphine.fr; isabelle.huault@dauphine.fr

J. P. Gond
Cass Business School, London, UK
e-mail: Jean-Pascal.Gond.1@city.ac.uk

© The Author(s) 2019
F.-X. de Vaujany et al. (eds.), *Materiality in Institutions*, Technology, Work and Globalization, https://doi.org/10.1007/978-3-319-97472-9_4

because the prominent sociological approaches of materiality have onto-logical assumptions regarding social reality that differ from those of institutional theory. In particular, institutional theory has a long-lasting interest for institutionalization. We refer here to institutionalization in a broad way as the extent to which actors orient their actions toward a common set of standards and practices (Scott 1995). Most sociological approaches to materiality have yet a much more flexible view of social reality, insisting on the permanent reconfiguration of the relations between artifacts and actors. Exploring how institutional logics research could engage with materiality, Jones et al. (2013) have reviewed three prominent theories: social construction of technology (SCOT), actor-network theory (ANT) and textuality. Those three approaches eventu-ally provide different ways to conceptualize relations between humans and artifacts but do not provide a view of how artifacts contribute to gradually shape practices and procedures so that they eventually con-verge and become institutionalized. Such approaches tend to insist on the ever-ongoing diversity and change of relations between actors and artifacts. Regarding institutional analysis, current research mostly focuses on how artifacts become institutionalized (e.g. Rao et al. 2003; Jones and Boxenbaum 2014; Jones and Massa 2013) but not how arti-facts contribute to institutionalization.

Our intention in this chapter is to contribute to bringing materiality into institutional analysis by exploring the role of artifacts in the institu-tionalization of new practices. More specifically, our study was motivated by the following research question: *What are the effects of artifacts on the institutionalization of practices in an emerging field?*

To answer this question, we first discuss the possible combination of research on socio-materiality with institutional theory to develop an analysis of materiality within the tenets of institutional theory that could contribute to explain the role of artifacts within institutionalization. In particular, we draw from Hodder's (2016) work on how artifacts and human are entangled and how such processes become irreversible. Second, we draw from an in-depth case study of the emergence of socially responsible investment (SRI) in France and the convergence of practices in managing SRI funds. We focus on the adoption of the artifacts developed by ARESE (Agence de

Rating Environnementale et Social des Entreprises), a non-financial rating agency among the French SR (Socially Responsible) funds. Those years when the practice of SRI took off are commonly named the "ARESE years" (Loiselet 2003). Central to the action of ARESE was the creation of artifacts to articulate their in-house system elaborated to measure corporate social performance and the demands of SRI fund managers.

Based on our theoretical framework and empirical study, we present a model of the effects of artifacts on the institutionalization of a new practice. We find that artifacts can have four types of effects, which contribute to the institutionalization of new practices. Artifacts create interest in new practices by enabling those practices and legitimizing them. They also constrain those practices by limiting the involvement of actors and restricting their actions. The creation of interest combined with the constraints produces the entanglement that eventually can lead to the institutionalization of practices.

We then discuss how considering materiality, among other aspects, can contribute to research on institutional processes as well as on activities such as institutional work. We also suggest some directions regarding the introduction of materiality within institutional theory.

An Approach to Artifacts in Institutionalization Process

We build on the analysis of the assessment that there are significant differences between the most popular approaches to artifacts and institutional theory. As Modell et al. (2017) recently discussed and analyzed, this is especially striking when comparing ANT and institutional theory. We see this is an opportunity rather than a problem. The opportunity would be to consider how to develop an approach to materiality and artifacts within the tenets of institutional theory. In other words, what institutional theory can bring to our understanding of artifacts. In this chapter, we intend to do so by engaging with the specific point of how artifacts contribute to institutionalization.

Artifacts as the Missing Masses of Institutionalization

Just as they used to be the missing masses of sociology (Latour 1992), artifacts remain currently the missing masses of the institutionalization process and, more generally, of current institutional analysis (Pinch 2008). That artifacts are being largely ignored is not specific to institutional research but is a more general tendency within organizational studies, which pay little attention to such artifacts (Knorr-Cetina 1997; Rafaeli and Pratt 2006, p. 1), with "over 95% of the articles published in top management research outlets do not take into account the role of technology in organizational life" according to Orlikowski and Scott (2008, p. 433). This lack of focus on the role of artifacts includes the institutionalization process—that is, the process whereby some practices and procedures are stabilized, diffuse and eventually become taken for granted in a field (Meyer and Rowan 1977; Tolbert and Zucker 1996). To explore the role of artifacts in institutionalization processes using the currently dominant approaches to socio-materiality in organizational research is difficult because those approaches have in general a much more flexible view of relations between artifacts and actors whereby stability can never be assumed. To do so, we suggest to build from two streams of research. First, we draw from institutional theory and, consequently, consider the symbolic aspect of artifacts, in particular how they can impact legitimacy. To account for how artifacts can influence practices that eventually become stable and more difficult to change, we turned to an approach of artifacts developed by Hodder (2016) to account for the irreversible entanglement of actors and artifacts.

The Legitimation Impact of Artifacts

A significant difference between institutional theory and other approaches, such as ANT, is the interest in symbolic aspects that transcend materiality (Boxenbaum et al. 2016). Institutional theory has historically focused attention on symbolic aspects, being interested in why organizations engage in activities that are legitimate in the symbolic realm rather than the material one (Suddaby 2010, p. 15). Central here is the importance of legitimacy defined as appropriateness to sets of norms, values or beliefs (Suchman 1995, p. 574).

When considering institutionalization, the issue is then to understand how artifacts can contribute to the legitimation of a behavior or practice that might become, over long periods of time, taken for granted. Research suggests that artifacts are designed to comply with sets of norms and practices already in use, potentially mixing the characteristics of existing systems with innovation so that innovation would be perceived as more familiar and legitimate to potential adopters (Jones 2001, postface in this volume; Hargadon and Douglas 2001; Silva and Backhouse 1997) to overcome the liability of newness. Yet, while the contribution of artifacts to legitimizing innovation can help explain initial adoption, it does not explain how practices become later entrenched in the habits of actors. To explain how artifacts contribute to the irreversibility of institutionalization, we turn to the notion of entanglement as developed by Ian Hodder.

Hodder's Entanglement Approach

Hodder's approach to the interaction between actors and artifacts is based on an initial critique of ANT for lacking to account for irreversibility in relations between humans and artifacts. Whereas the ANT approach argues that relations between humans and artifacts are constantly evolving, being tight or loose depending on circumstantial attachments, so that the process is constantly uncertain, Hodder develops an alternative argument. Building on his fieldwork in archeology, he argues that once the development and use of artifacts started, it leads to increasing entanglement between humans and things. While ANT authors insist on the flexibility of relations between humans and artifacts and constant change within them, Hodder's perspective insists on the increasing entanglement between humans and artifacts and considers their stabilization. As such we see in Hodder's approach an analysis of human-artifact interactions consistent with the interest of institutional theory in institutionalization as a process whereby some practices and procedures are stabilized, diffuse and eventually become taken for granted in a field. In particular, the entanglement perspective can contribute to advance our understanding of how artifacts influence the institutionalization process whereby some practices and procedures become taken for granted in a field.

Hodder insists on the notion of entanglement to account for the relations between actors and artifacts. Entanglement ensues from the development of interdependence between those entities. Along with other approaches (e.g. Orlikowski 2007; Latour 2000; Leonardi and Barley 2010), Hodder indicates that artifacts are both enabling and constraining for humans. To account for those effects, he insists on the dependencies that are therefore created, distinguishing between dependence and dependency. Dependency refers to the *enabling effects of things*. Actors realize the benefits they can gain from using things, including having activities that they could not otherwise have. Dependency refers to the *constraining aspect* of the relation. Things will shape the way humans behave and then reduce their freedom. The focus on dependence and dependency rather than on relationality draws attention to the dialectical relation whereby humans and things are entrapped in their relations to each other. Interactions between humans and artifacts are both positive and negative. As Hodder notes (2014, p. 20) "the entrapment is enticing and productive."

The Dynamic Aspect of Entanglement

Hodder explicitly considers that the more traditional model of a network between humans and non-humans as developed by Latour and ANT scholars is not adequate to account for the dynamics of the entanglement because within the ANT approach, humans and non-humans are always free to associate or not. A consequence is that, according to ANT, the network requires continuous attention because of a constant risk of dissolution, or as Preda (1999, p. 363) puts it, constant "social, technical, *and* financial maintenance, surveillance, and repairs." The notion of entanglement intends to capture a dynamic of exponential increase that other approaches to relations between artifacts and humans do not capture. As humans develop more artifacts, they become more engage with artifacts and become more depend on them. It becomes very difficult for humans to renounce to those artifacts because they enable action.

Eventually problems raised by entanglement are not solved by renouncing to engage with artifacts but by developing new artifacts. As Hodder notes "It is in our nature to try and fix our problems now by fiddling and fixing and so becoming more entangled in things and technologies. It is in our very being to devour things." (2014, p. 34).

This approach suggests that artifacts are a major aspect of institutionalization process. They work as vehicles for institutionalization because they enable practices and, once adopted, as actors increasingly depend on them, things constrain actors and ensure the reproduction of practices and their further institutionalization. Hodder does not argue that actors will always blindly adopt things and use them. Rather, he distinguishes between unsettled times, where actors become aware of problems and look for artifacts to solve them, and settled times, when they use those artifacts in their day-to-day practices. In this view, there are moments and contexts where humans seem to dominate over artifacts, and other moments and contexts where artifacts seem to dominate over humans.

To illustrate how combining the emphasis of institutional theory on symbolic aspects with Hodder's entanglement approach can provide insights into institutionalization, we then turn to the example of the initial steps of institutionalization of fund managers' practices in the emerging field of socially responsible investment in France.

Case Description and Method

Our illustration is SRI fund management in France, and the role of ARESE's strategies in institutionalizing it. ARESE was an organization that pioneered the activity of social and environmental rating and has been identified as an institutional entrepreneur (Déjean et al. 2004; Penalva-Icher 2007) due to its central role in the structuration of the emerging field. ARESE consisted in providing investors with information on the corporate social performance (CSP) of rated corporations. This implied, primarily, the production and diffusion of artifacts. Three of those artifacts in particular had a significant role in the institutionalization of new practices related to SRI: paper reports on companies, Excel spreadsheets and, finally, dedicated financial indexes. *Paper reports on companies* included ratings on five criteria (human resources, environment, clients and suppliers, relationship with shareholders and engagement with the community) from ++ (max) to − (min) and some details about those dimensions. *Excel spreadsheets* provided a more detailed view. Each criterion was sub-divided along three dimensions: leadership (the corporation's policy), implementation (corporation's means to implement this policy) and results (the actual results of the policy). Rating was then provided under two forms for each criterion and sub-division: from ++ to − and under a quantified form based on a scale from 1 to 100. Those ratings were completed by a *dedicated financial index* named ARESE Sustainable Performance Indices (ASPI) Eurozone developed by ARESE based on the top 120 companies in the Eurozone based on CSR criteria and using the DJ EuroStoxx index as a benchmark.

These artifacts were widely adopted by fund managers as the industry started and ARESE eventually achieved an 85% market share among fund managers in 2001 (see Annex 1). Interviewees suggest that without this agency the market for SRI might have never taken off.

Data and Method

This chapter is based on a broader qualitative study of the emerging activity of SRI in France from 1997 to 2002. Drawing from this broader research, our aim here is to contribute to an understanding of the importance of artifacts in the institutionalization process of the activity. Our research logic is mainly abductive, moving back and forth between our theoretical approach and the data, and our research method is mainly qualitative.

Data Collection

We draw from two PhD dissertations. One on the development of SR funds (Déjean 2004), one on the notion of corporate societal performance and as such engaged in an in-depth analysis of ARESE's strategy (Gond 2006). This allowed us to have material drawn from two different perspectives covering both the actions of the institutional entrepreneur (ARESE) and the way it was received by actors in the emerging field—that is, SR fund managers. We also used more than 60 interviews with members of the field of socially responsible investment, which were made when the field was structuring in the 2000s. This included not only all the persons who participated in the creation or development of ARESE and all the SR fund managers involved in the creation of this activity in banks but also some executives involved in the decision to create the funds. This allowed us to compare and contrast the different positions of these actors, thereby providing a certain degree of control over results by widening the range of data sources. Interviews were semi-structured and lasted from 30 minutes to four hours. They were conducted, taped and transcribed over an extended period from 2000 to 2005. We managed to have half a dozen more retrospective interviews to complete our data and discuss our analysis as we moved into it.

We also collected material about and related to the artifacts that ARESE developed for SR fund managers. This includes the artifacts themselves—that is, the datasheet, the Excel spreadsheets and the four different ASPI, which were publicized as the "ASPI family" of indexes (see Annex 2 for a more detailed description).

Among those secondary sources, we distinguished two sets. First, we gained access to internal documents used by the main actors in this activity. This includes archives and internal documents of the banks as provided by fund managers. Those fund managers provided internal working documents in which the procedures were detailed as well as the way they were assessing the performance of those funds. We accessed archive and internal documents from five European extra-financial rating agencies, including ARESE. Accessing the documents of several agencies allowed us to better understand the reasons for the success of ARESE and the specificity of its action and methods. Second, we reviewed the three main French professional SRI newsletters—the *ORSE, Novethic* and *SRI-in-Progress* newsletters from 2001 to 2003.

An in-depth knowledge of the field was gained from this set of data and familiarity with the field gained from long-lasting relations. It is important to insist that the analysis in this chapter focuses on the creation of the field. Things have been changing significantly since then. We elaborate further on this in the discussion section.

Data Analysis

Data analysis was conducted in three steps.

First, we ordered the collected data through a "facts database" (Yin 1989). That database chronicles the key facts related to the creation and diffusion of the artifacts developed by ARESE, and the institutionalization of practices among SR fund managers. The building was iterative, going back and forth between the data and the analysis. We drew from primary sources and triangulated them with the secondary sources. Those secondary sources also helped us to better understand the mechanisms of the activity. For example, it emerged from analyzing the secondary data that references from ARESE and its ASPI index were both used in public and internal presentations to legitimize the activity by many SRI fund founders. We then developed a narrative account (Eisenhardt and Bourgeois 1988) to chronicle the creation and diffusion of the artifacts developed by ARESE and the practices of the SRI fund managers. We captured what specific artifact had what impact on the institutionalization of practices in SRI fund management.

Second, we coded the material focusing on how artifacts enable and constraint actors and how that interplays in the development of institutionalization.

To complement this analysis, we conducted complementary interviews with five more actors, both former ARESE executives and SRI fund managers. We asked them questions related to our findings to check their robustness. Those actors were chosen both on the basis of their centrality to the emergence of SRI in France and of our enduring relations with them. This proximity allowed us to obtain detailed and genuine information, especially since they had changed jobs since (Boiral 2003).

The Role of Artifacts in the Institutionalization of Socially Responsible Investment in France

Creating Interest

Creating interest from the potential clients—that is, the SR fund managers and banks' executives—was central to ensure diffusion. This task was not obvious. Several other organizations were trying, at the same time, to develop this activity and to convince fund managers to buy their services and were failing (Leca et al. 2006). Moreover, the market study that ARESE's funders had ordered was negative, suggesting that there was not enough interest for such a rating agency to be profitable.

Artifacts developed by ARESE proved useful to create an interest both among the bank's executives in banks and among fund managers trying to create SR funds.

Legitimizing

The artifacts developed by ARESE contributed to legitimizing the emerging field of SRI because they were aligned on the existing cognitive schemes of the bankers and were designed and presented in a way that prevented them from hurting those schemes. Two such cognitive schemes were incorporated into the artifacts: profitability and quantification.

ARESE always insisted that the tools were meant to help fund managers in managing funds that would be both socially responsible and profitable. An ARESE analyst indicated:

We would always mention it somehow. We already had some slides about it. It was [another ARESE analyst] who was in charge of all the financial simulations, so we would do simulations and put them on slides. The question of performance would be come again all the time. The message was always the same, and it has not changed since: at first sight, you are not going to lose money with it. (*An ARESE analyst*)

Another aspect was the quantification of data (Déjean et al. 2004, 2006; Leca and Naccache 2006). While other emerging non-financial rating agencies offered qualitative evaluations of corporate social performance, ARESE opted for quantification, an approach that better complied with the established habits in use in the financial markets and was perceived as a sign of seriousness. A founding analyst at ARESE mentioned that

We'd use statistical and exploratory analysis… to justify our seriousness, to say: "Look, it's simply through analysis, we have a system of analysis—a complex black calculating box. It gives us a result that's relevant, and we can make sense of the data precisely because we can make correlations, interpret trends." (*An ARESE analyst*)

Those efforts to comply with the existing views of financial executives also included avoiding going against their cognitive schemes. A major issue for the fledgling SRI field in France was that the "negative screening" approach that was dominant in the US had a rather bad reputation among French financial executives. Negative screening was a selection strategy whereby fund managers exclude entire industries, such as weapons, pornography and tobacco, and do not invest in any corporation involved in those areas (sin stocks). This reflects the religious and political elements of SRI that are also conveyed in social movements that aim to change corporate behavior and, consequently, society (see Schepers and Sethi 2003). This raised two issues for financial executives. First, they felt uncomfortable with the political activism related to those sorts of practices. Second, consistent with financial theory (Markowitz 1952), top executives in banks argued that to reduce the universe of investment—something done drastically by negative screening—would increase the risk without necessarily having a positive impact on the potential return on investment. Hence, negative screening was rejected in France, as in Europe, as too "narrow-minded approach, overly reliant on personal moral and ethical principles, and inappropriate within the disciplines of the financial world" (Louche and Lydenberg 2006, p. 19). Fund managers starting SR funds would forcefully reject this approach. As one of them indicated:

> With ethical funds, ethics is considered as an obligation to forget about financial performance. We do think differently. In this respect, we talk about sustainable development, about SR funds and we avoid ethical funds because for investors ethics is synonymous of no financial performance. (*A fund manager*)

ARESE complied with this approach and distanced from the ethical aspect of SRI. It insisted that its tools were crafted to serve fund managers, not for activists, with the objective to reach financial performance (Déjean et al. 2013). The ARESE website was very clear regarding the financial performance goal:

ARESE provides investors and fund managers with social and environmental information with a logic based on sustainable development (...). SRI consists in integrating social and environmental criteria in investment decision without giving up financial performance (...). Clearly oriented toward financial performance, SR funds are for the moment not numerous in France.[1]

Artifacts were designed to allow "positive screening" (select the best values based on corporate social performance) and not provide the exclusionary screens that would be useful for negative screening (for a comparison between ARESE and KLD, the dominant US rating agency, see Igalens and Gond 2005).

The artifacts were meant to legitimize both ARESE and the fund managers toward financial executives by complying as much as possible with the cognitive schemes existing in the field to render diffusion easier. As diffusion ensued, the adoption of ARESE artifacts became a way for fund managers willing to develop SR funds to gain legitimacy. Consistently with the tenets of institutional theory, newcomers would imitate the existing fund managers and adopt the same artifacts. Such a fund manager indicated:

> We also saw other rating agencies (...) and this is ARESE that we considered as the most competent, with at that time a horizon larger than the others. It was better when considering the investment universe and considering that everybody else was working with them, we felt they were the ones with the largest basis of analysts and information, hence we followed a little bit the norm (...) We do not exclude to work with someone else other than ARESE, but at the moment in France, they are the only ones. They work almost with all the funds and SAM [another rating agency] only worked with two or three funds. (*A fund manager*)

Even though ARESE was not actually the "only ones," competitors were largely ignored. Eventually, diffusion succeeded and by 2001, 85% of the funds used ARESE rating (see Annex 1).

---

[1] ARESE's website in 2000.

Enabling

The adoption of ARESE artifacts by fund managers was not only ceremonial, but they actually enabled those managers to run their funds, something that those managers would arguably have had a hard time to do without those artifacts.

The major issue that fund managers had to face was the shortage of manpower. As top executives in banks were initially suspicious regarding SR funds, they would often provide those fund managers with limited support. As a consequence, they limited the investment regarding manpower and fund managers had to work with limited teams. Most often, those teams had to do analyses *and* manage funds. As fund management would need some regular attention, they had little time for analysis. A person formerly responsible for SR fund management in a major financial establishment indicated that back in 1997—the time when the activity took off thanks to ARESE—there were only two persons to manage the SR funds. In this context, resorting to artifacts was crucial. A fund manager indicated thus:

> I'm the only manager and at the moment. I rely on ARESE's works (…) Again, I don't really look at the ethical behavior of a corporation myself, we really rely on ARESE which does this as a full time job. You have to have your proper job. (*A fund manager*)

A frequent aspect of artifacts is that they allow to do more with less manpower (Hodder 2016). This aspect proved important for fund managers willing to engage in SRI. In particular, fund managers could delegate to ARESE, through its artifacts, the analysis of and focus on fund management. A fund manager indicated:

> This is not our work right now. At the moment, we know what we're doing, we know what's into ARESE's blackbox. There is a moment finally when you have to trust ARESE and consider that this is their domain (…). We clearly opted for a distinction between the jobs, based on this idea that it was important to use each one's competences. (*A fund manager*)

Artifacts allow fund managers to overcome the shortage of manpower and specialize in what they knew best. This was made all the easier as the artifacts to be compatible with their existing practices.

The enabling aspect of artifacts was made even easier by the ARESE design of the artifacts to make them easier to use for fund managers. To do so, ARESE developed artifacts that would be very close to the ones already used by professionals in finance. The artifacts were designed to serve fund managers and to reduce the cognitive and practical costs associated with the adoption of new tools.

Non-financial information was quantified and packed in such a way that it would fit into the traditional decision-making process used by fund managers. The first two ratings (see Annex 1) were provided through booklets with four or five pages for each corporation, including some specific comments on the corporation policy and the final ratings. Soon, ARESE's analysts found out that this presentation was too long and complex for fund managers who were used to simpler tools, larger databases and statistical analysis. Datasheets for each corporation were reduced to one to two pages of comments with ratings being presented prominently. Eventually, most funds managers would essentially rely on the Excel file provided with the forms. Former ARESE analysts indicate:

> Then you've got numbers, ratings, and that allows you to all possible sorts of combinations to adapt the product to financial analysis and to the way portfolio managers work. (*Former ARESE analyst*)

The tool was well adapted to the current practices of fund managers, releasing them from the burden of analysis and allowing them to save time to manage the funds' performances.

> We had a tool that corresponded to the way analysts work. We used to say "you have the financial filter, after the financial filter which is based on companies' turnover, cash flow etc., quantified figures, you have a rating which is based on other numbers, and which allows you to develop other numbers […]. So you see that would not complicate things, it could fit into the method analysts used to work. It was compatible." (*Former ARESE analyst*)

Constraining Action

While artifacts enabled action, they constrain them at the same time. The combination of both effects is what leads to entanglement (Hodder 2016). Hodder suggests that entanglement is the sum of four types of dependence: humans depend on things (HT), things depend on other things (TT), things depend on humans (TH) and humans depend on humans (HH). He insists that an important part of the entanglement process is things depending on things. When artifacts need to be combined with others to produce the operational chain that is necessary for humans to obtain what they want, the dependence on humans increases. In this part, we examine how this material environment has been constraining for human actors and has oriented their actions. Artifacts would both limit human involvement and restrict human actions. Interesting that while this was constraining, it was not perceived as such by humans. Consistently with what Hodder (2014) argues actors acknowledge the constraining effects but mostly insist on the enabling ones, which shows that both aspects of the human-artifacts interactions are inextricable.

Limiting Involvement

As fund managers adopted ARESE's artifacts, they delegated to those artifacts entire parts of the SR fund management. This was initially the case with the socially responsible part of the funds. A fund manager indicated:

> We strongly delegate the ethical management to ARESE, we delegated it entirely. We have no influence on that. We focus on financial management, ARESE send use the ethical management. (*A fund manager*)

Limited involvement was indeed intentional because evaluating corporate social performance implied dealing with a huge amount of data.

> We subscribe to ARESE because we consider there is too much information; we need a professional with a vision of sustainable development matching ours, someone who tries to have a managerial view of companies, who really

does an homogenous and coherent work for on all the companies, that clear out the field for us, that's why we use those rates. (*A fund manager*)

Initially, SR fund managers would not build the competences to perform such an analysis. Indeed, they renounced acquiring such competences. The artifacts would then limit their involvement in the process to the selection of values.

We don't have the competences to evaluate whether a company has a good social policy or a good environmental policy (...) As long as we do our job of selection, but this is a selection of selection, we are not competent to say whether ARESE is right when it states that the wage policy at Peugeot is good or bad. I don't know, we don't have to judge, we take them as they are. (*A fund manager*)

Involvement was further limited in 2001 and then in 2002 when ARESE introduced its ASPI indexes released as a broad-based equity index tracking the financial performance of values from the Down Jones EuroStoxx financial universe. This contributed to allowing fund managers to develop passive management based on trackers that mimic the performance of the index. For example, the ASPI Eurozone was the first index released by ARESE and was accompanied by a sustainability tracker—the *Easy ETF ASPI Eurozone.*

As the tools were developed, they offered increasingly convenient ways to develop and manage SR funds by connecting existing fund management artifacts with ARESE artifacts and automatize procedures. "Operational chains" (Hodder 2016; Leroi-Gourhan 1943; Lemonnier 1993) were then constituted with artifacts providing corporate social performance analysis upstream and artifacts supporting fund management downstream. While this proved legitimacy and enable fund managers, it also constrained their action.

Restrict Action

While limiting involvement and enabling fund management with less human resources, the artifacts also restricted action. The information and evaluation provided would limit the "universe" of investment and fund managers would refrain from venturing outside this universe.

Consequently, the evolution of the SR funds' portfolios followed the evolution of ARESE universe (Déjean 2005). As ARESE moved beyond the French market—CAC 40 and then SBF 120—and started rating European stocks—Eurostoxx 600 (see Annex 1 for details)—through a group named SiRi with other prominent European extra-financial rating agencies, SR funds started buying stocks beyond the French market. Fund managers indicated:

> ARESE had an investment horizon at the beginning that was a little tight, so it was problematic for us because the fund has a benchmark which is half SBF 120 [French index] and half Eurostoxx [European index]. So initially ARESE was mainly rating French stocks. After one year, ARESE had a much larger sample and it allowed us to extend the investment basis and now they cover almost all the Eurostoxx. (*A fund manager*)

> When we started this fund in June 1999 it was only invested in French stocks because at that time, ARESE had no other offer. And then, since ARESE created the SiRi group with their European and North American partners we extended to European middle caps in 2000. (*A fund manager*)

Not only would the universe of investment be limited by the artifacts but the ponderation of criteria in the funds would also depend on the artifacts.

> At the creation ARESE themselves told us that those criteria were the ones for which they had the more information, the more data, that they focused the more one, where they could provide the richer analysis like. So that's why for this product [the fund] we overweight human resources and relations with suppliers. It's like for us all the structure of the portfolio is determined by ARESE ratings, and what we do is just to adjust at the margin. (*A fund manager*)

A former analyst at ARESE accounts for sales meetings with fund managers, indicating:

> At the very beginning as it was totally new and the client had no expertise, there was no expertise from clients. The model, the first phase at least until

2000, 2001, may be even 2002 the model was the model of "third guarantor." That is, clients didn't know anything about the business, they needed a label, a logo they could show, someone that could guarantee quality. (…) People would ask us what our ratings looked like. It would take 2 or 3 hours for us to explain the scoring methods (…) after a couple of hours the guy would ask us: 'how do you use it? What would you recommend? We would tell them, there are several methods: you could use it to reduce your investment universe or to overweight or underweight some stocks in your portfolio, or you could use the sole qualitative part to have a general idea. Most did not dare departing from ratings. People would use ratings as a constraint to define the portfolio, either by eliminating the worst ratings (…). (*ARESE Analyst, 2009*)

While a departure from the ratings was possible, it remained limited. Several fund managers indicate that they selected among the ARESE criteria.

ARESE has five criteria, we took four of them. (*A fund manager*)

We launched four [SRI] funds for which we apply ARESE criteria, but we weight them sometimes differently. (*A fund manager*)

Our criteria depend on the nature of the funds, but they also depend on ARESE criteria. (*A fund manager*)

Discourse and Artifacts

While the present study focuses on artifacts, ARESE also used discourse to convince the fund managers and the executives. ARESE's discourse and ratings were aligned. The aims of both the discourse and the design of the artifacts were to create some interest from the financial community. Hence, the communication and the rating system were designed accordingly.

If ARESE did only one thing, it was to call itself social rating agency. [Before] there was only research organizations, small organizations created by former union leaders, former NGOs employees or religious groups [...] and there was not idea, no intend, to rate and create a tool that might be useful for finance professionals, as they were opposing finance profession-als. Their approach is just a conflicting approach, and not an approach based on complementarities. (*An ARESE funder*)

It was framed to be redundant with the priorities and needs of the financial community and the targeted clients: fund managers. The official presentation of the agency indicated that:

> Our core business is to realize analysis and rating on the corporations' soci-etal and environmental sustainability. This evaluation allows to orient long range investment decisions and contributes to integrate the social and envi-ronmental information to complement traditional financial analysis. (…) ARESE is a tool serving investors willing to take into account the criteria related to sustainable development.

ARESE diffused at the same time the idea of SRI and the tools neces-sary to implement it (Penalva-Icher 2007, p. 318). ARESE ratings reduce rhetoric to figures that investors could manipulate, and to index they can use them as a benchmark. Since fund managers insist that they are always evaluated on the performance of the fund, ARESE would always men-tion this dimension in the presentations they were doing of the rating system.

> We would always mention it somehow. We already had some slides about it. It was [another ARESE analyst] who was in charge of all the financial simulations, so we would do simulations and put them on slides. The ques-tion of performance would be come again all the time. The message was always the same, and it has not changed since: at first sight, you are not going to loss money with it. (*An ARESE analyst*)

The ARESE discourse can be analyzed as a classic example of framing (Benford and Snow 2000). ARESE would identify a problem (the need for tools to manage SR funds), offer a solution (their specific artifacts) and show potential clients the benefit for them (they would not be losing money and might make some). Reference to the dominant logic of finance—that is, profitability—helped in legitimizing the artifacts.

The discourse was certainly important in supporting the diffusion of the artifact and creating interest. Yet, while the discourse favored the diffusion of the artifact, it is the artifact that enabled fund managers to operate and eventually influenced their practices.

Discussion and Provisory Conclusion

Through this study, our intention was to illustrate how the combination of approaches can contribute to better understand how artifacts contribute to institutionalization. A model emerged from this study points to four mediating mechanisms (Fig. 4.1) by which artifacts might influence the institutionalization process. Artifacts are used to create interest and legitimize the activity of those adopting them. Artifacts can also allow actors to reduce their involvement and to delegate some work to the artifacts, and by doing so restrict the actions of those who adopted the artifacts. The combination of enabling and constraining is what provokes the entanglement between actors and artifacts, eventually leading to actors adopting the same behavior imposed by the same artifacts, which

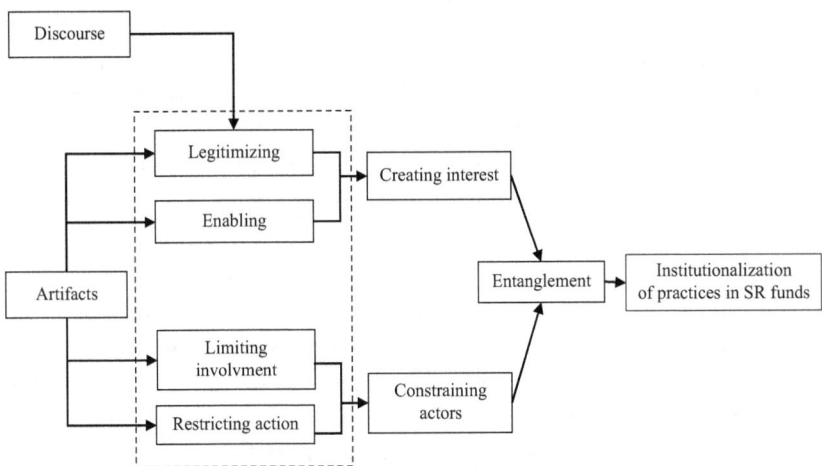

Fig. 4.1 An emerging model of the effects of artifacts in early institutionalization

leads to the institutionalization of practices. This is not to say that all fund managers had exactly the same practices. Artifacts enable and constraint actors but actors develop tactics to achieve their goals by adapting artifacts and do bricolage to bypass the limits of artifacts (Beunza and Stark 2009). In the present case, some fund managers told us how they directly access and retrieve information from companies to overcome the limits of ARESE artifacts. Nevertheless, what emerge are patterns of behavior in this emerging field that showed a relative permanence over time.

In what follows, we intend to discuss and reflect upon the approach adopted in this chapter and this illustration, points to the directions that are suggested and notes some of the shortcomings of our approach while acknowledging that there are certainly many others.

An Approach to Materiality in Institutional Theory

In this chapter, we intended to contribute to the integration of materiality within institutional theory. For more than one decade now, institutional analysis has mostly focused on discourse and discourse analysis and has rather neglected other aspects of social reality (Leibel et al. 2018; Levay and Scully 2007). Ensued more recently, a series of "turns" as institutional theory took a visual turn (Meyer et al. 2013), an emotional turn (Voronov and Vince 2012) and a material turn (Boxenbaum et al. 2016; Jones et al. 2013) to name some. Eventually, those turns could be more turns for a theory that will keep on spinning, and might well, at some point, lose any direction as divergent agendas accumulate without a proper or specific direction (David and Bitektine 2009). In order to avoid this, we intended to follow Suddaby's (2010, p. 15 emphasis by us) recommendation that while "institutional theory can benefit from insights of other approaches, *it must remain true to the central puzzle and questions that define it*" and remain within the ontological and epistemological tenets of institutional theory (for more discussion on ontological and epistemological trends, please refer to the introduction of this volume).

Building on Suddaby's remark, we asked what would be specific about an institutional approach to the material dimension. Based on this, we tried to develop an approach that would be consistent with the ontological and epistemological assumptions of institutional theory. We also paid attention to Modell et al.'s (2017) recent discussion about the problematic association of institutional theory with socio-material approaches such as ANT that have very different, potentially incompatible, perspectives. Based on those perspectives, we believe it is possible to elaborate approaches to socio-materiality that might be specific to institutional theory.

Trying to do so, we focused in the present chapter on the specific aspect of institutionalization, a central puzzle in institutional theory. Existing institutional research brings the specific perspective that legitimacy is crucial to facilitate adoption and accounts for how imitating existing material assemblages can help gain legitimacy and favor adoption. To account for the irreversibility in the institutionalization process, we then turned to Hodder's approach to materiality because it considers entanglement and irreversibility as important aspects, something that we could not find in other approaches to socio-materiality, and resonates with the prominent concern in institutional theory with institutionalization as an ongoing process toward the stabilization of behaviors.

We argue that adopting this sort of approach that would combine the specific insights of institutional theory with approaches to socio-materiality can help in building specific institutional approaches to materiality, which might provide interesting insights both to institutional theory and to research on socio-materiality.

Institutionalization

While institutional theory has recently integrated the material dimension, artifacts are often considered as instantiations of institutionalized practices or underlying logics (Jones and Massa 2013) or as carriers of institutions (Scott 2003). Their specific role in the institutionalization process has been less researched. The present chapter points to the creation of interest and the constraining aspects as a combination whereby artifacts diffuse and shape actors' practices. The combination of artifacts and consistent discourse contributes to legitimizing the activity, while artifacts enable fund managers to do more with less (i.e. less human resources), creating interest for the activity. At the same time, because of the limited affordances those artifacts offer to users, they constrain their action and lead to a convergence of behaviors in a field and their stabilization. Institutionalization here is to be understood in a broad sense because actors can not only use artifacts as such but can also develop tactics to achieve their goals by adapting artifacts and do bricolage to bypass the limits of artifacts (Beunza and Stark 2009). For example, some fund managers told us how they directly accessed and retrieved information from companies to complete the information they would get through ARESE artifacts. Actors are not more "material dopes" that they would be "cultural dopes." Yet, the collective adoption of artifacts contributes to the institutionalization of convergent behaviors.

Building on Hodder's (2016) approach to entanglement suggests that once diffusion is achieved, the use of artifacts become irreversible. Hodder's assumption is that because humans are increasingly entangled with artifacts that enable them to do more, there is no way back. Humans will not renounce artifacts but will only be able to replace them by other artifacts, most likely in increasing number. This is consistent with what we observed in SRI in France. ARESE ceased to be a prominent actor when banks started developing internal analyses and other non-financial rating agencies entered the field (Penalva-Icher 2007). ARESE artifacts were replaced or complemented by more artifacts that altogether contributed to the structuration of SRI as a well-established activity, distinct from traditional fund management because the tools and practices are not exactly the same. The integration in the decision-making process of a non-financial information layer provided through increasingly sophisticated tools and analysis is eventually what distinguishes SRI from mainstream fund management.

Potentially, this suggests the possibility of tracing institutional evolutions and changes in the organizational field by tracing changes in the operational chains. Operational chains are a technological approach that seeks to reconstruct the succession of mental operations, technical gestures and relations between humans and artifacts around the production, use and eventually discard the objects, considering the sequence as socially embedded (e.g. Martinón-Torres 2002). Considering the operational chains developed to perform activities specific to the field, tracing how those operational chains are constituted and evolved, and how humans and artifacts become entangled in them might provide an interesting approach to examine institutional processes.

Artifacts and Institutional Work

The present study can also contribute to institutional work, as artifacts appear to be part of the ARESE purposive strategy to help structure the field of socially responsible investment in France. Consistent with existing works (e.g. Battilana et al. 2009; Gawer and Phillips 2013; Jones and Massa 2013; Lawrence and Suddaby 2006; Lawrence et al. 2009; Raviola and Norbäck 2013), it points out that institutional work is a purposive activity that includes the use of multiple means, including the use of not only discourse but also artifacts as well as other dimensions that are not considered in the present study (e.g. financial resources, social relations). It suggests that each mean used in institutional work might have a different impact. In the present case, discourse mainly creates an interest but artifacts seem more important to constraint action and eventually produce the entanglement that is necessary for a convergence of behavior to happen. Their combination proves useful to achieve the entanglement of actors and artifacts. Along with previous research (e.g. Gawer and Phillips 2013), the present study suggests that to distinguish between discourse, artifacts and other means of action used by actors engaged in institutional work might allow an examination of their specific effects in institutional processes. It might also inform us on the effects of using different means in combination.

Finally, the present chapter has important limits. Arguably, the most important comes from the data of our empirical study. We draw from a larger research whose focus was not initially on the impact of artifacts on the emergence and stabilization of practices in SR funds but on the broader topic of the emergence and institutionalization of SRI in France. While those data allow us to point to some aspects, they are insufficient to reconstruct the precise operational chains composed to enable SR fund management. As such, the empirical part of this chapter should be considered as a limited illustration. Conducting research focusing on operational chains during institutional processes rather than in retrospect would certainly provide better results. More than an inductive study, the present chapter intends to be an invitation to institutional researchers to engage with new approaches to materiality such as the one developed by Hodder.

Second, all artifacts do not operate according to ARESE's rating. This case, as well as the example of financial rating agencies (e.g. Fitch, Standard & Poor's, Moody's) suggest that ratings are especially powerful artifacts that have a major impact on the investment-making decisions. While our case study allows an analysis of several dimensions of the way artifacts influence institutionalization and actors' practices, it is not possible to infer from it that *any* artifact will have the same effects. We need to learn more about the articulation between the constraining and allowing dimensions of artifacts, the way they articulate, whether some artifacts allow more than they constraint, while other artifacts would do the opposite, and, if so, what could explain those differences. Third, this chapter only focuses on the early stages of the institutionalization process. In the present situation, artifacts are used by the institutional entrepreneur to diffuse its institutional project. This is not to say that we oppose previous research, which suggests that during the institutionalization process, artifacts acquire an autonomy of their own. Yet, our empirical research does not allow to document this. To document how artifacts eventually achieve a position beyond the reach of their creators would call for longer research that would document institutionalization processes beyond the early stage on which we focus. Nevertheless, we anticipate that this study could open avenues for future research that would combine approaches to materiality while remaining within the tenets of institutional theory.

Annex 1: Evolution of the ARESE Rating and Its Diffusion (1997–2002)

Year	1998	End 1998	1999	2000	2001	2002
Artifacts						
Presentation of the final datasheets	Booklets with several pages 4 classes A B C D (a sign + or – is added)	Descriptive sheets (3–9 pages) 4 classes A B C D (a sign + or – is added)	Shorter sheets Excel files 5 classes: / – / ––	Sheets are systematically limited to 2 pages 5 classes: ++ / + / = / = / – / ––	Two-page sheets except for the CAC 40 (4 pages) 5 classes: ++ / + / = / – / ––	Two-page sheets except for the CAC 40 (4 pages) 5 classes: ++ / + / = / – / ––
Excel spreadsheet ASPI indexes			Excel files	Excel files	Excel files ASPI Eurozone/ ASPI Country	Excel files ASPI Europe/ ASPI Global
Covered "universe"						
Rated stocks	CAC 40	SBF 120	SBF 120 + Some European values	EUROSTOXX 600	EUROSTOXX 600	EUROSTOXX 600 + Small caps
Number of corporations covered	40	120	120 + 80	250–300	250–300	350–400
Market						
Number of funds using ARESE	0	4	9	22	34	80
Number of SRI funds in France	7	12	17	33	42	59
Market share	NS	33%	53%	67%	85%	
Money managed by SRI funds (in millions Euros)	312.3	324.5	511	722.2	921.3	1250

Sources: ARESE, Terra Nova Conseil, Novethic

Annex 2: The Artifacts Developed by ARESE

The Excel Spreadsheet

Above a financial universe, each company is rated on five "widely accepted stakeholder themes," the ARESE criteria:

- Community and international civil society
- Corporate governance
- Customers and suppliers
- Health, safety and the environment
- Human resources and international labor standards

ARESE analysts assess and rate a company's non-financial performance for each criterion on the basis of a three-step methodology that assesses a company's commitment to:

- Leadership: the role of management in institutionalizing each stake-holder criterion into company policy and strategy
- Implementation: the programs and actions undertaken by the company to put policy and strategy into real practice for each criterion
- Results: the degree, level and consistency of the realization of policy and strategy and stakeholder satisfaction for each stakeholder criterion supported by quantified performance data

Assessment	Scoring scale
Leadership	0–100
Implementation	0–100
Results	0–100
Final score	0–300

The awarding of points corresponds to a framework of key factors under each of the L-I-R steps for each criterion in the ARESE methodology. These key factors reflect general stakeholder and sustainability best-practice concepts identified by ARESE. Each key factor will also encompass a number of constituent sub-factors, which reflect more specific and particular best practices measures.

Finally, companies are ranked and awarded a rating on each of the ARESE criteria. Each rating is designed to be illustrative of a company's performance on each criterion vis-à-vis other companies in its respective industry sector.

Every key factor is awarded points on the basis of the dimensions contained in the following analytical framework:

Dimension	Scoring	Significance
Strategic planning	0–100	Planning and control
Consistency	0–100	Consistency with sustainability
Dissemination	0–100	Internal dissemination
Involvement	0–100	Stakeholder involvement
Trend	0–100	Extent of implementation
Cohesion	0–100	Consistency of application
Objectives and targets	0–100	Achievement of objectives and targets

Each dimension is scored on a 100-point scale using 25-point increments from 0 to 100. The neutral note is 50. And, if information or data are absent from any dimension, this dimension will not be assessed and is neutralized in the scoring process.

Finally, fund managers and investors receive an Excel file allowing them to find, for each company, six ratings: a global rating and a rating for each of the five criteria.

ARESE corporate sustainability ratings per criterion	
Pioneer	++
Advanced	+
Average	=
Below average	−
Unconcerned	−

Asset managers and investors compose their portfolio with these ratings with specific averages corresponding to the characteristics of socially responsible funds (more or less, environmental, social, community involvement etc.).

The ASPI Index

The financial index called ARESE Sustainable Performance Indices (ASPI).

ASPI is a family of ARESE indices. The ASPI family of indices was customized by Stoxx Limited.

The first one was ASPI Eurozone. It was launched on 28 June 2001 at the Palais Brongniart of the Paris Bourse. Between 2001 and 2002, ARESE launched many indices: ASPI Country, ASPI Europe and ASPI Global.

Regarding the launch of ASPI, Genevieve Ferone, Chairman of ARESE, commented "the launch of ASPI is an important landmark in the development, growth and institutionalization of corporate sustainability and SRI in Europe. Leading investors, corporations and stakeholders have made clear their need for SRI indices which reflect European values of best practice. ASPI will play an important role in satisfying this demand" (ARESE Release Press).

And Scott Stark, Managing Director of Stoxx Limited, added that "the launch of ASPI is an important signal for the market and its future development. Investors are becoming more and more conscious of the importance of a sustainable development showing financial and social maturity" (ARESE Release Press).

The ASPI Eurozone Guidelines (February 2002) indicates (page 4):

Leading institutional investors, corporations and stakeholder groups have made clear their demand to ARESE for SRI indices that reflect cutting-edge sustainability thinking and which offer a positive assessment of company performance. In that vein, it is anticipated that the ASPI will:

- Offer consistent standards and definitions of sustainability and SRI
- Encourage dialogue and debate on sustainability and SRI
- Promote the stakeholder agenda
- Encourage investment in companies that match the ASPI criteria thus spurring the growth of sustainable policies and practices and
- Serve as the basis for the launch of investment funds, trackers and benchmarks for socially responsible investing

The ASPI Eurozone is a European equity index tracking the financial performance of the Eurozone's leading companies in terms of corporate sustainability. More specifically, it is a broad-based equity index tracking the financial performance of the Eurozone's top 120 sustainability performers (from the DJ EURO Stoxx benchmark financial universe).

Companies are selected for inclusion within the ASPI family of indices on the basis of the social and environmental ratings of ARESE.

The ASPI indices are rooted in a positive approach toward corporate sustainability: companies are selected for inclusion solely on the basis of positive screening, selecting companies adopting and moving toward good and best practices. There is no company exclusion, the selection is based on the five criteria described above (see section "The Excel Spreadsheet").

ARESE's ratings for each of its criteria translate respectively into five ASPI scores for each company:

ARESE assessment	ARESE rating	ASPI score
Pioneer	++	4
Advanced	+	3
Average	=	2
Below average	–	1
Unconcerned	–	0

The five ASPI scores (on each of the five criteria) are averaged, leading to a mean sustainability score that determines a company's overall ranking in the ASPI (the highest score getting the highest ranking).

The Data Sheets

Fund managers can also use a synthetic data sheet (one or two pages) for each rated company. This document allows them to have qualitative data with the rating. The company profile is presented (figures, shareholders, sales, activity sector). And, for each five criteria, ARESE gives information about the progress of the company. These data aim at underlining the more striking facts during a period. They can be viewed as an abstract for the company's sustainable activity.

References

Battilana, J., Leca, B., & Boxenbaum, E. (2009). Agency and institutions: A review on institutional entrepreneurship. *Annals of the Academy of Management, 3*, 65–107.

Benford, R. D., & Snow, D. A. (2000). Framing processes and social movements: An overview and an assessment. *Annual Review of Sociology, 26*, 611–639.

Beunza, D., & Stark, D. (2009, August). *Reflexivity and systemic risk in quantitative finance.* Paper presented at the Politics of Markets conference, Berkeley.

Boiral, O. (2003). ISO 900: Outside the iron cage. *Organization Science, 14*, 720–737.

Boxenbaum, E., Huault, I., & Leca, B. (2016). Le tournant « matériel » dans la théorie néo institutionnelle. In F. X. de Vaujany, A. Hussenot, & J.-F. Chanlat (Eds.), *Théorie des organisations, nouveaux tournants*. Paris: Economica.

David, J. D., & Bitektine, A. B. (2009). The deinstitutionalization of institutional theory? Exploring divergent agendas in institutional research. In D. Buchanan & A. Bryman (Eds.), *The SAGE handbook of organizational research methods* (pp. 160–175). Thousand Oaks: Sage.

Déjean, F. (2004). Contribution à l'étude de l'investissement socialement responsable. *Les stratégies de légitimation des sociétés de gestion.* unpublished. Unpublished PhD dissertation.

Déjean, F., Gond, J.-P., & Leca, B. (2004). Measuring the unmeasured: An institutional entrepreneur's strategy in an emerging industry. *Human Relations, 57*(6), 741–764.

Déjean, F., Gond, J.-P., & Leca, B. (2006). La quantification comme instrument de légitimation ? Une analyse du rôle joué par ARESE dans la construction de l'Investissement Socialement Responsable en France. In P. de la Broise & T. Lamarche (Eds.), *Responsabilité sociale: vers une nouvelle communication des entreprises?* (pp. 177–199). Villeneuve-d'Ascq: Septentrion Presses Universitaires.

Déjean, F., Giamporcaro, S., Gond, J.-P., Leca, B., & Penalva-Icher, E. (2013). Mistaking an emerging market for a social movement: A comment on Arjaliès' social-movement perspective on socially responsible investment in France. *Journal of Business Ethics, 112*(2), 205–212.

Eisenhardt, K. M., & Bourgeois, L. J. (1988). Politics of strategic decision making in high-velocity environments: Toward a midrange theory. *Academy of Management Journal, 31*, 737–770.

Gawer, A., & Phillips, N. (2013). Institutional work as logics shift: The case of Intel's transformation to platform leader. *Organization Studies*, 1–37.

Hargadon, A., & Douglas, Y. (2001). When innovations meet institutions: Edison and the design of the electric light. *Administrative Science Quarterly, 46*, 476–501.

Hodder, I. (2014). The entanglements of humans and things: A long-term view. *New Literary History, 45*(1), 19–36.

Hodder, I. (2016). *Studies in human-thing entanglement*. Published online. http://www.ian-hodder.com/books/studies-human-thing-entanglement

Igalens, J., & Gond, J.-P. (2005). Measuring corporate social performance in France: A critical and empirical analysis of ARESE data. *Journal of Business Ethics, 56*(2), 131–148.

Jones, C. (2001). Co-evolution of entrepreneurial careers, institutional rules and competitive dynamics in American film, 1895–1920. *Organization Studies, 22*(6), 911–944.

Jones, C., & Boxenbaum, E. (2014). Let's get concrete!: How materials and aesthetics drive institutional change. https://hal.archives-ouvertes.fr/hal-01103155/

Jones, C., & Massa, F. G. (2013). From novel practice to consecrated exemplar: Unity Temple as a case of institutional evangelizing. *Organization Studies, 34*, 1099–1136.

Jones, C., Boxenbaum, E., & Anthony, C. (2013). The immateriality of the material in institutional logics. *Research in the Sociology of Organizations, 39A*, 51–75.

Knorr-Cetina, K. (1997). Sociality with objects. Social relations in postsocial knowledge societies. *Theory, Culture & Society, 14*(4), 1–30.

Latour, B. (1992). Where are the missing masses? Sociology of a few mundane artifacts. In W. Bijker & J. Law (Eds.), *Shaping technology, building society: Studies in sociotechnical change* (pp. 225–258). Cambridge, MA: MIT Press.

Latour, B. (2000), « Factures/fractures. De la notion de réseau à celle d'attachement », in A. Micoud & M. Peroni (dir.), Ce qui nous relie, La Tour d'Aigues: Éditions de l'Aube, p. 189–208.

Lawrence, T., & Suddaby, R. (2006). Institutions and institutional work. In S. Clegg, C. Hardy, & T. B. Lawrence (Eds.), *Handbook of organization studies* (2nd ed., pp. 215–254). London: Sage.

Lawrence, T., Suddaby, R., & Leca, B. (2009). Introduction: Theorizing and studying institutional work. In T. Lawrence, R. Suddaby, & B. Leca (Eds.), *Institutional work: Actors and agency in institutional studies of organization* (pp. 1–27). Cambridge: Cambridge University Press.

Leca, B., & Naccache, P. (2006). A critical realist approach to institutional entrepreneurship. *Organization, 13*(5), 627–651.

Leca, B., Gond, J.-P., Déjean, F., & Huault, I. (2006). Institutional entrepreneurs as competing translators: A comparative study in the French social evaluation industry. *Academy of Management*, Atlanta.

Leibel, E., Hallett, T., & Bechky, B. A. (2018). Meaning at the source: The dynamics of field formation in institutional research. *Academy of Management Annals, 12*(1), 154–177.

Lemonnier, P. (Ed.). (1993). *Technological choices: Transformation in material cultures since the Neolithic.* London: Routledge.

Leonardi, P. M., & Barley, S. R. (2010). What's under construction here? Social action, materiality, and power in constructivist studies of technology and organizing. *Annals of the Academy of Management, 4*, 1–51.

Leroi-Gourhan, A. (1943). *L'Homme et la Matière.* Paris: Albin Michel.

Levy, D. L., & Scully, M. (2007). The institutional entrepreneur as modern prince: The strategic face of power in contested Fields. *Organization Studies, 28*(7), 971–991.

Louche, C., & Lydenberg, S. (2006, March 23–26). *Socially responsible investment: Differences between Europe and United States, IABS 2006 Annual Meeting.*

Markowitz, H. (1952). Portfolio selection. *Journal of Finance, 7*(1), 77–91.

Martinón-Torres, M. (2002). Chaîne Opératoire: The concept and its application within the study of technology. *Gallaecia, 21*, 29–43.

Meyer, R., Höllerer, M., Jancsary, D., & van Leeuwen, T. (2013). The visual dimension in organizing, organization, and organization research: Core ideas, current developments, and promising avenues. *Academy of Management Annals, 8*, 1–56.

Orlikowski, W. J. (2007). Sociomaterial practices: Exploring technology at work. *Organization Studies, 28*(9), 1435–1448.

Orlikowski, W. J., & Scott, S. V. (2008). Sociomateriality: Challenging the separation of technology, work and organization. *Academy of Management Annals, 2*(1), 433–474.

Penalva-Icher, E. (2007). *Réseau et Régulation d'un marché financier 'socialement responsable': en attendant la concurrence...* PhD dissertation. Université des Sciences et Technologies de Lille. Unpublished.

Pinch, T. (2008). Technology and institutions: Living in a material world. *Theory & Society, 37*(5), 461–483.

Preda, A. (1999). The turn to things: Arguments for a sociological theory of things. *The Sociological Quarterly, 40*, 347–366.

Rafaeli, A., & Pratt, M. G. (2006). Introduction. Artifacts and organizations: More than the tip of the Iceberg. In A. Rafaeli & M. Pratt (Eds.), *Artifacts and organizations* (pp. 1–5). New York: Lawrence Earlbaum.

Raviola, E., & Norbäck, M. (2013). Bringing technology and meaning into institutional work: Making news at an Italian business newspaper. *Organization Studies, 34*, 1171–1194.

Schepers, D. H., & Sethi, S. P. (2003). Do socially responsible funds actually deliver what they promise? Bridging the gap between the promise and performance of socially responsible funds. *Business and Society Review, 108*(1), 11–32.

Scott, R. (1995). *Institutions and organizations.* Thousand Oaks: Sage.

Scott, W. R. (2003). Institutional carriers: Reviewing modes of transporting ideas over time and space and considering their consequences. *Industrial and Corporate Change, 12*(4), 879–894.

Silva, L., & Backhouse, J. (1997). Becoming part of the furniture: The institutionalization of information systems. In A. S. Lee, J. Liebenau, & J. I. DeGross (Eds.), *Information systems and qualitative research* (pp. 389–414). London: Chapman & Hall.

Suddaby, R. (2010). Challenges for institutional theory. *Journal of Management Inquiry, 19*, 14–20.

Voronov, M., & Vince, R. (2012). Integrating emotions into the analysis of institutional work. *Academy of Management Review, 37*, 58–81.

Yin, R. K. (1989). *Case study research: Design and methods.* Thousand Oaks: Sage.

Part II

Space and Time

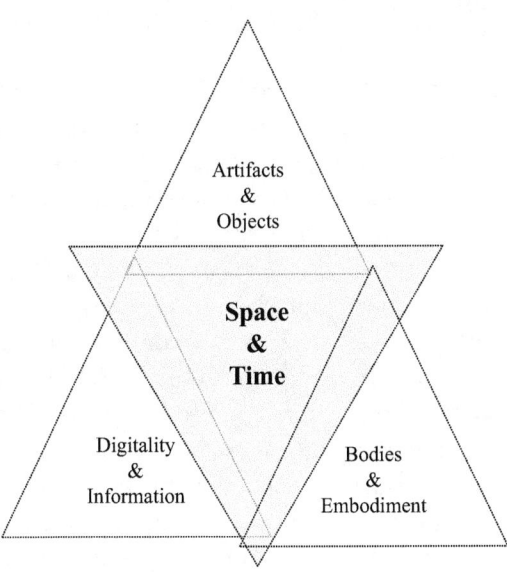

Key Questions

- Which roles do space and time play in processes of legitimation?
- To what extent do actors deliberately mobilize space and time for institutional effects?
- How can space and time be conceptualized ontologically in relation to institutions?
- Through which epistemological stances can space and time be studied empirically to better illuminate the material dimension of institutions?
- Which new methodological and theoretical approaches to the study of space and time carry potential for further developing institutional theory?

The second part of the book, entitled "Space and time", comprises three chapters that all address space as it relates to theoretical, methodological, epistemological and/or ontological components of institutional theory. In Chap. 5, Lise Arena and Ali Douai investigate how business studies were initially legitimated on the Oxford University campus. Engaging with both the epistemological and the methodological layers, they formulate a historical approach to studying materiality and institutions that relies on historical data to retrospectively examine how materiality shapes institutional dynamics. In Chap. 6, Anouck Adrot and Marie Bia-Figueiredo engage with space in relation to information flows and information holes in a firefighting organization. They look at how the pursuit of organizational legitimacy contributes to shaping spaces. Ontologically speaking, space stimulates practitioners to improve operations and information flows. The chapter's main contributions are methodological and epistemological in as much as space is evoked as a novel approach to institutional knowledge production. Finally, Chap. 7, written by François-Xavier de Vaujany, Sara Winterstorm-Varländer and Emmanuelle Vaast, examines how organizations use space to develop or maintain their legitimacy, notably through walking practices that they include in their legitimacy claims. This chapter engages with ontology and epistemology to explore, respectively, the nature of space and the production of knowledge on the role of spaces in legitimation. Figure 1 represents each of the three chapters' engagement with the multiple layers of materiality in institutions.

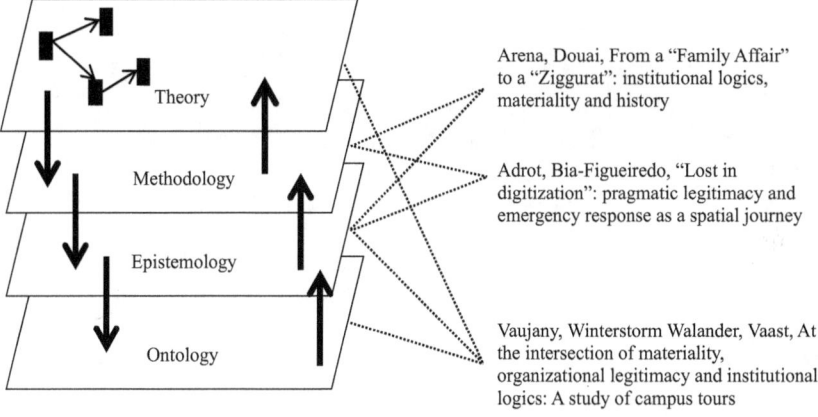

Arena, Douai, From a "Family Affair" to a "Ziggurat": institutional logics, materiality and history

Adrot, Bia-Figueiredo, "Lost in digitization": pragmatic legitimacy and emergency response as a spatial journey

Vaujany, Winterstorm Walander, Vaast, At the intersection of materiality, organizational legitimacy and institutional logics: A study of campus tours

Fig. 1   Reflexive journey on space and time through the chapters

5

From a "Family Affair" to a "Ziggurat": Institutional Logics, Materiality and History

Lise Arena and Ali Douai

Introduction

A Process of Institutionalization in a Highly Institutionalized Organization

The University of Oxford is usually described as a highly institutionalized organization, that is, as being inert, homogenous in terms of values and

An earlier version of this chapter has been presented at the "Organizations, Artifacts and Practices" workshop, Lisbon, June 2016. The authors appreciate the helpful comments of the participants of that session, especially Steward Clegg, and of the organizers who selected the paper for publication in this book. They also appreciate the helpful suggestions from the anonymous reviewers in helping to shape this chapter. The authors also owe a great debt of gratitude to very many people because of the manifold interactions with interviewees, archivists and Oxford fellows who participated in the institutionalization of management education. They are indebted to many more than could possibly be listed here, but a very great debt of gratitude is due to Clark Brundin, Dorothy Cooke, Anthony Hopwood, Bill Impey, Uwe Kitzinger, Colin Mayer, Ashley Raeburn, Richard Smethurst, Rosemary Stewart, Bob Tricker, Roger Undy and Bob Vause. Authors are also grateful to Collin Harris, superintendent of the Special Collections Reading Rooms at the Bodleian Library for his help regarding the files on management studies.

L. Arena (✉) • A. Douai
Université Côte d'Azur, CNRS, GREDEG, France
e-mail: lise.arena@unice.fr; ali.douai@unice.fr

© The Author(s) 2019   **113**
F.-X. de Vaujany et al. (eds.), *Materiality in Institutions*, Technology, Work and Globalization, https://doi.org/10.1007/978-3-319-97472-9_5

behaviours and conservative of a Victorian tradition. In this context, the establishment of management education naturally becomes an object of scrutiny, given the apparent orthogonality between Oxford's characteristics and the initial supposed lack of prestige of management as an academic discipline. The interest for this issue becomes particularly pregnant when knowing the dominant narrative: management education in Oxford is meant to be born in 2001, when the Saïd Business School (SBS) opened its doors and gave de facto management education the same status as other academic disciplines, as the result of a macro-movement. However, historical methods and institutional theory acquire relevance when we consider the following elements: (1) the establishment of management education in 2001 marked the end of a long-drawn-out process of institutionalization which started in 1953 with the first Oxford University Business Summer School and which involved a variety of actors, of dimensions (symbolic, material, etc.) and of unexpected events; (2) this process took place in an organization in which routinized practices and tacit rules played a central role in all spheres of daily life; and (3) materiality (mainly in terms of objects and spaces) is seen as a key dimension of these practices and rules. This field of study can be considered as a "textbook case" of the institutional fact in all its aspects.

Agency and Material Turns in Institutional Theory

In the last decade, literature on the history of business education had significantly grown. Essentially, two approaches can be identified: highly contextualized and actor-centred monographies (e.g. Engwall 2009) and an analysis in terms of "national models" (e.g. Pettigrew et al. 2014; Khurana 2007). Yet, few contributions integrate both levels, discuss these processes in terms of institutionalization and highlight the role of situated practices. Our study sheds light on the institutionalization of management education by invoking historical methods and neo-institutional theory since we interpret the former as a long, multilevel and non-deterministic process that involved multiple actors, dimensions, logics and unexpected sequences in an inert environment.

In recent years, the emphasis in neo-institutional theory has largely shifted from macro-structural analysis—focused on the links between institutional pressures, imitation and conformity of behaviours in organizational fields—to an agency-based perspective that focuses on diversity and change in more micro-settings, by highlighting the role of institutional entrepreneurs (Battilana et al. 2009) and, more recently, of institutional workers (Lawrence et al. 2011). This shift has entailed an increasing interest for "micro-practices" and has logically—though not mechanically—led to a material turn in neo-institutional theory (Boxenbaum et al. 2016). The role of material dimensions in the (re)production and change of various institutional orders (Jones and Massa 2013; Monteiro and Nicolini 2015) can be seen as a new frontier in neo-institutional theory. As Pinch (2008: 466) insists: "we neglect the material aspect of institutions at our peril, especially if we want to understand institutional change". The institutional logics perspective (Thornton et al. 2012) represents the most recent and systematic approach to institutional change, which tries to articulate its symbolic and material dimensions.

Aims of the Chapter

On the one hand, this article challenges the emphasis of the "management education" literature on "national models" (Arena 2011a) and the macro-forces of change in heterogeneous organizational fields (Locke 1998). In contrast, we try to provide an original understanding of the institutionalization process in Oxford that highlights the key roles of *embedded actors* (Greenwood and Suddaby 2006) and of *materiality*, as recent insights in neo-institutional theory suggest. The aim is to overcome the "one-point-in-time" view (2001 and the creation of the Saïd Business School) and rather to address a long-lasting and complex process of institutionalization, which was driven by varying combinations of *institutional entrepreneurship* and *institutional work*. This micro-process of change was largely built, as Thornton et al. (2012: 4) would argue, from "translations, analogies, combinations and adaptations" of institutional logics.

On the other hand, this chapter argues that a comprehensive understanding of the institutionalization process of management education in Oxford can only result from a combination of the core concepts of neo-institutional theory—institutional entrepreneurship (IE), institutional work (IW) and institutional logics (IL) —that still consist of three distinct and parallel literatures on institutional change. In our conceptual framework, materiality, as we approach it, that is as artifacts that both enable and extend institutional agency (cf. Monteiro and Nicolini 2015), plays the pivotal role for the consistency of this combination. Moreover, this study highlights the hybridization between competing institutional logics, and thus the construction of compromises, as a key feature of this process.

The section "Conceptual Framework" provides the conceptual framework that guides our analysis of the institutionalization of management education in Oxford. The section "Historical Methods and Data Collection" describes the historical method used to reassemble the fragmented trajectories, phenomena, events and data used in this chapter. The section "The Three Episodes" focuses successively on three key episodes of this institutionalization process. The section "Discussion and Concluding Remarks" discusses our main insights and concludes.

Conceptual Framework

One of the main challenges for institutional approaches in the social sciences is to provide a robust framework, which helps both to explain how institutions influence actors' behaviour and to understand how these embedded actors might, in turn, change institutions, that is a framework that solves the famous "paradox of embedded agency" (Holm 1995).

In organization theory, DiMaggio (1988) introduced the concept of *institutional entrepreneurship* to overcome the macro- or structuralist bias for which he and other scholars were criticized. Battilana et al. (2009: 72) define institutional entrepreneurs, "whether organizations or individuals, a[s] agents who initiate, and actively participate in the implementation of, changes that diverge from existing institutions, independent of whether the initial intent was to change the institutional environment and whether the changes were successfully implemented". This concept has been challenged for involving a heroic vision, a narrow analysis of the conditions of their emergence and a failure to account for the collective nature of institutional change. Battilana et al. (2009) provide a renewed model that considers the process of institutional entrepreneur from *the emergence* of an institutional entrepreneur to the *implementation* and possible institutionalization of the changes he initiates. The model considers two key categories of enabling conditions: organization characteristics and actor's social position. Oxford has never been a monolithic block: multiple institutional logics—founded on and mobilizing specific material and spatial arrangements—have always been developing and clashing, and it is also continuously submitted to changes in the global field of higher education. Considering the actor's social position, analysing the status and the relative position of the institutional entrepreneur in the organization become crucial. Battilana et al.'s model also sheds light on the concrete actions of an institutional entrepreneur to implement divergent change. Using symbolic and material resources to develop a vision for divergent change and to mobilize allies behind the vision are two types of actions that are to be taken into account in our context. The section "The Three Episodes" will highlight the key role of an initiator and identify his "enabling conditions" and his actions as an institutional entrepreneur.

The latter types of actions (mobilizing allies) contribute to filling the gap between institutional entrepreneurship and institutional work concepts. IW is defined as "the purposive action of individuals and organizations aimed at creating, maintaining or disrupting institutions" (Lawrence and Suddaby 2006: 215). The collective dimension of IW is underlined: "the creation of new institutions requires institutional work on the part of a wide range of actors, *both those with the resources and skills to act as entrepreneurs and those whose role is supportive or facilitative of the entrepreneur's endeavours*" (*ibid.:* 219, italics added). This definition highlights three main aspects: it depicts actors as goal-oriented and reflexive; actors' actions are at the centre of institutional processes; and it considers the role of actors' work to maintain existing institutions (Lawrence et al. 2013). IW allows considering both the role of IE aiming at developing an institutional logic and those types of actors who work to maintain a divergent institutional logic. It follows that the issues of conflicts, power relationships and *the construction of compromises* can come to the fore of the analysis. Lawrence and Suddaby (2006) provide a typology of nine forms of institutional work that actors can perform when they attempt to create, maintain or disrupt institutions: vesting, defining, advocacy, constructing identities, changing norms, constructing normative networks, mimicry, theorizing and educating. Not all these forms are relevant for our analysis, and their combination as well as the context of conflict characterizes institutional complexity. At this stage, it is useful to precisely state the two main aspects of the materiality-institutions that will be illustrated later: (i) the key role of material arrangements—including specific role of time and space modalities—in instantiating, diffusing and institutionalizing novel ideas, practices and institutional logics. Materials (the specific use of objects, the training and the use of the body and engagement in certain practices in a social and spatial context) are envelopes of meanings and may be strategically mobilized in a process of institutional entrepreneurship or institutional work. It follows that as artifacts instantiate institutions, practices are also shaping existing artifacts (Boxenbaum et al. 2016) and (ii) the key role of materials or artifacts as a vector of the construction of new practices. This suggests that they play an active role in constituting and perpetuating the very fabric of social life in an organization. Here, artifacts are not just only a vector of institutional process: they may influence and even disturb them. Hence, it suggests that artifacts constitute an active element of institutional entrepreneurship or institutional work processes (Monteiro and Nicolini 2015). From an ontological viewpoint, it follows that one cannot radically distinguish between the "subject" and "object" of institutional work (see Carlile et al. 2013): agency includes the long-lasting co-construction of "workers", space and objects aiming at institutionalizing institutional logics.

The *institutional logics* perspective positions itself as a meta- and integrative theory, which allows the linking of micro-processes of change with more macro-institutional logics. It thus claims to understand how actors are influenced by and create or modify elements of IL, which necessarily articulates symbolic meanings and material practices (Thornton et al. 2012). They are the "socially constructed, historical patterns of cultural symbols and material practices, including assumptions, values, and beliefs, by which individuals and organizations provide meaning to their daily activity, organize time and space, and reproduce their lives and experiences" (*ibid.*: 2). From this perspective, society is a system consisting of institutional orders and their associated logic. The sets of 'material practices and symbolic constructions' exist thus at the societal level and are also "available to organizations and individuals to elaborate" within fields. Two aspects are to be noted at this stage: the institutional logics theory tries to explain institutional diversity rather than homogeneity in any field; individual/organizational behaviour must be located in the institutional context, and this context both regularizes behaviour and provides an opportunity for agency and change.

As Gawer and Phillips (2013: 2) state, "despite the attention on how logics change and the parallel interest in institutional work, little work has been done applying insights from the literature on institutional work to improve our understanding of how logics change". Yet, change in institutional logics or the emergence of a new one in an organization depends on the institutional work carried out by actors in the field, as exemplified by the establishment of management education in Oxford. It could be argued that while the institutional logics perspective seems "relevant to explain how organizations change through the emergence and/or maintenance of multiplicity of conflicting logics", the dominant view is that institutional logics-based contributions lack "micro-foundations as little attention has been paid to how individuals 'manipulate and switch institutional logics'" (Gond and Leca 2012: 3). We argue that a coherent combination of the institutional entrepreneurship, institutional work and institutional logics concepts delivers the analytical basis for addressing the complex micro-process of institutionalization, interpreted as the gradual stabilization of a new institutional logic, itself resulting from a compromise between two opposed logics.

About this issue, Thornton et al. (2012) provide some interesting insights. In their attempt to build a theory of action and institutional change, they start by warning us against the institutional entrepreneurship concept (in its "old" sense) and the absence of "a theory of how institutional entrepreneurs discover their ideas and are embedded in or autonomous from the social systems that motivate their ideas" (*ibid.*: 9). The bridge between Battilana et al. (2009), on the one hand, and Thornton et al. (2012), on the other, is thus the notion of "enabling conditions". The key is the principle that "without some mechanism for partial autonomy of social structure and action, a theory of institutions cannot explain institutional origins and change" (Thornton et al.: 51).

Opportunities for agency and change come from the availability of multiple and contradictory institutional logics in the field. Individuals learn through social interactions and socialization. The contradictory relationships between institutional logics, eventually located at multiple levels, may provide individuals and organizations with opportunities for agency and change. The underlying model of human behaviour insists on its "situated, embedded [and] boundedly intentional" dimensions. On the one hand, institutional logics focus on embedded actors by *activating situated identities and goals*. On the other hand, the activated identities and goals shape social interactions. When an organization exhibits multiple and contradictory institutional logics, this activation and these social interactions may "generate communication and resource flows, [...] social practices and structures, including institutional work" (*ibid.*: 85).

In a pluralist context, "micro processes of change are built from translations, analogies, combinations, and adaptations of more macro institutional logics" (*ibid.*: 4). Several forces or mechanisms, including institutional entrepreneurs or "cultural entrepreneurs" (*ibid.*: 60), can explain the migration or transposition of elemental categories—both symbols/meanings and material practices—across institutional logics (eventually from higher-order logics). In Battilana et al.'s terms (2009: 68–69), "institutional entrepreneurs develop and assemble in narratives rhetorical arguments that refer to established institutional logics. They build their discourse based on institutional logics which, they anticipate, will resonate with the values and interests of potential allies".

In our framework, this IE-IW-IL combination is supported by the notion of materiality. Thornton et al. (2012: 51) clearly state that "without a method to integrate the symbolic and the material aspects, institutional change cannot occur". As already mentioned, the institutional logics perspective has remained largely "immaterial". In recent years, several authors have embraced the idea that materials play a central role in processes of institutional entrepreneurship (Gawer and Phillips 2013), of institutional work (Raviola and Norbäck 2013) and of the institutionalization of institutional logics (Jones and Massa 2013). In this chapter, special attention is paid to the temporal and spatial dimensions of material practices by which institutional entrepreneurs and workers try to change or maintain an institutional logic.

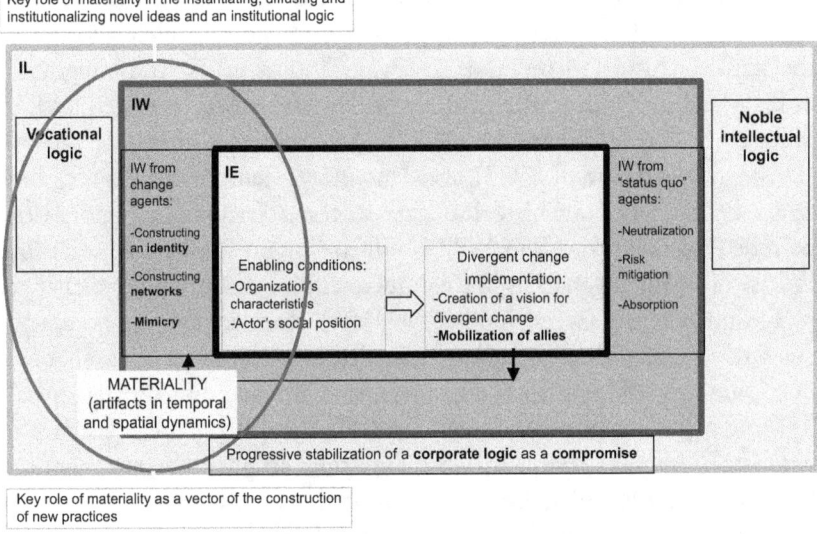

Fig. 5.1 The conceptual framework

Figure 5.1 provides a global view of our conceptual framework. In our context, IE's enabling conditions and types of actions are first to be analysed and linked to IW. The forms of IW will vary, whether they are done by change agents or by "status quo" agents. IW's purpose it to reinforce or institutionalize an IL. Materiality contributes to bridge these notions by highlighting the active role of artifacts in practices of institutional entrepreneurs and workers.

Historical Methods and Data Collection

In line with its conceptual framework, this chapter uses historical methods to analyse the establishment of management education in Oxford as the outcome of complex phenomena in which various causes interact and multiple actors coexist, fight and compete. To a large extent, this choice of method echoes a more general "historic turn" in organization and management studies that has been initiated by scholars such as Kieser (1994) before being more diffused by contributors such as Booth and

Rowlinson (2006). In this respect, Bucheli and Wadhwani (2014) had recently provided a systematic, up-to-date and very complete account of the status of historical methods in organization studies. The integration of historical methods in the field is not new and could be traced back to Weber (1922) or Chandler (1977). Yet, while institutional theory (DiMaggio and Powell 1983) also "integrated temporal dynamics into research that relied on historical data to test assertions in remote time periods (Haveman and Rao 1997)", efforts remain to be made regarding the use of historical analysis in the understanding of institutional change.

To Suddaby and Greenwood (2009: 183), there are three main advantages to use historical methods in institutional analysis: they enable a *processual* view of institutional change, therefore avoiding "linear causality" and allowing possible "messy causes"; they offer "the construct of *path dependency*" showing that present strategic positions are inherited from past choices and actions; they implicitly postulate that institutional arrangements are "*socially* constructed" and "allow researchers to avoid their own capture by a prevailing institutional logic". These three advantages nicely fit the issues raised in this chapter, namely the understanding of a long drawn-out institutionalization *process* as a result of a series of organizational drama, unexpected events and varieties of material and symbolic settings; the current status (e.g. multidisciplinary and research-oriented) of management education and the actual strategic position of the Saïd Business School as results of past strategic actions; and the role of institutional change agents in the social construction of management education at Oxford.

Our ambition to go beyond an analysis in terms of structures and macro-level contexts that condition organizational change first lead us to focus on agency and the discursive practices conducted by individuals inside Oxford. The explanation of agents' activities and of their interactions requires an "understanding of the subjective motives and contextualised worldviews of the actors being studied" (Wadhwani and Bucheli 2014: 10). This more discursive-oriented approach to institutions enables providing a better understanding of the nature of institutions rather than only studying their effects (Phillips and Malhotra 2008). In line with this ambition, we use an ethnographic form of history based on micro-history (Clark 2004) or "history-in-action" (Whittle and Wilson 2015) to deconstruct official historical narratives and to scrutinize agency at the individual level. This method enables researchers who cannot be present "with notebooks, tape recorders, and cameras, at the events they describe" to sometimes "discover a cache of sources" from witnesses that can tell "what it was like to be there" (Rowlinson et al. 2014: 266). In addition to the study of discursive practices, our analysis gives primacy to the role of materiality in institutional change (Boxenbaum et al. 2016). In this perspective, "history-in-action" also enables us to capture material assemblages that eventually participated in the stabilization of management education in Oxford and that result, therefore, from historically contingent arrangements.

The analysis relies on two main categories of data. It combines data from the time studied (recorded in writing or embodied in an artifact) and retrospective data (memoirs written much later, oral history interviews about something that happened in the past) (Yates 2014: 275). Over seven years, data were collected in the archives of the Bodleian Library (Oxford University) and include Oxford University Exam regulations and decrees, press releases, correspondence and internal reports, mainly from the Board of the Faculty of Social Studies. This archival work had been enriched by individual interviews with academics who participated in this institutionalization process, personal memoirs, internal press of the University of Oxford (Oxford University Gazette, Oxford Today), higher education reports (in particular the Robbins report and the Franks Report) and two privately printed books (Graves 2001; Bevan 2015). Based on the examination of this unexplored material, three key episodes—that illustrate a material and discursive assemblage—are selected to provide a better understanding of the overall institutionalization process.

The Three Episodes

The following section aims at describing three key episodes that we consider as illustrative of three institutional logics: vocational, intermediary and corporate. Each institutional logic reflects a specific spatial and temporal assemblage that is captured by a detailed historical analysis of each episode. Overall, the analysis shows the relevance of not isolating spatial from temporal dimensions when understanding the role of materiality and discursive practices in institutional change. The understanding of materiality in space has to be apprehended as a dynamical process including different levels of permanencies, witnessing the institutional stability of an organization (Table 5.1).

Episode 1: "A Family Affair": Oxford Centre for Management Studies, Templeton College (1969–2008) and the Establishment of a Vocational Logic

The first episode describes the establishment of the vocational logic initiated by Norman Leyland who was a key actor in the creation of the Oxford Centre for Management Studies (OCMS) in 1969, which later became Templeton College in 1983. The first Oxford degree in business introduced in 1965 was preceded by failures to get business training programmes established at Oxford. This was mainly due to a lack of interest displayed by industrialists in recruiting trained graduates in management and the attitude of the University in considering business as a vulgar profession and hence not noble enough to be taught at the University (Arena 2011a: 255–257).

We consider Norman Leyland—an economist of the firm at the periphery of the core economists' community—as the key institutional entrepreneur who introduced a vocational logic, different from the noble

Table 5.1 Three key institutional actors in the institutionalization of a business school in Oxford

Episodes	Date	Key actor	Institutional logics
Episode 1: "A family affair"	1965	Norman Leyland as an institutional entrepreneur	Vocational
Episode 2: "Dissecting the body corporate"	1992	Clark Brundin as an institutional worker	Intermediary (between vocational and corporate)
Episode 3: "The railway station"	2001	John Kay as an institutional worker	Corporate

intellectual one that prevailed. He initiated a vision of management studies at Oxford and gathered people around him to help in establishing its legitimacy. Considered a pure Oxford product, Leyland was familiarized with Oxford's tacit rules and organizational characteristics. He occupied some administrative positions (e.g. Bursar of Brasenose College) that favoured his institutional entrepreneur position. He was also part of the initiative of the Oxford Business Summer School (first organized in 1953) which was an annual summer event addressed at businessmen who were willing to learn standard economics. Because he was at the periphery of "mainstream" economics at the time, his probable lack of academic recognition eased his initial desire to introduce a new institutional logic that was, to a large extent, antagonist with the Oxford's Victorian heritage logics.

A Changing Institutional Field as a Trigger for New Institutional Logics The Robbins and the Franks reports as "enabling conditions" for agency— The 1960s witnessed substantial institutional changes in British higher education, particularly conveyed by two national reports: the Robbins Report of the Committee on Higher Education (1963) and the Franks Report of Commission of Inquiry (1966). The Robbins Report formulated 178 recommendations which first aimed at expanding student numbers in higher education. More importantly to our concern, the Report wanted university education to relate more to the changing needs of business and professions of the "modern world". The desire to develop more practical and specialized knowledge was explicitly mentioned for the first time and some commentators perceived the Robbins report as a critique of Oxford. For instance, to Halsey (1994: 722, italics added):

> there was not a simple opposition of left and right. Oxford's critics attacked from all quarters. From the left the thrust was against a traditional bastion of privileged inequality. But the *Times* and *Encounter* also carried the views of a wider group who felt that Oxford was *not responding adequately to the meritocratic requirements of the scientific and managerial professions.*

The Robbins Report gave rise to the creation of a specific commission concerned with Oxford University and chaired by Lord Oliver Franks.

The Franks Report was received by Oxford Congregation as a signal and a resolution of a need for administrative reform. In particular, the University was expected to play a more active part in the search for external funding, that is, "in the securing of money for research from governmental and non-governmental sources and should be prepared to put the full-weight of Oxford behind suitable applications" (Franks 1966, "38th recommendation": 414). Overall, the institutional changes initiated by these reports significantly contributed to the distance taken from the Victorian heritage described *supra*. In this respect, the role of Franks in the desire to get closer to managerial needs was crucial (in 1963, he already suggested a need for business schools to be established in England).

We identify these reforms as a trigger for institutional change: also seen as what we earlier called "enabling conditions" for change, as Oxford saw them as a threat of its academic excellence. To Silver (2003: 201), "Oxford not only did share the prevalent "expansionism" of higher education, it set its face against the forces of expansion in order to protect its social and academic patterns". In line with the argument developed in this chapter's conceptual framework, these contradictory institutional logics between the government and Oxford's governance created "some mechanism for partial autonomy of social structure and action", which gave rise to opportunities for agency.

Leyland's ambition to establish management education faced antagonism from the academic community. This desire not to develop a business school in Oxford was strongly evidenced by the Wright report produced in 1962 on this issue. Interestingly, a financial offer for such a report was initially made by the American Educational Trust (founded by McKinsey & Company Inc.), but the "special committee on management studies" (formed by the Board of the Faculty of Social Studies and chaired by the economist John Hicks) rejected this offer mainly because this operation closely conducted with a "firm of management consultants" could have caused "embarrassing publicity" for Oxford. However, there were some "more-forward looking dons at Oxford" and one of them, Norman Chester, Warden of Nuffield College, "was so incensed by the attitude of his colleagues" that he persuaded his own college to finance a study conducted by John Wright, economist at Trinity College, who toured American business schools for three months and came back with some recommendations (Raeburn 1995: 2).

Yet, the Wright report's conclusions were rather inconclusive: he acknowledged the significant effort made into the development of management education and the "useful research" done in the leading US business schools, but he argued that this successful research was not in any way integrated with the teaching programme of the schools. For him, "without additional staff, not much more could be done than broaden the University Business Summer School" (Graves 2001: 15).[1] The only solution was to introduce management studies "on the grounds that they bear some useful relation to [...] existing studies" (Wright 1962: 42). It is relevant to note that Leyland was part of this Committee. Although he did not share the report's conclusions, the organization's characteristics of Oxford in which he evolved could be considered as another set of "enabling conditions" that let him develop a vision. These characteristics are described by Smethurst as such "[in Oxford] there aren't really very strong powers to stop people doing things. It's a source of great advantage to the university because it does mean that people with energy and enthusiasm can produce all kinds of centres and institutes" (personal communication, 2010).

After much debate, the "activists" in the University slowly managed to edge Oxford into accepting some initiative in this "controversial field" (Raeburn 1995: 3). Because of his marginal social position, Leyland mobilized people (outside his own circle) to facilitate change and use more central figures to legitimate his entrepreneurial activities. It was at this stage that he and Chester contacted Clifford Barclay, a 50-year-old London businessman, who agreed to help financially to get a privately funded centre in management studies going. Hence, the OCMS was incorporated in 1965 as a company limited by guarantee. The Centre was not recognized as a university institution but obtained the status of an "associated institution". This status gave Oxford the comfort to maintain

---

[1] The idea of establishing a Diploma in Management Studies also arose, but the committee stated that "because the background of the students would be very miscellaneous; the studies in which such people could usually engage in common, at anything more than a very elementary level, are not easy to find... A general Diploma would, inevitably, be a low-grade Diploma; and we see no advantage in the provision of that sort of training in Oxford" (Graves 2001: 15).

management studies as a peripheral activity (outside Oxford institutions) while at the same time making one step towards its integration (in associating it). The aim of the Centre was to pursue management studies primarily through "post-experience" courses run for executives from business and from public administration. On the academic side, the University's contribution was the creation of a Diploma in Management Studies that held its first examination in Trinity Term 1968.[2] Leyland became the first Director of the Centre.

The creation of a network of actors (strengthened in collaboration with Chester and Barclay) who help legitimate his new institutional logics became gradually more visible. The nature of the institutional logic Leyland sought to introduce echoes the desire of his collaborators, who planned to develop more vocational education (addressed to graduates) as well as non-vocational adult education (addressed to post-experience managers). The role played by Barclay was crucial.[3] As Graves (2001: 20) reported, "over his business life he must have seen the misery that insolvency causes and decided that much of it could have been avoided with a little more mental application". Hence, to him, the OCMS was an opportunity to "induce a spirit of intellectual inquiry about management subjects and to provide a man with analytical skills to improve his business performance and the quality of his decisions and thus make him, to a considerable extent, "self-educating", over the rest of his career" (*ibid.*).

The young firm of Ahrends, Burton and Koralek was chosen to design the building on the Kennington site. In this chapter, the building's architecture is seen as a key element in instantiating, diffusing and institutionalizing the new vocational logics, carried out by Leyland. Put differently, it extends institutional agency as defined earlier.

First, the *location* of the site is quite significant, as unlike any other Oxford faculties or colleges, it was set up at Oxford's periphery. Commentators agree on the fact that the site overlooked "the dreaming spires" but lay in the "wrong side both of the railway line and of the Ring

[2] Further details about the initial content of the B.Phil. in Management Studies could be found in Arena (2011a: 275–280).

[3] Among several positions he took, at that time, Barclay became a governor of the London School of Economics, treasurer of Coleg Harlech in Wales, which fostered adult education for working people, and he contributed to the Hebrew University in Jerusalem (Raeburn 1995: 3).

Road" (What is Templeton? 1988: 83). This confirmed the idea that the set-up of this management centre was thought "if not within the University, at least in Oxford" (Snow 1995: 5).

Second, the design of the building illustrated Leyland's desire of *modernity* as it is depicted as an "unorthodox building", which was to "shock when you [drove] up to it—no aping of Oxford's ivy-clad gothic" (What is Templeton? 1988: 83). The building is characterized by the "widespread use of zinc cladding which, combined with greyish concrete, makes the building relatively unobtrusive from the road" (*ibid.*). It was even reported that the ugliness of the building—also known as 1960s brutal—impressed those visiting the place for the first time, as the Duke of Edinburgh called it "another building fit for battery hens". Yet, all this fit Leyland's ambition:

> As I can't do what they do in the army to change people's ideas, I want the building to startle them. (Leyland in Graves 2001: 156)

Third, the architecture also materialized the *unstable nature of management education* at the time. Retrospectively, the main architect Richard Burton remembered in an interview:

> Leyland said that he had no idea where Management Education was going; however, he expected us to produce a plan that could respond to that unknown factor. (Burton 1991, in Graves 2001: 156)

The material aspect of the building could also be seen as a trigger of action, and in particular of potential growth, since the building was "to be infinitely expandable in all (horizontal) directions for all possible purposes—hence modular syntax of the architecture" (What is Templeton? 1988: 83). Each of the three basic types of accommodation (communal, academic and residential) was designed in such a way that it could take its own identity and maintain its own growth potential, without losing the cohesion of the whole. The emergence of new practices was also strongly encouraged by the materiality of the OCMS. Two examples could be briefly exposed here: first, the Barclay room included a bespoke round table which was meant to ease dialogue between participants and to exhibit the absence of epistemic hierarchy between academics and industrial experts.

Second, the kitchen played a central role. New practices in attracting American post-experience managers to senior management programmes were institutionalized with the help of Gourmet's Oxford programmes introduced in 1976 (Impey, *in* Arena 2011b: 139). Bill Impey, the Chef, claimed that from his own experience from the early years of the Oxford Centre for Management Studies when we lodged our senior executives in Oxford's finest hotel while our building was under construction, I learned that poor food could aggravate or blow up minor problems. (*ibid.*)

During the following years, the OCMS encountered several financial difficulties. When Uwe Kitzinger became the Director in 1980, he argued that "Oxford is a collegiate University. (…) The attempt to create a Faculty of Management, which is not dominated by the Faculty of Economics, will never work. We have to turn the Management Centre into a college" (Tricker 2006: 21). At this point, to avoid financial issues, Kitzinger fired "an arrow into the blue" (Raeburn 1995) and persuaded the editor of the *American Oxonian*, the house magazine of North American Rhodes Scholars Alumni to publish an article entitled "College in Search of a Founder". After some weeks, John Templeton, who had been a Rhodes Scholar at Balliol, contacted Uwe Kitzinger and negotiations led to a conditional offer of five million dollars. After John Templeton's benefaction, three years later, Templeton College was born. Templeton was then seen as preserving the independence of the discipline from the University, as had been Leyland's preferred option.

Overall, this vocational logic initiated by Leyland was not sustainable since it was unstable. Mrs Clifford Barclay depicted this episode as a "family affair": "They were all like family, you know: we were friends with them all" (in Graves 2001: 195). Yet, this institutional logic was not strong enough institutionally, as evidenced by the 1989 research selectivity exercise who gave a 2 for business and management in Oxford; this being the median figure but rather below the mean of 2.4. The Planning and Development Committee expressed the need for the University to see "an improvement in both the graduate teaching offered in its name at TC and in the research done there which is attributed to the University" (General Board of Faculties 1990: 767).

Episode 2: The Oxford School of Management Studies and the Old Radcliffe Infirmary (1991–2001)—"Dissecting the Body Corporate"

The second episode describes the corporate logic initiated by Oxford University governance itself in the construction of the Oxford School of Management Studies in 1991, which was first located in the old Radcliffe Infirmary. This School constituted an embryonic relatively "modest" version of the actual "expensive and ambitious" Saïd Business School, which was funded by Wafic Saïd and which opened its doors in 2001 after a series of "kerfuffle and behind-the-scenes negotiation" (Beckett 1999; Currie 1999).

A Changing Institutional Field as a Trigger for New Institutional Logics: The Moser Report By the end of the 1980s, Oxford initiated a fundraising campaign as a response to the national economic climate. "Very severe financial problems" were encountered by British universities due to "Mrs. Thatcher and her ministers", who were, therefore, "unwittingly the cause of the next flurry of interest in management study in Oxford" (Tricker not dated, OX91A: 1). This financial climate coupled with the increasing competition taking place between business schools on the international scene led Oxford to start thinking about the eventual creation of an MBA programme. Consequently, the University set up a small working group under Sir Claus Moser (Warden of Wadham College), which was composed of economics dons and of Templeton Fellows (Raeburn 1995: 5) and which became known as the Moser Committee. The Moser "Report on the future of Management Studies", published on May 1988 in the *Oxford University Gazette* (p. 766), included major recommendations:

> That there should be an Oxford University School of Management responsible for all Management education within the University (possible involving a change of status of Templeton College);
>   [...] That a full-time, two-year MBA course should be introduced consisting of a "generalist" first year and a "specialist" second year—students with the appropriate qualifications would be entitled to exemption from the generalist year and would proceed immediately to the specialist year.

(Extract from the General Board of the Faculties, Hebdomadal Council, Vol. CLXXIX, 20 April 1988, p. 39)

Soon, what happened to be called the "Templeton problem" caused to enquire about the tense relationship between a new school of business and Templeton College. Some Templeton fellows perceived the operation as a "takeover of Templeton College by a new University School for Management Studies", consisting of taking over "the assets of Templeton, to appoint its fellows as university lecturers and adopt the Templeton name as the Templeton School of Management Studies" (Raeburn 1995: 6). To the Moser Committee, this operation rather implied a natural process of evolution within the University; the assets of Templeton College being used to enrich the new School of Management Studies:

> Templeton College would not be the School of Management Studies, but would be incorporated as a central part of it. [...] In this connection we would wish to recognise the current tenure position of the academic staff, and, indeed, the employment rights of all those working at Templeton College: they should become University employees at appropriate grading. (Moser Report 1988: 7)

The consideration of the "Templeton problem" in the Moser report is a significant element in our analysis since it is considered to be "key to understanding the future path plotted for Management Studies at Oxford" (Snow 1995: 7). Signs of unease about the report in some parts of Templeton evidenced the difficult institutional assemblage that was about to take place in this context of co-existence between Templeton College and the School of Management Studies.

Institutional Work In 1990, after almost a century of ongoing debate, Congregation agreed that the University should establish a business school. To manage the "Templeton problem", the University governance appointed a single Director—Clark Brundin—simultaneously acting for Templeton College and for the new School to come, in 1992. In an interview, we conducted with Clark Brundin in 2009, he admitted that this position was "one of the hardest jobs [he] did in [his] life and being a Vice-Chancellor [at Warwick] was much easier" (personal interview).

Brundin was no stranger to Oxford, since he came there from the University of California at Berkeley almost 30 years earlier, in 1963, as a lecturer in engineering. It was at this time that Brundin met Leyland, who was teaching on and had helped organize the Engineering Science and Economics joint honours programme. Brundin followed the progress of the OCMS and kept in touch through a membership of the Business Summer School Steering Committee. Brundin's successive positions in University's administration made him the right candidate, since as "the business school concept was then (in April 1992) so new", it needed "careful piloting through the Byzantium of University politics (Brundin's knowledge of *Microcosmographia Academica* came in useful)" (Graves 2001: 137). In 1985, he was persuaded to become Vice-Chancellor of the University of Warwick, "where his reputation as a planner had preceded him" and was then brought up to Oxford in 1992.

At that stage, the whole operation was led by this one figure who soon, and unsurprisingly, became a target for general criticisms from both sides—the University was looking for a business academic capable of imagining and building a new department from scratch, while the College was looking for an eminent academic or businessman, capable of adding lustre to the College's reputation.

Materiality as a Sign of Non-permanency and Unstable Institutionalization
Materiality plays a crucial role in the representation of the transitory nature of this institutionalization. Two particular material elements are preponderant in evidencing this non-permanency: (1) the location of the new School, which consisted of a breaking point with its previous peripheral location and (2) the unusual internal arrangement and occupation of space for a business school new venture, which was still a working hospital.

Although Congregation had already approved to locate the School on the grounds of Templeton College, Brundin believed that it should be positioned at the centre of town; claiming that if the school was left on a fringe location, it will remain a fringe activity. His idea was therefore to show that the School of Management Studies was a different entity from Templeton College, which was eased by the failure to get any fundraising on the Kennington site despite all the efforts made by the development Director attached to Templeton since 1988. The general feeling was that the difficulty to get fundraising was probably due to the fact that no benefactors would be willing to invest in a fringe site not emblematic of Oxford, both in terms of location and architecture. Hence, as soon as Brundin took office, he started to look for a temporary space in the town centre, with the support of the Vice-Chancellor and the Registrar, who was also Brundin's sailing friend. After all, the whole idea of Oxford is to have departments and colleges collaborating between each other beyond disciplinary divisions, and having the business school in town was facilitating these interactions and assisting the integration of MBA students into the academic and social life of the University.

Hence, in 1992, an embryonic Oxford School of Management Studies emerged in the Old Radcliffe Infirmary and began to host some courses in Management. To Brundin, "it was a huge space with office and nurses' space" (personal interview, 2009). Some space of the working hospital was converted into a lecture theatre, a library and some offices to welcome the first intakes of students in Management in 1993. The conversion of this space was funded by the University, while the Oxford's School in Management Studies was still waiting for a benefactor.

Brundin remembered:

> It was actually converted quite well because it ran all the way through so that the entrance of the business school wasn't through the main entrance to the old Radcliffe Infirmary. That was how you would get to the offices. You got into the School from the back, right on to the end of that wing that is between the Radcliffe Infirmary and Somerville. The whole wing was the Business School. The students went in through that. There was adequate space. (Brundin, personal interview, 2009)

The project to establish a 12-month MBA degree was implemented and a new institutional logic was driven by Brundin. This new logic was based on the development of a dynamic new venture attracting approximately 50 international students coming from 22 countries, developing graduate studies in management, gathering significant fundraising and ensuring the School's reputation. Hence, the idealized view provided by Brundin is somewhat nuanced by Desmond Graves' memories:

The rooms were not ideal; they had formerly been parts of the hospital which was still active on other floors. The new School would begin dissecting the body corporate somewhere between neurosurgery and the mortuary. (Graves 2001: 140)

Another Oxford fellow remembered:

It was awful, because it was still also a working hospital. Of course, it was the only space they could find. But, it wasn't doing anything. It didn't have any courses at all. I remember turning up to a meeting there, expecting this dynamic new venture and actually I got to the front door of the place and I saw two young boys in their pyjamas on their wheelchair coming out of the chest clinic who were having a cigarette. It wasn't quite the new venture you could have imagined it would be. (Interview with an anonymous Oxford fellow, 2009)

Yet, despite the criticisms, the written press noted the quality of the students "operating out of the old Radcliffe Infirmary" and who "have paid 15.000 to enrol on the University's fledgling one-year MBA programmes have the highest GMAT (Graduate Management Admissions Test) scores in Europe" (Currie and Griffiths 1999). This temporary process of institutionalization eventually gave rise to a third and last episode, which witnessed the openings of the actual Saïd Business School.

Episode 3: The Saïd Business School, the Oxford Rewley Road Station and the Establishment of a Corporate Logic (From 2001 Onwards)—"the Oxford Ziggurat"

It was as late as 1996, coinciding with Clark Brundin's retirement and after three years of discussion, that Oxford University announced a £20 million donation by the Syrian-born businessman Wafic Saïd.[4] Initially, this third episode gathered three categories of actors conducting institutional work

---

[4] Further details on this could be found in the article: "Cash for Colleges", *Times Higher Education*, October 25, 1996.

on the period: "change agents", "Templeton "statut quo" agents" and "University "statut quo" agents".

Institutional Work in Action: A "Clash Between the Priorities of a Businessman in a Hurry and Those of a 900-Year-Old University" The first category of institutional workers gathered all the forces which were in favour of the creation of a business school and of its funding by Wafic Saïd. The major actor behind these forces was John Kay, a distinguished Professor of Economics at the London Business School who also founded London Economics, a consultancy firm, and who was recruited in 1996. Press coverage described this recruitment as the ideal appointment: "An academic and an entrepreneur, as well as an influential proponent of stakeholding, he seemed just the person to run a 'joined-up' school combining Oxford's strengths in economics, engineering and law with a shot of Nineties enterprise" (Caulkin 1999). Kay was supported by the Vice-Chancellor as well as by Oxford's governance, which recruited him.

When Kay was appointed, he believed that "the first priorities were to establish a development strategy to identify the early steps needed to implement that strategy, and to put forward proposals for the operational management of the school" (Kay 2000: 3). Although he had been an Oxford tutor in the past, he was still considered an "outsider" by the Oxford governance. Initially, this did not prevent him from holding "enthusiastic meetings" with senior colleagues, which led to the production of a 50-page report and to the establishment of a strategy. Yet, retrospectively, Kay sees the implementation of this strategy as constrained by the inertia deployed by two other categories of institutional workers described as infra (the "status quo" agents). The institutional work he had to engage in aimed at getting the new venture project and the proposal made by Wafic Saïd accepted by the ultimate authority arena in Oxford: Congregation—the "parliament" of all the faculty of the University, some 4500 members including academic staff; heads and other members of governing bodies of colleges; senior research and administrative staff. To turn the project into a world-class business school, the question of international recruitments and corresponding salaries were soon put on the table. This issue that Kay had to resolve was shaking

Oxford's tradition in salary equality between disciplines. To him, it was not.

> [...] possible to attract internationally distinguished business school faculty if a newly appointed lecturer is paid less than £20.000 and the standard professional salary is around £40.000. (Would you listen to a lecture on corporate finance or option pricing from someone earning for less than the pay of the receptionist at an investment bank?) (Kay 2000: 4)

His "outsider" characteristics made Kay's institutional work even more difficult to engage in a community where most participants had worked in Oxford for all or most of their careers. Put differently, Kay had to deal with elements of "ritual", of "games" played according to "implicit rules" (*ibid.*). Kay's role as an institutional worker and change agent interfered with two other categories of institutional workers, both considered "status quo" agents.

First, in line with their opposition during the initial establishment of a business school outside of their own premises, Templeton College members were not in favour of the establishment of this new venture. To one Templeton Emeritus Fellow, so far as Clark Brundin became Templeton College's sole negotiator in 1992, the agreement to co-operate (between the College governing body and the University) in the development of the new school collapsed.[5] This dissatisfaction could be materialized while looking at the subsequent "transfer" of Templeton fellows to the business school, later in 2002. In the business school's strategy and while the governance decided to sell the executive education part, which still remained on the Kennington site, the deal was that all Templeton fellows would be transferred to full members of the business school and of the faculty. According to one commentator:

> There were one or two fellows at Templeton that didn't like it, they didn't mind the idea but they didn't want to be called lecturers and so they were not willing to sign [for the merger]. (Interview conducted with an Oxford don, 25/3/2010)

---

[5] Interview conducted on 23rd July 2009 at Egrove Park, Oxford.

While Templeton's opposition to the establishment of the Saïd Business School did not come as a surprise, the second category of status quo agents was less expected on the University side. In fact, after having written a 50-page paper on the strategy of the project, Kay was advised by the University to turn the document into specific proposals, which would then be considered individually by diverse relevant committees. Retrospectively, he writes, "But a plan to establish a new institution rests on a serious of interlinked initiatives. You cannot discuss courses, staffing and buildings independently of each other, even if there were different committees for all these things". (Kay 2000: 3). These "status quo" agents mainly belonged to other disciplines than management and made the implementation of the initial strategy harder. Kay remembers:

> In my time at the University, I do not think I encountered a single person who admitted they were opposed to the University establishing a business school. But I heard dozens of objections to the procedures used to establish it. And because the process and procedures of the University are so ill defined there is always an arguable case for these criticisms. (Kay 2000: 2)

To a large extent, this institutional work done by other Oxford academics to prevent the School from opening had been facilitated by the initiation of a public debate in the press regarding the source of the donation, as Wafic Saïd had been accused to be a Syrian arms dealer (Alderson 2001). While the project to build the business school on a green playing field site near Merton College (in the centre of Oxford) had been submitted to vote, Congregation voted 259–214 against the business school proposals in November 1996. This rejection was mainly explained by "concerns over the site, Saïd's business background and his level of control over the School" (Currie 1999). The University had given an undertaking that no building would ever take place on this ground (Beckett 1999). After the rejection of this new plan by Congregation, John Kay threatened to resign if the dons rejected the plans one more time. To Anthony Hopwood (Kay's successor) and others, this failure exemplified a "clash between the priorities of a businessman in a hurry and those of a 900-year-old university" since, in the Oxford context, "the remarkable thing is not how slowly the new school has taken root but how fast" (Caulkin 1999). Later on, John Kay admitted his failure to establish the new venture as such:

> I had hoped to help create a business school which would rate 5 in the next research assessment exercise and would be in, or close to, the top 25 institution in surveys such as that of the Financial Times. This is short of the world class business school which the University sought, but a springboard to it. My judgement was, and is, that this goal is attainable but not within the constraints the University imposed. (Kay 2001)

Materiality as a Sign of Permanency of a Corporate Logic: From Rewley Road Railway Station to the Oxford Ziggurat Congregation's rejection in November 1996 was followed by "a lot of kerfuffle and much behind-the-scenes negotiation" (Currie 1999). To John Kay, the main problem was coming from Oxford's system of governance, which does not give executive functions to academics owning executive titles. Put differently, Kay argued that this form of governance was hardly understood by outsiders used to "normal management processes" (Kay 2000). He noted:

> Outsiders expect to negotiate agreements with responsible officers on the basis that the results of such negotiation will be honoured. But this expectation cannot be satisfied, because the individuals who conduct the negotiations lack appropriate authority. This situation was a constant source—at first of incomprehension, then of frustration—to Said, who spent five years trying to persuade the University to accept a £20m gift. (Kay 2000: 5)

Despite Congregation's vote, Wafic Saïd did not pull out and in June 1997, a new site for the school was found, despite its unusually low quality for a high-standard new venture. The site was located opposite Oxford railway station and was occupied by a prefabricated listed building—the old wooden London Midland and Scottish station—which had to be packed flat and sent off to railway enthusiasts in Buckinghamshire. The location of the railway bridge acted as a gate to the city centre. As put in *The Guardian Education*, at the time:

The old Midland Railway station that stood here previously was a scion of Joseph Paxton's Crystal Palace. What remains of it has been shipped to the Quainton Road railway centre, Buckinghamshire. This was where the old Brill branch of the Metropolitan Line chugged slowly to the foot of Brill Hill before it stopped. Once there were plans to extend the line to Oxford, so that the city of dreaming spires would have become a London suburb. (Glancey 2001: 2)

Planning permission, including pulling down the listed building, was required. By the end of June, Congregation voted 342–55 to accept the plans and, in December 1998, Oxford City Council eventually granted planning permission.

This choice of location indicates the difficulty to establish the school on more standard Oxford University premises and signifies the long-drawn-out process of an unstabilized project. This emergent nature has also been materialized by the resistance expressed by 30 "eco-warriors" who occupied the trees that were meant to be removed by the construction of the school. At the time, the *Oxford Mail* commented on this:

It must have seemed so simple at the start. Move a few lanes of traffic, shift a tatty tyre depot, and let Oxford's Transport Strategy roll. That was before the eco-warriors arrived to spoil the party. (…) Before the junction can be widened the LMS building needs to go. But it is now home to between six and 30 squatters who know their rights and could take months to evict. (*Oxford Mail*, 1998)

Protesters came from Oxford's long-established group of green activists and many had taken part in direct action from Newbury to Manchester. While this all started with concern about trees, the building and its historic side became used for direct action. One activist interviewed in the press protested against the changes to the Park End junction: "Because it was being used as a tyre place I had a view of it as an old shed, but now I've started things like painting the pillars blue and yellow, like the Crystal Palace itself" (E. Pope, in *Oxford Mail*, 1998). The unstable process of the business school's establishment was reinforced by John Kay's sudden resignation in 1999 after two years of a five-year contract. This provoked the publication of a large amount of articles in the press, arguing that John Kay "disappeared on holiday for the whole of his notice period" (Beckett 1999), pursuing the "on-off saga" (Davies 1999) of "Wafic Said's dream of building a business school in Oxford [which] has been dogged by controversy since its inception" (Currie and Griffiths 1999).

Yet, the school eventually opened on 5 November 2001. Its architecture symbolized the importance of materiality in the capture of more permanency. The design of the new venture is the work of leading architects, Jeremy Dixon and Edward Jones, who were also responsible for the Royal Opera House in London. The building combines modern materials (handmade bricks) with an academic tradition (classical outdoor amphitheatre, columns and cloisters). It also combines Roman and Middle-East architectures: "there is a touch of ancient Rome at its very best - a touch, too, of the very early mosques, including that of the eighth century Ibn Tulun mosque in Cairo" (Glancey 2001: 2).

Press reports of the time exemplify the material dimension of the School when comparing its lobbies to "highly considered corporate headquarters, and Mies's Seagram Building on New York's Park Avenue" (*ibid.*). A corporate logic had been reached and clearly established as exemplified by the lecture rooms:

> Instead of a dais facing banks of seats, the seats wrap around the lecturer, who, as a result, is forced to interact with students. The students here, mostly postgraduates with an average age of 29, are treated very seriously. As they pay £30,000 per year, this is hardly surprising. (*Ibid.*)

This section had shed light on three key episodes in the institutionalization of management education in Oxford that are illustrative of three institutional logics: vocational, intermediary and corporate. Results drawn from our historical ethnography could be understood in terms of material and discursive arrangements, especially through their spatial and temporal dimensions. These results that could be summarized here are represented in Table 5.2.

Table 5.2 Three historical episodes, three institutional logics and their material (spatial and temporal) dimensions

Type of institutional logic	Main characteristics	Spatial dimensions	Temporal dimensions
Vocational *Oxford Centre for Management Studies, Templeton College (1969–2008)* "A family affair"	First vision of management studies at Oxford, **conflicting with the "noble"** existing logic inherited from the Victorian heritage Putting **businessmen at the heart of the logic** (cf. the nature of the Oxford Business Summer School and the key role of Clifford Barclay) Searching for **external funding** enabled by the Franks Report (e.g. financial support offered—before being rejected—by the American Educational Trust founded by McKinsey & Company Inc.) Development of **post-experience courses** in management	OCMS and Templeton College developed **at the periphery** of Oxford: on the "wrong side both of the railway line and of the Ring Road" A building designed to "shock when you [drove] up to it—**no aping of Oxford's ivy-clad gothic"** The form of the Barclay room bespoke **roundtable** to exhibit the absence of epistemic hierarchy between academics and industrial experts The kitchen to attract American post-experience managers to senior management programmes (cf. Gourmet's Oxford programmes)	**Non-permanency** reflected by the status of "associated institution" The material aspect of the building reflecting the **lack of a stable vision:** "Leyland said that he had **no idea where Management Education was going;** however, he expected us to produce a plan that could respond to that unknown factor" The material aspect of the building as a trigger of **potential growth** since the building was "to be infinitely expandable in all (horizontal) directions for all possible purposes—hence, the modular syntax of the architecture"

(continued)

Table 7.2 (continued)

Type of institutional logic	Main characteristics	Spatial dimensions	Temporal dimensions
Intermediary *The Oxford School of Management Studies and the old Radcliffe infirmary (1991–2001) "Dissecting the body corporate"*	Early gradual acceptance to **establish a business school** leading to the "Templeton problem"—tense relationship between a new school of business and Templeton To manage the "Templeton problem", the University governance appointed **a single Director**—Clark Brundin—simultaneously acting for Templeton College and for the new school to come **Embryonic version** of the actual Saïd Business School while waiting for a benefactor **Resistance from actors** belonging to the first vocational logic	**More central location** of the school as a breaking point with its previous peripheral location: Brundin believed that it **should be positioned at the centre of town**; claiming that if the school was left on a fringe location, it will remain a fringe activity	**Non-permanency** captured by an unusual internal arrangement and occupation of space for a business school new venture which was still a **working hospital**: "it was a huge space with office and nurses' space"
Corporate *The Saïd Business School (From 2001 onwards) "the Oxford Ziggurat"*	**Final stage of institutionalization** as a compromise between vocational and intermediary logics **Conflict with "status quo"** agents opposed to institutional change	**The most central location** as opposed to the railway station which eased access to Oxford from London businessmen	**Permanency** of this last stage of institutionalization materialized by a modern building funded by Wafic Saïd—combines modern materials (handmade bricks) with an academic tradition (classical outdoor amphitheatre, columns and cloisters)

Discussion and Concluding Remarks

This chapter analyses a long-lasting and process complex of institutionalization in an inert organization. The emergence and late stabilization of management education in Oxford is the history of a successive and contested hybridization of institutional logics that depended upon various types of institutional work carried out by social actors. Each type exhibits a combination between both the material and symbolic dimensions of actions that aim at legitimating emerging practices. Overall, this chapter offers three types of contributions: at an *ontological* level, it argues that agency and the importance of micro-practices are central entities in the construction of institutional workers, space and objects aiming at institutionalizing institutional logics. Hence, at an *epistemological level,* this chapter challenges the traditional view based on macro-determinants to understand institutional change and considers micro-forces to this change based on the articulation, of space, temporality and materiality. Consequently, the last contribution could be assessed at a *methodological level* as historical ethnography is used to capture materiality in the organization of space.

At least two points deserve attention in this concluding discussion: the need for an explicit articulation between neo-institutional theory and historical approaches and the need to go beyond the opposition micro-versus macro-determinants of institutional change. We argue that historical methods are particularly relevant when what is at stake is understanding institutional change in a highly institutionalized context. Unlike an emergent context, values, social positions and power are consolidated (cf. Thornton et al. 2012: 65). Although an IL is defined "as socially constructed, *historical patterns* of cultural symbols and material practices" (emphasis added), most of IL-based studies tackle short-time periods of change or institutionalization and the effects of IL on actors' behaviour. Not so much attention is paid to the gradual, uneven and non-deterministic process of the sedimentation of an IL in a highly institutionalized organization. Changes result from long-term processes whose concrete forms cannot be anticipated a priori: unexpected events and pathways become the rule and only the ex post reconstitution of events/ facts, with all its potential bias, can lead us to a robust understanding of these processes. Concerning IW, it should be stressed that actors' purposes and strategies, in these contexts, cannot be seen as linearly related to "preferences", which would derive from "objective" conditions or positions: though not absent, they are fuzzily and continuously (re)defined in a *path-dependent* and "interactionist" setting (in which identity, goals, etc. are not "congealed"). The concept of IE, in these contexts, should also be moulded quite differently: highlighting and understanding the role of actors' social positions, of organization and field characteristics requiring the mobilization of complex and (firstly) dispersed data and processes: micro-history is well-suited for this task, as we demonstrated in Part IV.

From this set of concerns, it follows that a strict distinction between the micro- and macro-forces of institutional change lacks relevance here. Micro-forces (agency-based approaches) cannot be disconnected from macro-forces: macro-transformations (material or ideological) contribute to the (re)definition of actors' interests and provide them with the set of material or symbolic resources that they could mobilize to initiate a change at the organizational level. Micro- and macro-levels are also articulated at the "meso" (organizational) level: the latter is the space of junction between the formers and the space in which social compromises between competing interests are shaped. These compromises ensure the (relative) stabilization of the organization and of the institutional field as a whole, that is, in which micro- and macro-forces are realigned to ensure a relative stability of "life" in the field.

References

Alderson, A. (2001, March 18). Do I deserve to be labelled a Syrian terrorist? Andrews Alderson interviews Wafic Saïd for the *Sunday Telegraph*.

Arena, L. (2011a). *From economics of the firm to business studies at Oxford: An intellectual history (1890s–1990s)*. D.Phil. thesis, University of Oxford.

Arena, L. (coord.). (2011b). "Gourmet's Oxford: Des cours de cuisine britannique dans une école de gestion", Rubrique Clin d'œil. *Entreprises et Histoire*, 65(4), 139–141.

Battilana, J., Leca, B., & Boxenbaum, E. (2009). How actors change institutions: Towards a theory of institutional entrepreneurship. *The Academy of Management Annals, 3*(1), 65–107.

Beckett, F. (1999, September 9). MBA: It's back to business at Oxford. *The Independent.*

Bevan, J. (2015). *Bringing business to Oxford: The story behind the Saïd Business School.* Oxford: Saïd Business School.

Bodleian Library Archives, University of Oxford, File: Management studies.

Booth, C., & Rowlinson, M. (2006). Management and organizational history: Prospects. *Management & Organizational History, 1,* 5–30.

Boxenbaum, E., Hault, I., & Leca, B. (2016). Le tournant matériel dans la théorie néo-institutionnaliste. In F. X. de Vaujany, A. Hussenot, & J.-F. Chanlat (Eds.), *La théorie des organisations: Les tendances actuelles.* Paris: Economica.

Bucheli, M., & Wadhwani, R. D. (2014). *Organizations in time – History, theory, methods.* Oxford: Oxford University Press.

Carlile, P. R., Nicolini, D., Langley, A., & Tsoukas, H. (2013). *How matter matters – Objects, artifacts and materiality in organization studies.* Oxford: Oxford University Press.

Caulkin, S. (1999, July 25). Dreaming spires wake up to modern business school reality. *The Guardian.*

Clark, E. A. (2004). *History, theory, text: Historians and the linguistic turn.* Cambridge, MA: Harvard University Press.

Currie, J. (1999, January 15). The Saïd Business School: From blueprint to spire. *The Times Higher Education.*

Currie, J., & Griffiths, S. (1999, January 15). All sewn-up: Oxford bags-of-money. *The Times Higher Education.*

Davies, R. (1999, May 26). Sainsbury millions for business school. *The Evening Standard.*

DiMaggio, P. (1988). Interest and agency in institutional theory. In L. Zucker (Ed.), *Institutional patterns and culture* (pp. 3–32). Cambridge, MA: Ballinger.

DiMaggio, P., & Powell, W. (1983). The iron cage revisited: Institutional isomorphism and collective rationality in organizational fields. *American Sociological Review, 42,* 147–160.

Engwall, L. (2009). *Mercury meets Minerva, business studies and higher education – The Swedish case* (2nd extended ed.). Stockholm: Stockholm School of Economics – EFI The Economics Research Institute.

Franks, O. (1966). *Report of commission of inquiry,* University of Oxford, chaired by Lord Oliver Franks. Volume I: Report, recommendations, and statutory appendix. Oxford: Clarendon Press.

Gawer, A., & Phillips, N. (2013). Institutional work as logics shift: The case of Intel's transformation to platform leader. *Organization Studies, 34,* 1035–1071.

General Board of the Faculties, Hebdomadal Council, University of Oxford, (1988–1990).

Glancey, J. (2001, December 10). Oxford's Saïd business school: When worlds collide. *The Guardian G2,* p. 10.

Gond, J. P., & Leca, B. (2012). *Theorizing change in a pluralistic institutional context: What can economies of worth and new – Institutionalism learn from each other?* Document de travail du LEM 2012-15, University of Lille, Lille.

Graves, D. (2001). *Templeton College, The Oxford centre for management studies, the first thirty years, "a family affair".* Oxford: Oxford Centre for Management Studies Association. Privately printed.

Greenwood, R., & Suddaby, R. (2006). Institutional entrepreneurship in mature fields: The big five accounting firms. *Academy of Management Journal, 49,* 27–48.

Halsey, A. H. (1994). The franks commission. In B. Harrison (Ed.), *The history of the University of Oxford: The twentieth century* (pp. 721–736). Oxford: Oxford University Press.

Haveman, H. A., & Rao, H. (1997). Structuring a theory of moral sentiments: Institutional and organizational coevolution in the early thrift industry. *American Journal of Sociology, 102*(6), 1606–1651.

Holm, P. (1995). The dynamics of institutionalization: Transformation processes in Norwegian fisheries. *Administrative Science Quarterly, 40*(3), 398–422.

Jones, C., & Massa, F. (2013). From novel practice to consecrated exemplar: Unity Temple as a case of institutional evangelizing. *Organization Studies, 34*(8), 1099–1136.

Kay, J. (2000, December 20). A lost cause? *Prospect Magazine.*

Kay, J. (2001). Oxford University: Facing the future (prospect reply). Article published in the author's blog: https://www.johnkay.com/2001/01/29/oxford-university-facing-the-future-prospect-reply/

Khurana, R. (2007). *From higher aims to hired hands – The social transformation of American business schools and the unfulfilled promise of management as a profession.* Princeton: Princeton University Press.

Kieser, A. (1994). Why organization theory needs historical analysis – And how this should be performed. *Organization Science, 5,* 608–620.

Lawrence, T. B., & Suddaby, R. (2006). Institutions and institutional work. In R. Stuart, S. Clegg, C. Hardy, T. B. Lawrence, & W. R. Nord (Eds.), *The Sage handbook of organization studies* (2nd ed., pp. 215–224). London: Sage.

Lawrence, T. B., Leca, B., & Suddaby, R. (2011). Institutional work: Refocusing institutional studies of organization. *Journal of Management Inquiry, 20*(1), 52–58.

Lawrence, T. B., Leca, B., & Zilber, T. B. (2013). Institutional work: Current research, new directions and overlooked issues. *Organization Studies, 34*(8), 1023–1033.

Locke, R. R. (Ed.). (1998). *Management education*. Dartmouth: Ashgate.

Monteiro, P., & Nicolini, D. (2015). Recovering materiality in institutional work: Prizes as an assemblage of human and material entities. *Journal of Management Inquiry, 24*(1), 61–81.

Moser Report. (1988, May 5), *Oxford University Gazette*, p. 766.

Oxford University Examination Regulations and Decrees: Michaelmas Term 1965 to Trinity Term 1969.

Pettigrew, A. M., Cornuel, E., & Hommel, U. (2014). *The institutional development of business schools*. Oxford: Oxford University Press.

Phillips, N., & Malhotra, N. (2008). Taking social construction seriously: Extending the discursive approach in institutional theory. In R. Greenwood, C. Oliver, R. Suddaby, & K. Sahlin (Eds.), *The SAGE handbook of organizational institutionalism* (pp. 702–720). London: Sage.

Pinch, T. (2008). Technology and institutions: Living in a material world. *Theory and Society, 37*, 461–483.

Raeburn, A. (1995). *Management studies at Oxford*. Personal unpublished memoirs.

Raviola, E., & Norbäck, M. (2013). Bringing technology and meaning into institutional work: Making news at an Italian business newspaper. *Organization Studies, 34*(8), 1171–1194.

Rowlinson, M., Hassard, J., & Decker, S. (2014). Research strategies for organizational history: A dialogue between historical theory and organization theory. *Academy of Management Review, 39*(3), 250–274.

Silver, H. (2003). *Higher education and opinion making in twentieth-century England*. London: Routledge.

Snow, P. (1995). Management studies at Oxford. *Journal of Management Development, 14*(5), 5–8.

Suddaby, R., & Greenwood, R. (2009). Methodological issues in researching institutional change. In D. Buchanan & A. Bryman (Eds.), *The Sage handbook of organizational research methods* (pp. 176–195). London: Sage.

Thornton, P. H., Ocasio, W., & Lounsbury, M. (2012). *The institutional logics perspective: A new approach to culture, structure and process.* Oxford: Oxford University Press.

Tricker, R. I. (not dated). OX91A, personal archives.

Tricker, R. I. (2006). Oxford'smanagementmyths. *Oxford Magazine,* 8th Week, Hilary Term, pp. 20–21.

Wadhwani, R. D., & Bucheli, M. (2014). The future of the past in management and organization studies. In M. Bucheli & R. D. Wadhwani (Eds.), *Organizations in time – History, theory, methods* (pp. 3–30). Oxford: Oxford University Press.

What is templeton? *The Journal of the Oxford Society, XL*(2), 1988.

Whittle, A., & Wilson, J. (2015). Ethnomethodology and the production of history: Studying 'history-in-action'. *Business History, 57*(1), 41–63.

Wright, J. F. (1962, June). *Draft report to members of the committee appointed by the Board of the Faculty of Social Studies to examine the implication of establishing Management Education in the University.* Mimeograph, Oxford University Archives, Bodleian Library.

Yates, J. (2014). Understanding historical methods in organization studies. In M. Bucheli & R. D. Wadhwani (Eds.), *Organizations in time – History, theory, methods* (pp. 265–284). Oxford: Oxford University Press.

6

"Lost in Digitization": A Spatial Journey in Emergency Response and Pragmatic Legitimacy

Anouck Adrot and Marie Bia Figueiredo

Introduction

Pragmatic legitimacy refers to the overall evaluation of an entity's capacity to address other organizations' needs. From this perspective, pragmatic legitimacy builds on interorganizational interactions and the way an organization practically addresses its partner's needs through its missions (Díez-Martín et al. 2013). Such perception becomes crucial in interorganizational systems structured in networks and characterized by intense collaboration (Provan et al. 2008), such as the emergency sector.

For emergency organizations, pragmatic legitimacy is not only important but also particularly volatile. While organizations can benefit from

A. Adrot (✉)
Université Paris-Dauphine PSL, Paris, France
e-mail: Anouck.adrot@dauphine.fr

M. Bia Figueiredo
LITEM, Univ Evry, IMT BS, Université Paris-Saclay, Évry, France
e-mail: marie.bia_figueiredo@imt-bs.eu

© The Author(s) 2019   **151**
F.-X. de Vaujany et al. (eds.), *Materiality in Institutions*, Technology, Work and Globalization, https://doi.org/10.1007/978-3-319-97472-9_6

shifts of pragmatic or moral legitimacy ('t Hart et al. 2009), the same shifts can endanger their survival as well. Public authorities decide to fund an emergency organization on the basis of their evaluation of its capability to address needs when an emergency occurs. Given that these capabilities get easily questioned when dysfunctions occur during an emergency response, organizations in the emergency sector have carefully been adapting their practices and competencies to strengthen, maintain and defend their pragmatic legitimacy.

More specifically, organizations conduct major transformative investments that, at the same time, generate radical changes in work practices. In line with this view, Suchman outlined the influence of legitimacy dynamics on an organization's functioning (1995). Going further, the influence of legitimation on organizational dynamics was also documented (Drori and Honig 2013). However, scholars have approached legitimacy as an institutional matter, primarily. As a result, they have overlooked how an organization's concern for its pragmatic legitimacy practically affects its daily operations and stakeholders. Lacking this view, practitioners can experience difficulties in judging the overall relevance of the reshaping an organization's activities in order to support its legitimacy.

As explained by Drori and Honig (2013), considering legitimation without taking into account organizational and practical contexts can lead decision-makers to misleading conclusions. This view advocates approaching pragmatic legitimacy not from a pure institutional perspective but rather by expanding its investigation to its materiality—literally, "what matters" from it (Vásquez and Plourde 2017). In the emergency sector, some organizations' willingness to defend their own legitimacy results in the enactment of deep changes in their management of information. More than ever, information management constitutes a strategic input to support pragmatic legitimacy, which results in the use of new tools to process higher amounts of information by emergency responders and a changing perception of the importance of information in emergency response.[1] However, our understanding of the

---

[1] While this chapter focuses on the material impact of an organization's pursuit for legitimacy, other chapters highlight how organizations rely on material properties to claim and support legitimacy. In Chap. 7, De Vaujany, Winterstorm and Vaast offer a complementarity view to this chapter by exploring the material properties of symbolic management. In Chap. 8, Santos explores the role of material properties of digital artifacts in discursive strategies related to legitimacy claim. The performativity of pursuit for legitimacy and its reliance on materiality are not exclusive but rather the two sides of the same coin.

materiality of some emergency organization's pursuit for legitimacy remains partial as uncertainty regarding its effects on operations persists. Therefore, this chapter aims to address this research question: "What is the influence of an organization's pursuit for pragmatic legitimacy on emergency response?"

Drawing on Bachelard's work on space (1927, 1938), this chapter explores the materiality of pragmatic legitimacy through a spatial journey into the operations of a firefighting organization that we label Sigma. Our analysis highlights how Sigma's digitization, initially designed to strengthen its legitimacy, partially endangered its action. More specifically, the proposed framework reveals how a balanced occupation of multiple spaces, a traditional lever to frame and regulate emergency action, collapsed as the organization was striving to enhance its pragmatic legitimacy. Practically, legitimacy issues conducted Sigma members to deal with emergencies by focusing on some of its aspects rather than by maintaining an overall awareness of the spaces that matter in emergency response. Emergency response as a narrowing journey impeded information processing and knowledge production, eventually questioning the organization's capacity to address its stakeholders' needs.

In the coming sections, we present pragmatic legitimacy as a major stake in the emergency sector, as well as its materializing into emergency action. We also argue the relevance of approaching this topic through the notion of space. We then provide a quick description of our methodology, as well as our proposal of space as a framework to address the research question. We fully employ the proposed framework to detail the practical implications of a pragmatic legitimacy quest on information transmission during a specific incident. In the concluding remarks of the chapter, we discuss the implications or our result and the relevance of relying on materiality and space as an intermediary concept.

Conceptual Background

Competing for Pragmatic Legitimacy for the Best, and the Worst

Legitimacy was reported by Suchman as the general perception or assumption that the activities of an entity are desirable and appropriate within some established institutional system (1995). Multiple forms and sources of legitimacy coexist. Suchman first identified moral legitimacy as the overall perception that an organization is doing good through its action. Second, organizations gain cognitive legitimacy when their activities make sense to its observers. Third, pragmatic legitimacy means that an organization's actions are perceived by other actors as appropriate to address their needs. In other words, pragmatic legitimacy stems from the absence of questioning (Meyer and Scott 1983) of the effectiveness of an organization in its supporting its stakeholders' needs.

Because legitimacy affects an organization's access to resources in the long term, its building is necessary for organizational survival (Diez-Martin et al. 2013). In the meantime, an organization's legitimacy can get easily questioned by its environment (Stout 2012), in particular when institutional conditions change (Dacin et al. 2002). An organization's stakeholders' needs can change, thereby accounting for its legitimacy gain or loss. Increased access to information, fostered by our societies' digitization, can also generate deep power shifts among competing institutions that correspond to opportunities but also threats to legitimacy. Nowadays, information plays an important role in legitimacy-related dynamics, as illustrated by an increasing reliance on digital space to show off one's legitimacy (Souto-Otero and Beneito-Montagut 2016). As a result, organizations struggle to gain, maintain and defend their legitimacy (Ashforth and Gibbs 1990).

Organizations strive to support their legitimacy through their whole life cycle (please refer to Zimmerman and Zeitz 2002 for more details on legitimacy building). When organizations detect opportunities and threats related to their legitimacy, they seem to opt for reaction, rather than denial (Lamin and Zaheer 2012). To do so, they can rely on multiple levers, coming from a structural isomorphism to the strengthening of informal social ties with institutional representatives (Deephouse 1996), or even the emergence of a narration devoted to promoting the organization's utility (Golant and Sillince 2007). They also promote their own professional identity and jurisdictional boundaries (Abbott

1998, 2014). The jurisdictional claims highlight the importance of rhetoric in strategies intending to promote pragmatic legitimacy (Suddaby and Greenwood 2005).

Such efforts to support and maintain pragmatic legitimacy are not without material impact on organizational life, which means that they have a significant impact on social and material subsistence (Thornton and Ocasio 1999). First, pragmatic legitimacy materially impacts organizations through the reshaping of their funding. Private but also public sectors have been characterized by strong financial implications from legitimacy, such as budget redefinition, sometimes vividly experienced by organizational members (Hoque 2005). Second, legitimacy matters through its role as a major pressure lever to promote innovation (Verhoest et al. 2007). Finally, competition for legitimacy generates crises that require compromises (Taupin 2012) that can result in the reshaping of professional standards and equipment. In the same vein, previous research has outlined that a contradiction between an organization's actual prerogatives and its claimed legitimacy can have severe effects on an organization's functioning. Anomic situations can emerge from this contradiction, where individuals get confused about their mission and their right to achieve it (Aballéa 2013), and sometimes stop using the worktools they are familiar with (Adrot 2017).

Competing for pragmatic legitimacy has financial, organizational and material consequences on organizations. The emergency sector, far from making an exception, is also concerned by legitimacy issues (Hughes and Palen 2012; Kendra and Wachtendorf 2003). Meanwhile, previous research has scarcely documented institutional challenges that emergency responders can face, even though it has highlighted the importance of other dimensions that are highly related to institutional matters, such as symbols, power and rituals (Hart 1993), and information (Comfort 2007; Majchrzak and More 2011; Osatuyi and Mendonça 2013). Information, being a crucial operational resource for emergency response, lies at the core of legitimacy not only from an operational but also from an institutional perspective.

Information at the Core of Legitimacy

Emergency response relies on intense collaboration and coordination within a heterogeneous set of actors, including private, public organizations and agencies (Kapucu 2005). Emergency response—in more or less critical settings—is thus regulated both by numerous institutional ties between responders and information flow. However, information remains an important source of uncertainty regarding an emergency organization's pragmatic legitimacy.

Information constitutes a primary need, not only for emergency responders but also for decision-makers and citizens. Being part of a "goal-oriented" organizational network (Kilduff and Tsai 2003), each emergency organizations addresses its environment—that can quickly become extremely uncertain—by relying on information. In the utmost routinized operations, information remains a crucial and timely needed resource to address events, allocate resources and anticipate risks related to operations. In more critical settings, emergency organizations manage operational—and sometimes unexpected—interorganizational interdependencies that conduct emergency responders to share large amounts of information. To that extent, an organization's pragmatic legitimacy in the emergency sector depends on its ability to transmit and share information.

While information fuels the pragmatic legitimacy of an emergency organization, its liberalized access in digitizing societies also aggravates its volatility. Open access to information generates controversies regarding the capacity of leading organizations to handle an emergency (Comes et al. 2017). For example, in the aftermath of Katrina, lines of controversies about the federal and state organizations' capacity to alert and share information immediately spread widely over multiple media (including international reports, official Rex reports and essays). In addition, information access can generate power shifts in decision-making and operation (Comfort 2007) that question institutionalized organizations' legitimacy on the stage of a crisis. For instance, the emergence of collaborative mapping tools empowers local and citizens' communities (such as in the case of the Kenyan post-election rise of violence in 2008) as well as the international communities of practice (consider the example of the distribution of geographical data among thanks to Twitter in the aftermath of the

2010 Haiti earthquake). Ad hoc organizations can emerge as information providers that appear to be more capable to address citizens and authorities' needs for information than traditional organizations.

In addition, emergency organizations' efforts to strengthen their informational capabilities do not grant operational excellence. The influence of information on pragmatic legitimacy has incented emergency organizations to massively invest in information systems and adapt their work practices to support information production and transmission. In line with this view, information technologies have been increasingly taken into consideration as a key resource to promote timely information access and distribution on the stage of emergency response (including humanitarian incidents, disasters but also exercises). However, beyond any emergency organization's intent to develop its capabilities to produce and transmit information, uncertainty persists regarding its practical and material effects on emergency action. Not only investments in information systems can have surprising outcomes on work practices (Orlikowski 1996; Vaast and Walsham 2005). In addition, organizations' eagerness to produce and process bigger amounts of information does not always support operations, in particular when an incident strikes (Dawes et al. 2004).

From Pragmatic Legitimacy to Emergency Action: A Spatial Journey

Subsequently to the spatial turn, Management and Organization Studies started taking into consideration the notion of space in organization life (Van Marrewijk and Yanow 2010). Since then, numerous studies have highlighted that space reveals organizational phenomena that would remain invisible otherwise, such as legitimation. Previous research has highlighted that the way groups design, customize and occupy spaces does not only reflect the institution's history but also competition for visibility and legitimacy (Yanow 2010; Van Marrewijk 2009; Van Marrewijk and Yanow 2010). Consistently with this view, multiple chapters of this book detail how topological and material features of spaces are designed or used in order to strengthen, when not show off, groups' legitimacy (in particular in Chaps. 5 and 7 in this book). We propose in this chapter a phenomenological approach to space as a valuable lens to explore pragmatic legitimacy and its materiality.

Even though spaces mostly refer to tangible areas, this notion does not restrict to bounded physical areas such as campuses, gardens, avenues or landscape. Spaces correspond to phenomenological experiences, may they relate to tangible arrangements or not. In line with this view, Bachelard (1938) proposed that a space exists mainly through one's experience of losing oneself somewhere. Losing oneself somewhere can be a rich, dialectical and transactional experience, comprising the exploration of the "somewhere" parts and embranchments, experimenting and continuously integrating new information to change one's perspective and position in the space.[2] Thus, space does not necessarily restrict to a physical place but rather can refer to one's moving into reasoning, a relationship or even organizational action.

We detail here in our rationale for approaching organizational action as what Bachelard describes as a spatial journey. Rather than strictly resulting from a sum of individuals' rationality, organizational action corresponds to a progressive shaping of decision and actions, fueled by a dynamic imbrication of individual and collective responses to past action, interactional flows and disrupting events (Lorino 2018). Similar to a wandering in an intricate set of avenues, innovation and decisions primarily fuel on seemingly unexpected discoveries and surprises (Cunha et al. 2006). Also, they involve a great deal of trial-and-error, improvisation (Miner et al. 2001) and dialectical interactions (Zeitz 1980). Losing and finding one's way into a space involves a very similar journey to an organization's apprehending its environment and framing collective action.

Collective action in the context of emergency response particularly fits Bachelard's description of a spatial journey. Emergency organizations, ideally, continuously adapt their responses to their sense-making of the situation (Landgren 2005; Weick 2010; Weick et al. 2005). They massively rely on discursive interactions to improvise (Adrot and Garreau 2010) and show proficiency in dealing with competing perspectives

---

[2] In Chap. 7, De Vaujany Winterstorm and Vaast also propose to approach space as a phenomenological experience but from a distinct perspective, based on the respective works of Augoyard (1979) and De Certeau (1980) on walking practices.

(Weick and Sutcliffe 2003) to shape collective action. Stated otherwise, emergency organizations approach any situation as an unknown somewhere and somehow admit their own blindness to adapt their progress through the situation.

By approaching emergency response as a spatial journey, we open the scope of investigation of pragmatic legitimacy to its material aspect, in particular how it affects emergency response. Materiality, far from restricting to physical assets, also refers to "what matters" (Vásquez and Plourde 2017). Materiality can also stem from seemingly intangible reality because of the weight of its meaning and its performativity (Gagliardi 1990). From this perspective, our ontological perspective on emergency response and legitimacy is essentially pragmatist and echoes realist ontological canons. While parts of the truth remain unreachable for organizations, individual and collective experiences still allow to approximately approach them (Outhwaite 2003). We further detail our ontological and epistemological stances as well as our methodology in the next section.

An Exploratory, Pragmatist and Grounded Research Design

First of all, the research design of this work is essentially exploratory, which is relevant given the scarcity of knowledge on the operational implications of organizations' competition for legitimacy. Grounded theory strongly fits the exploratory dimension of our research design (Strauss and Corbin 2008). Consistently with this approach, we had very little preconception regarding legitimation and the nature of its impact on an organization's operations. In line with grounded theory principles, we conducted a systematic comparison of coding and a constant confrontation of the categories that were emerging from data with practitioners. To do so, we completed more than 30 hours of observation as well as almost 40 hours of interviews, in addition to archive analysis. Through data collection and analysis, the researchers asked the interviewees if the categories and the emerging model fitted their understanding of a situation. Such confrontation helped us attain a semantic saturation of the framework.

This research draws on pragmatism and scientific realism (Cherryholmes 1992). Pragmatism's ontology well fits what was observed on the field. In particular, we quickly realized that the reality was partially, dynamically and subjectively approached by individuals through their interactions and experiences (Shalin 1986).

Our sampling in this work is primarily theoretical, in that the specificities of the case under study make its investigation particularly relevant to address the research question. As a case study, we chose a firefighting organization that we label Sigma and that has been striving from the early 2000s to adapt to a changing institutional context, associated with institutional pressures for a greater access to information. This institutional pressure resulted from a deep governance shift that affected budget allocation between public services. The threat of budget reduction, as well as the quick digitization of operational processes, compelled Sigma to defend its pragmatic legitimacy. Space, as a core category that emerged from data, corresponds to the concept that depicts the phenomenological journey of firefighters.

From this perspective, we do not explore how legitimacy can be impacted by particular events. Rather, we focus on the long-term evolution of legitimacy in the context of digitization. Our underlying rationale is that legitimacy on the spur of an incident does not only depend on how actors behave but also grounds on previous crises, organizational history and deep, yet invisible and latent, institutional dynamics.

The History of Sigma: From Legitimacy Shifts to Digital Transformation

Consistently with theory, Sigma's legitimacy corresponds to its perception by a large range of actors, coming from authorities (including members of the departmental council), citizens, media (and in particular social media) as well as the members of its advisory board, and so on. Numerous studies, essays and testimonies highlight the multiple sources of legitimacy of Sigma. Sigma's pragmatic legitimacy stems from the fact that firefighters significantly contribute to the authorities' duty of civil safety (Derbouilles 2001). In addition, through its history, Sigma has developed

a particularly strong moral legitimacy, in particular, due to the grateful-
ness of the population toward life-saving and firefighting activities.
Finally, Sigma's cognitive legitimacy results from its compliance with legal
frames and the increased transparency in its processes and doctrines.

For the last 20 years, however, several deep social changes have shaped
the institutional landscape of Sigma. First, in 1996, the parliament cham-
bers acknowledged the need to support synergies between emergency
responders, in terms of resources and equipment use as well as investments. Consistently with this thinking, the newly released law stipulated
that fire services' administration and institutional representation should
reorganize at the level of departments. This law had major implications
on Sigma funding and operational management. By 1996, French services mostly had been funded and supervised by municipalities.
Subsequently to the release of the law, fire services became a departmental
emergency organization, which practically implied the creation of trans-
versal and regional advisory boards. From the release of this law, Sigma
got involved in regional institutional dynamics.

More specifically, Sigma experienced the 1996 law both as an opportunity and as a threat to its legitimacy at a regional level. From one side,
the law enabled Sigma to get involved in the handling of a larger spectrum of risks, thereby expanding its pragmatic legitimacy. However,
regarding its operations and finance, Sigma had then to account to a
larger range of stakeholders, coming from local, departmental to regional
and national actors. In addition, the composition of the advisory boards
of the department's fire services changed in a manner that implied loss of
power in the definition of their own budget.

In 2004, a second law further institutionalized the supervision of civil
safety at a departmental level. As a result, Sigma began, in due course, to
provide the necessary information for decision-makers not only at the
local level but also at the departmental or regional level. In addition to
these institutional shifts, the society's digitization generated a shift in
Sigma's stakeholders' expectations. Increasingly, official documents, legal
frames and reports documented the need for civil safety actors to provide
their authorities with reliable and precise information. While such expec-
tation does not exactly fit firefighting's traditional competencies, Sigma
undertook a long-term organizational transformation, including massive

technological investments associated with an important portfolio of IT projects, additional training sessions devoted to information and the definition of new competencies and work practices.[3]

The need for Sigma to promote its pragmatic legitimacy conducted to the completion of multiple transformation projects that included the definition of new competencies related to information production and processing, which was not without impact on Sigma's functioning. In particular, information processing activities—such as the management of citizen's calls and information transmission to operational actors on the field—located in a new building. In addition, Sigma recruited individuals who had light experience in firefighting but would still master information management and processing. The newly recruited fellows experienced criticism from their colleagues but immediately got acknowledged for their proficiency to deal with alerts and information processing. However, despite the traditionally strong cohesion (Auger and Reynaud 2007), all these topological, cultural, material and managerial changes increasingly questioned the feeling of belonging to a unique profession and the fire services appeared less and less as a unified set of missions, values and tempers.

A Spatial Journey in Emergency Response

We detail in this section our conceptualization of emergency response as a spatial journey. We present the framework—emerged from data—that not only provides a comprehensive view of Sigma's operations in emergency settings but also reveals the practical and material dimensions of its pursuit of pragmatic legitimacy.

Emergency response as a spatial journey is inherently phenomenological and thus comprises multiple experiences—for example, sets of perceptions, impressions and emotions, discussion and practices—that we label as occupational. An occupation corresponds to a "personally constructed,

---

[3] The standard features of the technology implemented—not to be developed in this chapter—account for its transferability and quick spreading. The transferability of technology goes beyond the scope of this chapter but is examined in other chapters in this book, such as Chaps. 8 and 9 and the postface.

one-time experience within a unique context" (Pierce 2001, p. 138). From an ontological perspective, occupation "is an important mode through which human beings, as organisms in environment as a whole, function in their complex totality" (Dickie et al. 2006, p. 83).

Data revealed emergency response fueling on a mingling of multiple spaces, dynamically occupied by Sigma's members. These spaces, detailed in the remainder of the section, are inherently material and performative in that they guide and shape collective action. Spatial occupation plays a key role by enabling Sigma to grasp its environment, make sense and elaborate responses to an incident. In addition, data suggests that Sigma's action does not fuel on one space only, but rather relies on a moving focus that offers a balanced occupation of multiple and interdependent spaces. Both at inter-individual and collective levels, dialogical reasoning and interactions articulate Sigma's spatial journey.

Occupying one space calls for more occupation in other related spaces, as it comprises preliminary sense-making to better apprehend other spaces. As detailed in the coming lines, occupying a specific space conducts individuals to have a look, reflect or act on objects contained in this space and then report information produced on virtual platforms, which can conduct them to consider others' needs for information and constraints related to the topology and the objects, thereby making suggestions in case. Data also suggested that collective action required a balanced occupation of the spaces by Sigma's members. On the contrary, coordination got impeded when actors got stuck in one or several spaces, and did not manage to articulate their occupation of a specific space to the others. We describe the six spaces that emerged from data in the remainder of this section. We then detail the relational ontology of the emergency response as a spatial journey by detailing the articulation between the spaces.

Self

"Self" as a space covers all that matters regarding one's identity, both at the individual and collective levels, not only from an emotional but also from a cognitive perspective. As outlined by James in his work (1890),

Self has two dimensions that comprise on the one side the "bodily, material, social (…) aspects" of the Self (Lorino 2018, pp. 135–136) and the "sense of personal identity and continuity/sameness across time, a feeling of distinctness from others and a sense of personal volition reflected in the continuous appropriation and rejection of ideas" (Lorino 2018, pp. 135–136, citing James 1950). In some cases, "Self" only corresponds to what Sigma members experience, feel and think as individuals, like fear and apprehension. In other cases, it can also cover introspective efforts about one's identity, prerogative, profession or values.

Others

"Others" literally corresponds to the alter-entities that are distinct from what actors identify as "Self". More practically, "Others" refers to stakeholders who are likely to affect or be affected by Sigma's action, as well as the information produced from and by others. This space primarily refers to citizens in some cases and to organizations in other cases. Actors frequently refer to and explore this space during an incident because a collective response to an incident takes place according to a command chain that comprises a large spectrum of actors, including private and public organizations. Given that Sigma needs to abide by its predefined role within the command chains, responders are aware of their need to transmit and share information to address the command chain's needs.

Objects

"Objects", as space, comprises the material artifacts involved in operations or any response from Sigma to an incident. An artifact is a "product of human action", which "aims at solving problems" and is "perceived by the senses" (Gagliardi 1990, p. 3). While artifacts are not necessarily intangible—such as procedures or routines—the data generated suggests that the perception, analysis or manipulation and use of objects, which constitute tangible artifacts, correspond to a specific space. This space covers a large spectrum of equipments that Sigma members are familiar with—such as uniforms or vehicles—, working tools—such as protocols, procedures, programs—or even mundane objects that are not used on a regular basis but can be grasped by Sigma members to address an incident. In this case, "Objects" is an important space for Sigma actors who need to find innovative solutions on the spur of the moment. "Objects" is a particularly important space from an operational standpoint: Objects are essential to complete action on the field and alleviate the victims' suffering as soon as possible. That said, "Objects" does not solely refer to tangible artifacts that can be useful but also to matters related to objects that can represent constraints on a response. For instance, Sigma members might share information about a vehicle in which some victims remain trapped.

Topology

"Topology" does not only cover the stage of the incident but also the different locations where emergency response takes place, such as hospitals and crisis cells. From an epistemological perspective, "Topology" refers to the knowledge and understanding of a place, an essential lever for collective action in firefighting. When responding to an incident, firefighters need to plan their action and coordination on the basis of topological constraints. Three elements are essential to "Topology": (i) topological structural features, (ii) topological contingent features and, finally, (iii) the level of understanding of the two former points. Topological structural features are particularly diverse and cannot be exhaustively documented in this chapter. They represent an extended spectrum of matters, coming from the distance between the stage of the crisis and other locations to its functionality. Other features can be contingent, such as the direction and the strength of the wind, which have a strong influence on the evolution of a fire and are taken into consideration by firefighters with precision and care. Finally, the level of understanding of the topology, which depends on its functionality, also deeply impacts collective action. In some cases, topological characteristics get exhaustively documented. Some train stations, for instance, correspond to highly attended and crowded places, which conducts firefighters to develop a precise understanding of their structure and the roads around and within the station that can be used to deal with an incident as quickly as possible. In the same vein, firefighters develop a methodology to analyze topology in an ad hoc fashion. For instance, when an incident is large, Sigma formalizes topology by dividing it into sectors.

Virtuality

This space corresponds to what happens and matters on virtual platforms devoted to sharing information, such as a collaborative platform for a communication exchange or even social media such as Twitter and Facebook. It vividly embodies institutional pressure by corresponding the emergence of Sigma's new competencies in information collection and processing. Unsurprisingly, this space's occupation relates to Sigma's expectations regarding its pragmatic legitimacy. From an operational perspective, "Virtuality" is also important from an operational perspective as it enables Sigma and the "Others" to make sense of a situation collectively. In particular, Sigma shares information about the topology of an incident, the human and material resources deployed in "Virtuality". Sigma can also receive some messages, which enables the organization to know more about the "Others".

What If

"What if" corresponds to the set of assumptions collectively induced and framed by the firefighters from information related to other spaces. "What if" also relates to the risks inherent to a specific location or an incident that responders need to take into consideration to make a decision or adjust collective action. For instance, when incidents occur in industrial zones, Sigma proceeds to an analysis of the sanitary risks, the damages or disturbances that can impact the population due to the specificities of the incident itself. Sigma also takes into consideration the factors that might aggravate the impacts of the incidents on the population, such as the proximity of dense areas, transportation networks that can be blocked by the event and generate traffic jams and accidents, or even the wind force that could expand the perimeter of a fire.

Table 6.1 provides an overview of the various spaces presented herein.

Table 6.1 Spaces definition

Space	Definition
Self	All that matters regarding one's identity, both at the individual and collective levels, not only from an emotional but also a cognitive perspective
Others	The alter-entities that are distinct from what actors identify as "Self"
Objects	Comprises the material artifacts involved in operations or any response from Sigma to an incident
Topology	The stage of the incident and the different locations where emergency response takes place, such as hospitals and crisis cells
Virtuality	What happens and matters on virtual platforms devoted to sharing information
What if	The set of assumptions collectively induced and framed by the firefighters from information related to topology or objects

Spatial Imbrication Through Occupation

Emergency action as a spatial journey is ontologically relational. In line with the pragmatist thinking, relational ontology means that parts of a phenomenon have no independent existence (Lorino 2018), that reality shapes through a continuous flow of interactions and transactions (Shalin 1986; Tsoukas 2009). From this perspective, there is no explanatory value in excluding one space from the framework or focusing on one space solely. Rather, emergency action as a spatial journey results from Sigma members' dynamic occupation of the various spaces that we previously detailed, which supports the progressive shaping of emergency action. We detail in the coming lines the major interactions between the spaces.

Topology

Topology inherently relates to the other spaces. Practically speaking, firefighters need to fully understand the overall structure of a topological space to approach "Objects" in order to deduce where to find the appropriate resources to deal with the situation. In addition, "Topology"—which covers not only their objective characteristics but also the nature of their understanding by firefighters—affects access to their own equipment, including vehicles and medical resources. "Topology" also fuels "Virtuality", in particular, through the use of maps that are very frequently shared on collaborative electronic platforms. The topological analysis of a situation is also essential to frame hypotheses regarding constraints of action and thus fuels "What if". Collectively, firefighters deduce potential risks that can affect personal safety from topological features and from their own understanding of these features. From this perspective, topology matters most when "Self" and "Others" are involved in a crisis response.

Self

"Self" and the "Others" are intricately related spaces because Sigma members need to rely a lot either on their colleagues or on their counterparts. In other cases, "Self" corresponds to Sigma as a whole for its members, which is unsurprising given Sigma's strong cohesion. In such settings, "Self" covers Sigma's organizations' identity, which is very dependent on "Others" as a space also. "Self" as a space continuously matters during a response to an incident because self-reliability is an important condition for an efficient response to an incident and depends much on the other spaces. As a result, Sigma members generate important volumes of information that relates "Self" to immediate experience and understanding of a situation, regarding the specificities of the place where the incident took place—"Topology"—or the equipment needed—"Objects"—or the risks related to the situation—for example, "What if". As a procedure, when an incident occurs, the first responders usually describe to their coordinators where they are standing, what they are doing and what they are seeing on the incident stage. From this evaluation, Sigma analyzes needs and constraints that shape the response and reports to "Others". "Self" therefore corresponds to an essential source of information and action and strongly relates to alternate spaces, such as "Others".

Objects

By providing information about potential constraints and solutions to problem-solving, "Objects" allows the framing of the strategies and human resources needed to deal with a situation, thereby permitting occupying "Self". The same framing of hypotheses about risks and constraints boils down to "Objects" fueling "What if". In a reciprocal fashion, "What if" also conducts Sigma members to be creative with material artifacts and explore the possibilities of action associated with equipment or any other objects. To that extent, the occupation of "Objects" grows from "What if". In addition, "Objects" intensely relates to "Virtuality" in that Sigma often shares information about available resources through virtual communication. One reason for that is that equipment is a resource in limited quantities. Consequently, when "Objects" as a space matters, "Virtuality" also becomes important for Sigma.

What If

"What if" is essential to make sense of the situation because examining the inherent risks of an incident conducts actors to identify its most crucial aspects. "What if" intensely draws on occupation from other spaces and fuels other spaces with additional ideas. In addition, this space conducts actors to consider the topological nature of the place where the incident occurs, such as the transportation axis connected to the incident and the proximity of vulnerable resources such as water. Finally, identifying risks related to the incident and its location conducts actors to dispatch tasks and responsibilities. For instance, when incidents occur at the administrative frontier of two distinct sub-regions, colleagues might be consulted or even involved and additional tasks of coordination are subsequently planned. For this reason, this space is particularly important to Sigma in its anticipation of resource allocation and tasks.

Virtuality

Sigma members generally attribute a special status to their interactions within this space because it somehow formalizes information and makes it official. To that extent, occupying "Virtuality" often makes Sigma members jump to the space of "Others" and "Self". By fueling "Virtuality", Sigma members also have to rephrase information and comments about "Topology", "Self" and "Objects", which conduct them to reoccupy these spaces in order to check and refine the information produced.

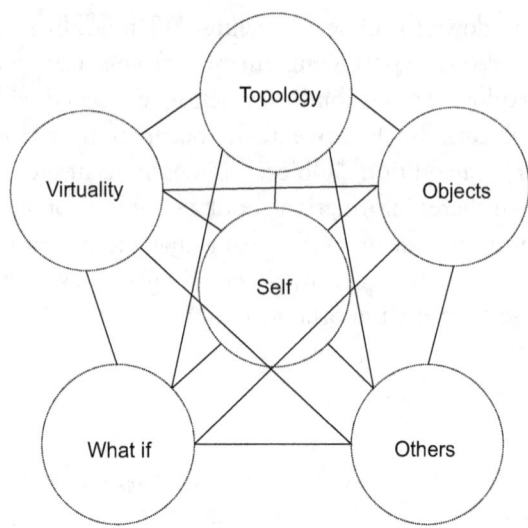

Fig. 6.1 Emergency response as a spatial journey

Figure 6.1 depicts space as a framework and represents its six components as well as their imbrication (represented by the black ties).

When Spatial Balance Got Broken: Analysis of the Operational Implications of Legitimacy Quest Through Space

On multiple occasions, Sigma's quest for legitimacy influenced the way
its members processed information. Representing emergency action as a
spatial journey supports a full consideration of the implications of Sigma's
pursuit of legitimacy and highlights that information transmission, interactions and practices can focus on some spaces rather than others. As a
result, Sigma restricted its handling of its environment to a partial proportion of it. The practical implication of restrictive reliance on the whole
set of spaces account for coordination failure and lower operational
performance.

For instance, during an exercise, Sigma firefighters confronted a brutal
refusal of access to the field from the other organizations. According to

the initial scenario of the exercise, Sigma had to handle a fire near a chemical plant that could potentially result in an explosion and leaks of toxic substances, affecting inhabitants near the plant. Other organizations involved in the exercise were competitors to Sigma for institutional legitimacy.

According to Sigma's competitors who had taken the lead of response and blocked access to the field, the objects present on the stage of the incident were highly explosive and toxic, which motivated a drastic restriction of access to the response perimeter. Given Sigma's expertise in explosive substance and chemical risk, such restriction was unfunded. Because of that, some Sigma members remained close to the stage of the incident to keep arguing with other organizations about their own legitimacy and prerogatives in this specific situation. Doing so, they focused their energy on the matter of their own prerogative in comparison with others. They hardly directed their attention toward the topological and material matters that were essential components of the support that they could bring to response. As a result, "Self" and "Others" attracted energy, action and information at the expense of "Topology" and "Objects", as well as "What if". Shocked by the absurdity of the situation, they eventually decided to stop providing information to the collaborative platform dedicated to crisis collaboration and coordination between local emergency responders, thereby rarifying interactions and information in "Virtuality".

In the meantime, some other Sigma firefighters were involved in a departmental crisis cell and were in charge of providing expertise about the risks related to the incident to the whole cell. They were also in charge of providing updates about Sigma's progress and course of action on the field. In that matter, Sigma members occupied "Topology" and "What if" by reflecting on hypotheses in relation to the wind force and resulting toxicity of the air nearby the plant. However, to frame their hypotheses, they needed additional topological information about the location of the buildings and the chemical nature of the objects in the fire. Lacking information from the field about the topology of the incident and the objects involved in the response, they could not provide strong and reliable expertise, which implied increased stress related to Sigma's legitimacy within the crisis cell. Lacking information and action to report with respect to "Topology" and "Objects", Sigma members could hardly fuel "What if". In addition, their attention remained stuck on the political and institutional negative implications of their lack of expertise and focused on "Self" and "Others". When they tried to contact their colleagues through the virtual platform, they realized that the lack of access to the field had compromised information production. As a result, Sigma members could not enrich their own action from "Virtuality" and their attention focused predominantly on their interactions with other organizations and "Others". However, other organizations started questioning Sigma's willingness to collaborate by sharing information. As a result, Sigma approached "Virtuality" as an issue intricately related to "Others" rather than as a source of information and reflection about other spaces.

The whole set of spaces that supports the sharing of Sigma's technical expertise—including risks, material, the topology of the incident stage—and draws collective action less attracted some Sigma members' attention in comparison with the other spaces that are more related to institutional stakes such as "Self" and "Others". By not occupying "Objects", "Topology" and "What if", Sigma was less capable of shaping strategies to cope with the incident. By abandoning "Virtuality", Sigma stopped information and its expertise with its stakeholders. The constant pressure on pragmatic legitimacy eventually led Sigma to overlook its institutional strength, including its specific expertise on topology, risks and equipment. Paradoxically enough, Sigma's reaction to pressure resulted in the endangering of its own pragmatic legitimacy.

Figure 6.2 depicts the collapse of balance in terms of spatial occupation. As represented, Sigma primarily occupies "Self" and "Others". In addition, "Virtuality" was primarily experienced as a problem in relation to "Others", as its fueling by "Topology" and "Objects" rarified. Being able to provide information about Sigma's operations from the field was stressful with respect to others' perception of Sigma functioning and contribution to collective action. "What if" appears atrophied on the figure: "Topology" being primarily discussed in relation to Sigma's access to the field (which corresponds to "Self"), attention was less devoted to the potential hazards that could affect crisis response, at the expense of collective action.

Due to a lack of mutual informational and experiential enrichment between spaces, Sigma members collectively endangered their own capability to address other's needs, thereby undermining their own prag-

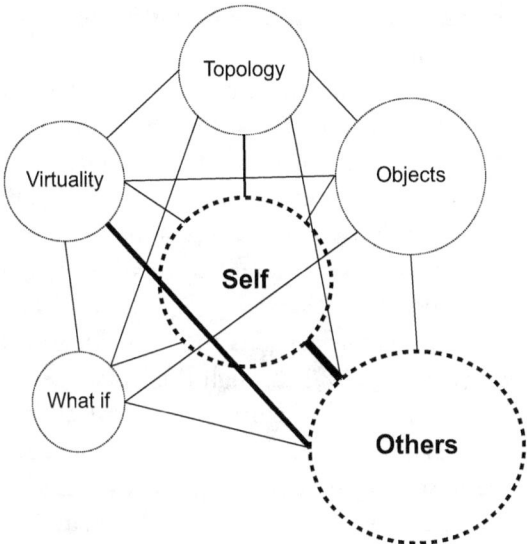

Fig. 6.2 Distorted spatial balance

matic legitimacy. In addition, the collective response to the incident during the exercise was delayed due to the waiting times for updates from the field and information provided about the situation.

Conclusion

As Greenwood et al. explain, an "overarching theory of legitimation remains unfinished business" (2008). This chapter addresses this call by highlighting, from a material perspective, the operational shifts generated by an emergency organization's pursuit of pragmatic legitimacy.

In order to support its pragmatic legitimacy, Sigma initially intended to improve its information sharing through digitization. However, the institutional pressure associated with Sigma's need to obtain legitimacy prevented the actors from optimally using their resources. Rather than providing finer and more reliable information to its stakeholders, Sigma got trapped into a strong focus on the others, thereby impeding its own legitimacy. Such findings have several implications on current knowledge on institutional pressure.

First, our findings reveal that organizations do not always benefit in a positive manner from their pursuit for pragmatic legitimacy. While the literature highlights institutional pressure as a source of innovation in public organizations (Verhoest et al. 2007), our analysis based on space allows us to challenge this assertion. We pose that institutional pressure for pragmatic legitimacy also has potential negative effects on an organization's capacity to operate.

Going further, our analysis suggests that individuals fully experience legitimacy stakes (Hoque 2005) through their practices. They not only experience legitimacy stakes through information transmission but also through the six spaces that regulate informational flows. However, adapting their practices to support pragmatic legitimacy, organizations can face coordination and operational dysfunctions. This material dimension of legitimation implies that organizations, when encouraged to abide by institutional injunction—such as the need to provide information to stakeholders—should be accompanied to fully benefit from innovation that are meant to promote their legitimacy and survival. From this perspective, this chapter echoes previous calls for constantly putting into perspective institutional legitimacy and the daily context of an organization's members (Drori and Honig 2013).

Approaching legitimacy through its materiality does not only enable proposing managerial guidance over its pursuit. Rather, it opens a window over the conceptual and epistemological richness of materiality. From a conceptual perspective, materiality not only refers to what matters, has a significant impact or vividly expresses in social and material subsistence (Thornton and Ocasio 1999). Rather, materiality also covers this very subsistence, its features and properties, may they be physical and intangible (Jones et al. 2013).[4] While the chapter originally departs from materiality as its performativity (Vásquez and Plourde 2017), empirical investigation conducted us to thoroughly examine the specific features of

---

[4] In Chap. 9, Thomas, Abrunhosa and Canales, through their investigation of the role of digital objects, discuss the need to reconceptualize materiality to relate its features to institutional matters. Going further in the postface, Candace Jones offers promising avenues for institutional research, including the durability, transferability, relationality as essential features of materiality.

several forms of materiality, including artifacts (such as equipment, vehicles, helicopters), digitality (including the use of a digital collaborative platform), bodies (through matters related to one's physical safety) and space (through topology). From an epistemological perspective, our research has outlined materiality as a heuristic springboard to understand the ties between its various areas (for more discussion on the numerous conceptual ties between the various areas of materiality, please refer to Chap. 1), as well as the complex impact of institutional life on daily operations. We relied on space as an entry to depict through six spaces the shaping of information transmission by the pursuit of pragmatic legitimacy. From this perspective, the value of materiality is not only conceptual but also epistemological and methodological.[5]

Therefore, our chapter fully embraces the spatial turn not only by putting into perspective institutional and operational dynamics, but also by proposing space as an intermediary concept (Van Marrewijk and Yanow 2010). In line with this view, even though practitioners have been knowing for a long time that organizational transformation much depends on changes related to human resources (Kochan and Dyer 1993), our analysis suggests that transformation also requires a constant monitoring of the influence of institutional dynamics on operations, in particular, by taking into consideration its material and spatial dimension. Going further, organizations ought to complete a clear preliminary diagnosis of the existing strengths and potential side effects of pragmatic legitimacy defense. Otherwise, organizations take the risk to engage in a lost crusade.

As a second source of implication, this chapter experiments the possibilities of reflection and action offered by the notion of space. Inspired by pragmatist thinking (Dewey 1908; James 1975; Lorino 2018) the proposed framework depicts emergency response as a spatial journey. Not only it offers insights on pragmatic legitimacy and its materiality, but it

---

[5] Several chapters in the book rely on some area of materiality as a springboard to better understand other approach other aspects of materiality. In Chap. 5, Arena and Douai explore the physical and spatial emergence of Saïd Business through their archives, another kind of materiality. In Chap. 10, Felix, Arena and Douai produced their own digital artifacts to approach spatial occupation, body expression and emotion. Likewise, in Chap. 11, Norhorm and Kirkegaard investigate body plasticity and institutional ideation through a documentary.

also serves as a "reflection in action" concept (Yanow and Tsoukas 2009). Initially, our approach to space was purely analytical. While we were conceptualizing our own understanding of collective action, frequent discussion of the emerging framework with the interviewees—initially aimed at a refinement of the framework from a purely scholarly perspective— eventually resulted into a representation of firefighters' ontology that transcribed their own approach to their work practices. Constant confrontation between conceptualization and empirical sources of knowledge fits pragmatism principles, in that we strove to produce knowledge that could possibly impact the reality (Dewey 1908).

Thus, after each interview, we systematically submitted the framework to the interviewees to confront its substance to the firefighters' operational reality. Some of them also suggested additional spaces, which conducted us to recode data and include "Self" as a core element of the framework. Interestingly, data suggested that even though not being strictly aware of the diverse spaces that we had identified, Sigma more or less intuitively regulated emergency response on the basis of the spatial imbrications. The proposed framework thus participated and still participates in practical reflexivity and thoughtful collective action. Consistently with Raelin's approach, we aim at contributing to public learning from research as *"the ability to uncover and to make explicit (...) what one has planned, observed or achieved in practice"* (Raelin 2001, p. 11).

References

Aballéa, F. (2013). L'anomie professionnelle. Déprofessionnalisation et désinstitutionnalisation du travail. *Recherche et formation, 72*, 15–26.

Abbott, A. (1998). Professionalism and the future of librarianship. *Library Trends, 46*(3), 430–443.

Abbott, A. (2014). *The system of professions: An essay on the division of expert labor.* Chicago: University of Chicago Press.

Adrot, A. (2017). Dynamiques émergentes, matérialité et transmission d'information dans les organisations mises en difficulté : l'étude d'un réseau inter-organisationnel entre 2003 et 2013. Revue COSSI, n°2-2017. https://revue-cossi.info/numeros/n-2-2017-bricolages-improvisations-et-resilience-organisationnelle-face-aux-risques-informationnels-etcommunicationnels/661-2-2017-revue-adrot

Adrot, A., & Garreau, L. (2010). Interagir pour improviser en situation de crise. Le cas de la canicule de 2003. *Revue Française de Gestion, 36*(203), 119–131.

Ashforth, B. E., & Gibbs, B. W. (1990). The double-edge of organizational legitimation. *Organization Science, 1*(2), 177–194.

Auger, P., & Reynaud, E. (2007). Le rôle de la confiance dans la gestion du risque d'incendie. (French). Trust and management in fire interventions. (English). *Revue Française de Gestion, 175*(6), 155–169. https://doi.org/10.3166/ RFG.175.155-169.

Augoyard, J. F. (1979). *Pas à pas. Essai sur le cheminement quotidien en milieu urbain*. Paris: Seuil.

Bachelard, G. (2005). From Essai sur la connaissance approchée (1927). In G. Gutting (Ed.), *Continental philosophy of science* (pp. 176–183). Malden: Blackwell Publishing.

Bachelard, G. (1938). *La formation de l'esprit scientifique*. Paris: Vrin.

Cherryholmes, C. H. (1992). Notes on pragmatism and scientific realism. *Educational Researcher, 21*(6), 13–17.

Comes, T., Adrot, A., & Rizza, C. (2017). Decision making with uncertainty. In K. Poljanšek, M. Marín Ferrer, T. De Groeve, & I. Clark (Eds.), *Sciences for disaster risk management: Knowing better and losing less* (pp. 404–437). Brussels: Publications Office of the European Union.

Comfort, L. K. (2007). Crisis management in hindsight: Cognition, communication, coordination, and control. *Public Administration Review, 67*, 189–197.

Cunha, M. P., Clegg, S. R., & Kamoche, K. (2006). Surprises in management and organization: Concept, sources and a typology*. *British Journal of Management, 17*(4), 317–329.

Dacin, M. T., Goodstein, J., & Scott, W. R. (2002). Institutional theory and institutional change: Introduction to the special research forum. *Academy of Management Journal, 45*(1), 45–56.

Dawes, S. S., Cresswell, A. M., & Cahan, B. B. (2004). Learning from crisis – Lessons in human and information infrastructure from the World Trade Center response. *Social Science Computer Review, 22*(1), 52–66.

De Certeau, M. (1980). *L'invention du quotidien, t. I, Arts de faire*. Paris: Folio essais. Reedited in 1990.

Deephouse, D. L. (1996). Does isomorphism legitimate? *Academy of Management Journal, 39*(4), 1024–1039.

Derbouilles, L. (2001). Contribution à l'étude du service public local d'incendie et de secours. *Annuaire des collectivités locales, 21*, 715–724.

Dewey, J. (1908). What does pragmatism mean by practical? *The Journal of Philosophy, Psychology and Scientific Methods, 5*(4), 85–99.

Dickie, V., Cutchin, M. P., & Humphry, R. (2006). Occupation as transactional experience: A critique of individualism in occupational science. *Journal of Occupational Science, 13*(1), 83–93.

Díez-Martín, F., Prado-Roman, C., & Blanco-González, A. (2013). Beyond legitimacy: Legitimacy types and organizational success. *Management Decision, 51*(10), 1954–1969.

Drori, I., & Honig, B. (2013). A process model of internal and external legitimacy. *Organization Studies, 34*(3), 345–376.

Gagliardi, P. (1990). *Symbols and artifacts: Views of the corporate landscape* (Vol. 24). Berlin: Walter de Gruyter.

Golant, B. D., & Sillince, J. A. (2007). The constitution of organizational legitimacy: A narrative perspective. *Organization Studies, 28*(8), 1149–1167.

Greenwood, R., Oliver, C., Suddaby, R., & Sahlin-Andersson, K. (2008). *The Sage handbook of organizational institutionalism.* London: Sage.

Hart, P. (1993). Symbols, rituals and power: The lost dimensions of crisis management. *Journal of Contingencies and Crisis Management, 1*(1), 36–50.

Hoque, Z. (2005). Securing institutional legitimacy or organizational effectiveness? A case examining the impact of public sector reform initiatives in an Australian local authority. *International Journal of Public Sector Management, 18*(4), 367–382.

Hughes, A. L., & Palen, L. (2012). The evolving role of the public information officer: An examination of social media in emergency management. *Journal of Homeland Security and Emergency Management, 9*(1). ISSN (Online) 1547-7355. https://doi.org/10.1515/1547-7355.1976.

James, W. (1890). *The principles of psychology* (Vol. 1). New York: Henry Holt and Company.

James, W. (1975). *Pragmatism* (Vol. 1). Cambridge, MA: Harvard University Press.

Jones, C., Boxenbaum, E., & Anthony, C. (2013). The immateriality of material practices in institutional logics. In *Institutional logics in action, Part A* (pp. 51–75). Bingley: Emerald Group Publishing Limited.

Kapucu, N. (2005). Interorganizational coordination in dynamic context: Networks in emergency response management. *Connections, 26*(2), 33–48.

Kendra, J. M., & Wachtendorf, T. (2003). Reconsidering convergence and converger legitimacy in response to the World Trade Center disaster. In L. Clarke (Ed.), *Terrorism and disaster: New threats, new ideas* (pp. 97–122). Bingley: Emerald Group Publishing Limited.

Kilduff, M., & Tsai, W. (2003). *Social networks and organizations.* London/Thousand Oaks: Sage.

Kochan, T. A., & Dyer, L. (1993). Managing transformational change: The role of human resource professionals. *International Journal of Human Resource Management, 4*(3), 569–590.

Lamin, A., & Zaheer, S. (2012). Wall Street vs. Main Street: Firm strategies for defending legitimacy and their impact on different stakeholders. *Organization Science, 23*(1), 47–66.

Landgren, J. (2005). Supporting fire crew sensemaking enroute to incidents. *International Journal of Emergency Management, 2*(3), 176–188.

Lorino, P. (2018). *Pragmatism and organization studies.* New York: Oxford University Press.

Majchrzak, A. N. N., & More, P. H. B. (2011). Emergency! Web 2.0 to the Rescue! *Communications of the ACM, 54*(4), 125–132. https://doi.org/10.1145/1924421.1924449.

Meyer, J., & Scott, R. (1983). Centralization and the legitimacy problems of local government. In J. Meyer & R. Scott (Eds.), *Organizational environment: Rituals and rationality* (pp. 199–216). Newbury Park: Sage.

Miner, A. S., Bassoff, P., & Moorman, C. (2001). Organizational improvisation and learning: A field study. *Administrative Science Quarterly, 46*(2), 304–337.

Orlikowski, W. J. (1996). Improvising organizational transformation over time: A situated change perspective. *Information Systems Research, 7*(1), 63–92.

Osatuyi, B., & Mendonça, D. (2012). Temporal modeling of group information foraging: An application to emergency response. *Information Processing & Management, 49*(1), 169–178.

Outhwaite, W. (2003). Realism and social science. In M. Archer, R. Bashkar, A. Collier, T. Lawson, & A. Norrie (Eds.), *Critical Realism: Essential Readings* (pp. 282–296). Routledge.

Pierce, D. (2001). Untangling occupation and activity. *American Journal of Occupational Therapy, 55*(2), 138–146.

Provan, K. G., Kenis, P., & Human, S. E. (2008). Legitimacy building in organizational networks. In L. Blomgren Bingham & R. O'Leary (Eds.), *Big ideas in collaborative public management* (pp. 121–137). New York: M.E. Sharpe.

Raelin, J. A. (2001). Public reflection as the basis of learning. *Management Learning, 32*(1), 11–30.

Shalin, D. N. (1986). Pragmatism and social interactionism. *American Sociological Review, 51*(1), 9–29.

Souto-Otero, M., & Beneito-Montagut, R. (2016). From governing through data to governmentality through data: Artifacts, strategies and the digital turn. *European Educational Research Journal, 15*(1), 14–33.

Stout, M. (2012). *Logics of legitimacy: Three traditions of public administration praxis.* Hoboken: CRC Press.

Strauss, A. L., & Corbin, J. (2008). *Basics of qualitative research: Techniques and procedures for developing grounded theory.* Thousand Oaks: Sage.

Suchman, M. C. (1995). Managing legitimacy: Strategic and institutional approaches. *Academy of Management Review, 20*(3), 571–610.

Suddaby, R., & Greenwood, R. (2005). Rhetorical strategies of legitimacy. *Administrative Science Quarterly, 50*(1), 35–67.

't Hart, P., Tindall, K., & Brown, C. (2009). Crisis leadership of the Bush presidency: Advisory capacity and presidential performance in the acute stages of the 9/11 and Katrina crises. *Presidential Studies Quarterly, 39*(3), 473–493. https://doi.org/10.1111/j.1741-5705.2009.03687.x.

Taupin, B. (2012). The more things change… Institutional maintenance as justification work in the credit rating industry. *M@n@gement, 15*(5), 529–562.

Thornton, P. H., & Ocasio, W. (1999). Institutional logics and the historical contingency of power in organizations: Executive succession in the higher education publishing industry, 1958–1990. *American Journal of Sociology, 105*(3), 801–843.

Tsoukas, H. (2009). A dialogical approach to the creation of new knowledge in organizations. *Organization Science, 20*(6), 941–957.

Vaast, E., & Walsham, G. (2005). Representations and actions: The transformation of work practices with IT use. *Information and Organization, 15*(1), 65–89.

Van Marrewijk, A. H. (2009). Corporate headquarters as physical embodiments of organisational change. *Journal of Organizational Change Management, 22*(3), 290–306.

Van Marrewijk, A., & Yanow, D. (2010). *Organizational spaces: Rematerializing the workaday world.* Northampton: Edward Elgar Publishing.

Vásquez, C., & Plourde, M. C. (2017). Materiality and organizing. In C. R. Scott & L. Lewis (Eds.), *The international encyclopedia of organizational communication* (pp. 1484–1499). Chichester, UK: Wiley.

Verhoest, K., Verschuere, B., & Bouckaert, G. (2007). Pressure, legitimacy, and innovative behavior by public organizations. *Governance, 20*(3), 469–497.

Weick, K. E. (2010). Reflections on enacted sensemaking in the Bhopal disaster. *Journal of Management Studies, 47*(3), 537–550. https://doi.org/10.1111/j.1467-6486.2010.00900.x.

Weick, K., & Sutcliffe, K. M. (2003). Hospitals as culture of entrapment: A reanalysis of the Bristol Royal Infirmary. *California Management Review, 45*(2), 73–84.

Weick, K. E., Sutcliffe, K. M., & Obstfeld, D. (2005). Organizing and the process of sensemaking. *Organization Science, 16*(4, Frontiers of Organization Science, Part 1 of 2), 409–421.

Yanow, D. (2010). Giving voice to space: Academic practices and the material world. In A. H. Van Marrewijk & D. Yanow (Eds.), *Organizational spaces: Rematerializing the workaday world* (pp. 139–158). Cheltenham: Edward Elgar.

Yanow, D., & Tsoukas, H. (2009). What is reflection-in-action? A phenomenological account. *The Journal of Management Studies, 46*(8), 1339–1364.

Zeitz, G. (1980). Interorganizational dialectics. *Administrative Science Quarterly, 25*(1), 72–88.

Zimmerman, M. A., & Zeitz, G. J. (2002). Beyond survival: Achieving new venture growth by building legitimacy. *Academy of Management Review, 27*(3), 414–431.

7

At the Intersection of Materiality, Organizational Legitimacy and Institutional Logics: A Study of Campus Tours

François-Xavier de Vaujany,
Sara Winterstorm Varlander,
and Emmanuelle Vaast

Earlier drafts of this chapter were presented at APROS conference in December 2015, the fourth Organizations, Artifacts and Practices (OAP) workshop in June 2014 and the workshop "Giving visual and material form to ideas, identity and imagination: architecture, urbanism and sustainable construction" in May 2014. We thank all participants for their precious feedbacks and comments.

F.-X. de Vaujany (✉)
Université Paris-Dauphine PSL, Paris, France
e-mail: Francois-Xavier.deVAUJANY@dauphine.fr

S. W. Varlander
Stockholm School of Economics, Stockholm, Sweden

Stanford University, Stanford, CA, USA
e-mail: sara.winterstorm.varlander@hhs.se

E. Vaast
McGill University, Montreal, Canada
e-mail: emmanuelle.vaast@mcgill.ca

© The Author(s) 2019
F.-X. de Vaujany et al. (eds.), *Materiality in Institutions*, Technology, Work and Globalization, https://doi.org/10.1007/978-3-319-97472-9_7

183

Introduction

During the last decade or so, the phenomenon of campus tours, also called 'the Golden Walk' (Hoover 2009, 2010; Miller 2012) has become increasingly widespread, particularly among US universities, as they have been considered an effective student recruitment practice. Facing tightened budgets, universities have had to expand their recruitment efforts to generate substantial applicant pools (Padjen 2002). Furthermore, higher education has often been labeled as a business, selling intangible products to students, who are increasingly wary of debt and consumer savvy (Padjen 2002; Washburn and Petroshius 2004), and who consider multiple factors in their choice of college or university. Thus, universities today are facing conflicting demands and pressures, dictated by various institutional logics[1] (Jarzabkowski et al. 2013 b; Greenwood et al. 2010). On one hand, the industry or market logic prescribes business-like practices and goals. On the other hand, the social logic dictates values such as individual learning and the cultivation of the citizens (Gumport 2012; Carnoy and Rhoten 2002; Kondakci and Van den Broeck 2009).

In this complex and changing institutional context, it is crucial for universities to acquire and maintain their legitimacy[2] (e.g. Meyer and Rowan 1977; DiMaggio and Powell 1983; Elsbach 1994; Scott 1995; Lounsbury and Glynn 2001; Suddaby and Greenwood 2005). Building legitimacy is imperative for organizations to be perceived as "more meaningful, more predictable, and more trustworthy" (Suchman 1995, p. 575) and to receive more support and resources from external stakeholders

---

[1] Other chapters in the book examine conflicting institutional logics in universities, which reveal that multiple areas of materiality relate to this topic. In Chap. 9, Morgan-Thomas, Abrunhosa and Canales explore the role of digital objects in the orchestration of conflicting institutional logics. In Chap. 5, through historical investigation, Arena and Douai analyze the emergence of Saïd Business School as a stand-alone unit and its institutionalization in Oxford University.

[2] Please refer to Chaps. 6, 8 and 12 for complementary empirical approaches to legitimacy. In Chap. 6, Adrot and Bia-Figueiredo examine the materiality of a firefighting organization's pursuit for legitimacy. In Chap. 8, Santos analyzes digital entrepreneurs' reliance on the materiality of digital artifacts to frame discursive strategies and legitimacy claims. In Chap. 12, de Vaujany proposes three ontologies to explore legitimacy, including the ontology of sculpture and the ontology of bubbles.

(Ashforth and Gibbs 1990). To sustain legitimacy, organizations may rely on different broad modalities of justification, or institutional logics that can dictate various goals and subsequent practices of legitimation.

Thus far, while studies have explored how institutional logics are invoked in symbolic management practices when firms compete for resources (Jones et al. 2010), very few have studied how institutional logics are instantiated in the material context of organizations (Jones et al. 2013). In order to start addressing this gap in the literature, here we argue that campus tours constitute a particular, walking-based, practice that is simultaneously discursive, material, visual and embodied (de Certeau 1980; Schatzki 2001; Rose and Tolia-Kelly 2012; de Vaujany and Vaast 2016), and that aims at establishing legitimacy by invoking the material context of the university in its legitimacy claims. Through the lens of de Certeau (1980) and his attention to walking as a particular practice that 'makes space talk', we address how materiality, through the practice of walking, is involved in symbolic management that aims at promoting an adherence to diverse, conflicting institutional logics. Specifically, our research question reads: *How do the walking practices of campus tours invoke materiality to make legitimacy claims?*

The organization of the chapter is as follows. We first introduce key issues related to organizational legitimation, followed by an introduction of our lens of walking as a practice in which space is made alive and invoked in legitimacy claims. We then outline the method we employed before presenting our findings and resulting propositions related to how institutional logics are enacted in legitimation practices and the role of materiality therein. We conclude with a summary of this work's contributions, limitations and promising future research avenues.

Organizational Legitimation

How organizations acquire and maintain their legitimacy in complex and changing institutional contexts has been a significant topic in institutional theory (e.g. Meyer and Rowan 1977; DiMaggio and Powell 1983; Elsbach 1994; Scott 1995; Lounsbury and Glynn 2001; Suddaby and Greenwood 2005). Organizational legitimacy corresponds to "a generalized perception or assumption that the actions of an entity are desirable, proper, or appropriate within some socially constructed system of norms, values, beliefs, and definitions" (Suchman 1995, p. 574). The process of legitimation is essential for organizations to gain support and resources from multiple stakeholders (Ashforth and Gibbs 1990).

Organizations can pursue legitimacy in various ways (Ashforth and Gibbs 1990; Oliver 1991; Suchman 1995). Ashforth and Gibbs (1990) consider that organizations may resort to substantive or symbolic management in their legitimation efforts. In this chapter, the focus lies on symbolic management that implies that an organization may change the ways in which it portrays itself to appear more consistent with stakeholders' expectations. As the number of organizational relationships tends to grow and organizational fields become more complex (Kraatz and Block 2008), it becomes impossible for each and every stakeholder to have deep substantial knowledge about an organization, which explains why symbolic management has become increasingly strategic to organizations. Also, managers may resort to symbolic management, since it does not require any substantial changes of the underlying processes and infrastructure of the organization but rather involves control over, and creativity with, the resources at hand. Thus, in contrast to substantive management, which implies that organizations try to create real, material change in their goals, structures and processes, or in alterations of socially institutionalized practices (such as role performance and coercive isomorphism), symbolic management does not involve specific material *changes* in the ways organizations operate. However, materiality (in particular that of communication practices themselves) still remains important in symbolic management, which we argue can be tightly and powerfully connected to—and amplified by—the material context of the organization. The materiality of an organization (e.g. buildings, statues, technologies, facilities, pieces of art, morphology of the area, etc.) is thus selected, visualized or incorporated into organizational narratives by means of specific communication practices, where walked campus tours are central.

Organizations engage in symbolic management when they try to espouse socially acceptable goals, while actually pursuing less acceptable ones. One example would be organizations that espouse ethics policies without actually implementing processes for monitoring compliance with those policies. Organizations deploy various symbolic management strategies. For instance, through denial and concealment, some organizations may attempt to hide information about their activities or outcomes that would risk undermining their legitimacy. Organizations may also attempt to redefine their means and ends. Since legitimation is mainly a retrospective process, an organization has the freedom to interpret and account for how its past is aligned with current social values (Maclean et al. 2012). Closely related to this are the implications that removing the organization from a situation may negatively impact its image or claim to legitimacy. Finally, ceremonial conformity implies that an organization may claim legitimacy by adopting certain highly visible and salient practices aligned with social expectations, while not changing the underlying infrastructure of the organization. These practices are adopted solely for their symbolic value.

Organizations engage in symbolic legitimation efforts depending on whether the organization faces a need to extend, maintain or defend its legitimacy (Ashforth and Gibbs 1990). Our research focuses on legitimation claims aiming at maintaining legitimacy, which is the case when organizations have "attained a threshold of endorsement sufficient for ongoing activity" (Ashforth and Gibbs 1990, p. 183). To maintain their legitimacy, legitimation efforts especially entail symbolic management-related activities.

The literature on organizational impressions and symbolic management (see e.g. Elsbach 1994) considers that organizational members, and specifically managers, are instrumental in their communications as they signal the appropriateness and effectiveness of organizational activities to internal and external stakeholders (Golant and Sillince 2007). In this chapter, we follow this tenet and adopt a practice lens that highlights, in a fine-grained way, how walked campus tours are instrumental for universities to make legitimacy claims and how tours constitute a clear illustration that shed light on the intertwining of the institutional and material dimensions involved in legitimation. More specifically, drawing on de Certeau (1980, 1984), we delve into the practice of walking and movement to understand this intertwining.

A Practice-Based, Mobile View of Legitimation Process

In this chapter, we view legitimation and campus tours as a 'practice', which implies that we are interested in "the fine details of how people use the resources available to them to accomplish intelligent actions, and how they give those actions sense and meaning" (Gherardi 2012, p. 2).

There are several important differences between practice theories and other theories of a social nature. One key difference is that what is thought of as the creation of shared meanings is argued to be created not in the human mind, as mentalists would argue (e.g. classical structuralism and interpretivism); nor is it located in symbolic interactions (e.g. theory of communicative action, symbolic interactionism); or as post-modernists would claim, in 'texts' (e.g. post-structuralism and various forms of post-modernism). Instead, practice theory argues that meaning is created in 'practices', which implies that the loci in focus include the body, cognition, things, knowledge, language/discourse, structure/process and human agency and their embeddedness in practice (Bourdieu 1972; de Certeau 1980; Giddens 1984; Sandberg and Dall'Alba 2009).[3]

Put simply, "practices are loci – spatial and temporal – in which working, organizing, innovating or reproducing occurs" (Gherardi 2012, p. 2) and are "embodied, materially mediated arrays of human activity centrally organized around shared practical understanding" (Schatzki 2001, p. 2). Hence, activity is the central element of practice; and it is the set of activities that form a pattern that makes a practice (Gherardi 2012). The activities are composed of humans and non-humans, sayings and doings, and there is not a privileged place for any of these elements, but rather, they are seen as intertwined. Thus, practice theorists aim to go beyond problematic dualisms (de Certeau 1980; Reckwitz 2002), for example, between mind and body or human and material (Gherardi 2012). Recent work in a post-humanist vein has been strongly influencing practice theory (Schatzki 2001); and science and technology scholars such as Latour (1987, 2005), Callon and Latour (1986), Knorr-Cetina (1997), Pickering

---

[3] For additional discussion on the imbrication between the various aspects of materiality, please refer to Chap. 1, introduction.

and King (1995), Pinch (2008) and Suchman (2007) have articulated, albeit in different ways, the role of non-humans, such as technology, buildings and artifacts, in the production and reproduction of social life (Feldman and Orlikowski 2011).

Thus, this implies that practice theorists attribute an important role not only to humans but also to non-humans such as artifacts, technology and space. In this chapter, we take this lens to practices, as we are particularly interested in understanding practices as extending beyond humans and including the contexts, spaces and places in which humans act and interact. De Certeau (1984), a major source of practice-based studies, has acknowledged space as central to practice through his example of walking in the space of a city, where he shows how the practice of walking creates the link between the morphology of space and practice. On the one hand, he argues that when walking in a space, there are the expected behaviors that a space will dictate (e.g. crossing a street at the crosswalk, walking on the pavement and not the street itself, sitting on a bench in a park). On the other hand, there is the instantiation of the space through 'speech acts', where space is incorporated into a narrative, particular artifacts are pointed out and commented on and so on. This latter process can be creative in the sense that people can circumvent expected behaviors and produce new or unexpected relationships with the space. For de Certeau, it is through the practice of walking that the city 'expresses itself' as a space and its meaning is created. There is not one particular meaning of a space, but rather it is through walking that various meanings are created that can circumvent, reduce, extend or divert 'the grammar' of space. Thus, through the practice of walking, space can take on a variety of different meanings. The walking practice of a campus tour hence becomes one of many possible ways of experiencing a campus and of making legitimacy claims.

Building upon Augoyard (1979), de Certeau (1980) argues that the practice of walking in space combines two stylistic figures: the synecdoche and the asyndeton. In a synecdoche, a word is employed "in a sense which is part of another meaning of the same word". In short, "it names a part instead of the whole which includes it" (de Certeau 1984, p. 101). Thus, a synecdoche "expands a spatial element in order to make it play the role of 'more'" (Ibid., p. 101). For example, a bicycle or a piece of furniture in a shop window stands for the whole street or neighborhood. It "replaces totalities by fragments", "amplifies the detail and miniaturizes the whole" (p. 101). The asyndeton accomplishes the reverse. Instead of amplifying details and making broad claims based on fragments, an asyndeton skips, omits and neglects spaces traversed. It is a strategy of 'cutting out' and it undoes continuity by creating "less" and "open gaps in the spatial continuum" (p. 101). In short, through these stylistic figures, some parts of space disappear while others are exaggerated, distorting and fragmenting the space and making it something that invokes different logics. Through the lens of these pedestrian figures, in the empirical context of universities, the walked campus tour makes legitimacy claims that are creatively crafted (invoking different logics) that make sense through walking and that are linked to the spatial context of the organization. Thus, as we build upon de Certeau's lens of walking, we also adhere to Jarzabkowski et al.'s (2007, p. 6) mandate that "micro-phenomena (…) be understood in their wider social context" and claim that "actors are not acting in isolation but are drawing upon the regular, socially defined modes of acting that arise from the plural social institutions to which they belong".

In this chapter, we argue that a practice lens inspired by de Certeau and his focus on movement will extend this initial understanding of the role of materiality in institutional theory. A focus on practices, and movement in space in particular, will yield an understanding not only of the rhetoric dictated by logics, but also how material artifacts are invoked in legitimacy claims to subscribe to or take distance from particular logics.

Method

Empirical Settings

Our empirical inquiry focuses on a context where the relationships between practices, materiality and legitimacy are most vividly at stake: university campus tours.

The notion of campuses has a long history and originates from the USA (Turner 1984; Scotto 2014). Basically, "the word campus, more than any other term, sums up the unique physical character of the American college and university [...] But beyond these purely physical meanings, the word has taken on other connotations, suggesting the pervasive spirit of a school, or its genius loci, as embodied in its architecture and grounds" (Turner 1984, p. 4). The 'language' of campuses has varied from one century to another and one place to another. Initially, the American higher educational system was influenced by the British ideal where students and teachers lived and studied together. In turn, this layout of universities was modeled on monasteries where all main functionalities were present and formed 'the campus' (Scotto 2014). Since the 1980s, these campuses have also been increasingly shown and performed in the practice of 'campus tours' for key external stakeholders, in particular, prospective students and their parents, sponsors and tourists (Magolda 2000). The importance of tours of physical spaces to 'impress' visitors has long been established (Kuh 1990; Braxton and McClendon 2001; Atkinson and Hammersley 1994). For centuries, showing a place, emphasizing its history, its beauty, its technical or aesthetic performance, has been a way to legitimate an organization and its leaders. Historical examples abound. In particular, in the seventeenth century, the French King Louis the XIV wrote a text titled "How to show gardens of Versailles, by Louis the XIV" ("La manière de montrer les jardins de Versailles par Louis XIV"). It has, however, taken on a special urgency and criticality for many organizations, given the multiplicity of stakeholders they face and the diversity of institutional logics that may govern them.

University campuses and campus tours thus provide a suitable case for studying the intersection between materiality, legitimation practices and institutional logics. First, they constitute events that are highly ritualized and done by many universities worldwide. This implies that it is an established practice and creates a potential for comparison and contrast. Furthermore, campus tours are occasions in which organizations encounter potential stakeholders, and the management of legitimacy is at stake. Their situated nature in a material context was also a determining factor for choosing campus tours as a vehicle to study legitimation efforts through communication practices. Lastly, for the last 30 years or so, higher education, particularly in the USA, has been characterized by a transformation where market mechanisms and industry standards have seeped into the field and challenged the legitimating ideas of universities as social institutions. Gumport (2012), followed by other scholars

(Carnoy and Rhoten 2002; Kondakci and Van den Broeck 2009), made the case that higher education in the USA has become shaped by two competing logics—the industry (or market) logic and the social logic. (Table 7.1 describes the key values, root metaphors, key stakeholders and key criteria for legitimacy as prescribed by the different logics.) These logics are field-level logics and may in turn be expressed and enacted in multiple ways 'on the ground' (McPherson and Sauder 2013). The legitimation practices of campus tours become one way (among others) in which organizational members seek to manifest, negotiate and reject adherence to the logics of the field. A campus tour can assert the openness of a university and its social orientation (which involves a sense of non-profitability and a general access to knowledge), but also emphasize the innovative, business orientation (which draws on the market logic with an ambition for excellence, selection and knowledge for the elite of society). Narratives can be used to emphasize, for example, success stories of alumni who are now economic leaders, involvement of students in charities and so on; these narratives would invoke very different artifacts (e.g. big lecture hall, small classrooms, luxurious entry hall, comfortable rooms, dormitories, etc.).

The social logic implies that knowledge is viewed as something that all citizens have the right to and it emphasizes the free or affordable access to universities as well as inclusivity and diversity. It emphasizes how universities interact and contribute to the broader social environment and its culture, norms, history and techniques, as well as socially pressing issues such as equality and ethics. The social logic also views universities as

Table 7.1 Key characteristics of the two logics in higher education

Logics	Industry or market logic	Social logic
Key values	Performance, functionality, differentiation, competitive advantage	Justice, equality, accessibility, diversity
Root metaphors	Machines	Tradition
Key stakeholders involved in the logic	Customers	Citizens
Key criteria for legitimacy	Efficiency, tangibility, value, innovation	Sustainable development, equality

Adapted from Gumport 2012

historical institutions, where certain myths and traditions are seen as important.

The market or industry logic sees universities more from a business-like perspective. When the market logic is enacted, individuals pay attention to the functional characteristics of the university and its practical, immediate values (e.g. buildings, classrooms, ITs, sports stadiums and amphitheaters) as well as their sophistication, exhaustiveness or modernity. Individuals also put forward the qualities of the campus, its education and competitive advantage, drawing differentiation on an economic and/or strategic rhetoric and how they sustain the value customers will be willing to pay for.

Data Collection Methods

Our data collection was based on participant observations of real-life campus tours in order to collect rich and contextual data. Our sample was based on multiple observations at nine different universities in the USA and Europe performed between April 2013 and July 2014. The campus tours lasted for approximately 60–180 minutes. Notes were taken during and right after the tours, which were extended to include details we did not have time to elaborate on during the actual tour. Our observations followed an observation guideline (see Appendix 1). The guideline was elaborated after a first exploratory tour at McGill University in April 2013. The dimensions it includes derived from cross-discussions among co-authors. We identified dimensions likely to describe the modalities, context, focus, objectives and process of the tours.

Each tour generated between 5 and 10 pages of typed notes, and in total, we gathered more than 60 pages of notes. We followed a disciplined approach to our field-note taking and always expanded and finalized the notes within the same day of the tour. This was to ensure that the notes would include a maximum of detail and be as accurate as possible. Numerous photos were also taken at each site in order to remember details of the context, such as certain artifacts or the arrangement of spaces.

In addition to observational data, we also collected archival data, such as campus maps, articles and books, and information about the history of the campuses and the universities. This information (detailed in Table 7.2) enabled

Table 7.2 Overview of data collection

Universities explored	Period of observation	Collected data	Key spaces involved in the campus tour	Main artifacts shown	Tour schedule
Mc Gill University, Montreal, Canada	April 2013 Participation in two campus tours	Participant observation of two campus tours (around 1 hour each) Pictures (12), maps, leaflets, screen printings of the website Articles and books about the history of McGill University	One campus (of two)	Buildings, statues	1 hour (Two per day) Online registration
La Sorbonne, Paris, France	September and October 2013	Participant observation of two campus tours Maps, leaflets, screen printings of the website Articles and books about the history of La Sorbonne and the Université de Paris Pictures (9)	A main, historical building (Maison Sorbonne)	Buildings, big historical lecture hall, paintings, status	Two hours (by appointment from Monday to Friday and on one Saturday per month) Registration by email
Stanford University, Stanford, CA, USA	September and October 2013	Participant observation of one campus tour Pictures (24), maps, leaflets, books and articles about the history of Stanford University Pictures (19)	The oldest parts of campus	Sports facilities, oldest buildings, big lecture halls, buildings named after famous people or where famous researchers have worked or are working	1 ½ hours (twice a day, year round, open to all). No registration needed

(continued)

Table 7.2 (continued)

Universities explored	Period of observation	Collected data	Key spaces involved in the campus tour	Main artifacts shown	Tour schedule
UC Berkeley, Berkeley, CA, USA	November 2013	Participant observation of one campus tour. Maps, leaflets, screen printings of the website. Articles about the history of UC Berkeley Pictures (11)	The oldest parts of campus	Sports facilities, library, old buildings and artifacts	1 ½ hours (on specific days year round). Registration via online registration system required
Vienna University of Economics and Business, Vienna, Austria	May 2014	Participant observation of one campus tour. Maps, leaflets, screen printings of the website Pictures (12) and videos (3)	New campus	Modern new buildings (library, student center)	45 minutes (upon request)
London School of Economics & Political Sciences, London, UK	June 2014	Participant observation of one campus tour. Maps, leaflets (e.g. 'LSE explorer'), screen printings of the website Pictures (18)	Entire campus	Old building, the Shaw library, fourth-floor restaurant, student service center, library, Lincoln's inn fields, new academic buildings, Saw Swee Hock student center, Peacock theater, the towers, Clement house, LSE Garrick	Annual tours. Self-guided tours (with big map LSE explorer). Maps and recommendation to do the tour offered at the students' center. Duration: 1 ½ hour on average to cover the 12 recommended spots

(continued)

Table 7.2 (continued)

Universities explored	Period of observation	Collected data	Key spaces involved in the campus tour	Main artifacts shown	Tour schedule
San Jose State University, San Jose, CA, USA	July 2014	Participant observation of one campus tour Maps, leaflets provided at check-in Pictures (10)	Entire campus	Student services center, various departments, Malcolm X plaza, Tommy Smith and John Carlos statues, library, sports facilities and dorms	Close to daily tours year round. Duration: 1 hour. Registration via online system required
San Francisco State University, San Francisco, CA, USA	July 2014	Participant observation of one campus tour Maps, leaflets provided at check-in Pictures (8)	Entire campus	Student services center, various departments, student union, library, science buildings	Close to daily tours year round. Duration: 1 hour. Registration via online system required

us to understand more about the background and to place the narrative told during the tour in a broader context. The maps were also used to get a clear understanding for the sites of each campus that the tours presented, as well as obscured.

To systematize our data collection, we applied an observation guide (see Appendix 1), which aligned with our interests in capturing the legitimation processes and how these were framed in a narrative anchored in space and materiality. Our real-life experience of campus tours confirmed that multiple logics were at play in this setting and that university members invoked the material context of the organization to promote and/or reconcile the logics on which the organization drew.

Analysis

Our analysis of the qualitative data started with an open coding of the data set, in particular our field notes (Charmaz 2006). We coded our data in a grounded way (Corbin and Strauss 1990) by completing open and axial coding of our memos (see Appendix 2), which was followed by a discussion and comparison of the emerging codes. At this stage, what emerged as particularly salient was the various ways in which the buildings, spaces and artifacts of the universities were invoked during the tour in ways that clearly suggested an adherence or rejection of particular institutional logics.

In a second round, after iterating with the literature and de Certeau (1984) in particular, we coded the data again with the ambition to understand more clearly the various forms of practices that organizational members undertook to create links between materiality and logics during the tours. This led to a more fine-grained categorization of various forms of de Certeau's (1984) 'synecdoches' and 'asyndetons' (see Table 7.3 for an overview of our coding scheme).

Table 7.3 Overview of coding scheme

First-order codes	Empirical examples	Examples of logics connoted	Theoretical constructs	Axial coding	Proposition
Isolated artifacts pointed out as descriptive of the university	Berkeley: presentation of a dinosaur skeleton intertwined with a story of how students and professors cooperated in crafting the dinosaur, which was delivered in thousands of pieces	Social logic: emphasis on learning, equal opportunities, student support and involvement and the role of the university in society	Legitimacy claims based on object-focused synecdoches	Drawing on materiality to infer adherence to particular logics	Proposition 1: practices, performed in the material context of walking campus tours, can rely upon "legitimizing synecdoches" that highlight certain parts of a campus to legitimize the entire organization
Unique spaces pointed out as descriptive of the university	Stanford University: the guide points to the Bill Gates building and says that this is where Google started and that Google's server was located in a Lego box in that building, hence the colors of the Google logo, he says. He then points to the Hewlett and the Packard buildings, two buildings that are built in a much more modern style. He says that both Hewlett and Packard went to Stanford and that they got together in the so-called HP garage and started their company	Market logic: emphasis on the unique and successful innovations that the university has fostered	Legitimacy claims based on spatial synecdoches		Proposition 2: the material practice of walking allows organizational members to make legitimacy claims by invoking 'reconciling synecdoches' that invoke space to mediate potential conflict between logics
Territories pointed out and used as an entryway to an unrelated description of the university	Stanford University: the tour arrives at the area in front of the main quad, the oval, which is where the Palm drive leads up to the university. It is a big open space and the Palm Drive, a street with palm trees planted on each side, can be seen the whole way down to Palo Alto. It is a stretch of approximately 1 km. The guide talks a bit about the education at Stanford. He says that as a prospective student, you apply to Stanford and not to specific courses, and once you are accepted you choose from 3 different undergraduate schools. He says he now wants to talk about transportation and mentions that there are more bikes than people on campus, but that he prefers to walk everywhere. He says that some people use skateboards	Social logic: emphasis on the accessibility of the university and environmental friendliness of alternative transportation	Legitimacy claims based on territorial synecdoches		Proposition 3: the material practice of walking allows organizational members to make legitimacy claims by invoking 'interpretively flexible synecdoches'

(continued)

Table 7.3 (continued)

First-order codes	Empirical examples	Examples of logics connoted	Theoretical constructs	Axial coding	Proposition
Avoidance of places	McGill University: we move on to a corridor linking two buildings and enter into the anthropology department, which is avoided (we do not go straight and avoid a liminal corridor) and is not commented by our guide. This is another period of silence	Avoidance of undesirable places and/or departments that do not fit into the narrative and the desired symbolic	Legitimacy claims based on focused asyndetons	Avoiding or downplaying materiality to show adherence to or refrain from particular logics	Proposition 4: the material practice of walking allows organizational members to make legitimacy claims by invoking 'concealing asyndetons'
Transition between places	San Jose State University: on the way from the office of student affairs, where the tour started, we pass several anonymous gray cement buildings. The guide does not comment on these and instead engages in a narrative that explains the various forms of support available to students of the university	Certain transitional spaces are passed, yet neglected since they do not fit into the narrative and the desired symbolic	Legitimacy claims based on transitional asyndetons		
Hidden places pointed out as descriptive of the university	LSE: the guide emphasizes that the access to the New Academic Building is restricted to LSE staff and students, creating a sense of prestige and exclusivity	Market logic: emphasizing that the school is only for a selected few	Legitimacy claims based on imaginary asyndetons		Proposition 5: the material practice of walking allows organizational members to make legitimacy claims by invoking 'evoking asyndetons'
Making the audience experience a particular atmosphere	San Jose State University: the tour walks inside one of the buildings through a long hallway. It seems to be a way to show one of the oldest and most historical buildings and it is a pretty nice building with an old feel to it. It signals 'old and traditional university' which most other buildings definitely do not. The guide does not make any comments when inside	Social logic: the history and embeddedness in a long history and tradition	Legitimacy claims based on ambient asyndetons		

Creating Links Between Legitimacy Claims and Space Through the Walked Campus Tour

In this section, we build and justify four propositions related to the relationship between legitimizing practices (in particular, those focused on asyndetons and synecdoches), materiality and institutional logics emerging from our data.

Proposition 1 Practices, performed in the material context of walking campus tours, can rely upon "legitimizing synecdoches" that highlight certain parts of a campus expected to legitimize the entire organization.

In a context of institutional complexity with multiple logics (Friedland and Alford 1991; Kraatz and Block 2008), which impose conflicting demands and pressures on organizations and their members (Jarzabkowski et al. 2013a, b; Greenwood et al. 2010), walking was a way for organizational members to invoke artifacts and narratives to mobilize and emphasize the adherence to particular logics. Particularly, it was a way to create "legitimizing synecdoches". We define legitimizing synecdoches as the walked practice of invoking particular places and artifacts in legitimacy claims.

This was visible in all of the campus tours that we observed. In some cases, a campus tour seemed to draw on mainly one particular logic in its legitimizing synecdoches. In other cases, multiple logics were blended with equal emphasis. In yet other cases, there was a dominant logic with additional elements from other logics. Independent of one of the several logics being promoted, it was clear that universities engaged in a practice of carefully choosing only a selected few out of many possible spaces and artifacts to promote during the campus tour. For example, at San Jose State University (SJSU), which adhered mostly to the social logic, the starting point of the tour took place at the student services center, which was largely emphasized. The center was invoked to tell a narrative of all the various types of services that students could receive for free, such as counseling, course advice and preadmission services, the guide acknowledging that everyone can have a hard time at some point during their studies. The fact that the tour started at the student services center gave the audience a sense of accessibility to these services, as well as established credibility to these claims. Throughout the tour, the social logic of a university that is accessible and open to everyone continued to be emphasized by pointing out particular spaces that were carefully selected. For example, when arriving at the building in which the bookstore was located, the guide, pointing at the bookstore, emphasized that books can be purchased on credit allowing for more payment flexibility for students with financial difficulties. Another example is how two statues of Afro-American men located at the 'Malcolm X plaza'—'Tommie Smith and John Carlos', former students known for their historic demonstration as medalists in the 1968 Olympic games—are invoked in a narrative about the university's focus on diversity. The guide vividly describes the statues in detail and how Smith's raised right black-gloved fist represents black power. The scarf around the neck represents pride and the box he is carrying with an olive sapling represents peace. The other statue is of Carlos, with his raised left black-gloved fist representing unity in America, and the beads around his neck signifying the lynching suffered by Black people, the guide explains. She further emphasizes that students successfully fought for the statue to be placed at the center of campus instead of being located at the sport's center, which was the original idea. Diversity is important to the campus, the Latin tour guide says with emphasis.

A contrasting example of a university that drew largely on the market logic, putting forward the competitive and functional elements of the campus, was Stanford. For example, when the tour arrived in front of the main quad, the guide, who was also a student of the university, engaged in a narrative that emphasized the vastness of the campus, stating that it is the second largest in the world after the University of Moscow. The large auditoriums were also pointed out as places that had hosted numerous famous speakers such as Hillary Clinton, Al Gore and the Dalai Lama. Thus, these particular places came to be invoked in the campus tour as something larger, illustrative of a broad claim of superiority and elitism along the lines of the market logic. Another example of amplification is when the tour passed the computer science buildings named after Bill Gates and the Hewlett and Packard buildings, where the guide points out that the original server of Google is still in the basement of one of the buildings on campus; and that the founders—Sergey Brin and Larry Page—had studied at Stanford. These particular buildings were invoked to make legitimacy claims that again drew on the market logic, stating the innovativeness and the many companies that had spurred from the university.

As yet another illustration of how walking was a way for organizational members to invoke artifacts and narratives to mobilize and emphasize the adherence to particular logics, the University of Sorbonne drew largely on historical artifacts and spaces to craft legitimacy claims drawing on the social logic. Historical artifacts have a very strong symbolic power through their longevity and can be invoked and put forward when more market-oriented, competitive and functional resources are lacking. In the case of Sorbonne University, the working spaces of former Professors Pierre and Marie Curie (who attended the university in the beginning of the 1900s) were pointed out. Also, the grandiose scene of the amphitheater was pointed out and interwoven with a narrative revolving around Marie Curie and her historical keynote speech which was held there, which was an event often categorized as the turning point in the history of the role of women in French academia. Thus, these examples show how historical artifacts are invoked in the practice of campus tours as a resource to bring up equality and diversity, connoting the social logic. It could also be argued that this emphasis on historical spaces and artifacts was a way to compensate for a lack of infrastructure, or a 'real' campus to show (as Sorbonne is spread out in several different buildings throughout Paris and does not have a campus in the American sense).

The examples above illustrate a practice that, on one hand, was about selectivity of a few among many possible spaces and artifacts that could have been shown during the campus tour, and on the other, an emphasis and amplification of these particular spaces and artifacts. This resonates with de Certeau's (1984) notion of synecdoche and we therefore refer to this as 'legitimizing synecdoches' due to the connection that we establish with legitimacy. For synecdoches to work, walking is clearly imperative. During a guided tour, the selectivity and exaggeration done through the invocation of synecdoches become less problematic than in other forms of communication. This is because, even if not emphasized, many of the spaces and artifacts are oftentimes still visible. Thus, the problem of making 'false' claims is less present in this form compared to other forms of communication where distortion, exaggeration and selectivity, the making of 'more' (de Certeau 1984) would be seen as false advertising and potentially threaten legitimacy. When organizations of today make legitimacy claims drawing on the social logic to claim sustainability, for example, it is often received with suspicion and skepticism among stakeholders (Gond 2010; Butler 2011). However, by pointing out material manifestations of the logic by employing legitimizing synecdoches, legitimacy claims may become more credible. The walked format, in particular, allows the audience to gain a lived experience of a large part of a campus, yet only a few spaces and artifacts are chosen to become interwoven into the narrative of legitimacy claims.

Proposition 2 The material practice of walking allows organizational members to make legitimacy claims by drawing on 'reconciling synecdoches' that invoke space to mediate potential conflict between logics.

Synecdoches are not only useful as a way to make legitimacy claims drawing on one particular logic. "Reconciling synecdoches" refer to how spaces were invoked to alleviate potential conflict between logics, as a form of strategy to make legitimacy claims compatible despite invoking competing logics simultaneously. This definition extends Swan et al.'s (2010, p. 1334) view of individuals crafting compatibility out of seemingly incompatible logics. They stated that "despite creating a patchwork of seemingly contradictory modes of working", individuals can blend logics "artfully and selectively [...] to lend legitimacy to their practices". It also alludes to Pache and Santos (2013) argument that individuals can respond to competing logics by attempting to 'integrate' them. We show that materiality has an important role in this practice.

A first illustrative example of how the campus tour managed to alleviate a conflict between logics was when the tour guide on the Stanford campus tour invoked the church to show the university's adherence to ethics (connoting the social logic) rather than being a religious institution (hence avoiding connoting a religious logic, which does not characterize today's higher education, but was largely present and guided the activities of universities a century or so ago). This maneuver was done by spending

a relatively long period of time of the tour in the church, where participants were instructed to tour it in silence, particularly focusing on the
inscribed messages on its walls. A text about the church states that these
inscriptions were selected by Mrs. Stanford and represented her religious
faith. However, before entering the church, the tour guide framed them
as being ethical guidelines to students rather than religious ones. At the
same time, the fact that the tour did indeed spend a considerable amount
of time in the church, providing the opportunity for the audience to live
the space and project their own interpretations of it, signaled an importance attributed to religious institutions, and hence dissolved a possible
tension between the two logics. In this example, the church was invoked
in the pedestrian figure of a synecdoche to signify a 'more' that expanded
beyond the most obvious connotation of a religious logic. Yet again, this
example shows how synecdoches are employed to exaggerate and emphasize the adherence to particular logics. In addition, it also demonstrates
that through possibilities that are offered by walking in a space, by experiencing it, synecdoches invite multiple interpretations of a space that
allow for mediation of conflicts between logics. Through the walked campus tour, which is simultaneously a narration and a movement in space,
multiple interpretations and experiences are invited that would be much
harder to navigate in other forms of communication.

A second example from the campus tours at Stanford was the attempt
to balance the market logic that they drew largely upon (as described
under proposition 1), with elements of the social logic. For example, the
campus tour guide at Stanford repeatedly pointed out recycling bins,
construction sites (framed as building more environmentally friendly
buildings), electric bus shuttles, the large number of bikes on campus and
the nearby train station (alluding to the accessibility to campus via train
to all). In this way, seemingly mundane artifacts and spaces were invoked
as synecdoches, that is, manifestations and materializations of the social
logic.

Another example is drawn from the campus tour of VU Vienna. This
campus is very recent, and was designed by numerous famous architects
and ended up being highly expensive (≈500 million euros). During the
tour, the great architecture was continuously emphasized by pointing out
the various buildings, explaining the thoughts behind each of them and

the respective architects. Thus, each building came to represent a logic of the market, where universities compete for their students not only based on the degrees and knowledge they provide but also on their aesthetics and functional and infrastructural aspects of the campus. Simultaneously, the tour guide used synecdoches to make 'more' out of the natural materials chosen in the new buildings, the natural light and the so-called lakes on campus, as well as the closeness to a vast natural park, which altogether aimed at connoting a social logic where nature and environmental values are more salient. Thus, this practice apparently reconciled incompatible logics by invoking various material aspects of the campus.

The London School of Economics tour also illustrates this point, creating both an adherence to the social and market logics. Starting the tour with the Old building gave a sense of longevity and social importance to a relatively young institution (compared to Oxford or Cambridge universities). Moving then to recent, modern and grandiose places of the campus (student service center, Lincoln's Inn Fields acquired in 2013 and the new academic building) in contrast gave a sense of the global competitiveness, expansion and growth of LSE, adhering to a market logic of business-like growth.

A final example of this practice of making the incompatible compatible is the campus tour at McGill, which aimed to reconcile the competing social and market logics by prioritizing its immersion and interaction with its local context of Montreal and the Quebec area (social logic) while simultaneously emphasizing that it is a university that competes in the global arena for the most talented students (market logic). This is a long-standing challenge for McGill, as it at times sees protesters at its doorsteps who bemoan that its courses are offered in English. As a way to resolve this conflict, the tour guide invoked several synecdoches to make 'more' out of artifacts in the storytelling during the campus tour. First, a long period of time was spent in front of the tomb of the founder McGill, referring to his English origins, making the tomb a manifestation of the European impregnation of the university, hence exaggerating the presence of the tomb to become a symbol for something larger—the adherence to a market logic that acknowledges internationalization and globalization—while acknowledging its history and longevity and thus drawing on the social logic.

Thus, synecdoches allow for multiple interpretations and reconcilia-
tion of logics, since they can be framed as multifaceted. To reconcile
multiple logics in practices of legitimation is a complex exercise. The
examples above show how the very flexibility of space itself (de Vaujany
and Vaast 2014) and how it is simultaneously walked and narrated can be
helpful in the management of tensions. Thus, this practice was possible
due to the interpretive flexibility of materiality, which implies that they
can be invoked to put forward various logics, that is, an artifact does not
signify a logic in itself, but it is the context in which it is invoked and the
narrative surrounding it that creates its meaning in relation to institutional logics. This flexibility creates possibilities for actors to 'play' with
artifacts and craft legitimation practices that are coherent, but may simultaneously put forward multiple and competing logics. This practice resonates with previous studies that have found that organizational members
can employ 'interpretive flexibility' and 'strategic ambiguity' to frame
artifacts in various ways in order to cater to the needs and agendas of various stakeholders (Orlikowski 1992; Barley et al. 2012).

Proposition 3 The material practice of walking allows organizational
members to make legitimacy claims by invoking 'concealing asyndetons'
in order to make legitimacy claims.

Our empirical data also showed that a common practice during campus tours was to hide or avoid (deliberately) particular spaces and artifacts. "Concealing asyndetons" implies that the walked practice allows for
an avoidance of undesirable spaces and artifacts that do not fit the desired
legitimacy claims. The tour at Sorbonne University is one example where
this strategy was implemented to make legitimacy claims. During the
campus tour, there was much emphasis placed on how the space relates to
the republic (laic) governance system of the state, emphasizing that the
university is a social institution and part of the broader society. Several
artifacts were used as synecdoches of this governance system, such as the
statue of the Marianne, which is a symbol of the French Republic.
However, in order to craft this adherence to the social logic, the campus
tour was also forced to invoke a strategy of asyndetons—of avoidance of
certain artifacts, such as the Fleur de Lys, that were symbolic of the historical monarchic governance system.

In the case of San Jose State University, we also found the use of the legitimizing strategy of asyndetons. For example, the tour guide points out the business school building, which is a pretty tall and fairly new building. The surrounding concrete buildings from the 1960s or so are not mentioned and instead the audience's attention is directed to another modern building that has just been constructed. This is clearly a strategy of concealing and downplaying in order to make legitimacy claims.

In summary, the guided walk of campus tours allows for a subtle way for organizations to select and disregard particular places and artifacts that they consider undesirable and that would risk undermining legitimacy. While the audience has the experience of a transparency of the campus that is laid out for them, the asyndetons are invoked to hide or downplay particular spaces or artifacts.

Proposition 4 The material practice of walking allows organizational members to make legitimacy claims by invoking 'evoking asyndetons' in order to make legitimacy claims.

Finally, our findings also showed that organizational members at times employed a strategy to make legitimacy claims that involved the creation of imagery or particular atmospheres during the walked practice. We define this as "evoking asyndetons". Here, the campus tour guide could describe, vividly, a space or artifact that would be out of sight to the audience, yet making legitimacy claims based on this invisible materiality. This involved a great deal of storytelling as well as the audience's own imagination. It also required more trust compared to the pointing out of artifacts and spaces that were before the eyes of the beholders. One example of this was during the campus tour at Berkeley, where the tour guide pointed to a building hidden behind a grove and explained that it hosts the College of Natural Resources, which does research on environmental sciences, nutrition and political management. This building, the guide emphasized, also hosts the first undergraduate library in the USA. This was clearly a legitimacy claim that drew on the social logic. However, the materiality that was invoked to support this claim remained invisible, yet had an important role. Another example is drawn from the tour at San Jose State University, where the tour guide brought the audience through a long and beautiful hallway that was atypical of the architecture of the rest of the buildings on campus and which was located in an older building. The guide did not talk much during the passing in the hallway, yet this passage seemed to feature an important symbolism, namely that the university has a long history and traditions worthy of an old institution. Here, the storytelling was left to the audience's imagination and by instantiating an atmosphere that was historical, it could be expected that the audience would equal their experience with that of touring an older, more ancient institution. Thus, the particular atmosphere that the hallway provided was a way to connote the social logic by emphasizing, through an atmosphere created by movement in a particular space, the (not quite so) long history of the university and its roots.

Discussion

Our propositions shed light on how campus tours provide embodied experiences of the intangible activities of universities. They constitute opportunities for stakeholders to get to know an organization through sensory experiences such as seeing, touching, smelling. Since many contemporary service-oriented organizations, such as universities, engage in complex, abstract and immaterial activities, such embodied experiences of the organization's physicality and performing activities take on a heightened importance (de Vaujany and Vaast 2014). Gieryn (2002, p. 40) argued that materiality, such as buildings, provides an "institutional reality to the intangible such as academic disciplines or specialties" and helps "convert the abstraction of [academic] discipline into something more palpable, stable, and enduring". That legitimation practices and logics are linked is well known. However, what institutional scholars have not yet greatly examined is the way in which artifacts are used to show adherence to particular logics and how these can be mobilized in legitimation practices in ways aimed at promoting legitimacy. Research on legitimation has so far remained at a symbolic and discursive level and artifacts have mostly been absent. This chapter attempts to address this gap in the literature. Our propositions outline the different roles that artifacts and spaces take on as they are invoked in legitimacy claims in the walked campus tour.

First, legitimation practices based on walking can reflexively select and combine different institutional logics. Through the invocation of artifacts into narratives, an organization chooses to put forward certain claims while concealing others. Spaces and artifacts provide a material reality to the desired logics and claims and are thus powerful, concrete tools in legitimation practices. Thus, we allude to how material practices direct attention and inform meaning-making among stakeholders. This is an important distinction from the more common preoccupation regarding how values shape practices.

Second, materiality can also be used to resolve conflict and altering meanings due to the interpretive flexibility of materiality, and the playfulness or artfulness of organizational members (Swan et al. 2010).

Third, for the same reason of interpretive flexibility, invoking materiality allows organizational members to downplay institutional logics and create alternative, credible legitimation practices. If universities lack resources or infrastructures to make market-related claims for functionality, for instance, campus tours may highlight, instead, the historical features of buildings and present narratives that emphasize other sources of meaning and legitimation. Thus, the walked practice allows not only for putting forward but also for concealing and hiding undesirable materialities that may risk undermining the desired legitimacy claims. This practice of 'concealing' is important and has thus far been largely ignored in studies on the how individuals enact logics on the ground. Even in institutional studies that promote the visual, there has been a neglect of that which is 'not' seen (Meyer et al. 2013).

Fourth, materiality, and particular spaces and sites, allows for the creation of experiences that foster the imagination among stakeholders to, for example, historical or prospective times. It is more about an aesthetic springboard for invoking logics, rather than a cognitive one, and it cannot easily be translated into language (Langer 1957). Aesthetics are often referred to as the "non-rational of organizational life" (Warren 2008). The aesthetic experience is triggered by material things, and it is also a highly embodied, sensory mode of being in the world (Warren 2008). While aesthetics has been largely ignored in institutional theory, our findings open up a new line of inquiry that promotes a need for a deeper understanding how aesthetics are linked to institutional logics as well as how this 'non-rational' medium can be used to make legitimacy claims.

This research adds to the emerging field of understanding the micro-foundations of institutional theory, where scholars have started to show an interest for how institutions are enacted in the everyday practices of individuals (McPherson and Sauder's 2013; Smets and Jarzabkowski 2013), as well as the role of materiality (Jones et al. 2013) and visuality (Meyer et al. 2013; Puyou and Quattrone 2018) in altering, disrupting or maintaining institutional logics. Materiality has been conceptualized as an actor in several theoretical fields, in particular research on organizational space, science and technology studies, actor-network theories and some evolutionist views of organizations (Jones et al. 2013; de Vaujany and Mitev 2013). Also, in the literature about organizational space and spatial practices, the spatial and material dimensions of societies and more recently, organizations, have been largely explored (Gagliardi 1992; Kornberger and Clegg 2004; Dale and Burrell 2008; Yanow and Marrewijk 2010). Mainly in continuation of Lefebvre (1991) and the spatio-material aspects of seminal social studies (e.g. Marx et al. 1974; Bourdieu 1972; Giddens 1984, 1985), but also Merleau-Ponty (1945, 1964) and his view of experience or American pragmatism, it shows that organizations and organizing processes are interpenetrated by their spatial, temporal and material environment (Dale 2005; Pittz et al. 2017; de Vaujany et al. 2018). Finally, it illustrates the 'materiality turn' that has grown increasingly popular in IS and organization studies and posits practices as socio-material and materiality as constitutive of everyday life (Barad 2003; Latour 2005; Suchman 2007; Orlikowski 2007; Pozzebon et al. 2017). Materiality, in this view, "is not an incidental or intermittent aspect of organizational life; it is integral to it" (Orlikowski 2007, p. 1436). Nonetheless, this stream of literature has rarely investigated the relationship between spatial practices and legitimacy claims (Wasserman and Frenkel 2011; de Vaujany and Vaast 2014). Our tentative theory integrates these two streams and suggests the various ways in which materiality is invoked in legitimacy claims drawing on various institutional logics. Thus, materiality constitutes an important part of the 'tool box' of cultural elements (Swidler 1986) that organizational members may invoke to construct legitimacy.

This research also brings attention to mobility, i.e. walking, as a practice worthy of including in institutional analyses. By drawing on de Certeau's work, we zoomed in on a particular aspect of the micro-foundations of institutions that had not yet been examined, namely the important role of moving in instantiating the materiality of organizations and in asserting particular legitimacy claims. While practices have started to become an important focus for institutional theorists, there is still little effort put into theorizing about the constitution of practices. Practices are oftentimes used as a synonym to micro-level actions, but the elements of practices remain largely blackboxed. By acknowledging mobility as an important facet of practices, we start to unpack this concept. We find support for this among an emerging number of scholars in methodology, who have started to acknowledge the uniqueness and empirical value of walking practices (Anderson 2004; Evans and Jones 2011). However, there is still a dearth of research on the role of embodied mobility in and between organizations. Our research illustrates how the practice of walking provides visual experiences as well as embodied and material matter to institutions. Movement may be experienced merely as a visual flow (e.g. a passenger sitting on a train in motion). Yet, walking in the streets and spaces of cities, campuses or organizations allows for multisensory stimulation of the surrounding environment (Adams and Guy 2007), which provides "an immediacy as well as a kinaesthetic rhythm" (Middleton 2009 in Evans and Jones 2011, p. 850) that a focus on the visual alone does not capture. Thus, walking is not only about a 'transfer' from A to B but an occasion where the surrounding materiality is instantiated and brought to life through asyndetons and synecdoches (de Certeau 1980). Walking practices relate to, transfer and transform institutional logics, and give life to the material matter of organizations. While we agree that the recent preoccupation with the role of the visual in institutional theory is an interesting way to advance the inclusion of materiality (Meyer et al. 2013), our focus on movement underlines its limitations in accounting for the more embodied experiences that materiality provides when 'walked and lived'.

Conclusion

This chapter has examined how the walking practices of campus tours invoke materiality to make legitimacy claims and provided five tentative propositions that constitute the stepping-stone for an emerging theory on the links between materiality and legitimacy. It is a first attempt to shed light on the importance of incorporating mobility and materiality into any analysis of legitimation and institutional dynamics. In qualitative research, the challenge of representativeness is always lingering. In this work, in particular, we had no way of ascertaining that the tours we followed at particular universities were representative of the other tours we could have followed over the academic year. Moreover, our study focused on a subset of European and North American campuses, which provides a highly Westernized view on the phenomenon.

For future research, there is promise in contrasting campus tours to other tour contexts (e.g. corporate tours or museum tours), as this may reveal different instantiations of institutional logics. We also urge scholars to continue to deepen the exploration of how visuality and materiality participate in micro-institutional dynamics and may embody organizational legitimacy.

Appendices

Appendix 1: Observation Guideline of Campus Tours

The guide aimed at capturing the main verbal narrative that was told, as well as how this narrative related to places and artifacts during the tour.

- D1: How is the tour communicated? Our focus here was the tools, actors, organizational structures, etc. involved in the practice of legitimation.
- D2: Where is the meeting point?
- D3: Who is guiding the tour? What is the profile of the guide?
- D4: What is the narrative told during the tour? Are there specific aspects that are recurrently emphasized?
- D5: What is the trajectory of the tour? What were the main sites visited/artifacts shown? What is the appearance and aesthetics of these spots and artifacts?
- D6: Are there sites of the campus that are excluded from the tour? If so, which parts?
- D7: How are the artifacts and spaces enacted in front of visitors?

Appendix 2: The Distribution of Institutional Codes (Market Versus Social) for Each Tour

Tour	Number of sequences identified	Market logic	Social logic
Université La Sorbonne	6	1	8
McGill University	4	2	3
Stanford University	9	7	4
San Francisco State University	10	3	12
UC Berkeley	9	3	10
Vienna University	5	5	2
LSE	12	8	4
San Jose State University	8	1	7

References

Adams, M., & Guy, S. (2007). Editorial: Senses and the city. *The Senses and Society, 2*(2), 133–136.

Anderson, J. (2004). Talking whilst walking: A geographical archaeology of knowledge. *Area, 36*(3), 254–261.

Ashforth, B. E., & Gibbs, B. W. (1990). The double-edge of organizational legitimation. *Organization Science, 1*(2), 177–194.

Atkinson, P., & Hammersley, M. (1994). Ethnography and participant observation. *Handbook of Qualitative Research, 1*(23), 248–261.

Augoyard, J.-F. (1979). Pas à pas. *Essai sur le cheminement quotidien en milieu urbain.*

Barad, K. (2003). Posthumanist performativity: Toward an understanding of how matter comes to matter. *Signs, 28*(3), 801–831.

Bourdieu, P. (1972). Les stratégies matrimoniales dans le système de reproduction. *Annales, 27*, 1105–1127.

Braxton, J. M., & McClendon, S. A. (2001). The fostering of social integration and retention through institutional practice. *Journal of College Student Retention: Research, Theory and Practice, 3*(1), 57–71.

Butler, J. (2011). *Bodies that matter: On the discursive limits of sex.* New York: Taylor & Francis.

Callon, M., & Latour, B. (1986). Comment suivre les innovations? Clefs pour l'analyse sociotechnique. *Prospective et santé, 36*, 13–25.

Carnoy, M., & Rhoten, D. (2002). What does globalization mean for educational change? A comparative approach. *Comparative Education Review, 46*(1), 1–9.

Cetina, K. K. (1997). Sociality with objects. *Theory, Culture & Society, 14*(4), 1–30.

Charmaz, K. (2006). *Constructing grounded theory: A practical guide through qualitative research*. London: Sage.

Corbin, J. M., & Strauss, A. (1990). Grounded theory research: Procedures, canons, and evaluative criteria. *Qualitative Sociology, 13*(1), 3–21.

Dale, K., & Burrell, G. (2008). *The spaces of organization and the organization of space: Power, identity and materiality at work*. Basingstoke: Palgrave Macmillan.

de Certeau, M. (1980). L'invention du quotidien, t. I, Arts de faire. *Folio essais (éd. 1990)*.

de Certeau, M. (1984). Idéologie et diversité culturelle. *Diversité Culturelle, Société Industrielle, Etat national*. Paris: l'Harmattan.

de Vaujany, X., & Mitev, N. (Eds.). (2013). Introduction: Space in organization and sociomateriality. In *Materiality and space. Organizations, artifacts and practices* (pp. 1–24), Basingstoke: Palgrave Macmillan.

de Vaujany, F.-X., & Vaast, E. (2014). Dual iconographies and legitimation practices in contemporary organizations: A tale of the Former Nato Command Room. In *Materiality and time: Historical perspectives on organizations, artifacts and practices* (p. 33). London: Palgrave Macmillan.

de Vaujany, F. X., & Vaast, E. (2016). Matters of visuality in legitimation practices: Dual iconographies in a meeting room. *Organization, 23*(5), 763–790.

de Vaujany, F. X., Fomin, W., Haefliger, W., & Lyytinen, K. (2018). Rules, practices and information technology (IT): A Trifecta of organizational regulation. *Information Systems Research*. https://doi.org/10.1287/isre.2017.0771.

DiMaggio, P. J., & Powell, W. W. (1983). The iron cage revisited: Institutional isomorphism and collective rationality in organizational fields. *American Sociological Review, 48*, 147–160.

Elsbach, K. D. (1994). Managing organizational legitimacy in the California cattle industry: The construction and effectiveness of verbal accounts. *Administrative Science Quarterly, 39*, 57–88.

Evans, J., & Jones, P. (2011). The walking interview: Methodology, mobility and place. *Applied Geography, 31*(2), 849–858.

Feldman, M. S., & Orlikowski, W. J. (2011). Theorizing practice and practicing theory. *Organization Science, 22*(5), 1240–1253.

Friedland, R., & Alford, R. R. (1991). Bringing society back. In *Symbols, practices and institutional contradictions*. Chicago: University of Chicago Press.

Gagliardi, J. (1992). Dynamics of grinding brittle materials with coated abrasives. *American Ceramic Society Bulletin, 71*(11), 1641–1646.

Gherardi, E. F. X. (2012). Comprendre et accompagner le développement de l'enseignement bilingue en Corse. *L'enseignement des langues locales: institutions, méthodes, idéologies, Actes des quatrièmes journées des droits linguistiques*.

Giddens, A. (1984). *The constitution of society: introduction of the theory of structuration*. Berkeley: University of California Press.

Giddens, A. (1985). *A contemporary critique of historical materialism: The nation-state and violence* (Vol. 2). Berkeley: University of California Press.

Gieryn, T. F. (2002). What buildings do. *Theory and Society, 31*(1), 35–74.

Golant, B. D., & Sillince, J. A. (2007). The constitution of organizational legitimacy: A narrative perspective. *Organization Studies, 28*(8), 1149–1167.

Gond, J.-P. (2010). *Gérer la performance sociétale de l'entreprise*. Paris: Vuibert.

Greenwood, R., Díaz, A. M., Li, S. X., & Lorente, J. C. (2010). The multiplicity of institutional logics and the heterogeneity of organizational responses. *Organization Science, 21*(2), 521–539.

Gumport, P. J. (2012). Strategic thinking in higher education research. In M. N. Bastedo (Ed.), *The organization of higher education: Managing colleges for a new era* (pp. 18–41). Baltimore: The John Hopkins University Press.

Hoover, E. (2009, March 6). Golden walk gets a makeover from an auditor of campus visits. *Chronicle of Higher Education, 55*(26). Retrieved from http://www.chronicle.com/article/golden-walk-gets-a-makeover/21806

Hoover, E. (2010). Campus tours go Disney. *Washington Monthly, 42*(9/10), 35–41.

Jarzabkowski, P., Balogun, J., & Seidl, D. (2007). Strategizing: The challenges of a practice perspective. *Human Relations, 60*(1), 5–27.

Jarzabkowski, P., Spee, A. P., & Smets, M. (2013a). Material artifacts: Practices for doing strategy with 'stuff'. *European Management Journal, 31*(1), 41–54.

Jarzabkowski, P., Smets, M., Bednarek, R., Burke, G., & Spee, P. (2013b). Institutional ambidexterity: Leveraging institutional complexity in practice. *Research in the Sociology of Organizations, 39*, 37–61.

Jones, C., Boxenbaum, E., & Anthony, C. (2013). The immateriality of material practices in institutional logics. In M. Lounsbury & E. Boxenbaum (Eds.), *Institutional logics in action, part A* (pp. 51–75). London: Emerald Group Publishing Limited.

Jones, C., Livne-Tarandach, R., & Balachandra, L. (2010). Rhetoric that wins clients: Entrepreneurial firms use of institutional logics when competing for resources. *Research in the Sociology of Work, 21*, 183–218.

Kornberger, M., & Clegg, S. R. (2004). Bringing space back in: Organizing the generative building. *Organization Studies, 25*(7), 1095–1114.

Kraatz, M. S., & Block, E. S. (2008). Organizational implications of institutional pluralism. In *The Sage handbook of organizational institutionalism* (p. 840). London: Sage.

Kuh, G. D. (1990). Assessing student culture. *New Directions for Institutional Research, 1990*(68), 47–60.

Langer, S. (1957). *Philosophy in a new key*. Milton Keynes: Open University Press.

Latour, B. (1987). *Science in action: How to follow scientists and engineers through society*. Cambridge, MA: Harvard University Press.

Latour, B. (2005). *La science en action: introduction à la sociologie des sciences*. Paris: La Découverte/Poche.

Lefebvre, H. (1991). *The production of space* (Vol. 142). Oxford: Blackwell.

Lounsbury, M., & Glynn, M. A. (2001). Cultural entrepreneurship: Stories, legitimacy, and the acquisition of resources. *Strategic Management Journal, 22*(6–7), 545–564.

Maclean, M., Harvey, C., & Chia, R. (2012). Sensemaking, storytelling and the legitimization of elite business careers. *Human Relations, 65*(1), 17–40.

Magolda, M. B. B. (2000). *Teaching to promote intellectual and personal maturity: Incorporating students' worldviews and identities into the learning process*. San Francisco: Jossey-Bass.

Marx, K., Engels, F., & Lenin, V. I. (1974). *On historical materialism: A collection*. New York: International Publishers.

McPherson, C. M., & Sauder, M. (2013). Logics in action managing institutional complexity in a drug court. *Administrative Science Quarterly*. https://doi.org/10.1177/0001839213486447.

Merleau-Ponty, M. (1945). *Phénoménologie de la perception*. Paris: Gallimard, 2013.

Merleau-Ponty, M. (1964). *Le visible et l'invisible: suivi de notes de travail* (Vol. 36). Paris: Gallimard.

Meyer, J. W., & Rowan, B. (1977). Institutionalized organizations: Formal structure as myth and ceremony. *American Journal of Sociology, 83*(2), 340–363.

Meyer, R. E., Höllerer, M. A., Jancsary, D., & Van Leeuwen, T. (2013). The visual dimension in organizing, organization, and organization research: Core ideas, current developments, and promising avenues. *Academy of Management Annals, 7*(1), 489–555.

Middleton, J. (2009). 'Stepping in time': Walking, time, and space in the city. *Environment and Planning A, 41,* 1943–1961.

Miller, L. (2012). The library and the campus visit: Communicating value to prospective students and parents. *College and Library News,* pp. 586–589. Retrieved from http://crln.acrl.org/content/73/10/586.full

Oliver, C. (1991). Strategic responses to institutional processes. *Academy of Management Review, 16*(1), 145–179.

Orlikowski, W. J. (1992). The duality of technology: Rethinking the concept of technology in organizations. *Organization Science, 3*(3), 398–427.

Orlikowski, W. J. (2007). Sociomaterial practices: Exploring technology at work. *Organization Studies, 28*(9), 1435–1448.

Pache, A.-C., & Santos, F. (2013). Embedded in hybrid contexts: How individuals in organizations respond to competing institutional logics. *Research in the Sociology of Organizations, 39,* 3–35.

Padjen, P. (2002). Emergency medical services education—Evaluating the need for undergraduate and graduate degree programs in Wisconsin. *Prehospital and Disaster Medicine, 17*(S2), S82–S83.

Pickering, J. M., & King, J. L. (1995). Hardwiring weak ties: Interorganizational computer-mediated communication, occupational communities, and organizational change. *Organization Science, 6*(4), 479–486.

Pinch, T. (2008). Technology and institutions: Living in a material world. *Theory and Society, 37*(5), 461–483.

Pittz, T. G., Boje, D. M., Intindola, M. L., & Nicholson, S. (2017). COPE'ing with institutional pressures: A reintroduction of pragmatism to the study of organisations. *International Journal of Management Concepts and Philosophy, 10*(2), 113–129.

Pozzebon, M., Diniz, E. H., Mitev, N., Vaujany, F. X. D., Cunha, M. P. E., & Leca, B. (2017). Joining the sociomaterial debate. *Revista de Administração de Empresas, 57*(6), 536–541.

Puyou, F. R., & Quattrone, P. (2018). The visual and material dimensions of legitimacy: Accounting and the search for socie-ties. *Organization Studies.* https://doi.org/10.1177/0170840618765013.

Reckwitz, A. (2002). Toward a theory of social practices a development in culturalist theorizing. *European Journal of Social Theory, 5*(2), 243–263.

Rose, G., & Tolia-Kelly, D. P. (2012). *Visuality/materiality: Images, objects and practices.* Farnham: Ashgate Publishing, Ltd.

Sandberg, J., & Dall'Alba, G. (2009). Returning to practice anew: A life-world perspective. *Organization Studies, 30*(12), 1349–1368.

Schatzki, T. R. (2001). Practice mind-ed orders. In *The practice turn in contemporary theory*. London: Routledge.

Scott, P. (1995). *The meanings of mass higher education*. New York: McGraw-Hill International.

Scotto, C. (2014). The principles of campus conception: A spatial and organizational genealogy. What knowledge can we use from a historical study in order to analyze the design processes of a new campus. In F. X. de Vaujany, N. Mitev, P. Laniray, & E. Vaast (Eds.), *Materiality and time* (pp. 204–224). London: Palgrave.

Smets, M., & Jarzabkowski, P. (2013). Reconstructing institutional complexity in practice: A relational model of institutional work and complexity. *Human Relations, 66*(10), 1279–1309.

Suchman, L. (1995). Making work visible. *Communications of the ACM, 38*(9), 56–ff.

Suchman, L. (2007). *Human-machine reconfigurations: Plans and situated actions*. Cambridge: Cambridge University Press.

Suddaby, R., & Greenwood, R. (2005). Rhetorical strategies of legitimacy. *Administrative Science Quarterly, 50*(1), 35–67.

Swan, J., Bresnen, M., Robertson, M., Newell, S., & Dopson, S. (2010). When policy meets practice: Colliding logics and the challenges of 'Mode 2' initiatives in the translation of academic knowledge. *Organization Studies, 31*(9–10), 1311–1340.

Swidler, A. (1986). Culture in action: Symbols and strategies. *American Sociological Review, 51*, 273–286.

Turner, P. V. (1984). *Campus: An American planning tradition*. New York: MIT press.

Warren, S. (2008). Empirical challenges in organizational aesthetics research: Towards a sensual methodology. *Organization Studies, 29*(4), 559–580.

Washburn, J. H., & Petroshius, S. M. (2004). A collaborative effort at marketing the university: Detailing a student-centered approach. *Journal of Education for Business, 80*(1), 35–40.

Wasserman, V., & Frenkel, M. (2011). Organizational aesthetics: Caught between identity regulation and culture jamming. *Organization Science, 22*(2), 503–521.

Yanow, D., & Van Marrewijk, A. (2010). Giving voice to space: Academic practices and the material world. In *Organizational spaces: Rematerializing the workaday world* (pp. 139–158). Cheltenham: Edward Elgar.

Part III

Digitality and Information

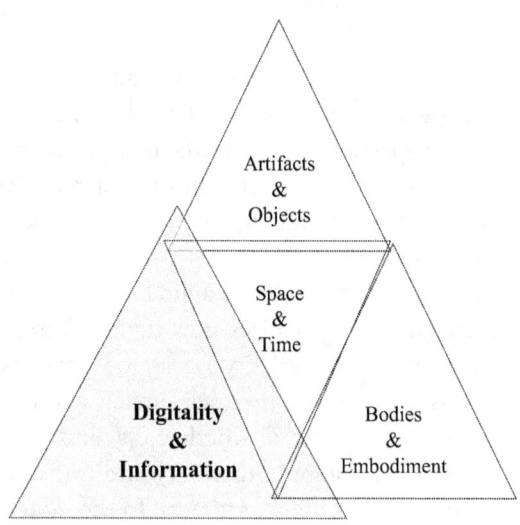

Key Questions

- What is the role of materiality of digital objects in institutional dynamics?
- To what extent do digitality features foster institutional disruption or permanence?
- How to conceptualize the material properties of digital artifacts?
- What does investigation on digitality reveal about the ontological status of materiality?
- From methodological and epistemological standpoints, to what extent can digitality offer avenues to generate fresh knowledge on institutions?

The third part of the book, entitled "Digitality and information" (a short definition of this topic can be found in Chap. 1), comprises three chapters that put into perspective digital artifacts and objects and institutional matters. In diverse ways, they complete a reflexive journey on materiality in institutions by digging into the theoretical, ontological, epistemological and methodological layers, thereby proposing promising avenues for future research on the role of digitality in institutional dynamics. Santos, in Chap. 8, conceptualizes how digital entrepreneurs in the game industry rely on the materiality of digital artifacts (blog, game application and websites) to claim their legitimacy, and more specifically demonstrate their handling of distinctiveness and conformity. His research expands to the ontology of digitality and leads him to examine the very material properties of digital artifacts. In the same vein, in Chap. 9, Thomas, Abrunhosa and Canales address the essential paradox of conflicting institutional logics by exploring the materiality of digital objects. Their analysis reveals that materiality plays the prominent role of orchestrating the emergence of conflicts between institutional logics. By doing so, they not only build theoretical ties between the concepts of affordance, digital objects and institutional logics but also encourage a reconceptualization of materiality from both an ontological and an epistemological standpoint. Felix, Arena and Conein provide an insightful methodological use of digitality in their investigation of institutional requirements and situated action. Through their analysis, they conceptualize the role of body and space in the adaptation of workers to institutional uncertainty. Figure 1 represents each chapter's digging into the multiple layers of materiality in institutions.

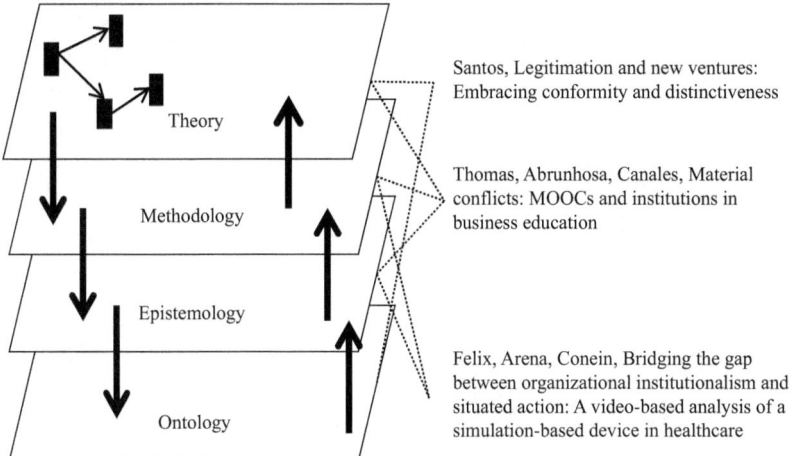

Santos, Legitimation and new ventures: Embracing conformity and distinctiveness

Thomas, Abrunhosa, Canales, Material conflicts: MOOCs and institutions in business education

Felix, Arena, Conein, Bridging the gap between organizational institutionalism and situated action: A video-based analysis of a simulation-based device in healthcare

Fig. 1 Reflexive journey on digitality and information through the chapters

8

Websites and the Discursive Legitimation of New Ventures: Embracing Conformity and Distinctiveness

Fernando Pinto Santos

Introduction

Previous studies suggest that to attain the support of key audiences such as investors and potential employees, entrepreneurs engage in legitimation efforts that follow institutionalized norms and expectations

I am indebted to Rebecca Piekkari from Aalto University and Eleanor Westney from M.I.T. and York University for their strong encouragement and support to this work. I would also like to thank Perttu Kähäri, Nina Granqvist, Toni-Matti Karjalainen, Inês Peixoto, Andreas Benker and Alexei Koveshnikov, from Aalto University, and Björn Wikhamn from University of Gothenburg, for their developmental comments on earlier versions of this manuscript. Moreover, I benefited much from the insightful lectures and discussions at the Scancor PhD Workshop on Institutional Analysis, in EMLyon. Thanks to all the participants and in particular to Woody Powell from Stanford University. His perspectives on institutions and materiality greatly influenced my work. I am also very grateful to Lasse Seppänen from Playraven who made this study possible. Finally, I am thankful to the Marcus Wallenberg Foundation that supported the development of this work.

F. P. Santos (✉)
Aalto University, Espoo, Finland
e-mail: fernando.santos@aalto.fi

© The Author(s) 2019
F.-X. de Vaujany et al. (eds.), *Materiality in Institutions*, Technology, Work and Globalization, https://doi.org/10.1007/978-3-319-97472-9_8

(Lounsbury and Glynn 2001; Navis and Glynn 2011). New organizations' practices thus become aligned, to some degree, with what the broader institutional environment establishes as appropriate or credible (DiMaggio and Powell 1983; Navis and Glynn 2011). At the same time, distinctiveness is also necessary to show that the organization offers something unique or valuable (Martens et al. 2007; De Clercq and Voronov 2009; Voronov et al. 2013). Furthermore, difference from others in the field is essential to create competitive advantages and induce favorable assessments of new organizations' plausibility (Navis and Glynn 2011; Tan et al. 2013; Zhao et al. 2016).

Little is known however about how entrepreneurs handle this tension between conformity to, and differentiation from, their organization's context (Navis and Glynn 2011; Zhao et al. 2016). In particular, the discursive aspects of the entrepreneurs' legitimation activities remain under-explored. This study empirically embraces these shortcomings based upon the case of a new venture in the mobile game industry. The research question is the following: how do entrepreneurs handle the tension between conformity to and distinctiveness from their organization's institutional context, when discursively striving for legitimacy? An understanding of the discursive means employed by entrepreneurs is particularly relevant to advance current knowledge on legitimation processes (De Clercq and Voronov 2009; Vaara and Monin 2010).

This research furthers the advancement of current studies on the legitimation of new ventures by providing a fine-grained view of how entrepreneurs present their organizations as both similar to, and different from, their institutional context. It reveals that legitimation is sustained by particular discursive strategies and that entrepreneurs can strive for conformity and distinctiveness in an implicit way. This study also highlights that the discursive pursuit of legitimacy is potentiated in the materiality of digital media. More broadly, this research adds to studies that address institutionalism, by highlighting that entrepreneurs' legitimation efforts potentially impact the wider discursive construction of their fields and by suggesting that the materiality of websites is particularly suited to influence this construction.[1]

---

[1] While this chapter explores how actors can deal with institutional expectations through discourse, Chap. 10 offers a complementary view to actors' dealing with institutionalism. In Chap. 10, Felix,

Institutions, Legitimacy and Discourses

A Discursive View of Institutions

Based on the premise that shared assumptions often influence actors' practices, institutions are regarded as common understandings about what are proper organizational structures and actions in a given field (Meyer and Rowan 1977; Zucker 1977; DiMaggio and Powell 1983; Tolbert et al. 2011). Previous studies have highlighted the discursive dimension of institutions and argued that it is mainly through discourses that information about actions gets spread and influences further actions (Phillips et al. 2004). In this view, "[i]nstitutions, as common cognitive understandings, are, importantly, also an emergent effect, or outcome, of ongoing processes of communication between diverse actors" (Cornelissen et al. 2015, p. 14). Within a discursive view of institutions, Lounsbury et al. (2003) proposed the concept of field frames. Field frames are discursive constructions that emerge from the efforts of different actors, providing meaning and order to fields of activity. These temporary conventions evolve over time, according to changes in actors' practices, interests and struggles over meaning and resources (Lounsbury et al. 2003).

The quest for organizational legitimacy is considered as the main motivation for organizations' alignment with the practices and discourses of their institutional context (DiMaggio and Powell 1983; Deephouse 1996). Legitimacy can be regarded as "a generalized perception or assumption that the actions of an entity are desirable, proper, or appropriate within some socially constructed system of norms, values, beliefs, and definitions" (Suchman 1995, p. 574). Hence, legitimacy reflects cultural alignment and consonance with field expectations and understandings (Scott 1995). While legitimacy ultimately results from audiences' judgments, legitimation refers to the purposive efforts made to accomplish it (Suchman 1995; Bitektine 2011). Thus, legitimation is a "process of social construction of legitimacy" (Bitektine 2011, p. 152) through

---

Arena and Conein explore situated action—including body expression—by actors who address organizational institutionalism.

which there is a purposive pursuit to influence the judgments and perceptions of others. This study is focused on this construction and will address entrepreneurs' discursive efforts.

New Ventures and Legitimation

Legitimacy is recognized as an important aspect for different kinds of organizations, and it assumes an especially preponderant role in the creation of new ventures. Given their lack of track record and the need to attract resources for growth, new ventures need to be judged as legitimate by key audiences such as investors and potential new employees (Lounsbury and Glynn 2001). Research that focuses on entrepreneurs' legitimation efforts has essentially addressed their impression management and symbolic activities, as well as their use of discourses (see Überbacher 2014). This research builds on this latter discursive approach to legitimation (Lounsbury and Glynn 2001; Martens et al. 2007; Garud et al. 2014).

Previous studies have highlighted that when striving for legitimacy, entrepreneurs must assess what the broader institutional context establishes as appropriate in order to align their discourses with institutionalized practices and norms (Lounsbury and Glynn 2001; Voronov et al. 2013). While institutional alignment is important, new ventures must also show distinctiveness in order to be regarded as plausible (De Clercq and Voronov 2009; Navis and Glynn 2011; Zhao et al. 2016). Although this tension between conformity and differentiation to the institutional context is recognized in previous works (e.g. De Clercq and Voronov 2009; Navis and Glynn 2011), little is known on how entrepreneurs can address it (Zhao et al. 2016). It has been suggested, for example, that distinctiveness claims must make meaningful the deviations from the institutional context (Navis and Glynn 2011). Furthermore, Lounsbury and Glynn (2001) have argued that entrepreneurs must strive for "optimal distinctiveness," that is, to balance normative appropriateness with strategic distinctiveness. However, current knowledge remains quite limited (Zhao et al. 2016). Furthermore, most of the current studies on "optimal distinctiveness" address its cognitive dimension. The present research complements these studies by focusing on the discursive construction of this tension between conformity and distinctiveness.

Finally, it is important to note that some studies essentially equal legitimacy with normative appropriateness to context (e.g. Deephouse 1999; van Werven et al. 2015) and others suggest a more nuanced view asserting that legitimacy implies both conformity and distinctiveness (e.g. Lounsbury and Glynn 2001; De Clercq and Voronov 2009; Voronov et al. 2013). This study follows this latter perspective.

Discursive Legitimation

Particular discourses seem to provide a more adequate basis for legitimation than others, and specific justifications have been considered as especially engaging or appealing (Vaara and Monin 2010). The works of Van Leeuwen and colleagues (e.g. Van Leeuwen and Wodak 1999; Van Leeuwen 2007) figure prominently in the literature on discursive legitimation. These linguists' pioneering work has distinguished and elaborated on four general discursive categories, characterized in Table 8.1. Vaara and Monin (2010) have transposed and expanded these works into organizational studies and identified two additional discursive legitimation strategies.

Table 8.1 Characterization of legitimation discursive strategies

Legitimation discursive strategies	Characterization	References
Rationalization	Emphasizing rational arguments and logic	Van Leeuwen and Wodak
Moralization	Referencing to value systems linked to particular discourses on morality. Adjectives like "good," "healthy" and "useful" are frequently used to hint at moral values	(1999), Van Leeuwen (2007)
Narrativization	Employment of a narrative discursive format to articulate legitimation	
Authorization	Using the authority of tradition, custom, law or even a person such as an expert, to sustain legitimation	
Exemplification	Using specific examples to establish legitimation	Vaara and Monin (2010)
Naturalization	Presenting something as effortless or natural by specific discursive means	

These legitimation strategies are frequently intertwined and overlap in discursive activities (Vaara et al. 2006).

Discourses and Materiality

Discourses are collections of texts, such as written documents and images, that bring ideas into being (Phillips and Oswick 2012; Phillips et al. 2004). Importantly, texts must be "spoken, written, or depicted in some way" and thus take a material form (Phillips et al. 2004, p. 636). It is precisely by being grounded in the materiality of some media that texts gain the ability to be shared and become influential (Czarniawska and Joerges 1996; Jones et al. 2013; Phillips et al. 2004; Lammers and Barbour 2006).

Materiality can be generically defined as the quality of persistence across places and time (Leonardi 2012). Hence, materiality refers to the properties of artifacts that "do not change from one moment to the next or across differences in location" (Leonardi 2012, p. 29). Thus, the concept encompasses not only physical artifacts but also technological ones, such as digital media and software (Suchman 2000; Orlikowski 2007; Volkoff et al. 2007). As Leonardi (2010, p. 2) explains, "Although it has no physical properties, software clearly does not exist in the conceptual domain because it provides hard constraints and affordances in much the same way as physical artifacts do." Leonardi (2012) illustrates his argument with the example of Microsoft Excel. Although software evolves by being updated from time to time, it is nonetheless stable and enduring in the moments in between the changes in different versions, and these qualities related to persistence over time allow users to work productively with the software. In this study, this encompassing perspective on materiality is followed.

Methods

This research addresses the case of a new organization—Playraven—in the mobile game industry in Finland. Data collection started in March 2014, sensibly nine months after the firm was founded, and while the first game was under development. At this stage, the founders of Playraven were still debating important strategic options, such as the games' distribution and revenue models, and they were actively searching for new members for the organization. Thus, the setting offered an interesting opportunity to follow the evolution of the new firm. Furthermore, the mobile game industry was a nascent and fast-paced growing market, and provided a rich institutional context. The data collection ended in September 2016.

This chapter builds essentially on the data that are publicly available. A central source of data is the communication developed by the venture and presented on its website and in its blog, in press releases, in public presentations by the CEO and in interviews to media. The data collection process evolved within a continuous search for the organization's communication. The website of the organization was essential in this regard, since it displays links to a wealth of resources, such as publications where Playraven's CEO interviews were published.

Furthermore, public data related to the mobile game industry more generally was collected, in order to gain a broad understanding of the case's context. These sources of public data include industry meetings and publications and also media archives, as well as communications from other ventures in the field. Although I developed over 20 interviews with Playraven's CEO and most of the members of the organization, as well as observations during regular visits to the company headquarters, these generally do not figure as direct sources of data in this chapter, since the focus has been on publicly available texts. Nonetheless, these were fundamental to the understanding of the case and its context.

The collection, analysis and interpretation of empirical material took place throughout the process of research, in an iterative way (Alvesson and Sköldberg 2009). The continuous and recurrent interpretation of the empirical material led me to address particular aspects of the literature that, in turn, directed my attention to emerging new aspects of legitimation efforts that were then further explored. I employed discourse analysis to address the empirical material (Phillips et al. 2004). The goal of this analysis was to understand how legitimation was discursively constructed in texts, as well as to grasp the context of this construction (Phillips et al. 2004; Philips and Oswick 2012). Thus, the texts collected were repeatedly read, notes were taken and there was a continuous search for discursive patterns that could help to grasp the construction of legitimation and aspects related to conformity and distinctiveness, according to this study's purpose. This process of analysis evolved with an increasing sensitivity (Alvesson and Sköldberg 2009) that allowed discernment of how legitimation was discursively expressed. Moreover, it was possible to uncover relationships between texts, as well as relating the empirical material to existing studies and theoretical frameworks. Two of these frameworks emerged as relevant in the process of analysis: (1) discursive legitimation strategies and (2) field frames.

Throughout the fieldwork, it became noticeable how Playraven's communication seemed to be developed following particular discursive mechanisms. This directed my attention to the literature on discursive legitimation, and from a further engagement with the empirical material, the collection of which was still ongoing, it was possible to confirm further the relevance of the theoretical framework against the background of the data. Discursive legitimation strategies were characterized in the previous section, and building on the literature mentioned, the existing categories were used as the basis for the coding. When proceeding with the analysis, the discursive strategy of "authorization" was not evident in the empirical material and following the practice of previous studies (Vaara et al. 2006; Vaara and Monin 2010) this strategy was disregarded. The concept of field frames emerged also from the iterative process of collection and analysis of data, against the backdrop of the existing literature. In the fieldwork, it became noticeable how the communication of different organizations in the field seemed to coalesce around some ideas that shared similarities. Analyzing the literature and further exploring the data set, the concept of the field frame gradually emerged as relevant. From the analysis of data, a field frame was identified revolving around the idea of organizational practices based on small teams working in parallel. This field frame was further explored in the later stage of this study and will be further elaborated in the next sections.

A View of the Game Industry and the Foundation of Playraven

The Mobile Game Industry

Mobile gaming devices have existed since the 1970s, and a few, such as Game Boy, have achieved relative success. With the widespread use of mobile phones by the end of the last century, some companies started developing games for these devices. However, the market was still only embryonic. Lack of standardization in mobile devices created significant technical challenges and the distribution of games ran into difficulties. The situation only started to change with the launch of the iPhone and Apple Store in 2007. For the first time, there was a mobile phone with adequate technical features for gameplay, such as a widescreen and the capacity to download software easily. Furthermore, Apple Store made possible the global distribution of mobile games that consumers could access without difficulty. With this new digital distribution channel, developers no longer needed the publishing companies that until then had dominated the market. Furthermore, with the rise of touchscreen devices such as smartphones and tablets, and with more digital distribution channels such as that of Google that followed Apple, an industry centered on mobile games emerged.

The Finnish game industry was particularly well prepared to compete in the mobile game market. Stimulated and often funded by diverse initiatives of Nokia, a few companies in Finland started developing games for mobile phones from around 2000 onward. After the launch of the iPhone, an increasing number of Finnish companies soon focused their efforts on the development of games for touchscreens. The experience accumulated in the development of games for mobile phones was important in this regard, as well as the growth of the entrepreneurial activities in the country, highly incentivized by governmental funds. Moreover, the success cases of some Finnish companies propelled the industry. In particular, two of these companies became prototypical in the field. In 2009, Rovio launched Angry Birds and the game became the first global success in Apple Store, enabling the company to grow rapidly and expand its activities to different areas. The second highly successful case is the one of Supercell. In October 2013, and with two mobile games for touchscreens on the market, 51% of the Finnish company was acquired for 1.1 billion euros. Supercell, founded only three years earlier, became one of the fastest-growing start-ups ever (Kuorikoski 2015). At the beginning of 2016, there were over 300 Finnish game companies operating and more than half of these were created in the previous two years. Over 80% of these companies develop games for mobile devices.

Playraven: A New Venture in the Mobile Game Industry

Five entrepreneurs founded Playraven in the summer of 2013, in Helsinki, with the goal of developing games for touchscreen devices like smartphones and tablets. The entrepreneurs—four Finnish and one Brazilian—are industry veterans, having worked both in traditional games for consoles and in mobile game development. In January 2014, Playraven obtained 1.7 million euros from venture capital firms and launched its first game in September. The game reached the top 10 charts in the strategy genre in 76 countries and was thus a moderate success. In December, the firm secured a new round of seed investment: 3.3 million euros. The games developed by Playraven are distributed in online stores like those of Apple and Google. In the spring of 2016, there were 24 people working at Playraven, with 3 teams developing games simultaneously.

Around 2013/2014, when Playraven was starting its activities, the mobile game industry was evolving at a fast pace. The sector had not yet clear and widespread normative understandings, and was characterized by constant technical innovations, by an exponential growth in the number of companies entering the market and by the introduction of new business models. As an example of the changes in the latter aspect, we have the sources of revenue. While around 2010 most of the games in Apple Store had a price, in 2012 and 2013 more and more games became available free. Around 2014, the most successful mobile games were free. In the free-to-play business model, the games can be downloaded for free. However, games display ads and/or players need to spend money to progress more quickly or to play with improved features. In sum, throughout 2013 and 2014, the mobile game industry was becoming established as a specific domain but was still very tied to the traditional game industry field. It was in this highly dynamic and continuously evolving context that Playraven was founded, as a member of the broader game industry, as well as of the nascent mobile game industry. To overcome the venture's lack of track record and influence audiences to make favorable judgments pertaining to the firm's plausibility and attractiveness, legitimation has been a key aspect of the entrepreneurs' communication.

The Pursuit of Legitimacy in the Game Industry

Playraven's CEO has been leading the efforts to present the organization as a legitimate organization. The main audiences of these efforts have been investors and potential new human resources. Additionally, being generally recognized by other organizations and the media, for example, as legitimate in the game industry, has also been important for the co-founders. The CEO has highlighted three areas in particular that have been important for the investors' judgments of Playraven's legitimacy as a new venture in the industry:

> They are investing in your team and your company, so you should talk to them mostly about your team, your company and your business strategy. Obviously, it's important to pitch your game, show a demo and have great materials, but don't get lost in talking about the details of the design – they are not developers, they invest in companies and you should talk about your company.

The three areas mentioned—team, strategy and company—have been presented prominently in the venture's communication and will now be analyzed in terms of legitimation. In Table 8.2, there are empirical excerpts pertaining to Playraven's team. The team presentation is developed with legitimation strategies of rationalization and exemplification that show conformity to the industry. Playraven's members are presented as having extensive experience and a background both in the traditional

234   F. P. Santos

Table 8.2 Legitimation strategies pertaining to Playraven's team

Discursive strategies	Empirical texts	Media
Rationa-lization	"Playraven is an independent game development studio founded in 2013 by veterans with AAA console, mobile and free-to-play experience from renowned studios such as Remedy Entertainment, Wooga and Digital Chocolate. In the past, the founders have shipped 50+ game titles, including the Xbox 360 hit Alan Wake (over three million copies sold)"	Playraven's website *(Press release 2014.01)*
Exempli-fication	"Stuart has joined as Lead Artist. He's been working in the games industry for over 10 years, previously with Rockstar and our friends at Remedy on Quantum Break. (…) Gabri is our new Player Support Lead, joining us from Supercell, where he has been serving Clash of Clans players worldwide since the early days. (…) Robin joins us from Rovio as Marketing Director"	Playraven's website *(Blog post, 2015.01)*

game industry and in the mobile game industry. This experience is backed up with figures (rationalization) and examples of games and other companies (exemplification).

In terms of what can be generically regarded as Playraven's business strategy, the venture is described as different from others in the industry, as illustrated in the table below (Table 8.3). With the same discursive strategies of rationalization and exemplification employed to present the team, and additionally strategies of moralization and naturalization, it is argued that the organization's approach to the market is essentially distinctive from others in the field. Building on the idea that the games on the market have not adequately followed the exponential growth of mobile devices, it is claimed that these generally continue to revolve around a few genres, and that stagnation essentially characterizes the range on the market (rationalization). Also, it is stated that consumers are not well served by this narrow range (moralization). Furthermore, it is argued that Playraven aims to disrupt the current state of the mobile market, just as Coca-Cola disrupted the soft drinks market (exemplification). Finally, it is explained that the venture was founded at a time when business opportunities and the technical features of mobile devices made it ideal to develop games in the strategy genre (naturalization).

Table 8.3 Legitimation strategies pertaining to Playraven's strategy

Discursive strategies	Empirical texts	Media
Rationa-lization	"Mobile gaming has become stagnant. Tablets and smartphones have matured into a market even greater than television, and yet revenues are dominated by titles that are 18–24 months old. (…) Our promise to our peers and our audience is to put forth original properties that shake the mobile scene out of its comfort zone"	Playraven's website *(Press release 2014.12)*
Moralization	"Audiences are not well served. Better can be done. The number of tablets and smartphones now exceeds the total number of television sets on the planet. We believe this massive audience can no longer be served with a "one size fits all" approach. New mobile gaming audiences with diverse tastes are out there, waiting to be served"	Playraven's website *(Press release 2014.01)*
Exempli-fication	"By definition I think the future is gonna be defined by new games eventually. Another way to look at it is, if we were a soda start-up would it make any sense for us to think that, "Coca-Cola sells a lot so, we need to make cola as a start-up". There would be no way to, survive with that kind of strategy. We would need to differentiate from the, rest of the market and look for openings"	YouTube website, Slush channel *(CEO public presentation at Slush conference, 2014.09)*
Naturali-zation	"Our dream is to create new classics and genres. Who knows, if we're lucky, maybe we'll make the next Civilization. Right now mobile is the perfect place to pursue that dream"	Publication website *(CEO interview to Nordic Game Bits, 2015.02)*

Playraven's organizational structure and practices are also prominently presented in the venture's communication. These can generically be seen as corresponding to the third area highlighted by Playraven's CEO in terms of what investors appreciate in a new venture—the company itself. The firm's practices and organizational structure have been presented via four discursive strategies: rationalization, moralization, exemplification and naturalization, as illustrated in Table 8.4. The discourses revolve around how the venture is organized and how it creates games. The discourses

Table 8.4 Legitimation strategies pertaining to Playraven's organizational structure and practices

Discursive strategy	Empirical texts	Media
Rationalization	"The way to do this in business you have to manage a risk. (…) That's why have three teams, working on three games, that are quite different and, looking for different audiences with different kinds of mechanics"	YouTube website, Slush channel *(CEO public presentation at Slush conference, 2014.09)*
Moralization	"We're bringing in a new team to make "Game 2" as we're so creatively calling it right now. (…) But they'll be free to make something their own"	Publication website *(CEO interview to Pocket Gamer, 2014.01)*
Exemplification	"We have to build an environment where people feel comfortable, about going to each other, even in the other team. And saying "I think your game has a problem". This is a bit similar what they do at Pixar actually, if you've read the book Creativity Inc. It's very very important to get candid feedback, and not have this sort of, politically correct, "well yeah your game is kinda cool""	YouTube website, PocketGamer.Biz channel *(CEO public presentation at Pocket Gamer conference, 2014.09)*
Naturalization	"Playraven was formed to foster an environment that advances creativity and autonomy"	Venture's website *(Press release 2014.12)*

present an implied idea of differentiation, where the practices are essentially described as unique and thus distinctive.

In around 2013, when Playraven was founded, explicit understandings and expectations about proper organizational structures and practices, as well as related communication—regarded as field frames in this study—were evolving. One of these field frames revolved around an organizational model based on independent teams working on new games, the one followed by the company Supercell. This field frame was not widespread around 2013. Thus, in Playraven's context, there were competing expectations about what would be proper practices for a mobile game company. Different actors in the field were discursively contributing to this frame, and at the time of Playraven's foundation and sensibly until the end of 2015, the evolving conventions articulated in the frame were not taken for granted. Although the mobile game industry rapidly accomplished legitimacy as a field in the early 2010s, the organizational practices were still being institutionalized during this period. Nonetheless, Playraven's founders decided to implement an organizational structure and practices based essentially on the frame mentioned: multiple teams working independently on new games. These practices, aligned with the ongoing discursive construction of the field frame in the field, became central to the legitimation of the venture. Importantly, these practices became foundational to Playraven's members' daily work as well as for the way the overall business strategy was being pursued. Thus, having aligned the practices of the venture with the field frame identified, the entrepreneurs inserted the organization into it. In particular, Playraven's founders have drawn from this frame as well as contributing to its reinforcement and further development over time, both through their organizational practices and their legitimation discourses.

In discursive terms, Playraven's entrepreneurs claim that having multiple teams enables them to manage creative risks (rationalization). It is also argued that freedom is an important aspect of the organization's practices (moralization). Furthermore, a case example from outside the industry, that illustrates the open environment culture at Playraven, is also employed (exemplification). Finally, an open environment that fosters creativity and autonomy is presented as almost effortless, as something that has just been part of the organization's practices since its foundation (naturalization).

Finally, a discursive narrative format has been central in the organization's communication. The narrative allows the bringing together of the three aspects just addressed—team, strategy and company—and the underlying discursive strategies in a coherent way, organized in a temporal sequence and with an overall sense of purpose entailed in this discursive format. Furthermore, the opposing ideas of conformity and distinctiveness underlie the narrative as logical and complementary elements (Table 8.5).

Table 8.5 Playraven's narrative legitimation strategy

Discursive strategy	Empirical texts	Media
Narrati- vization	"My name is Lasse Seppänen. I'm the CEO and co-founder at Playraven, a new start-up here in Helsinki (…) I started in the first wave of, mobile games back in 1998–1999. (…) [Playraven] first of all: 18 months old. (…) Our game portfolio consists of three games at the moment. (…) If we look at that list of what is actually on the top lists, those games have a lot of similarities. (…) Why are we seeing this discrepancy between a new mass medium and, a very narrow clustered offering of games? We believe it's because of the speed, of increasing the install base. IOS and Android, have grown really fast. Within just a few years a billion devices were added. (…) What do those people want? How do we find that? One thing is clear to me, one size no longer fits all. It just, makes no sense, with two billion devices out there"	YouTube website, Slush channel *(CEO public presentation at Slush conference, 2014.09)*

The narrative is an ongoing construction that has been evolving and that is continuously adapted to meet particular target audiences and also to be suited to particular communication purposes and media. Some aspects of the narrative have been emphasized, and others downplayed or even disregarded over time but still the discursive strategies of rationalization, moralization, exemplification and naturalization are usually employed. Thus, these discursive strategies serve as the building blocks of the more holistic narrative strategy.

Although Playraven achieved two successful rounds of funding (in January and December 2014) and attracted experienced human resources, the entrepreneurs have regularly reiterated the legitimacy claims over time. The search for talented human resources is regarded as ongoing, as it is more generally the need to attract investors. Thus, a regular reiteration of legitimacy claims is regarded by the Playraven's CEO as a necessary activity:

We have to break the noise and if we're very open about our message, which is different from everybody else's message and we keep repeating it everywhere, we create an image… in the professionals' minds.

The legitimation efforts of Playraven's entrepreneurs have been regularly expressed in oral accounts but also through different artifacts. Digital media, in particular, have been especially important in the instantiation of the entrepreneurs' legitimation intent. When the Playraven's CEO and vice-president met the first potential investors in the autumn of 2013, they showed a playable version of a game under development that the investors could experience on a touchscreen device. Furthermore, the Playraven's website has been particularly relevant in the entrepreneurs' efforts to legitimize their new firm.

Especially in 2013 and at the beginning of 2014, when Playraven had not yet launched its first game, the website was what entrepreneurs had to show to different audiences, such as investors and potential new employees. This strategic relevance of the website to stand out in the market and to streamline the communication of the firm has been fully embraced by the entrepreneurs since the foundation of the firm. New content has regularly been released on the website since then.

Playraven's website provides a wealth of content organized in four main sections: a blog, the company's presentation, job announcements and an archive of press releases. The blog has presented detailed accounts of the work being developed and explanations of some of the creative decisions, as well as unveiling features of games under development. In this blog, new content is regularly added, but all older posts remain available. The same is true of the Playraven's archive of press releases.

Together with verbal texts, the visual mode of communication is quite salient and a plethora of images pervade the website. These include images related to the games under development, such as hand-drawn plans, sketches and the design of environments and characters related to the conceptual development of games. Also, different images related to the inspiration for game development are displayed. Furthermore, screenshots of gameplay and video trailers of the games are also displayed. Finally, on Playraven's website, one can also find photos of the firm's facilities, meetings related to game development, new members of the organization and industry-related events such as conferences.

Moreover, the website also presents links to a wealth of other actors in the field and online resources. Through hyperlinks, there are connections to media websites where news or interviews with Playraven's members have been published. Also, industry-related events where the organization participated and diverse industry publications are accessible through Playraven's website. In particular, the firm has been included in lists such as "Europe's most exciting game start-ups" or "Facebook 2015 Games of the Year List as a Studio To Watch" and the links related to these lists are also available. Finally, hyperlinks make available connections to many other resources such as online stores where games are available and game players' fora. These connected resources significantly enrich the content of Playraven's website.

In particular, Playraven's website has been important to attract new employees to the organization, as illustrated by the comments of two of the firm's current members:

> Everything that I knew I was pretty much learning from the Internet, from their own site. And, when I came here for the... for the interview, I was learning a lot. That's about it, but not that much because they only had one game that was still actually unreleased. So, there was not that much information available.

> I heard about the first game, Spymaster, sometime when they started, publishing the blog, about it. It was really interesting, back then.

Thus, the website has since the firm's foundation assumed the role of a tangible touchpoint between the organization and different audiences. The website has from the beginning been developed exclusively in English and its global reach has been important. Some of the current employees, who joined the company from outside Finland, gathered information through the website before joining the firm. At the same time, the website has also been essential for reaching international investors.

While Playraven's website makes the entrepreneurs' legitimation efforts widely accessible to others, conversely, online communication by other field actors also make discourses available that have been influential on the industry. Naturally, the influence of online communication should be regarded together with the influence of different other communication activities and events such as meetings, discussions and presentations in the industry. Nonetheless, it became evident in the fieldwork of this research that websites had a prominent role in the discursive construction of the mobile game industry field in Finland. In Fig. 8.1, there are illustrative empirical excerpts of discourses revolving around organizational structures and practices in the field. This particular aspect of Playraven's legitimation, addressed earlier, can be clearly seen as part of the evolving discursive construction of the field, and thus the emphasis on it here. The organizational practices discursively articulated in the field frame are based on small game development teams, and related aspects, such as organizational flexibility, creative freedom, the goal of taking risks when developing games and the ability to abandon projects as early as possible (in the field's jargon: kill the game). In Fig. 8.1, there are fragments of discourses that briefly illustrate how Playraven's communication can be seen as part of a wider space to which different actors have contributed through time. The illustrations include excerpts from actors such a news publication, a non-profit governmental organization (Neogames), and the Finnish ventures Supercell, Small Giant Games, Kopla Games and Frogmind, just as examples of actors in the field.

Discourses are thus what brought into being the identified field frame, in the Finnish mobile game industry. Importantly, the discourses above were materialized in websites which made them accessible in the public domain, and endowed with the potential to reach widespread audiences. Over time, with the discursive contribution of different actors, and with an increasing employment of the practices articulated in the frame, these practices became more institutionalized. Around 2016, it became taken for granted that new ventures in the mobile game should be organized in small multiple teams, with autonomy and creative freedom, and inserted in an organizational environment with low bureaucracy. This is evident in the widespread adoption of these practices observed in 2016 in the mobile game industry in Finland. In this process of field institutionalization, the contribution of the discursive legitimation of new organizations was essential.

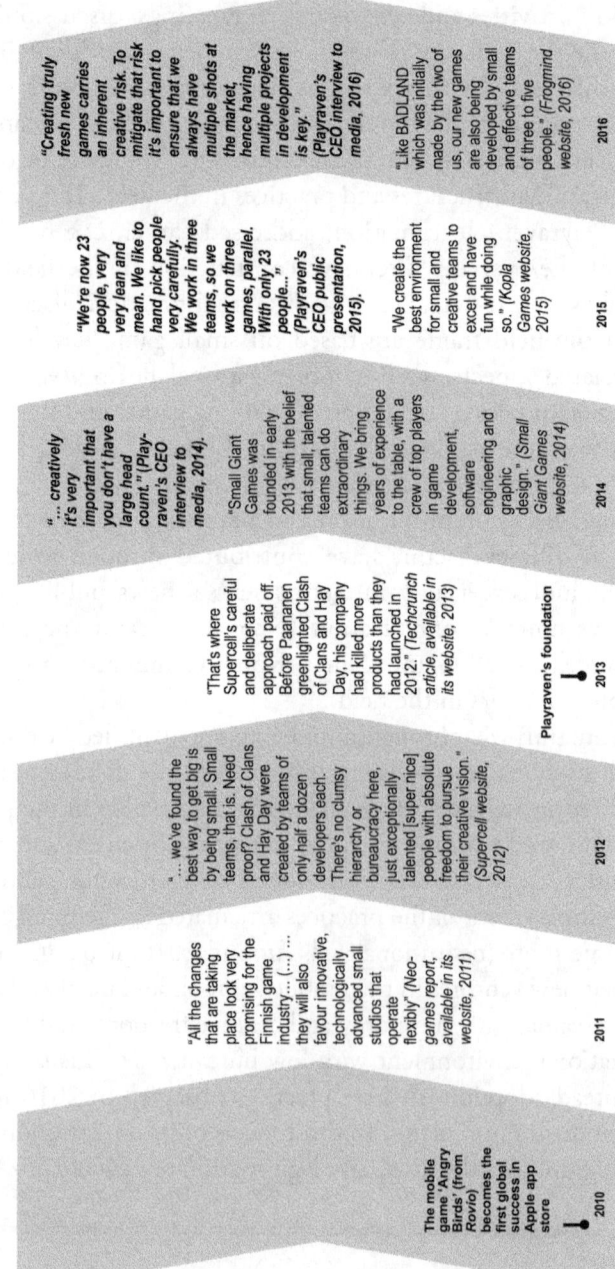

Fig. 8.1 Fragments of discourses circulating in the mobile game field in Finland, through time. Playraven's discourses are highlighted in bold and italics

Legitimation and the Material Qualities of Websites

The tension between conformity and distinctiveness is discursively addressed in different ways by Playraven's entrepreneurs. First, claims pertaining to the organization's team essentially show conformity to the organization's institutional field and the ones related to strategy are presented as distinctive from it. While these claims are opposite, they are discursively constructed with similar legitimation strategies, which help to tone down the differences in the claims. Previous works have suggested that the same discursive strategies can be used to legitimize or delegitimize (Vaara et al. 2006; Vaara and Monin 2010). However, this study advances a more nuanced view on discursive legitimation. This research shows that claims related to institutional conformity and distinctiveness are part of legitimation efforts and that the same discursive strategies are used to pursue both types of claims.

A second aspect of how conformity and distinctiveness are handled in legitimation efforts relates to a possible implicitness, when fields' conventions are still evolving, as in the case studied. In the firm's first two years of activity, Playraven's practices were presented with an implicit conformity that is understandable only to those aware that the simultaneous work of multiple teams in game development was a practice successfully followed by some companies in the mobile game field at the time. Anyone not aware of the field frame that articulated these practices would judge the claims as distinctive in the field. Thus, in the case of Playraven, conformity to mobile game industry practice remained implicit and only understandable to those aware of the field frame mentioned.

Previous research has highlighted the fact that different audiences embrace their own particular evaluative lenses and have their own particular standards for judging legitimacy (Castelló et al. 2016; Zhao et al. 2016). This study empirically suggests that when fields are forming and beliefs are not widespread, different audiences will judge conformity and distinctiveness according to their own understandings. In particular, this study advances the concept of the field frame as especially useful to grasp this perspective. The ideas articulated in field frames are not widespread or taken for granted and thus reach only some actors in the field. As temporary conventions, field frames are constructions that might evolve or not into institutionalized beliefs. This enables one to understand how actors in a field may be socialized to valuing or ignoring particular aspects pertaining to the legitimacy of organizations when developing their specific evaluative lens (Fisher et al. 2015; Zhao et al. 2016).

Finally, the narrative discursive strategy has also been important to make the presentation of the opposing ideas of conformity and distinctiveness coherent. By bringing together claims that both conform to the institutional field and are distinctive from it, as well as claims that can be implicitly judged in both ways, the narrative provides an explanation of how the different ideas presented are related. In this view, conformity and distinctiveness are not opposing forces but rather logical elements that function together (King and Whetten 2008). Presentation in a narrative provides them with an underlying explanation that enables them to make sense (Polkinghorne 1987; Vaara et al. 2016).

While this study helped to unearth micro-discursive aspects of legitimation strategies, there is potential to explore further how entrepreneurs discursively build on their fields. Future research may address, for example, how claims of conformity and distinctiveness evolve as institutionalization unfolds over time. Another aspect worth studying is the implicitness that emerged in this study as a mechanism to cope with and to build on evolving field expectations. This perspective holds promise to reveal interesting insights in entrepreneurial legitimation. It is also relevant to address the evaluation of legitimation efforts by different audiences in future studies, as well as how these audiences' ongoing judgments might influence legitimation efforts.

Importantly, this research contributes to a view of discursive legitimation as materially anchored, and where material qualities are deemed as an important aspect of the pursuit of legitimacy (De Vaujany and Vaast 2013, 2014; Jones et al. 2013). In particular, this study suggests that the materiality of websites and the qualities enabled by it are especially relevant in the legitimation of new organizations. I will now discuss four key qualities that sustain legitimation, blending the insights of the case with the existing literature. First, by enduring though time and space, websites give tangibility to new firms. This tangibility may assume special relevance in the initial stages of entrepreneurial activity, in particular for firms whose commercial range is not physical and whose touchpoints with the markets tend to be reduced. For more than a year, before Playraven had launched any game, the organization's website provided the main reference point between the organization and its different audiences. Thus, the website contributed to endowing the firm with an ontological existence in contact with the markets. And this is especially relevant for legitimation efforts: through websites and other digital media, entrepreneurs are able to demonstrate the existence of their new firm to different audiences, regardless of their geographical location and the moment when they come into contact with the organization (Treem and Leonardi 2012). Furthermore, the website displays the entrepreneurs' discourses over time, enabling these to persist and stand out when faced with different legitimation audiences. In addition, websites hold the potential to achieve a wide reach, and through these digital media, a new venture's legitimation becomes globally available on screens. Finally, websites are easily accessible (an account is not required as is the case with social media), are usually located in a fixed domain (which does not happen with all online content, sometimes more fleeting) and can be accessed repeatedly at this location, which reinforces their role as the actual touchpoints of new organizations.

Second, by being editable (Kallinikos et al. 2013), websites offer the opportunity to renew legitimacy claims. The materiality of websites enables the implementation of changes over time, something that is not possible with physical documents, such as printed ones. This does not imply, however, that the content and structure of websites are continually being changed (Leonardi 2010). As the case of Playraven illustrates, websites' content can be composed of both continuity and change. On the firm's website, the blog posts, for example, extend from the early days of the firm; this content endures through time and page visitors can access all posts that have ever been published. At the same time, new content has been added through time. Thus, websites' materiality enables these digital media content to both endure and evolve over space and time. And this is also especially relevant to entrepreneurs' legitimation efforts: the website grounds the new firm in time, attesting to its existence and activities since its foundation (which is quite relevant from a legitimation perspective), while it promotes the cumulative enrichment of the discourses over time. The tension between conformity and distinctiveness in the legitimation discourses can thus be renewed as time unfolds and the institutional environments evolve. Hence, websites provide a pliable ontology for the organization, facilitating the co-existence of continuity and change.

Third, websites enable the employment of hyperlinks through which connections are established to other digital media content. Playraven's entrepreneurs have prominently been using these connections in the presentation of legitimacy claims on their firm's website. Hence, through this "hyper-intertextuality" enabled by websites' materiality, entrepreneurs are able to enrich their legitimation discourses by relating to other institutional actors, ideas and evidence (Barros 2014). Also, carefully choosing these hyperlink connections allows entrepreneurs to reinforce their claims of conformity and distinctiveness, creating an interplay that pushes further the tension already articulated in the organization's own texts. Thus, websites' materiality also endows the organization with what can be regarded as a distributed ontology: through these connections, the new venture expands further and attests to its ontological existence and its appropriateness and relevance in its field.

Fourth and finally, websites' materiality enables communication with different modes, which offer a variety of ways of presenting legitimacy claims (Kress 2010). Although this study was focused on verbal texts, Playraven's entrepreneurs employ other modes in their legitimation efforts, such as the visual. An aesthetic dimension expressed in images, drawings and videos, as well as in the graphic design elements of websites, for example, offers the potential to create engagement with legitimation audiences (Kornberger and Clegg 2011). In particular, the holistic manner in which visual communication is processed enables experiences that are not necessarily coupled with explicit verbal categories (Kress and Van Leeuwen 2001; Kress 2010) and allows the creation of claims without a logical predication, thus being especially adequate to influence by suggestion (Kress and Van Leeuwen 1996; Meyer et al. 2018). Also, as the visual mode of communication is more plastic and ambiguous than the verbal one (Meyer et al. 2013), it is particularly well suited to expressing the tension between conformity and distinctiveness in legitimation. Finally, by being accessible on screens, the multimodal content on websites assumes a vividness and larger-than-life presence, contributing to emphasizing the credibility (Barry and Elmes 1997; Meyer et al. 2018) and even authenticity (Graves et al. 1996) of the entrepreneurs' legitimacy claims.

More broadly, this research suggests that the legitimation efforts of entrepreneurs have the potential to enrich the discursive construction of institutional fields. As analyzed, Playraven's organizational practices can be seen within a discursive construction that has been evolving in the mobile game industry in Finland. This field frame has been revolving around a vision of game development by multiple independent teams with creative freedom as a proper practice in the mobile game field. The frame has been sustained by the discursive contribution of distributed actors in the field. And, Playraven's presentation of its organizational structure and practices has been inserted into this ongoing discursive construction. By presenting its practices as legitimate in discourses with underlying rational, moral and natural arguments, and also with examples, Playraven has contributed to the ongoing discursive construction of the mobile game field. Hence, over time, the entrepreneurs' legitimation strategies have reaffirmed the field frame's discursive construction and strengthened it with the particular examples, rationales, analogies and other discursive elements employed by Playraven. At the same time, legitimation has further expanded the frame by the intertextual connections established in the organizations' communication. Furthermore, by yielding a tension between claims that emphasize conformity and distinctiveness, the venture has enriched, more generally, the discursive construction of the field.

These insights push forward the perspective suggested by De Clercq and Voronov (2009, p. 801) that "legitimization is a reciprocal process, whereby not only do newcomers seek legitimacy as entrepreneurs to participate effectively in a field, but that by their very attempts to comply with field-imposed expectations, they legitimize the field." In particular, this study addresses the discursive aspect of legitimation and field construction and embraces the evolving nature of discourses and fields by building on the concept of the field frame. Thus, this work suggests a close recursive relation where entrepreneurs' legitimation discourses build on evolving field frames and enrich these through the articulation of particular discursive legitimation strategies. By pursuing a self-interested legitimation of their ventures, entrepreneurs became potentially involved in the ongoing and distributed discursive construction of their field.

In these co-constitutive dynamics between new organizations and their institutional fields, the materiality of websites—and, in particular, the qualities discussed here of endurance over time and space, editability, hyper-intertextuality and multimodality—assumes an especially relevant role. The importance of digital media in legitimation remains largely under-addressed (for exceptions, see e.g. Coupland and Brown 2004; Barros 2014; Castelló et al. 2016) and this study highlights, in particular, the qualities of websites that derive from their materiality as especially well suited to sustain new ventures' legitimation efforts and subsequently their potential to influence fields. While organizations commonly develop a significant number of discursive activities, these often have a limited impact and potential to influence institutional settings (Phillips et al. 2004; Nicholls 2010). Phillips et al. (2004, p. 640) have theorized that actions related to attaining and maintaining legitimacy are more likely to leave "enduring residue" that can impact the institutional settings. While this study empirically corroborates this perspective, it additionally reveals the importance of the communication media's materiality in the potential to influence institutional settings. In order to become influential, ideas must be objectified, instantiated and shared (Czarniawska and Joerges 1996; Santos et al. 2016), and materiality is essential in the diffusion and institutionalization of new ideas (Jones and Massa 2013).

In the highly connected and digitalized contemporary markets, the material qualities of websites emerged in this study as especially relevant, and future research may explore the qualities discussed both on websites and in other digital media (see Fischer and Reuber 2014; Castelló et al. 2016). Moreover, new organizations can be regarded as becoming involved in "institutional work" (Lawrence et al. 2009), and this is one of the paths that is relevant to develop further in future research, since there are intriguing opportunities for studies that address how entrepreneurs and new ventures can influence institutional arrangements (Battilana et al. 2009; Nicholls 2010; Phillips et al. 2004; Cornelissen et al. 2015). In particular, a view of agency as being distributed across the actions of multiple institutional actors is yet another related avenue of research that is worth exploring in future studies (Battilana et al. 2009).

Conclusions

This study shows that entrepreneurs pursue the legitimacy of their organizations by employing particular claims articulated through discursive strategies. While some of the claims conform to the institutional context, others are presented as distinctive from this context. However, the same discursive strategies are employed to present both conformity and distinctiveness, which tones down the opposition between these. Furthermore, this research shows that narratives present these opposing claims as complementary parts of a broader and temporally sequenced account. This study also reveals that discursive conformity or distinctiveness can potentially be developed in implicit terms. When there are understandings on some aspects of a field's activities that are not yet taken for granted and widespread, the judgment of conformity or distinctiveness will be formed against the backdrop of one's own awareness of the field's evolving expectations. Thus, entrepreneurs can present their organizations according to their understanding of particular audiences' expectations, in order to conform to or be distinctive from the field, in the view of those audiences.

This research also highlights the fact that the discursive pursuit of legitimacy is grounded and potentiated in the materiality of communication media. In particular, the materiality of websites and the qualities that it supports were found to be especially well suited to this pursuit. Endurance over time and space, editability, hyper-intertextuality and multimodality are key qualities that prominently sustain the legitimation of new organizations in contemporary markets as well as the potential of these firms' communication to influence the overall discursive construction of fields.

References

Alvesson, M., & Sköldberg, K. (2009). *Reflexive methodology: New vistas for qualitative research*. London: Sage Publications.

Barros, M. (2014). Tools of legitimacy: The case of the Petrobras Corporate Blog. *Organization Studies, 35*(8), 1211–1230.

Barry, D., & Elmes, M. (1997). Strategy retold: Toward a narrative view of strategic discourse. *Academy of Management Review, 22*(2), 429–452.

Battilana, J., Leca, B., & Boxenbaum, E. (2009). How actors change institutions: Towards a theory of institutional entrepreneurship. *The Academy of Management Annals, 3*(1), 65–107.

Bitektine, A. (2011). Toward a theory of social judgments of organizations: The case of legitimacy, reputation, and status. *Academy of Management Review, 36*, 151–179.

Castelló, I., Etter, M., & Årup Nielsen, F. (2016). Strategies of legitimacy through social media: The networked strategy. *Journal of Management Studies, 53*(3), 402–432.

Cornelissen, J. P., Durand, R., Fiss, P. C., Lammers, J. C., & Vaara, E. (2015). Putting communication front and center in institutional theory and analysis. *Academy of Management Review, 40*(1), 10–27.

Coupland, C., & Brown, A. D. (2004). Constructing organizational identities on the web: A case study of Royal Dutch/Shell. *Journal of Management Studies, 41*(8), 1325–1347.

Czarniawska, B., & Joerges, B. (1996). Travel of ideas. In B. Czarniawska & G. Sevón (Eds.), *Translating organizational change* (pp. 13–48). Berlin: De gruyter.

De Clercq, D., & Voronov, M. (2009). The role of domination in newcomers' legitimation as entrepreneurs. *Organization, 16*(6), 799–827.

de Vaujany, F. X., & Vaast, E. (2013). If these walls could talk: The mutual construction of organizational space and legitimacy. *Organization Science, 25*(3), 713–731.

de Vaujany, F. X., & Vaast, E. (2014). Dual iconographies and legitimation practices in contemporary organizations: A tale of the former NATO command room. In F. X. de Vaujany, N. Mitev, P. Laniray, & E. Vaast (Eds.), *Materiality and time* (pp. 33–58). Hampshire: Palgrave Macmillan.

Deephouse, D. L. (1996). Does isomorphism legitimate? *Academy of Management Journal, 39*(4), 1024–1039.

DiMaggio, P., & Powell, W. W. (1983). The iron cage revisited: Institutional isomorphism and collective rationality in organizational fields. *American Sociological Review, 48*, 147–160.

Fischer, E., & Reuber, A. R. (2014). Online entrepreneurial communication: Mitigating uncertainty and increasing differentiation via Twitter. *Journal of Business Venturing, 29*(4), 565–583.

Fisher, G., Kotha, S., & Lahiri, A. (2015). Changing with the times: An integrated view of identity, legitimacy and new venture lifecycles. *Academy of Management Review, 41*(3), 383–409.

Garud, R., Schildt, H. A., & Lant, T. K. (2014). Entrepreneurial storytelling, future expectations, and the paradox of legitimacy. *Organization Science, 25*(5), 1479–1492.

Graves, O. F., Flesher, D. L., & Jordan, R. E. (1996). Pictures and the bottom line: The television epistemology of U.S. annual reports. *Accounting, Organizations and Society, 21*(1), 57–88.

Jones, C., & Massa, F. G. (2013). From novel practice to consecrated exemplar: Unity Temple as a case of institutional evangelizing. *Organization Studies, 34*(8), 1099–1136.

Jones, C., Boxenbaum, E., & Anthony, C. (2013). The immaterial of the material in institutional logics. *Research in the Sociology of Organizations, 39*, 51–75.

Kallinikos, J., Aaltonen, A., & Marton, A. (2013). The ambivalent ontology of digital artifacts. *MIS Quarterly, 37*(2), 357–370.

King, B. G., & Whetten, D. A. (2008). Rethinking the relationship between reputation and legitimacy: A social actor conceptualization. *Corporate Reputation Review, 11*(3), 192–207.

Kress, G. (2010). *Multimodality: A social semiotic approach to contemporary communication*. Abingdon: Routledge.

Kress, G., & Van Leeuwen, T. (1996). *Reading images*. London: Routledge.

Kress, G., & Van Leeuwen, T. (2001). *Multimodal discourse: The modes and media of contemporary communication*. London: Arnold.

Kornberger, M., & Clegg, S. (2011). Strategy as performative practice: The case of Sydney 2030. *Strategic Organization, 9*(2), 136–162.

Kuorikoski, J. (2015). *Finnish video games. A history and catalogue*. Jefferson: McFarland & Company, Inc.

Lammers, J. C., & Barbour, J. B. (2006). An institutional theory of organizational communication. *Communication Theory, 16*(3), 356–377.

Lawrence, T. B., Suddaby, R., & Leca, B. (Eds.). (2009). *Institutional work: Actors and agency in institutional studies of organization* (pp. 1–28). Cambridge: Cambridge University Press.

Leonardi, P. (2010). Digital materiality? How artifacts without matter, matter. *First Monday, 15*(6), 1–15.

Leonardi, P. (2012). Materiality, sociomateriality, and socio-technical systems: What do these terms mean? How are they different? Do we need them? In P. M. Leonardi, B. A. Nardi, & J. Kallinikos (Eds.), *Materiality and organizing: Social interaction in a technological world* (pp. 25–48). Oxford: Oxford University Press.

Lounsbury, M., & Glynn, M. A. (2001). Cultural entrepreneurship: Stories, legitimacy, and the acquisition of resources. *Strategic Management Journal, 22*, 545–564.

Lounsbury, M., Ventresca, M., & Hirsch, P. M. (2003). Social movements, field frames and industry emergence: A cultural–political perspective on US recycling. *Socio-Economic Review, 1*(1), 71–104.

Martens, M. L., Jennings, J. E., & Jennings, P. D. (2007). Do the stories they tell get them the money they need? The role of entrepreneurial narratives in resource acquisition. *Academy of Management Journal, 50*(5), 1107–1132.

Meyer, J. W., & Rowan, B. (1977). Institutionalized organizations: Formal structure as myth and ceremony. *American Journal of Sociology, 83*(2), 340–363.

Meyer, R. E., Höllerer, M. A., Jancsary, D., & Van Leeuwen, T. (2013). The visual dimension in organizing, organization, and organization research: Core ideas, current developments, and promising avenues. *The Academy of Management Annals, 7*(1), 489–555.

Meyer, R. E., Jancsary, D., Höllerer, M. A., & Boxenbaum, E. (2018). The role of verbal and visual text in the process of institutionalization. *Academy of Management Review, 43(3)*, 392–418.

Navis, C., & Glynn, M. A. (2011). Legitimate distinctiveness and the entrepreneurial identity: Influence on investor judgments of new venture plausibility. *Academy of Management Review, 36*(3), 479–499.

Nicholls, A. (2010). The legitimacy of social entrepreneurship: Reflexive isomorphism in a pre-paradigmatic field. *Entrepreneurship Theory and Practice, 34*(4), 611–633.

Orlikowski, W. J. (2007). Sociomaterial practices: Exploring technology at work. *Organization Studies, 28*(9), 1435–1448.

Phillips, N., & Oswick, C. (2012). Organizational discourse: Domains, debates, and directions. *The Academy of Management Annals, 6*(1), 435–481.

Phillips, N., Lawrence, T. B., & Hardy, C. (2004). Discourse and institutions. *Academy of Management Review, 29*(4), 635–652.

Polkinghorne, D. E. (1987). *Narrative knowing and the human sciences.* Albany: State University of New York Press.

Santos, F. P., Burghausen, M., & Balmer, J. M. (2016). Heritage branding orientation: The case of Ach. Brito and the dynamics between corporate and product heritage brands. *Journal of Brand Management, 23*(1), 67–88.

Scott, W. R. (1995). *Institutions and organizations.* Thousand Oaks: Sage.

Suchman, M. C. (1995). Managing legitimacy: Strategic and institutional approaches. *Academy of Management Review, 20*(3), 729–757.

Suchman, L. (2000). Organizing alignment: A case of bridge-building. *Organization, 7*(2), 311–327.

Tan, J., Shao, Y., & Li, W. (2013). To be different, or to be the same? An exploratory study of isomorphism in the cluster. *Journal of Business Venturing, 28*(1), 83–97.

Tolbert, P. S., David, R. J., & Sine, W. D. (2011). Studying choice and change: The intersection of institutional theory and entrepreneurship research. *Organization Science, 22*(5), 1332–1344.

Treem, J. W., & Leonardi, P. M. (2012). Social media use in organizations: Exploring the affordances of visibility, editability, persistence, and association. *Communication Yearbook, 36*, 143–189.

Überbacher, F. (2014). Legitimation of new ventures: A review and research programme. *Journal of Management Studies, 51*(4), 667–698.

Vaara, E., & Monin, P. (2010). A recursive perspective on discursive legitimation and organizational action in mergers and acquisitions. *Organization Science, 21*(1), 3–22.

Vaara, E., Sonenshein, S., & Boje, D. (2016). Narratives as sources of stability and change in organizations: Approaches and directions for future research. *The Academy of Management Annals, 10*(1), 495–560.

Vaara, E., Tienari, J., & Laurila, J. (2006). Pulp and paper fiction: On the discursive legitimation of global industrial restructuring. *Organization Studies, 27*(6), 789–813.

Van Leeuwen, T. (2007). Legitimation in discourse and communication. *Discourse & Communication, 1*(1), 91–112.

Van Leeuwen, T., & Wodak, R. (1999). Legitimizing immigration control: A discourse-historical analysis. *Discourse Studies, 1*(1), 83–118.

van Werven, R., Bouwmeester, O., & Cornelissen, J. P. (2015). The power of arguments: How entrepreneurs convince stakeholders of the legitimate distinctiveness of their ventures. *Journal of Business Venturing, 30*(4), 616–631.

Volkoff, O., Strong, D. M., & Elmes, M. B. (2007). Technological embeddedness and organizational change. *Organization Science, 18*(5), 832–848.

Voronov, M., De Clercq, D., & Hinings, C. R. (2013). Conformity and distinctiveness in a global institutional framework: The legitimation of Ontario fine wine. *Journal of Management Studies, 50*(4), 607–645.

Zhao, E. Y., Fisher, G., Lounsbury, M., & Miller, D. (2016). Optimal distinctiveness revisited: Broadening the interface between institutional theory and strategic management. *Strategic Management Journal, 38*(1), 93–113.

Zucker, L. G. (1977). The role of institutionalization in cultural persistence. *American Sociological Review, 42*, 726–743.

9

Material Conflict: MOOCs and Institutional Logics in Business Education

Anna Morgan-Thomas, Agostinho Abrunhosa, and J. Ignacio Canales

Introduction

Although the notion of incompatibility is implicit in the research on conflicting institutional logics, few studies explicitly address it (Goodrick and Salancik 1996; Pache and Santos 2010) and little is known about the origin of conflicts (Greenwood et al. 2011). The chapter draws on the concept of materiality and theories of digital objects to explain how materiality affects the organizational templates and reasons for the conflict. The context of this chapter is Massive Open Online Course

A. Morgan-Thomas (✉) • A. Abrunhosa
Adam Smith Business School, University of Glasgow, Glasgow, Scotland
e-mail: Anna.Morgan-Thomas@glasgow.ac.uk; a.abrunhosa.1@research.gla.ac.uk

J. Ignacio Canales
Business School of the University of Aberdeen, Aberdeen, UK
e-mail: ignacio.canales@abdn.ac.uk

© The Author(s) 2019   **255**
F.-X. de Vaujany et al. (eds.), *Materiality in Institutions*, Technology, Work and
Globalization, https://doi.org/10.1007/978-3-319-97472-9_9

(MOOC) that contradicts the conventional organizing templates in Business Schools (BSs), but it emerges as a powerful force regardless. The focus on digital materiality (Ekbia 2009; Faulkner and Runde 2013; Kallinikos et al. 2013) helps clarify the current confusion concerning materiality as a concept and its role in institutional logics. Of importance is that we juxtapose and reconcile the substance of the physical matter and the substantive mattering of matter and that this treatment enhances the definition and the theoretical boundaries of the concept. The enhanced and more active role of materiality in institutional logics, which includes material orchestration of logics, is also proposed.

Despite significant research interest in conflicting institutional logics (Battilana and Dorado 2010; Fincham and Forbes 2015; Nicolini et al. 2016; Pache and Santos 2010, 2013a), the nature of conflict has received limited attention (Greenwood et al. 2011). The lack of precision concerning incompatibility of logics, its source, severity and consequences for the organizations is problematic for several reasons. If logics are indeed incompatible, then the presence and persistence of a growing number of hybrid organizations represents an inherent paradox (Fan and Zietsma 2017; Greenwood et al. 2011). Conversely, if conflicting logics may be successfully combined and reconfigured, as some research on hybrid forms suggest (Batista et al. 2015; Santos et al. 2015; Reay and Hinings 2009; Schildt and Perkmann 2017; Smets et al. 2012), then the whole notion of incompatibility of logics becomes questionable (Greenwood et al. 2011). To resolve these inconsistencies, further research into the incompatibility of logics and its sources seems urgently needed.[1]

This chapter addresses this gap. Specifically, building on the concept of materiality (Jones et al. 2013; Leonardi 2012) and theories of digital objects (Ekbia 2009; Faulkner and Runde 2009, 2013; Kallinikos et al. 2013), the chapter explores the material sources of conflicting logics. The

[1] In Chap. 5, Lise Arena and Ali Douai offer a complementary perspective on competing logics in Business Education. They explore the emergence of co-existing but competing logics through the history of Oxford University campus and the building of Saïd Business School. Through their investigation of space, they show how materiality fosters the hybridization of seemingly orthogonal institutional logics. That said, Chap. 5 explores institutional changes on a much longer time horizon, for example, several decades.

chapter focuses on the introduction of MOOCs in the teaching portfolio of commercial European Business Schools (EBSs). MOOCs are online courses that are aimed at an unlimited audience and accessible to any participant anywhere at any time (Ong and Grigoryan 2015). Like other types of e-learning, MOOCs typically include posted online resources such as videos of lectures, readings and problem sets (Anderson 2015). The key difference between MOOCs and traditional e-learning is that a typical online course has students registered to a particular institution, whereas MOOCs are open to anyone. The unlimited access denotes the underlying foundations in the open source movement and the related principles of free access, equality, connectivity, autonomy and diversity (Fournier et al. 2014).

The introduction of MOOCs in EBSs offers an excellent opportunity for the revision of the approach to conflict in institutional logics. The organizational field of executive education in Europe is characterized by significant tensions between competing goals and means including teaching versus research objectives (Thorpe and Rawlinson 2014; Thomas and Peters 2012), emphasis on applied versus theoretical knowledge (Chia and Holt 2014) and broad educational goals versus commercialism and market orientation (Schoemaker 2008). Unlike the North American model, where BSs tend to be appended to universities, EBSs tend to be stand-alone units (Chap. 5 offers an interesting depiction of Saïd Business School outside the premises of Oxford University campus). Thus, they are more exposed and sensitive to changes in the institutional field (Antunes and Thomas 2007). These organizations operate within a highly specific environment where detailed prescriptions define legitimacy, reputation and rules of behavior. For example, organization's status is highly dependent on its compliance with existing standards (e.g. AACSB, EQUIS, AMBA) and there is limited latitude for discretion in conforming to these criteria (Quinn Trank and Washington 2009).

The advent of MOOCs potentially disrupts existing organizational templates. EBSs have traditionally embraced "exclusivity" logics where substantial premiums are being extracted from tightly controlled access to business education. The exclusivity logic relies on premium pricing and high-quality offer (e.g. low staff–student rations, innovations in teaching, emphasis on premium faculty). By contrast, the emergence of MOOCs is underpinned by a set of radically contrasting principles involving open access to the teaching provision and unlimited participation (Anderson 2015; Finkle and Masters 2014). The ongoing failure to identify sustainable revenue streams from MOOCs presents a particular challenge to EBS whose business models relies on extracting high fees from students. The study of MOOCs in the context of EBSs thus offers an excellent opportunity to examine conflicting logics.

Using the case of MOOCs in EBS, we argue that in highly complex organizational settings, the incompatibility and the subsequent organizational response is best understood by exploring the material sources of competing logics. Though studies have examined sources of logics (Rao et al. 2003; Fincham and Forbes 2015) and the nature of their change (Micelotta et al. 2018), the logic evolution has been rarely linked with materiality (Jones et al. 2013). Past research tended to focus on the work of human actors (Lawrence et al. 2013) and material objects, and more specifically technologies, have been largely been overlooked in institutional work. A recent state-of-the-art review of literature on the institutional change (Micelotta et al. 2018) provides a stark illustration of this point: though recognizing agential and practice turn in institutional change, the review is largely silent about technologies and their implications. This is surprising given technologies' growing prevalence in multiple organizational arenas (Kallinikos 2009; O'Mahony and Ferraro 2007) and their transformative potential for institutions (Hinings et al. 2018). By focusing on MOOCs as digital objects (Ekbia 2009; Faulkner and Runde 2013; Kallinikos et al. 2013), the chapter offers an enhanced conception of materiality and its mattering. It thus contributes to efforts that aim to elevate materiality to a more central theoretical role (Jones et al. 2013). In doing so, the chapter attempts to add clarity to the concept of materiality in the field of organizational complexity and institutional logics (Orlikowski 2000; Morgan-Thomas 2016).

Materiality and Conflicting Institutional Logics

Institutional Logics

Research on institutional logics represents a vibrant and rapidly growing domain in organizational theory (Battilana and Dorado 2010; Fincham and Forbes 2015; Nicolini et al. 2016; Pache and Santos 2010, 2013b). The term "institutional logics" was first introduced by Alford and Friedland (1985) to describe the contradictory beliefs and practices found in contemporary institution and subsequent research applied the concept to show how broader belief systems affect the conduct of social actors. Contemporary conceptualizations depict institutional logics as templates for organizing that outline goals and values in specific domains (Thornton et al. 2012) and define them as "the socially constructed, historical patterns of material practices, assumptions, values, beliefs, and rules by which individuals produce and reproduce their material subsistence, organize time and space, and provide meaning to their social reality" (Thornton and Ocasio 2008, p. 804). Within the organizational field, research on institutional logics has explored the material and symbolic foundations of institutions (Thornton and Ocasio 1999; Thornton 2004), the shifts in institutional logics overtime (Lounsbury 2002; Nicolini et al. 2016; Rao et al. 2003; Thornton 2002) and incompatibility or competing institutional logics (Batista et al. 2015; Pache and Santos 2010; Santos et al. 2015).

The last decade has seen growing interest in conflicting institutional logics as enduring and persistent facets of institutional complexity (Greenwood et al. 2011; Santos et al. 2015). Multiple organizational settings seem to be defined by schisms where significant contrasts concern varying organizing principles (Reay and Hinings 2009; Pache and Santos 2013a) and understanding what is legitimate, reasonable or effective (Fincham and Forbes 2015; Batista et al. 2015). Early studies on institutional logics in particular tended to explore contrasts by focusing on domination and succession of new logics (Rao et al. 2003; Thornton and Ocasio 1999). Past research also examined the organizational response to this complexity within two broad lines of enquiry. The first strand, scholarship concerning hybrid organizing, shows how the conflicting logics affect the organizational structures and practices (e.g. Battilana and

Dorado 2010; Fincham and Forbes 2015; Pache and Santos 2010, 2013a; Santos et al. 2015). The other line of enquiry focuses on organizational coping with complexity and examines organizational work, strategies and approaches for dealing with complexity and addressing temporary evolvement, depth and nature of conflict (Batista et al. 2015; Kraatz and Block 2008; McPherson and Saunder 2013; Pache and Santos 2010).

Considering the nature of conflicts, past studies have offered important insight into the severity and the temporal dimension of conflicts. Conceptions of conflict have juxtaposed the differences between just two logics (Battilana and Dorado 2010; Pache and Santos 2010) and have drawn attention to the existence of multiple logics (McPherson and Sauder 2013; Smets et al. 2015). Though tensions may be temporarily resolved with settlements involving specific configurations of organizational structures (Greenwood et al. 2011; Smets et al. 2015) and the accompanying changes in members' conceptions of the norms and practices (Schildt and Perkmann 2017), conflicts may be severe and permanent facet of organizing involving an ongoing effort to cope (Kraatz and Block 2008). Such permanent, pervasive and sustained conflicts are frequently found in fields formed around issues that are inherently cross-jurisdictional (Zietsma et al. 2017) where tensions emerge from conflicting prescriptions (Ansari et al. 2013), diverse expectations of multiple actors involved (Reay and Hinings 2009) and varied understanding of the filed logics (Fan and Zietsma 2017; Zilber 2002).

Although the notion of incompatibility is implicit in research on conflicting logics, few studies explicitly define and address incompatibility of logics. Frequently, incompatibility is implicitly assumed and simply conveyed with adjectives such as "contested", "conflicting" or "competing" (Greenwood et al. 2011). Theorization relies on descriptions of contrasts as reflected by tasks, practices or roles (Reay and Hinings 2005; Thornton 2002, 2004). Admittedly, some studies have attempted to add precision to the degree of incompatibility, for example, Pache and Santos (2010) distinguish between conflicting goals or means to suggest that conflicts between goals are particularly challenging. The specificity and sources of conflicting logics have also received some attention and past studies suggest that contrasts between logics may be tempered by ambiguity concerning the conflicting templates (Goodrick and Salancik 1996; Thornton and Ocasio 2008).

Logic Incompatibility and Materiality

The study of incompatibility has drawn attention to the substantive content of institutional logics. Thornton and Ocasio (2008) have argued that the comparative conflict or conformity of institutional logics are reflected in both material and cultural characteristics of logics and that logics encompass both "material" and "symbolic" dimension (Thornton and Ocasio 1999; Thornton et al. 2012). The symbolic dimension captures informal, largely invisible and intangible elements such as norms, beliefs, ideation, symbols and meaning. By contrast, the material dimension includes more tangible and formal elements and includes structures and practices. Structures focus on formal rules, roles, units and patterns of their relationships, whereas practices denote activities, skills and knowledge enacted in roles (Jones et al. 2013; Townley 2002). Following Thornton and Ocasio (1999), the dominant conception of materiality in institutional logic research is narrow and encompasses structures and practices (Jones et al. 2013).

Despite the ostensive labeling, the "material" elements of institutional logics have rarely included material objects and the physical materiality of logics has been largely ignored (Jones et al. 2013). Rather, the mainstream research considers "material" to denote "mattering"; practices and structures are considered material through they are, arguably, ideological entities lacking physicality and substance (Jones et al. 2013). The absence of objects is surprising because objects are implicated in practices, that is, "practices operate through and on objects" (Friedland 2013, p. 37) and "when materials change, role relations and practices may change as well" (Jones et al. 2013, p. 65).

Few recent studies provide an exception to so conceived "materiality" and draw attention physical objects as important anchors of meaning and material manifestations of symbolic logics (Friedland 2013; Jones and Massa 2013). For example, Jones and Massa (2013) have shown that a shift from professional to commercial logic in architecture involved a move from one set of building materials (brick, stone and wood) to another (concrete, steel and glass). The authors argued that physical materials played an essential role in anchoring and institutionalizing new sets of practices and were important vehicles allowing the new ideas and symbols to catalyze, stabilize and spread.

Missing Materiality as a Pivotal Concept

Though the explicit recognition of materiality has begun to emerge as a theme within institutional logic (Friedland 2013; Jones and Massa 2013; Jones et al. 2012), past research has largely sidelined the material dimension (Jones et al. 2013). In fact, the review of literature shows three important gaps.

Firstly, physical objects remain largely invisible or peripheral to the analyses. Though multiple studies illustrate how changes in logics go hand in hand with objects such as educational textbooks (Thornton and Ocasio 1999), meals (Rao et al. 2003), musical instruments (Glynn 2000), money (Lounsbury 2007) and fuel (Hargadon and Douglas 2001), theoretical explanations that link objects and logics are largely absent. In fact, studies tend to place materials in the background of analyses and bring to the forefront theoretical explanations that do not encompass materiality. To illustrate, Rao et al.'s (2003) analysis of nouvelle cuisine has relied on the identity movements theory and has paid limited attention to the very objects (food ingredients, meals and menus) implicated in the new practices. Similar peripheral treatment of objects can be found in analysis by Hargadon and Douglas (2001), who examined the shift from gas to electricity logic and used the theoretical lens of design processes and technological systems to explain institutional change. Considering the focal position of objects in the emergence of new logics (Rao et al. 2003; Jones and Massa 2013) and their mattering for practices (Friedland 2013; Jones et al. 2013), the peripheral treatment of objects and the lack of conceptual definitions of materiality represent important oversights (for additional detail regarding the implications of a lack of conceptualization of materiality, please refer to the introduction of the book, Chap. 1).

Second, when physical materiality enters institutional logics, it tends to make a largely passive contribution and the mattering of matter is reactive to logics. A typical metaphor evoked to describe the role of objects is that of an anchor: objects reflect, embed or symbolically manifest institutional logics (Jones and Massa 2013). Though material manifestations unquestionably contribute to the spread and durability of institutions, the relationship between matter and logic is reactive in that logics precede materials and materials follow by instantiating logics and making them durable. Some current conceptualization of objects seems to go beyond this passive status and Friedland (2013), for example, argues that practices within institutional logics revolve around objects and that objects are not only the means of anchoring but also instruments of institutional change, the means by which practices are affected and oriented (Friedland 2013, p. 37). Thus, for Friedland (2013), material objects are pivoting points for the practices. As such, objects can be understood as an important extension of, and a necessary condition for, the practices and structures that scholars associate with the materiality of logics (Thornton and Ocasio 2008). This extended conception of the role of objects seems missing from the current research and yet to emerge is the analytical treatment of objects that acknowledges not only the material manifestation of logics but also the material orchestration of logics. We concur with Jones et al. (2013) in saying that a greater analytical emphasis on objects accompanied by a more active conception of their role would benefit future research on institutional logics.

Third, the research on institutional logics largely ignores one class of objects: digital technologies. That is, on rare occasion, such technologies may enter an institutional logic study to form a backdrop for analysis and be "absently present" (see Hinings et al. 2018). Past research on finance sector (Lounsbury 2007) or publishing (Thornton and Ocasio 1999) illustrates this treatment. Recent theoretical calls for greater attention to materiality explicitly recognize digital technologies and refer to digital objects such as Wikis and blogs (Jones et al. 2013), software (Friedland 2013) or computers (Jones et al. 2013). Though there seems some evidence of emerging interest in digital objects (O'Mahony and Ferraro 2007), large institutional scholarship has tended not to provide explicit treatment of digital technology. The avoidance may be understandable given the institutional prerogative to eschew technological determinism (Thornton et al. 2012). Nonetheless, digital technologies increasingly permeate organization in multiple institutional fields (Kallinikos 2009; Orlikowski and Scott 2008) and there is growing evidence of saturation of multiple organizational practices with information and communication technologies (ICTs)

(Kallinikos et al. 2013; Yoo et al. 2012). Given these trends, it seems imperative to account for digital objects and not to "shy away from trying to specify how materials underpin practices" (Jones et al. 2013 p. 65). Furthermore, considering that digital objects have been co-implicated in the emergence of new organizational forms and new ways of organizing (Boland et al. 2007; Yoo et al. 2010), and that broader research in management has examined both their symbolic role and the impact on practices (Kallinikos and Mariátegui 2011), digital technology seems a potentially fertile ground for institutional logics research.

Given the paucity of object and technology research, we argue that the analysis of digital technologies may foster conceptual refinement of the content of logics, sources of conflict and the material and symbolic aspects of practice. Most importantly, the analysis of digital technologies has the potential to clarify the status of "matter" in institutional logics because the discussions of materiality of digital objects (Ekbia 2009; Faulkner and Runde 2009) seem to echo the tensions between physical and non-physical materiality in institutional research (Jones et al. 2013). Specifically, the debate mirrors the contrasts between physical materiality, as advocated by Jones et al. (2013) and the non-physical mattering, as advanced by Thornton and Ocasio (2008). The lack of fit provides an excellent opportunity for further elaboration of the content of logics and the sources of conflict.

We propose to bring intangible nonetheless material digital objects into the theoretical realm of institutional logics. Using the case of European Business schools, their educational provision and focusing on one type of digital object, MOOC, we illustrate a shift in institutional logics. The object-centered shift in logic relies on non-physical yet material object (MOOC) and involves incompatibility and change in roles, structures and practices. Building on theories of digital objects, we explore how MOOCs re-orchestrate the institutional logic in business schools. To understand these implications, the following section explores digital materiality from the perspective of MOOCs, shows how materiality drives conflict and contrasts conventional organizational templates with new templates.

MOOCs, Materiality and Conflicting Logics

Digital Materiality

To understand materiality of MOOCs, it is helpful to engage with material properties of digital objects. We draw on theories of digital objects to elaborate on these properties (Ekbia, 2009; Faulkner and Runde 2009; Kallinikos et al. 2013). MOOCs can be categorized as digital artifacts, that is, man-made technological objects of non-physical nature (Ekbia 2009; Faulkner and Runde 2009). Whereas physical objects such as textbooks, buildings or meals have physical properties (i.e. form, shape, size, color and mass), the digital objects are syntactic entities composed of software codes (Faulkner and Runde 2013). For example, MOOCs consist of digital video lectures, interactive problems, images, presentations, online laboratories, discussion forums, text files, sound files and other digital objects (Breslow et al. 2013; Ong and Grigoryan 2015).

Similar to other syntactic objects, for example, websites or social media (Treem and Leonardi 2012), MOOCs have materiality that is not dependent on their physicality. Software codes can be inscribed, copied, shared and accessed from multiple devices (PCs, laptops, tablets or mobile phones) often simultaneously (Faulkner and Runde 2009). Though the physical devices are necessary for users to engage with digital objects, the implications of MOOCs, or their mattering for practice, derive from their non-physical properties and functionalities offered by software codes (Leonardi 2012). Codes enable creation, storage, editing, accessing and sharing of digital components such as online text, video, discussion boards and forums, all of which come together to generate a MOOC. All these objects are material in that they channel actions: some actions are made possible and others impossible or at least more difficult to achieve (Leonardi 2012). Similar to other syntactic entities (apps, social media, web pages or digitized images), MOOCs materiality is non-physical because it derives directly from the syntactic nature of a computer code. In sum, an important distinguishing feature of MOOCs is that their material features, the elements that have implications for practice, are non-physical and that the physicality is very loosely, if at all, implicated in the material outcomes of the object.[2]

Conceptually, the mattering of MOOCs for educational practices may be captured using the notion of affordance (Gibson 1986; Hutchby 2001). In the context of digital objects such as MOOCs, affordances represent possibilities for outcomes that derive from the use of a tool (Leonardi 2013; Volkoff and Strong 2013). Though affordances are tied to technologies—a piece of technology affords to achieve certain ends—they are neither the intrinsic properties of an object nor its users but emerge when the two interact (Leonardi 2012). From an ontological perspective, an affordance is a feature of the relationship between technology and its user, a concept that may help explain the generative mechanisms behind technology in use (Volkoff and Strong 2013).

Material implications of MOOCs are linked with the unique features of digital objects (Ekbia 2009; Faulkner and Runde 2009; Kallinikos et al. 2013; Treem and Leonardi 2012) and their affordances. Similar to other digital objects, MOOCs are editable and can be easily and relatively effortlessly modified and updated. Editability ties with modularity in that MOOCs consist of components (text, images, videos) and functionalities (programs and procedures) that are interchangeable and loosely coupled. The confluence of editability and modularity create the seemingly infinite possibilities of recombination, change or variation that contribute to rapid expansion of digital objects. Furthermore, MOOCs are interactive in that they offer a range of possibilities for action: users can activate functions or explore the content, they can browse, read, download, post, share or communicate. Finally, MOOCs are distributed, borderless and open and MOOC is seldom contained in a single source or institution. Rather, MOOC and is best conceptualized as a transient and temporary assembly *"made up of functions, information items or components spread over information infrastructures and the internet"* (Kallinikos et al. 2013, p. 360).

---

[2] Chapter 1—introduction—provides additional detail about the debate on the porosity of the different kinds of materiality, in particular objects and digitality. Besides, digitality being dependent on physical artifacts implies that information is not only shared in digital spaces and platforms but also accessible through multiple, mobile devices. Such porosity thereby sophisticates the transferability of materiality. In the postface of the book, Candace Jones provides insightful discussion on the transferability of materiality.

MOOCs and the Dominant Institutional Logic of EBS

The material properties of MOOCs as digital objects have implications for the symbolic and material content of logics in business school education. According to the dominant organizational template, an EBS is a market-oriented (Schoemaker 2008) and stand-alone entity (Antunes and Thomas 2007) that offers campus-based management education. Its main purpose is to train people in the practice of management as a profession and to develop new knowledge that may be relevant for improving the operation of organizations (Gordon and Howell 1959). As EBS pursues its main objective, it sustains itself by attracting a body of premium fee-paying students (Crainer and Dearlove 1999). This task is helped by reputation and accomplished by providing a tightly bundled and controlled offer that encompasses curriculum design, educational content, assessment, certification, employability and admissions.

The bundle is tightly controlled by the institution in response to stringent and detailed standards set by accrediting bodies such as EQUIS, AACSB or AMBA (Quinn Trank and Washington 2009). These standards drive cultural values such as academic value in the creation and dissemination of new knowledge or social value in generating graduates that have the potential to make significant contribution to organizations and societies (Hay 2008). Selectivity and premium fees mean that business schools are vehicles of social mobility (Crainer and Dearlove 1999) and play a significant role in the creation of elite networks (Hugstad 1983; Van Baalen and Moratis 2001). They are organized around material templates that set expectations concerning the content of logics that determine roles (teachers, researchers, administrative support) and practices (teaching, assessment, admissions, quality control).

The dominant EBS template appears in stark contrast with the new educational logics brought about by MOOCs. Aside from the difference in reliance on face-to-face (EBS) versus online delivery of courses (MOOCs), the main contrast between MOOCs and other online courses concerns enrollment and participation. Whereas the latter have students registered to a particular institution, MOOCs are available and open to anyone (Finkle and Masters 2014). MOOCs commonly do not have the application process and there is no requirement for a learner to apply for registration and therefore no possibility of rejection. Learners are free to decide if they meet the stated prior learning requirements (or ignore them). Similarly, students may easily ignore the structure of the learning tasks recommended by the course designer. Therefore, one might perceive MOOCs as free from the institutional constraints that a traditional EBS system imposes.

Considering the symbolic content of logics, MOOCs are associated with diametrically different social purposes based on the principles of free access, equality, connectivism and collaboration. For example, Yuan and Powell (2013) observe that "the development of MOOCs is rooted within the ideals of openness in education, that knowledge should be shared freely, and the desire to learn should be met without demographic, economic, and geographical constraints" (p. 6). The implicit link between MOOCs and open source movement entails the principle no-fee or near-no-free access to exclusive institution courses and instructors (Liu et al. 2014). These radical principles contrast sharply with the notion of profit-generating private business school (Crainer and Dearlove 1999). Unsurprising, the economic model behind MOOCs has received much attention within and beyond business school (Carruth and Carruth 2013; Dellarocas and Van Alstyne 2013; Hollands and Tirthali 2014; White et al. 2014).

From the perspective of the material content of an organizational template (Thornton and Ocasio 1999), MOOCs have implications for roles, structures and practices. For example, this mode of learning potentially unbundles educational offerings (Finkle and Masters 2014) and traditionally integrated functions such as research, curriculum design, educational content and resources, assessment and certification become separated and new roles emerge. In the process, teaching practices receive more attention and there is elevated appreciation for the profession of teaching, with the emphasis on learning processes as well as the development and design of courses (Daniel 2012; Firmin et al. 2014). MOOCs necessitate organizational adjustment and rearrangement of roles: learning technologists and instructional designers typically take center stage in the planning, design and execution of courses (Veletsianos and Shepherdson 2015). The focal role of a lecturer as the key architect and hierarchically most dominant contributor to learning may become eroded and lecturing staffs may be relegated to "subject matter experts" that sit alongside "technology" experts. The unbundling opens the possibility of offering new bundles of educational services within institutions but also potentially broadens the supply of courses to include pan-institutional provision and services from non-educational organizations in the private and not-for-profit sectors (Finkle and Masters 2014). Largely unregulated and evolving, MOOCs undermine conventional quality assessment structures (Margaryan et al. 2015).

In summary, when viewed from the perspective of institutional logics, the materiality of MOOCs seems directly implicated in the conflict of logics. The material properties of MOOCs, such as their open and distributed nature, editability, interactivity and modularity, offer a set of possibilities for actions that affect practices and in turn drive specific new templates for organizing business education. These properties provide the foundation for the incompatibility of logics and the source of conflict which, incidentally, encompasses both the organizational goals and the means. MOOCs affect both the ideological aspects of the institutional template (goals, values and principles) as well as it material content (roles, structures and practices). Moreover, the role of digital objects is not limited to a passive anchor or carrier of logics, as suggested by past research (Jones et al. 2013). Rather, digital objects generate conflict and actively orchestrate organizational templates, an issue thus overlooked in logic research.

Discussion

The chapter argues that MOOCs provide a fertile context for the examination of the sources of conflict in organizational templates. Building on the theories of digital objects, the chapter shows how traditional templates are affected by the emergence of new template and how the new template derives from material properties of digital objects. The digital materiality of MOOCs is instrumental in generating conflicts with the existing principles of organizing. The case of MOOCs in EBS offers important implications for the conceptualization of materiality and its relationship with institutional logics. The implications concern the origins of conflict, the content of logics and the shift in logics and pertain to the conception of materiality and its role in institutional logics.

New Conceptualization of Materiality

The case of MOOCs shows that materiality, in this case, the digital materiality of MOOCs, is intrinsically implicated in logic because it is closely tied to practices, roles and structures (Friedland 2013). Past studies have shown that changes in logics go hand in hand with objects and the examples include educational textbooks (Thornton and Ocasio 1999), meals (Rao et al. 2003) and musical instruments (Glynn 2000). In parallel to the past treatment of materiality in institutional logics (Jones et al. 2013), the case of MOOCs illustrates that objects may be central to the development of new institutional logics. In addition, it demonstrates that objects need not be material in a physical sense to affect logics and that non-physical objects such as MOOCs affect practices. By recognizing non-physical materiality, the arguments here are analogous to prior literature that focused on the role of syntactic objects in the context of changing organizational practices (D'Adderio 2011; Leonardi 2011).

In stressing the implications of digital materiality for logics, the chapter makes important theoretical contribution in re-conceptualizing materiality and clarifying its meaning. Past treatment of materiality in institutional logics has tended to overlook objects (Jones et al. 2013). This is largely because the notion of "material practice" advanced by Thornton and Ocasio (1999) had both equated materiality with significance and emphasized the importance of roles and structures as the "material" emblems of institutional logics. Although this conception of materiality as mattering is well aligned with the definition adopted in the current chapter (see e.g. Leonardi 2012), its application in institutional theory has paradoxically led to the oversight of matter in institutional theory. As a consequence, past research has tended to focus on "material practices" with corresponding emphasis on practices and structures accordingly (see Jones et al. 2013). This conception has left a limited space for objects in institutional logics and though they are present in analyses, they seem to be of limited conceptual interest.

A key implication of digital objects for institutional logics is that they invite an urgent review of the status of "material". A closer reading of the extant literature uncovers two contrasting approaches to materiality. On the one hand, Thornton and Ocasio's (1999) conception aligns with "material" as conveying the quality of being relevant or significant. On the other hand, for Jones et al. (2013) and Friedland (2013), the meaning of materiality closely relates to physicality and the material properties of objects. For them, materiality denotes physicality and captures the quality of being composed of matter and having physical properties of form, shape, mass, consistency, color and so on.

Like other non-physical objects, MOOCs do not seem to fit either definition. They are objects and therefore separate and independent from "material practices" outlined by Thornton and Ocasio (1999). Simultaneously, they are non-physical objects and their mattering cannot be tied to physical properties (see Jones and Massa 2013). To accommodate MOOCs, the definition of materiality must concurrently align with the notion of mattering as being relevant and significant (Thornton and Ocasio 1999) and as being an object: implicated in practice but nonetheless different from and exceeding the roles and structures (Jones et al. 2013). In other words, MOOCs imply re-conceptualization of materiality of objects that is not tied to their physicality. We argue that to enhance the conception of materiality, institutional logic may follow a definition of materiality derived from the theories of digital objects, which confers materiality as an implication of an object for practice that is independent from the objects physicality. The definition offers a broader conception of objects but also a flexible notion of mattering (Faulkner and Runde 2013). So conceived materiality may enable future institutional logic research to re-focus on and more easily accommodate objects, including non-physical objects.[3]

---

[3] Other proposals for materiality re-conceptualization can be found in this book. In Chap. 12, François-Xavier de Vaujany identifies three ontological avenues of legitimacy, including the ontology of sculpture and the ontology of bubbles. In the postface, Candace Jones proposes to view materiality as a carrier or through its performative role.

New Role of Materiality as an Orchestrator of Institutional Logics

Embracing a broader definition of materiality may also enhance the role of objects in institutional logics. Past studies on the implications of objects for institutional logics have focused on the passive role of objects and argued that objects largely anchor logics, that is, reflect organizational values, goals and organizing principle (Jones and Massa 2013). The discussions surrounding MOOCs and their implications for higher education suggest a different, more proactive notion of objects mattering (see Breslow et al. 2013; Finkle and Masters 2014). According to theories of digital objects, objects may play a much more active role in orchestrating practices (Faulkner and Runde 2013).

Admittedly, this broader role falls short of technological determinism, but it does not mean that objects directly influence institutional logics. Research on the institutional adoption of MOOCs illustrates that the technological possibilities do not necessarily translate into new practices, and that adoption may be limited and partial (Ong and Grigoryan 2015). Nonetheless, there seems an interplay between the objects and practices and by being implicated in practices, objects do more than just reflect it (Leonardi 2013; Orlikowski and Scott 2008). MOOCs' abilities to facilitate and constrain a broad range of activities implicated in learning and teaching offer new opportunities for educational practices and generate educational practices of a new kind. Stopping short of technological determinism, we concur with Friedland (2013), who argues that material practices revolve around objects, "which are the means by which practices are anchored, affected and oriented" (Friedland 2013, p. 37), and that objects are important because institutional logics necessarily "bind value, practice and object" (Friedland 2013, p. 37). The permeation of digital objects in multiple domains and at various frontiers of organizing is not just a facet of "anchoring": we argue that object-centered "orchestration" of logics deserves more attention.

References

Alford, R. R., & Friedland, R. (1985). *Powers of theory: Capitalism, the state, and democracy*. Cambridge: Cambridge University Press.

Anderson, J. Q. (2015). Individualisation of higher education: How technological evolution can revolutionise opportunities for teaching and learning. *International Social Science Journal, 64*(212–214), 305–316.

Ansari, S., Wijen, F., & Gray, B. (2013). Constructing a climate change logic: An institutional perspective on the "tragedy of the commons". *Organization Science, 24*, 1014–1040.

Antunes, D., & Thomas, H. (2007). The competitive (dis)advantages of European Business Schools. *Long Range Planning, 40*(3), 382–404.

Batista, M. G., Clegg, S., Cunha, M. P., Giustiniano, L., & Rego, A. (2015). Improvising prescription: Evidence from the emergency room. *British Journal of Management, 27*(2), 406–425.

Battilana, J., & Dorado, S. (2010). Building sustainable hybrid organizations: The case of commercial microfinance organizations. *Academy of Management Journal, 53*, 1419–1440.

Boland, R. J., Jr., Lyytinen, K., & Yoo, Y. (2007). Wakes of innovation in project networks: The case of digital 3-D representations in architecture, engineering, and construction. *Organizational Science, 18*(4), 631–647.

Breslow, L., Pritchard, D. E., DeBoer, J., Stump, G. S., Ho, A. D., & Seaton, D. T. (2013). Studying learning in the worldwide classroom: Research into edX's first MOOC. *Research & Practice in Assessment, 8*(March), 13–25.

Chia, R., & Holt, R. (2014). The nature of knowledge in business schools. *Academy of Management Learning & Education, 7*(4), 471–486.

Crainer, S., & Dearlove, D. (1999). *Gravy training: Inside the business of business schools*. San Francisco: Jossey-Bass Publishers.

Daniel, J. (2012). Making sense of MOOCs: Musings in a maze of myth, paradox and possibility. *Journal of interactive Media in education, 3*. Available online: https://jime.open.ac.uk/articles/10.5334/2012-18/

D'Adderio, L. (2011). Artifacts at the centre of routines: Performing the material turn in routines theory. *Journal of Institutional Economics, 7*(2), 197–230.

Dellarocas, C., & Van Alstyne, M. (2013). Money models for MOOCs. *Communications of the ACM, 56*(8), 25–28.

Ekbia, H. R. (2009). Digital artifacts as quasi-objects: Qualification, mediation, and materiality. *Journal of the American Society for Information Science and Technology, 60*(12), 2554–2566.

Fan, G. H., & Zietsma, C. (2017). Constructing a shared governance logic: The role of emotions in enabling dually embedded agency. *Academy of Management Journal, 60*(6), 2321–2351.

Faulkner, P., & Runde, J. (2009). On the identity of technological objects and user innovations in function. *Academy of Management Review, 34*(3), 442–462.

Faulkner, P., & Runde, J. (2013). Technological objects, social positions and the transformational model of social activity. *Management Information Systems Quarterly, 37*(3), 803–818.

Fincham, R., & Forbes, T. (2015). Three's a crowd: The role of inter-logic relationships in highly complex institutional fields. *British Journal of Management, 26*(4), 657–670.

Finkle, T. A., & Masters, E. (2014). Do MOOCs pose a threat to higher education? *Research in Higher Education Journal, 26*(1), 1–10.

Firmin, R., Schiorring, E., Whitmer, J., Willett, T., Collins, E. D., & Sujitparapitaya, S. (2014). Case study: Using MOOCs for conventional college coursework. *Distance Education, 35*(2), 178–201.

Friedland, R. (2013). God, love and other good reasons for practice: Thinking through institutional logics. *Research in the Sociology of Organizations, 39A*, 25–50.

Friedland, R., & Alford, R. B. (1991). Bringing society back in: Symbols, practices, and institutional contradictions. In W. W. Powell & P. DiMaggio (Eds.), *The new institutionalism in organizational analysis* (pp. 232–266). Chicago: Chicago University Press.

Fournier, H., Kop, R., & Durand, G. (2014). Challenges to research in MOOCs. *MERLOT Journal of Online Learning and Teaching, 10*(1), 1–15.

Gibson, J. J. (1986). *The ecological approach to visual perception.* Hillsdale: Lawrence Erlbaum Associates.

Glynn, M. A. (2000). When cymbals become symbols: Conflict over organizational identity within a symphony orchestra. *Organization Science, 11*(3), 285–298.

Goodrick, E., & Salancik, G. R. (1996). Organizational discretion in responding to institutional practices: Hospitals and caesarean births. *Administrative Science Quarterly, 41*(1), 1–28.

Gordon, R. A., & Howell, J. E. (1959). Higher education for business. *The Journal of Business Education, 35*(3), 115–117.

Greenwood, R., Raynard, M., Kodeih, F., Micelotta, E. R., & Lounsbury, M. (2011). Institutional complexity and organizational responses. *Academy of Management Annals, 5*, 317–371.

Hargadon, D. B., & Douglas, Y. (2001). When innovations meet institutions: Edison and the design of the electric light. *Administrative Science Quarterly, 46*, 476–501.

Hay, M. (2008). Business schools: A new sense of purpose. *Journal of Management Development, 27*(4), 371–378.

Hinings, B., Gegenhuberb, T., & Greenwood, R. (2018). Digital innovation and transformation: An institutional perspective. *Information and Organization, 28*, 52–61.

Hollands, F. M., & Tirthali, D. (2014). Why do institutions offer MOOCs? *Online Learning, 18*(3), 1–15.

Hugstad, P. S. (1983). *The business school in the 1980s: Liberalism versus vocationalism.* New York: Preager.

Hutchby, I. (2001). Technologies, texts and affordances. *Sociology, 35*(2), 441–456.

Jones, C., & Massa, F. G. (2013). From novel practice to consecrated exemplar: Unity Temple as a case of institutional evangelizing. *Organization Studies, 34*(8), 1099–1136.

Jones, C., Maoret, M., Massa, F. G., & Svejenova, S. (2012). Rebels with a cause: Formation, contestation, and expansion of the de novo category "modern architecture," 1870–1975. *Organization Science, 23*, 1523–1545.

Jones, C., Boxenbaum, E., & Callen, A. (2013). The immaterial of the material in institutional logics. *Research in the Sociology of Organizations, 39A*, 51–75.

Kallinikos, J. (2009). On the computational rendition of reality: Artifacts and human agency. *Organization, 16*(92), 183–202.

Kallinikos, J., & Mariátegui, J.-C. (2011). Video as digital object: Production and distribution of video content in the internet media ecosystem. *The Information Society: An International Journal, 27*(5), 281–294.

Kallinikos, J., Aaltonen, A., & Marton, A. (2013). The ambivalent ontology of digital artifacts. *Information Systems Quarterly, 37*(2), 357–370.

Kraatz, M. S., & Block, E. S. (2008). Organizational implications of institutional pluralism. In R. Greenwood, C. Oliver, K. Sahlin, & R. Suddaby (Eds.), *The SAGE handbook of organizational institutionalism* (pp. 243–275). London: Sage.

Lawrence, T. B., Leca, B., & Zilber, T. B. (2013). Institutional work: Current research, new directions and overlooked issues. *Organization Studies, 34*(8), 1023–1033.

Leonardi, P. M. (2011). When flexible routines meet flexible technologies: Affordance, constraint, and the imbrication of human and material agencies. *MIS Quarterly, 35*(1), 147–168.

Leonardi, P. M. (2012). Materiality, sociomateriality, and socio-technical systems: What do these terms mean? How are they different? Do we need them. In P. Leonardi, B. Nardi, & J. Kallinikos (Eds.), *Materiality and organizing: Social interaction in a technological world* (pp. 25–48). Oxford: Oxford University Press.

Leonardi, P. M. (2013). When does technology use enable network change in organizations? A comparative study of feature use and shared affordances. *MIS Quarterly, 37*(3), 749–775.

Liu, M., Kang, J., Cao, M., Lim, M., Ko, Y., Myers, R., & Schmitz Weiss, A. (2014). Understanding MOOCs as an emerging online learning tool: Perspectives from the students. *American Journal of Distance Education, 28*(3), 147–159.

Lounsbury, M. (2002). Institutional transformation and status mobility: The professionalization of the field of finance. *Academy of Management Journal, 45*, 255–266.

Lounsbury, M. (2007). A tale of two cities: Competing logics and practice variation in the professionalizing of mutual funds. *Academy of Management Journal, 50*, 289–307.

Margaryan, A., Bianco, M., & Littlejohn, A. (2015). Instructional quality of massive open online courses (MOOCs). *Computers & Education, 80*, 77–83.

McPherson, C. M., & Sauder, M. (2013). Logics in action managing institutional complexity in a drug court. *Administrative Science Quarterly, 58*, 165–196.

Micelotta, E., Lounsbury, M., & Greenwood, R. (2018). Pathways of institutional change: An integrative review and research agenda. *Journal of Management, 43*(6), 1885–1910.

Morgan-Thomas, A. (2016). Rethinking technology in the SME context: Affordances, practices and ICTs. *International Small Business Journal, 34*(8), 1122–1136.

Nicolini, D., Delmestri, G., Goodrick, E., Reay, T., Lindberg, K., & Adolfsson, P. (2016). Look what's back! Institutional complexity, reversibility and the knotting of logics. *British Journal of Management, 27*, 228–248.

O'Mahony, S., & Ferraro, F. (2007). The emergence of governance in an open source community. *Academy of Management Journal, 50*, 1079–1106.

Ong, S., & Grigoryan, A. (2015). MOOCs and universities: Competitors or partners? *International Journal of Information and Education Technology, 5*(5), 373–376.

Orlikowski, W. J. (2000). Using technology and constituting structures: A practice lens for studying technology in organizations. *Organization Science, 11*(4), 404–428.

Orlikowski, W. J., & Scott, S. V. (2008). Sociomateriality: Challenging the separation of technology, work and organization. *The Academy of Management Annals, 2*(1), 433–474.

Pache, A., & Santos, F. (2010). When worlds collide: The internal dynamics of organizational responses to conflicting institutional demands. *Academy of Management Review, 35*(3), 455–476.

Pache, A. C., & Santos, F. (2013a). Inside the hybrid organization: Selective coupling as a response to competing institutional logics. *Academy of Management Journal, 56*(4), 972–1001.

Pache, A. C., & Santos, F. (2013b). Embedded in hybrid contexts: How individuals in organizations respond to competing institutional logics. *Research in the Sociology of Organizations, 39*, 3–35.

Quinn Trank, C., & Washington, M. (2009). Maintaining the legitimacy of legitimating organizations: The institutional work of the AASCB and its constituents in business education. In T. Lawrence & R. Suddaby (Eds.), *Institutional work: Actors and agency in institutional studies of organizations* (pp. 236–261). Cambridge: Cambridge University Press.

Rao, H., Monin, P., & Durand, R. (2003). Institutional change in Toque Ville: Nouvelle cuisine as an identity movement in French gastronomy. *American Journal of Sociology, 108*, 795–843.

Reay, T., & Hinings, C. (2005). The recomposition of an organizational field: Health care in Alberta. *Organization Studies, 26*, 351–384.

Reay, T., & Hinings, C. R. (2009). Managing the rivalry of competing institutional logics. *Organization Studies, 30*, 629–653.

Santos, F., Pache, A. C., & Birkenholz, C. (2015). Making hybrids work: Aligning business models and organizational design for social enterprises. *California Management Review, 57*(3), 36–58.

Schildt, H., & Perkmann, M. (2017). Organizational settlements: Theorizing how organizations respond to institutional complexity. *Journal of Management Inquiry, 26*(2), 139–145.

Schoemaker, P. J. H. (2008). The future challenges of business: Rethinking management education. *California Management Review, 50*(3), 119–140.

Smets, M., Morris, T., & Greenwood, R. (2012). From practice to field: A multi-level model of institutional change. *Academy of Management Journal,* 55, 877–904.

Smets, M., Jarzabkowski, P., Burke, G., & Spee, P. (2015). Reinsurance trading in Lloyd's of London: Balancing conflicting-yet-complementary logics in practice. *Academy of Management Journal,* 58, 932–970.

Thomas, H., & Peters, K. (2012). A sustainable model for business schools. *Journal of Management Development,* 33(5), 470–486.

Thornton, P. H. (2002). The rise of the corporation in a craft industry: Conflict and conformity in institutional logics. *Academy of Management Journal,* 45, 81–101.

Thornton, P. H. (2004). *Markets from culture: Institutional logics and organizational decisions in higher education publishing.* Stanford: Stanford University Press.

Thornton, P. H., & Ocasio, W. (1999). Institutional logics and the historical contingency of power in organizations: Executive succession in the higher education publishing industry, 1958–1990. *American Journal of Sociology,* 105, 801–843.

Thornton, P. H., & Ocasio, W. (2008). Institutional logics. In R. Greenwood, C. Oliver, K. Sahlin, & R. Suddaby (Eds.), *The Sage handbook of organizational institutionalism* (pp. 99–129). London: Sage.

Thornton, P. H., Ocasio, W., & Lounsbury, M. (2012). *The institutional logics perspective: A new approach to culture, structure and process.* Oxford: Oxford University Press.

Thorpe, R., & Rawlinson, R. (2014). Engaging with engagement: How UK business schools could meet the innovation challenge. *Journal of Management Development,* 33(5), 470–486.

Townley, B. (2002). The role of competing rationalities in institutional change. *Academy of Management Journal,* 45, 163–179.

Treem, J. W., & Leonardi, P. M. (2012). Social media use in organizations: Exploring the affordances of visibility, editability, persistence, and association. *Communication Yearbook,* 36, 143–189.

Van Baalen, P. J., & Moratis, L. T. (2001). *Management education in the network economy.* Boston: Kluwer Academic Publishers.

Veletsianos, G., & Shepherdson, P. (2015). Who studies MOOCs? Interdisciplinarity in MOOC research and its changes over time. *International Review of Research in Open and Distributed Learning,* 16(3), 1–17.

Volkoff, O., & Strong, D. M. (2013). Critical realism and affordances: Theorizing IT-associated organizational change processes. *MIS Quarterly, 37*(3), 819–834.

White, S., Davis, H., Dickens, K., León, M., & Sánchez-Vera, M. M. (2014). MOOCs: What motivates the producers and participants? *Communications in Computer Science, 510,* 99–114.

Yoo, Y., Boland, R., Lyytinen, K., & Majchrzak, A. (2012). Organizing for innovation in the digitized world. *Organization Science, 23*(5), 1398–1408.

Yoo, Y., Henfridsson, O., & Lyytinen, K. (2010). The new organizing logic of digital innovation: An agenda for information systems research. *Information Systems Research, 21*(4), 724–735.

Yuan, L., & Powell, S. (2013). *MOOCs and open education: Implications for higher education* (JISC White Paper).

Zietsma, C., Groenewegen, P., Logue, D., & Hinings, C. R. (2017). Field or fields? Building the scaffolding for cumulation of research on institutional fields. *The Academy of Management Annals, 11,* 391–450.

Zilber, T. B. (2002). Institutionalization as an interplay between actions, meanings, and actors: The case of a rape crisis center in Israel. *Academy of Management Journal, 45,* 234–254.

10

Bridging the Gap Between Organizational Institutionalism and Situated Action: A Video-Based Analysis of a Simulation-Based Device in Healthcare

Catherine Félix, Lise Arena, and Bernard Conein

Introduction

This contribution lies at the junction between two intellectual traditions that often fail to be brought together in the organization studies literature, namely organizational institutionalism and situated and distributed approaches. Overall, it aims to make micro-foundations of institutional theory more explicit as satisfying an urging need already addressed by

We owe a great debt of gratitude to the Maison des Sciences de l'Homme et de la Société (MSHS) Sud-Est, which supported this pluridisciplinary research, and to Alain Percivalle, who gave us access to occurring natural data and took part in the simulation-based device at the hospital. Finally, we would like to thank the organizers of the OAP Seminar in Lisbon (2016) who selected our paper for publication and provided remarkable comments to improve the initial version of our work.

C. Félix (✉) • L. Arena • B. Conein
Université Côte d'Azur, CNRS, GREDEG, France
e-mail: lise.arena@unice.fr

© The Author(s) 2019
F.-X. de Vaujany et al. (eds.), *Materiality in Institutions*, Technology, Work and Globalization, https://doi.org/10.1007/978-3-319-97472-9_10

281

Powell and Colyvas in 2008 and not significantly advanced since. While providing a better account of material aspects of institutions, it also aims to enhance the role of artifacts and tools as currently accounted by the situated/distributed approach. The main objective in this chapter is to couple a reference to materiality of institutions with a reference to the manipulation of objects and equipment in a changing environment. The ambition to establish a dialogue between these two intellectual traditions is made possible by an observation of specific "naturally occurring data". It gives an access to recorded sequences of body actions that provide a fine-grained analysis of the relation between the setting as a local work-space and the arena as a broader institutional context. This method enables to capture a disadjustment between distinct levels of activities: *institutional environment* (public durable framework designed "ahead of time"), an *external plan* (defined as both an organizational programme and a scenario for acting) and *situated action* (real-time local interactional routines).

The fieldwork is conducted in an experimental hospital and focuses on the implementation of a digital artifact—a simulation-based training device personified in a lifelike virtual mannequin—initially designed to improve the training of teamwork skills in a health professionals' community (doctors, physicians and nurses). In line with the tradition initiated by workplace studies, it is argued that the workspace is made of material objects (cognitive artifacts and physical tools) and body movements that act as an external support for action when the environment is prepared and familiar.

This chapter's contribution to the book is therefore both theoretical and methodological, since video analysis appears as a tool to resolve some common opposition between organizational institutionalism and situated approaches. In line with its main objective, this chapter is divided into three main parts. The first section roots the analysis in the existing literature and provides a conceptual framework that combines both traditions of organizational institutionalism and situated action. To a large extent, it shows the limits of each intellectual tradition and offers a more integrated approach with the integration of material dimensions. The purpose of the second section is to expose and justify the video methods able to produce the retranscription of a short sequence of action, subject to the analysis. The last section of this chapter presents the results of an analysis of a medical setting and explores future avenues of research initiated by this chapter.

Bringing Organizational Institutionalism and Situated Action Closer

The nature of this first section is essentially conceptual and aims at providing a large picture of what organizational institutionalism and situated/distributed action are and how they can complement each other when one wants to enhance the material dimensions of both conceptual frameworks.

Putting Forward the Material Dimension of Institutions

The first argument of this chapter explores the material dimension of organizational institutionalism, in line with very recent contributions on this topic (Boxenbaum et al. 2016). This argument tries to scrutinize the articulation between material artifacts and body action in a context of institutional disadjustments.

Cognitive and Discursive Perspectives as a "Micro-motor" to Macro-lines" of Analysis Organizational institutionalism (OI) is rooted in organization theory and is the application of the institutional perspective to questions such as: "how and why do organizations behave as they do, and with what consequences?" (Greenwood et al. 2008, p. 1). This tradition of thought goes back to the end of the 1970s with two seminal papers published by Meyer and Rowan (1977) and Zucker (1977) that introduced what later became known as new institutionalism. Over the years and throughout the legitimation of new institutionalism up to the 1990s, its bulk remained to a great degree confined to a macro-level, mainly sectoral or global. Scholars alerted the community on two dangers that are still threatening current research: (1) focusing too significantly on macro-levels and therefore (2) producing a taxonomy of institutions rather than an explanation of processes underlying their evolution and persistence— that is "forgetting that labeling a process or structure does not explain it" (Zucker 1991, p. 106). This idea of searching for a "micro-motor" to "macro-lines of analysis" seeks to go beyond the bipolar structure-agency spectrum that kept both OI and more situated approaches at a distance from each other (Powell and Colyvas 2008, p. 276). While new institutionalism gave primacy to structure and the macro-level contexts that condition organizations, situated approaches have rather focused on agency, that is body action and the joint activities of individuals inside organizations.

To overcome these diverging paths, recent scholarship aimed at making micro-foundations of OI more explicit and at integrating in particular a cognitive perspective as well as a more discursive approach to institutions (Phillips et al. 2004; Phillips and Malhotra 2008; Harmon et al. 2015; Gray et al. 2015). These new approaches to institutions were a reaction to the tendency to adopt a "realistic" perspective in OI and to position "the social world as having an existence outside and independent of the meaningful linguistic activity through which it is constituted" (Philips and Lawrence 2012, pp. 480–481). To a large extent, this general fear was already expressed a decade earlier by Zucker, who claimed that "without a solid cognitive, micro-level foundation we risk treating institutionalization as a black box at the organizational level, focusing on content at the exclusion of developing a systematic explanatory theory of process, conflating institutionalization with resource dependency, and neglecting institutional variation and persistence" (Zucker 1991, pp. 105–106). Overall, the desire to use more interpretative methods to the understanding of institutions pays close attention to "subjective experiences such as social roles, routines, and patterns of interaction" made by actors in their institutionalized practices (Suddaby and Greenwood 2009, p. 181).

The First Steps into Integrating Materiality in Institutional Analysis Despite preliminary efforts to develop cognitive and discursive perspectives in OI, only very few existing contributions consider the material dimension of institutions. Very recently the authors have started considering the role of artifacts, materials, workspace and bodily actions into institutional analysis (Boxenbaum et al. 2016). While these first publications are central in the effort that has to be made on this "cross-fertilization", they essentially focus on a simple causal link between material artifacts and body action (Rao et al. 2003). What is neglected in fact is the grounding of materiality into the process of interactions. This missing element is exemplified by the small amount of empirical analysis concerned with the impacts of materiality on the emergence of routines that could be captured by observing the arrangement of artifacts in a prepared environment.

To a certain extent, this gap is consistent with the primacy given by scholars to the study of institutionalization processes. This particular emphasis in OI was already central to Berger and Luckmann (1967), who defined it as a process which "occurs whenever there is a reciprocal typification of habitualized actions by types of actors". They added that "put differently, any such typification is an institution". In this respect, defining institutions as cognitive structures directly results from the definition of institutionalization given by Meyer and Rowan (1977, p. 341), who claim that it involves the "processes by which social processes, obligations, or actualities, come to take on a rulelike status in social thought and action".

While mostly focusing on the institutionalization process and legitimacy, these authors invite future research in the field to examine the actual micro-processes through which organizations become more alike in form. Yet, this invitation leaves one question unanswered: what would happen when "habitualized actions" (or routines) that are constitutive of institutionalization are not sufficient to support action? Put differently, what would be the consequences of a disadjustment between these "habitualized actions" and individual action? This gap has been recently identified by Boxenbaum et al. (2016, p. 236), who argued that while artifacts are often considered as vectors of institutional processes (through instantiation of ideas); the way artifacts can influence and disturb institutional processes has not been analysed yet.

This idea to look at institutional readjustments between routines as body actions rather than exclusively at institutionalization processes per se echoes very few existing contributions that claim that "institutional agency is better conceived as both emergent and distributed" and that look at institutions as an assemblage between human action and material objects (Monteiro and Nicolini 2014, p. 61).

The Concept of "Action Arena" as an Account of Institutional Materiality Capturing the material dimension of institutions initially requires identifying the social space where humans and material artifacts interact. In this perspective, the contribution made by Elinor Ostrom is useful to our analysis. While Ostrom's research programme aimed at capturing institutional change, she put the concept of rules at the heart of her institutional analysis. To her, institutions are "shared concepts used by humans in repetitive situations organized by rules, norms, and strategies" (Ostrom 2007, p. 23). Overall, rules can then be thought as a set of instructions to create an action situation. Ostrom qualifies this situation as an action arena which refers to the social space where "participants with diverse preferences interact, exchange good services, solve problems, dominate one another, or fight" (Ostrom 2005, p. 14). To Ostrom, action arenas include both the "action situation" and "actors within it"—that is individuals (or groups) who are routinely involved in the situation (actors). A series of "exogenous variables" (such as the types of participants and their positions, their possible actions and information they have) structure the action situation. Although Ostrom assumes that agents have limited resources, bounded rationality (limited cognitive capabilities) and behave in an uncertain environment; her ambition is not to understand social action per se. Yet, she argued that action arenas are also framed by three clusters of "contextual variables": (1) the *rules-in-use* followed by participants—opposed to "rules-in-form" and defined as "informal" rules that might (or might not) be accepted by individuals in their everyday interactions (Ostrom and Basurto 2011, p. 318); (2) the physical and the material world (*bio-physical world*) within which the actors interact; and (3) the attributes of the more general *community* within which any action arena is placed. In fact, Ostrom's integration of materiality in her understanding of institutions is limited by the static nature of what she defines as an "action arena". To a large extent, the concept of "arena" implies to prepare a plan of action "ahead of time". The main limits to this approach are therefore the lack of account addressed to the dynamic dimension of action, in the emergence and disturbance of interactional routines. We believe that situated approaches could complement the institutional framework and integrate a more dynamic dimension of action in the understanding of institutional disadjustments. In particular, the process of online interaction with the local components of a workspace is scrutinized by workplace studies and is worth discussing further here.

Putting Forward the Material Dimension of Situated Action as Action Affordance

The conceptualization of "arena" by Ostrom could be complemented by a second argument that explores the material dimension of professional settings. This idea is based on the work of Kirsh (1995) and Lave (1988) on the spatial arrangement of artifacts and bodies in the workspace (Mead 1932). This argument seeks to make explicit how ecological factors drive the emergence of interactional routines by finding their inspiration in the ecological analysis of perception of Gibson (1986). Overall and partly in contrast with Ostrom's discussion of the concept of "arena", situated approaches focus on the dynamics of space arrangement (as opposed to the static nature of the institutional and more global dimension of an arena).

The Interplay Between Plan and Action: A routine Is Not a Plan Our main working hypothesis suggests that materiality grounded in technical artifacts and body movements impacts control of body action by activating execution routines. More precisely, it examines in what circumstances a "plan", acting as a programme made of instructions, could act as an efficient cognitive aid when the environment is far too complex to rely only on the affordances of physical objects, such as tools and equipment. In most everyday cases, skilled agents do not need to plan in advance if they could lean on highly prepared and adapted environment.

The importance of routines based on interactional contingencies and improvisations (Agre 1985, 1997) was explored in the early work of Lucy Suchman. She focused on the disadjustments (Suchman 2009) between "plans" as programme at the organizational level and "situated actions" at the interaction level.

By opposing verbal or written plan to the dynamics of moment to moment situated embodied interaction, she claimed that there is a continuous interaction or interplay between a rich prepared environment and a global plan of action. In her work, the plan is viewed as one among various resources an agent can use to act. The plan as programme should be opposed to the plan as resource. The classical view on planning conceives plan as a dense programme that will predict subsequent action as the routines emerge on the spot without deciding what to next ahead of time. Strictly, a plan is not affected by the agenda of real-time action as distinct "options presented by the world around them" (Agre 1997), p. 167).

The permanent interplay between plan and routine action can explain difficult cases where a specific action cannot be accomplished without one line re-thinking or without the reading of a written instruction. When such cases appear, as we will see in our empirical analysis, the agent comes across either a gulf of execution (the action cannot be executed in real time) or a gulf of evaluation (the information coming from the environment is available but cannot be processed) (Norman 1988).

The Workspace as a Setting and as an Arena

As a result of contributions made by Kirsh (1995), Hutchins (1995) and Lave (1988), the material and ecological dimension of action is made more explicit with a constant reference to the impact of equipment and tools as a guidance of interactional routines. The three authors emphasize the two sides of interaction between objects and human agents: the effect of materials on the emergence of interaction routines (effect of the arena on the setting) and the effect of dynamics of body actions for shaping a supporting environment (effect of the setting on the arena).

What G.H. Mead (1932) has called the manipulatory area is an accurate representation of what an analysis of the materials at the micro-level is. There is a clear affinity between G.H. Mead and J. Gibson. However, for Mead, the important point is an explicit reference to the dynamical relation between the physical materials at hand (seen and handle) and their placement in a workspace: "There is a distinction to be made, however, between the object in the manipulatory area that is both seen and handled, and the distant object that is both out of reach and also lies in a visual perspective". To Gibson, the spatial environment affords various actions when there is a natural coupling between the manipulative object and the body action. The performance of an action is based on the various perceptions of affordances one could have in the environment. Affordances provide a set of cues for acting without thinking as they are directly perceived.

The arena as equipment is an explicit reference to the spatial arrangement of materials at the macro-level. The materiality of institution is revealed in the action arena in the example of the supermarket as an arena: "The arena of grocery shopping in the supermarket, an institution at the interface between consumers and suppliers of grocery commodities" (Lave 1988, p. 152).

As a result, the environment should be conceived as a spatial structure as having two interactive parts: a dynamical part, the *setting* at the local level, where objects stand at reaching hand ready for use and for manipulation and a static part, the *arena* as a macro space of objects arranged and placed at distant and stored for future use. Put differently, the arena is a material reflection of an institution's properties. Design for use could be seen as an institutional design of the arena to stabilize the environment for long-term purposes and as a design for the setting to prepare the environment as a workspace for a real-time use (Fig. 10.1).

Overall, there is a tension between the arena and the setting. This tension results from a set of instructions created by the simulation device: a gap between the static infrastructure of the arena and the dynamical process of the setting. As we aim to highlight the relevance of understanding the setting, our work focuses on the analysis of the local site of work activities.

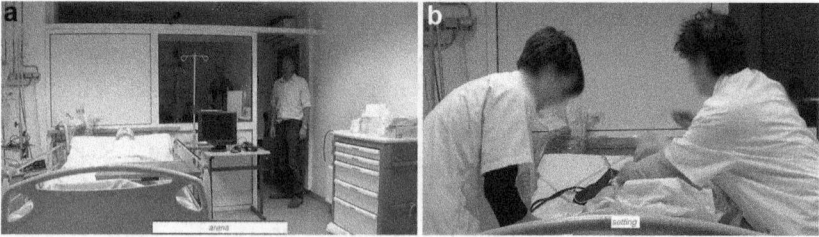

Fig. 10.1   (a) The "action arena" (*left*) as a static spatial arrangement of materials (here the experimental room) and (b) the "setting" (*right*) as a dynamical space of objects at "hand" (here the nurse and her assistant executing tasks required by a cardiopulmonary reanimation)

Video Analysis of Natural Occurring Data: A Matchmaker Between Organizational Institutionalism and Situated Action

This second section exposes video analysis as a method used to describe the action arena and to capture local interactions in a professional setting. We then introduce the case study and the main observations.

Video Methods to Capture Material Dimensions of Institutions and of Situated Action: The Case of a Simulated Cardiopulmonary Resuscitation in an Experimental Public Hospital

Borrowing from a Fine-Grained Descriptive Sociological Tradition Video methods enable access to the two institutional dimensions introduced in the previous section: namely to the action arena (seen as an institution) and to the setting (manipulatory area, i.e. dynamical aspect of the work-space). Video analysis is rooted in a fine-grained descriptive sociological tradition (Sacks 1984) that encourages researchers to locate interactional processes, whereby agents make everyday sense of their experience and configure their social environment. This approach claims that recorded data can reveal real-time natural processes. Recordings of "technology in action" made possible by video analysis enable access to multimodal interactions (gazes, gestures, tools, objects, artifacts and manipulations) (Goodwin 1981). This tradition is also rooted in the field of workplace studies, in the tradition of Lucy Suchman's work (Suchman 2009) and Heath and Luff's naturalistic studies of "technology in action" (Heath and Luff 2000) that focused on identifying the material architecture of professional environments. Overall, video analysis mainly takes into account temporal restitution of face-to-face interactions and coordination of work activities, including activities between distant parties through technological tools (Relieu 2006; Mondada 2006).

Video-recorded data are particularly relevant to evidence underestimated aspects of social and cognitive processes and therefore to assess the socio-material dimensions of organizations. The embodied task-resolving processes are "seen but unnoticed", not available to parties in the moment of action and after as well. Hence, these recorded data and their transcriptions could be shared with other researchers and studied by reviewing details of coordinated stances until the researcher can offer a relevant sense of what parties have produced in a specific timing. As Heath and Luff (2000, p. 23) put it: "video recording of workplace activities coupled with certain methodological assumptions drawn from conversation analysis and ethnomethodology provide the resources through which we explicate the practices, reasoning and procedures utilised by the participants themselves in the day-to-day practical accomplishment of their workplace actions and activities in the workplace". As video methods document coordination between a variety of embodied actions (talk, gestures and gazes) relying on the uses of material objects, it involves specific methodological challenges—such as configuring a video material device which can be attuned to the research focus—as well as ethical issues—such as obtaining participants' written authorizations to be recorded during their professional activities.

As regards transcriptions of these recorded sketches of verbal and non-verbal action, they aim at capturing the temporality of actions' achievement, in a step-by-step account of processes. Transcriptions' conventions are used to underline how the different parties manifest in details a mutual understanding of what happens in a series of moves. Here, we use multimodal transcriptions that aim at describing the interrelation between verbal and non-verbal actions such as gazes, gestures, tools manipulation and their progressive realization. Put differently, these transcriptions reflect the processual and embodied nature of interactions in professional settings as well as coordination between different scenarios and gestures that could also arise in practice.

Emerging Uses of Video Analysis in Organization Studies Video methods have only recently emerged in the field of organization studies and strategy research. For instance, in their article published in the *Strategic Management Journal*, Gylfe et al. (2016) stress the significance of human body and materiality in the practice of organizational strategy. Video methods enable them to show how middle managers' embodied cognition supports strategy implementation "by influencing nascent behavioral and cognitive changes among their subordinates" (Ibid., p. 133). To our knowledge, this very recent work is the first attempt to provide a "tool kit" of video methods in organization studies and is one of the few existing exceptions of published video-based work in strategy research which contribute to the crafting of a "visual agenda" in the field. This visual agenda aims to gather static (such as pictures, maps or webpages) as well as dynamic (such as films and video recording) visual data to provide a better understanding to the socio-material dimensions of organizational phenomena. To a large extent, this method is consistent with both recent "linguistic" and "material" turns in organization studies that claim that embodiment has to become a major programme of research into socio-materiality of organizations. Overall, this method is relevant for the pluridisciplinary tradition initiated by workplace studies and micro-sociology that also inspired recent advances in management and organization studies, such as practice-based studies (Gherardi 2000) or socio-material approaches (de Vaujany and Mitev 2013).

Material dimensions of our case study have to be found in an environment made of objects (such as a virtual mannequin, a sealed medical trolley, various medical tools) and of relationships between tasks and material support of these tasks. Situated approaches seek to provide a better understanding of the emergence of cues necessary to the task execution (setting) due to the environment's characteristics (replication of an emergency room). Our method is based on audio visual data recorded in the context of simulated emergency situations. This methodological choice enables to stress a temporal sequence of verbal and non-verbal actions (such as gesture, eye contact, objects manipulation) as well as the coordination between these two types of actions.

As in any video-based approach, our method has been constrained by the recording device, for example location of the video camera and the microphone, necessary to align camera angles with scientific objectives. A significant amount of literature on the subject has shown that expected biases of this video device is usually overtaken by participants being entirely devoted to the task they have to perform. To a large extent, because of their focus on tasks, they tend to "forget" the video camera device. The auto confrontation method that has been used confirms dis-adjustments between given instructions and action supported by the environment. Overall, our video analysis method eases the observation of embodied action.

Case Study and Data Collection Our case study scrutinizes the implementation of a simulation-based training device personified in a lifelike virtual mannequin. This implementation is conducted within a project called PACTE (Programme d'Amélioration du Travail en Equipe) and is based on professional activities' simulation techniques inspired by real scenarios of risky situations. The device is initially designed and controlled by the Haute Autorité En Santé (HAS-French National Authority for Health) and seeks to improve learning and team coordination in practice. Overall, the objective is to detect defect professional behaviours and faults committed by health professionals in their everyday activities. It is assumed that agents, when immerged in a specific simulated "scenario", will reproduce real professional situations and, in turn, reveal defaults in their individual or collective tasks. Our analysis essentially focuses on discrepancies between scenarios/scripts initially thought at the institutional level by the Haute Autorité de la Santé, on the one hand, and professional body practices/routines based on the uses of material objects during the simulation, on the other. These material objects include medical devices, furniture, screens and circulation space, all components of the arena of action that mainly act as guidance for action and for the emergence of routines.

More specifically, professionals in charge of the simulation locate the simulation exercise in a specific room that they consider as a relevant copy of a real intensive care room. This experimental room is meant to offer an adjusted environment for the realization of the scenario (which is in the case studied here: a cardiopulmonary resuscitation on the lifelike mannequin). The room is equipped with a medical bed, a computer to scan the patient, an automated external defibrillator (AED) and a medical trolley with the tools required to execute the different tasks (breathing support, drugs, etc.). The medical equipment required to conduct a cardiopulmonary resuscitation (CPR) is meant to be ready to use, in case of emergency, as in a real intensive care ward setting.

More than 20 hours of video data have been collected and gather simulation training sessions as well as debriefings with the simulation participants that follow those sessions. This method is useful to account for uses of material objects and body engagement in the accomplishment of routinized tasks in practice (Kirsh 1995). The data analysis leads us to the selection of a short video sequence (45 seconds) that identifies temporal discrepancies between instructions (resulting from initial scenarios) and actions (triggered by the use of material objects in routinized professional practices).

Observing Object Manipulation and Interactional Routines in a Dynamical Environment

The main activity scrutinized by our case study is concerned with tasks coordination between heterogeneous healthcare professionals whose competencies are evaluated in situ, that is during the simulation exercise. We chose to study the following video-recorded sketch of body actions: a nurse has to put a drip on a patient in time, when other practitioners (doctor and nurse's assistants) are challenged to reactivate heart beating and natural breathing. Technically, this specific sketch of action has been captured by one fixed video camera and one microphone in order to reduce potential trouble during the simulation session.

The video sequence starts with a very brief talk from the instructor to the healthcare professionals subject to the simulation exercise: "you are located in an intensive care ward, the patient has just arrived, he is unconscious".

This scenario's prescription reflects a more institutional level as it echoes a plan made ahead of time in the aim to improve professional skills of the medical team. This instruction is minimalist in order to frame the setting as realistically as possible, that is without providing any information that health professionals would not have in the real equivalent setting. Cardiopulmonary resuscitation simultaneously implies two main objectives: (1) reviving the patient's cardiac activity with the help of a cardiac massage, electroshock and an intravenous drug injection, and (2) an intubation of the patient, which enables artificial breathing.

The sequence of actions we analyse makes explicit the fine-grained processes of this resuscitation collective activity. In the simulation setting, doctors, nurses and nurse assistants play their respective (real) professional roles. This implies that tasks eventually enabling the resuscitation are distributed between teams' members, according to their expertise and to their degrees of responsibilities in real-life settings. For instance, the doctor is responsible for intubating the patient while the nurse is responsible for putting a drip on.

The sequence studied is very brief and actions last 45 seconds (from 00.00 to 00.45). In this time interval, our analysis of the different steps constitutive of tasks coordination results from (i) a series of screens captures and (ii) a written transcript reproducing verbal and non-verbal actions between the doctor, the nurse and the nurse's assistants. It is from the interrelation between verbal and non-verbal actions that we can make sense of what happened in this specific sequence of action.

Figures 10.2 expose two micro-sequences of actions: capture (a) shows the team of healthcare professionals as a locus of tasks distribution. The main objective is to preserve the synchronization among team members in order to accomplish several simultaneous actions.

Capture (b) illustrates another sequence of tasks distribution: while the doctor focuses on the patient's breathing, the nurse is busy opening the trolley's drawers to find adequate tools to put the drip on. This illustrates that during a cardiopulmonary resuscitation process, the different tasks have the same priorities and require simultaneous operations. This is exemplified by the simultaneous temporality of giving a cardiac massage (defibrillation) and injecting drug (such as adrenaline, most of the time). What is shown in Fig. 10.2 corresponds to standard steps in the tasks distribution processes: Each participant to the professional setting is

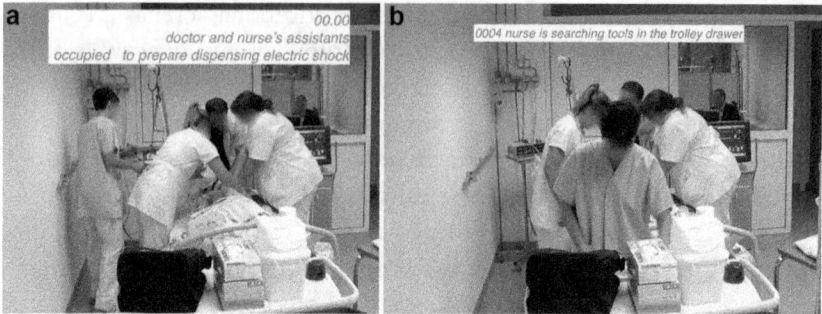

Fig. 10.2 (a) Task distribution in the healthcare team at 00.00 (*left*). (b) Attempt of task execution as the nurse searches material objects to put a drip on at 00.04 (*right*)

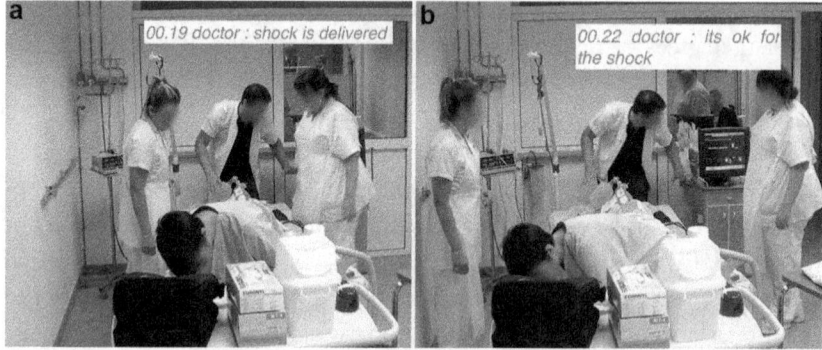

Fig. 10.3 (a) Doctor managing the nurse's assistants at 00.19 (*left*). (b) Doctor looking at the computer at 00.22—a software program drives shock deliveries according to the electrocardiogram information displayed on the screen (*right*)

in charge of a specific task; unless perhaps in the specific case of nurses' assistants use of AED.

Tasks Coordination in Action: Led by the Doctor Figures 10.3 and 10.4 (including two screen captures each) show how the doctor is leading tasks coordination during the simulation session, in line with the usual distribution of expertise (and hierarchical arrangement) in healthcare. The doctor monitors the nurse's assistants during the delivery of an electric shock. He uses the verbal expression "a shock is delivered" as an instruction for them to stop the cardiac massage.

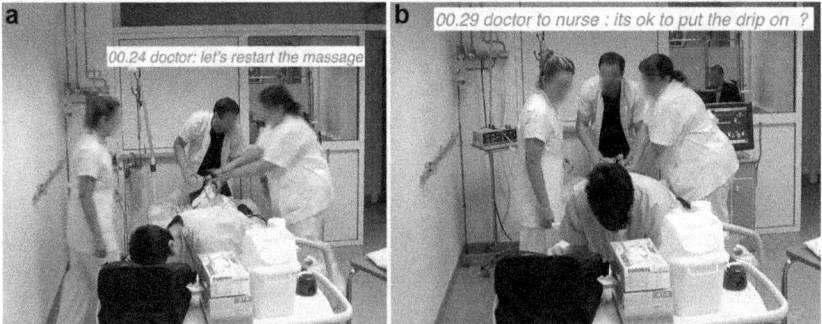

Fig. 10.4 (**a**) Doctor coordinating cardiac massage given by the nurse's assistants (along with defibrillation) at 00.24 (*left*). (**b**) Doctor instructing the nurse (for the first time in the scenario) to be ready to put the drip on at 00.29. At the same time, the nurse is still searching for the adequate tools in the trolley's drawers (*right*)

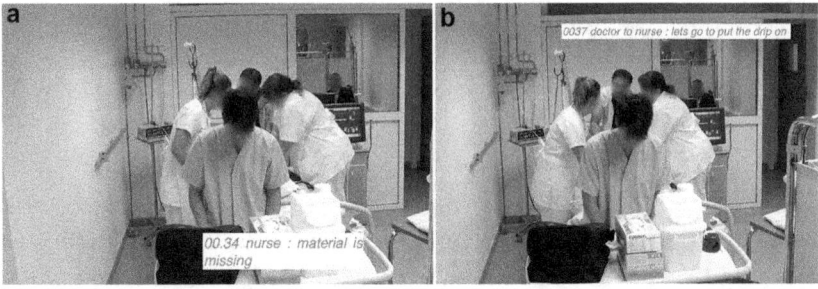

Fig. 10.5 (**a**) Nurse encountering a problem in her search of the adequate tools at 00.34 (*left*). (**b**) Doctor instructing the nurse (for the second time in the scenario) to put the drip on. Our verbal transcription shows that the nurse eventually finds the adequate material and informs the team when she says: "here it is, I finally found it" just a few seconds after the doctor's instruction at 00.37 (*right*)

Difficulties to Execute the Task on Time: Experienced by the Nurse Captures in 5 and 6 depict the nurse's attempt to execute the task given by the doctor. Her behaviour reflects the difficulties she encounters as a result of the non-availability of tools "at hand" to perform her work (Figs. 10.5 and 10.6).

Interestingly, this in-situ video-recorded sequence of actions has been complemented by an additional interview with the nurse. This interview

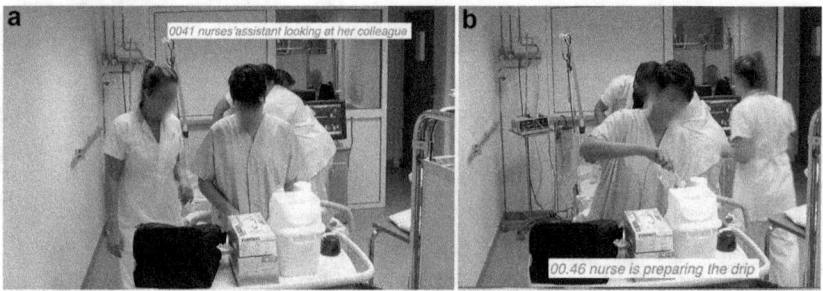

Fig. 10.6 (a) Nurse's assistant offering help to the nurse (NB: the nurse's verbal actions are not hearable). (b) Nurse is about to execute the task as she is on her way to put the drip on at 00.46 (*right*)

included a self-confrontation's[1] session that consisted of showing her the recorded sequence and interviewing her ex-post. To our questions concerning the difficulties she encountered in the task execution, she answered that the trouble was caused by the "mess in the medical trolley drawers", adding that she was "panicking" at that moment (cf. transcription in the appendix).

When Object Placements and Arrangements Do Not Support Action These series of captures enable to follow step-by-step an instance of routinized tasks disadjustment in a simulated environment. This disadjustment reflects a dysfunction between prescription and action. In Suchman's terms, the prescribed problem is replaced by the activity of following an instruction. In our video sequence, the prescription corresponds to the initial brief talk from the instructor to the healthcare professionals subject to the simulation exercise: "you are located in an intensive care ward, the patient has just arrived, he is unconscious". When the nurse fails to put the drip on time because she does not find the relevant tools "at hand", there is a disadjustment between her intended action (as following an instruction) and her body action (limited by the unfamiliarity of objects placements).

---

[1] Self-confrontation methods are considered as relevant approaches to study information-seeking behaviour, in a psychological trend devoted to working practices' analysis. Further details on this method could be found in Faïta (1997) and Clot et al. (2000).

Some additional contextual elements are worth mentioning here. First, it is not necessary for a nurse to be monitored by a doctor to put a drip on.[2] Second and in a similar vein, the nurse does not need to refer to any formal instructions in this specific task, since executing a cardiopulmonary process is a procedure learned by every single healthcare practitioner in their intensive care's professional training. Knowing what is needed to be done in time and how it needs to be done is thoroughly bounded to "embodied skills". Being skilled does not only result from learning but can be seen as grounded in day-to-day work experiences. Putting a drip on—in coordination with other tasks that need to be done—assumes that the relevant tool is ready at hand or easily reachable. Accomplishing routinized moves—such as opening a specific drawer first to find the adequate material—depends on environment opportunities.

In line with Kontos and Naglie's (2009) study of embodied caring, we believe that "The experienced nurse, (..) develops a tacit connection between her fingers and the catheter, and experiences an 'embodied takeover of a skill' wherein she probes with the catheter tip as if it were an extension of her fingers (Benner and Tanner 1987, p. 26). The importance of tacit knowledge for expertise has been identified in the practice of anaesthetists (Pope et al. 2003), where it has been demonstrated that knowledge of cannulating a vein, for example, is not imparted explicitly through texts but rather tacitly through clinical apprenticeship" (Kontos and Naglie 2009, p. 689) (Fig. 10.7).

Embodied knowledge could be viewed as linked to the perception and recognition of cues in the environment. This view echoes the embodiment of routines that aims to modify the spatial arrangement of an arena infrastructure into an everyday setting. Put differently, embodied routines transform the setting within the arena, by activating objects that are to be used. This conception of embodiment echoes Paul Dourish's definition of the term: "by embodiment I mean a presence and participation in the world, real-time and real-space, here and now. Embodiment denotes a participative status, the presence and occurrence of a phenomenon in the world. So, physical objects are certainly embodied, but so are conversations and actions" (Dourish 2001, p. 240).

---

[2] Yet, the kind of drugs given to a patient is decided by the doctor when the patient's health status results from a specific disease. In vital emergency cases, such as heart attack cases, adrenaline is the standard drug given.

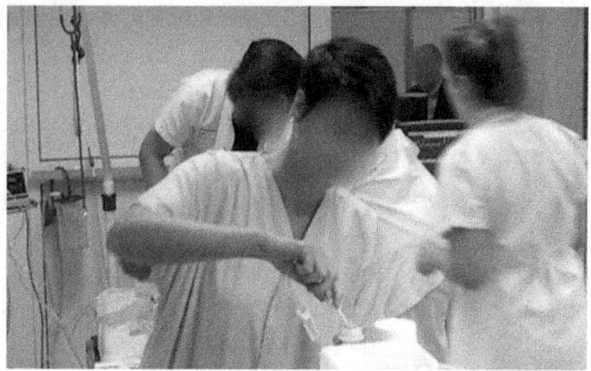

Fig. 10.7 Manipulating tools is grounded in routinized gesture scaffolded by local environment

In our case study, the action arena provides the ecological and material resources to this embodied knowledge implementation when the environment's configuration is "attuned" to the work which needs to be done.

As a result, in real resuscitation settings, situations in which a doctor addresses two successive requests concerned with the task of putting a drip on (here: "ready to put the drip on" and "let's go, put the drip on") to a nurse should be rather rare.

In real settings, in standardized conditions, medical trolleys are organized to support task's execution in time.[3] Every drawer is devoted to a specific category of material: the first one contains drugs, the second gathers catheter, needles and the third includes intubation tools as laryngoscope. Moreover, the medical trolley is controlled after every utilization and sealed for the next setting. This replication from real settings is part of the "arena" (in Ostrom's and Lave's sense) and belongs to the institutional plan, which was made ahead of real time and aimed at providing training devices for healthcare teams.

In our case study, screen captures show that nurse's routines to extract what she needs from the trolley's drawers are not supported by visual cues. She has to open all drawers to eventually find the adequate tools for her task execution. In the supposed equivalent simulated setting, the

---

[3] Prescriptions regarding medical trolley drawers' organization used for cardiopulmonary resuscitation could be found on http://www.infirmiers.com/etudiants-en-ifsi/cours/cours-reanimation-le-chariot-durgence.html

medical trolley is not organized as if a real resuscitation had to be performed in an emergency context. The material is not prepared to play its role of guiding for action.

Discussion and Conclusion

This chapter's ambition was both theoretical and methodological. First, it aimed at bringing closer two traditions of thought usually taken at a distance in the literature, namely organizational institutionalism and situated approaches. Then, the naturalistic observations gathered in our case study gave us access to a level of activities that provide data on real-time occurring actions.

Three main results can be drawn from our analysis.

First, we have shown that the simulation-based device re-enforces the gap between the level of body actions (interactional routines) and the level of instructions (the plan as programme). At the same time, the modalities of interactions between the two levels are structural as the execution of a routine cannot be predicted in advance. What can be re-enforced is mainly the interplay between routines and planned actions. This first result is meaningful since it prevents us from simply opposing a macro-level of an arena made of equipment and a micro-interactional level made of tools at hand. Rather, this first result is closer to David Kirsh's distinction between actions of stabilization done ahead of time and actions of tools placement performed online (Kirsh 1995). Our attempt to reconcile both levels is therefore based on the focus we put on activities without drawing a clear distinction between environment preparation done ahead of time and body movement with tools at reaching hand performed in real time.

Second, we emphasize that the simulation-based device has been designed without any active engagement from healthcare practitioners' community. Put differently, the device's main users are not contributing to the design process. The idea of design in use bear upon other principles based on joint commitments of the user and the designer.

Third, the setting is arranged by the users to prepare the tools to have them at hand and in time. Our analysis highlights two types of meaningful disadjustments between instructions and routines:

- when a cue in a work setting that needs to be perceived and assessed is not available (evaluation phase, cf. Norman 1991)
- when an instruction cannot be transformed into a bodily routine (execution phase)

In both cases, the workspace as made of materials, cognitive artifacts and physical tools and body movements cannot act as a permanent external support for evaluation and improvised execution.

In that case, the video analysis shows a disadjustment between purposeful action designed at the institutional level by the HAS and situated actions that follow routines in simulated professional settings. This disadjustment could be put closer to the concept of "organizational dysfunctions" that is not neutral, since identified by scholars as a possible cause of decline (Cameron et al. 1987). In our case, this organizational dysfunction could result from the perceived inability by nurses to perform a task in a simulated setting. In real equivalent professional settings, and during the course of professionals' action, healthcare professionals find relevant cues—materialized in objects—located in their work environment at reaching hand.

Hollan et al. (2000, p. 177) argued that "the human body and the material world take on central than peripheral roles", since "minds are not passive representational engines, whose primary functions is to create internal models of the external world. The relations between internal process and external ones are far more complex involving coordination at many different time scales between internal resources – memory, attention, executive function – and external resources – the objects, artifacts and at hand materials constantly surrounding us". Hence, the notion of "at hand materials" is a good illustration of why materials matter so much both to explain and to observe the use of medical artifacts in a work setting. Moreover, literature on simulation techniques in healthcare claims that "there is a widespread belief that simulation experiences (and effectiveness) improve proportionately as the precision of the replication of the real world improves" (Dieckman et al. 2007, p. 183). Yet, we argue that the degree of replication of the real world is inherently dependent on the ways simulated scenarios had been initially thought by the institutional frame. Scenarios/instructions that are meant to create the conditions for an everyday professional practice are not enough or dedicated to capture routines and dynamics that would emerge in a familiar environment. The strict adherence of specific routines to the setting (cf. Clark 1996) is broken by the simulation framework.

Overall, this chapter offers some new insights to go beyond these discrepancies between institutional plan and situated actions. In particular, the elaboration of a bottom-up design or design in use of the socio-technical device could reach a better involvement from healthcare professionals and develop a more contextualized oriented governance for the execution of actions. As Clark (1996, p. 66) put it, "the key it seems lies in the extent to which the individuals rely on highly structured environment which they create and then inhabit". This implies, therefore, that when the workspace is no more adapted and inhabited by the user, the disadjustment emerges.

Regarding the main chapter's ambition, one could argue that the existing gap between organizational institutionalism and situated action cannot be filled without referring to arguments still in tension. Efforts still have to be made to develop a "material based organizational institutionalism". Similarly, the step for situated action to reach an ecological and material-based approach still exists despite interesting arguments in G.H. Mead's conception of the workspace. Based on this first attempt to reconcile both approaches, next avenues of research have to bring even closer OI and situated approaches, on a material ground (seen as a common denominator). The clarification of the notion of action arena conceived as both an institution and a material device could be a good candidate for future research.

Appendices

Appendix 1

Video sequence transcription
  D: doctor, N: nurse

00.04   1. D: allez vite le massage
D: *come on let's go for the massage quickly*
Doctor holding oxygenation's mask on the face of the patient----to 11
ip on the machine --to 11
Drawers noise --to

00.07   2. D: : ( ) vite
hurry up

00.14   3 D: y a un choc qui est délivré a priori il devrait être délivré ?
there is a shock which is delivered in theory it should be delivered ?
electronic voice AED ---------------------------------------
----to 11

00.17   4 D: allez le choc est. délivré (.) on recule
here it goes shock is delivered(.) you have to be at distance
doctor's gesture to indicate shock imminence

00.20   5 D: c'est. bon pour le choc.
it's ok for the shock

00.23   6 D: allez on reprend l'massage ( )
let's go and start the massage again
Doctor oriented towards computer----

00.30   **7 D: c'est bon pour la perf ?=**
ready to put the drip on?
Doctor looking at nurse

0031   **8 N: = ouais je sais je sais (.) il manque du matériel**
yeah I know I know (.) material is missing
nurse is still searching for tools ---------------->

00.34   **9 D: allez la perf c'est posé ?**
Come on, is the drip on?
10 N: = ah c'est bon.
I found it

00.40   **The nurse finds the needle and intravenous drugs**
The nurse's assistant leaving the patient's bed and going near the nurse
The nurse seems to talk to herself
11 N: (inaudible)

00.42   *The nurse's assistant looks at the nurse*

Appendix 2

Transcription of the nurse's interview during the auto confrontation session.

R: researcher
N:nurse

Looking together at the video, the researcher asks nurse to describe the moment when she was searching tools in the trolley's drawers.

R: Is it the same material you use in real settings? Usually, have you got some cues concerning the material's locations?
N:the configuration is not the same at all that in the... that in our own ward
R: not the same at all
N:hmm
N:**completely different. material was not in the usual place, everything was messy in the trolley so ... so in fact I started panicking, I started panicking rather quickly**

References

Agre, P. (1985). *Routines*, MIT Memo 828.
Agre, P. (1997). *Computation and human experience*. New York: Cambridge University Press.
Benner, P. E., & Tanner, C. A. (1987). Clinical judgment: How expert nurses use intuition. *The American Journal of Nursing, 87*(1), 23–31.
Berger, T., & Luckmann, P. (1967). *The social construction of reality*. New York: Doubleday Anchor.
Boxenbaum E., Huault, I., & Leca B. (2016), Le tournant matériel dans la théorie néo-institutionnaliste. In F. X. de Vaujany, A. Hussenot, & J. F. Chanlat (Eds.), *Théorie des Organisations: Nouveaux Tournants* (pp. 227–238). Paris, France: Economica.
Cameron, K. S., Whetten, D. A., & Kim, M. U. (1987). Organizational dysfunctions of decline. *Academy of Management Journal, 30*(1), 126–138.

Clark, A. (1996). *Being there: Putting brain, body and world together again.* Cambridge: MIT Press.

Clot, Y., Faïta, D., Fernandez, G., & Scheller, L. (2000). Entretiens en auto-confrontation croisée : une méthode en clinique de l'activité. *Perspectives interdisciplinaires sur le travail et la santé, 2*(1), 1–20.

de Vaujany, F.-X., & Mitev, N. N. (Eds.). (2013). *Materiality and space: Organizations, artifacts and practices.* Basingstoke: Palgrave Macmillan.

Dieckman, P., Gaba, D., & Rall, M. (2007). Deepening the theoretical foundations of patient simulation as social practice. *Simulation in Healthcare: Journal of the Society for Simulation in Healthcare, 2*(3), 183–193.

Dourish, P. (2001). Seeking a foundation for context-aware computing. *Human Computer Interaction, 16,* 239–241.

Faita, D. (1997). La conduite du TGV, exercice de styles. *Champs visuels, 6,* 75–86.

Gherardi, S. (2000). Practice-based theorizing on learning and knowing in organizations: An introduction. *Organization, 7*(2), 211–223.

Gibson, J. J. (1986). *The ecological approach to perception.* Hillsdale: Lawrence Erlbaum Associates.

Goodwin, C. (1981). *Conversational organization, interaction between speakers and hearers* (pp. Xii+195). New York: Academic.

Gray, B., Purdy, J. M., & Ansari, S. S. (2015). From interactions to institutions: Microprocesses of framing and mechanisms for the structuring of institutional fields. *Academy of Management Review, 40,* 115–143.

Greenwood, R., Oliver, C., Sahlin, K., & Suddaby, R. (2008). Introduction. In R. Greenwood, C. Oliver, K. Sahlin, & R. Suddaby (Eds.), *The SAGE handbook of organizational institutionalism* (pp. 1–46). London: Sage.

Gylfe, P., Franck, H., Lebaron, C., & Mantere, S. (2016). Video methods in strategy research: Focusing on embodied cognition. *Strategic Management Journal, 37,* 137–148.

Harmon, D. J., Green, S. E., & Goodnight, G. T. (2015). A model of rhetorical legitimation: The structure of communication and cognition underlying institutional maintenance and change. *Academy of Management Review, 40,* 76–95.

Heath, C., & Luff, P. (2000). *Technology in action.* Cambridge: Cambridge University Press.

Hollan, J., Hutchins, E., & Kirsh, D. (2000). Distributed cognition: Toward a new foundation for human-computer interaction research. *ACM Transactions on Computer-Human Interaction, 7*(2), 174–196.

Hutchins, E. (1995). *Cognition in the wild.* Cambridge: MIT Press.

Kirsh, D. (1995). The intelligent use of space. *Artificial Intelligence, 73*(1–2), 31–68.

Kontos, P. C., & Naglie, G. (2009). Tacit knowledge of caring and embodied selfhood. *Sociology of Health & Illness, 31*(5), 668–704.

Lave, J. (1988). *Cognition in practice.* Cambridge: Cambridge University Press.

Mead, G. H. (1932). *Philosophy of the present.* Chicago: Chicago University Press.

Meyer, J., & Rowan, B. (1977). Institutionalized organizations: Formal structure as myths and ceremony. *American Journal of Sociology, 83,* 340–363.

Mondada, L. (2006). Video recording as the preservation of fundamental features for analysis. In H. Knoblauch, J. Raab, H.-G. Soeffner, & B. Schnettler (Eds.), *Video analysis.* Bern: Lang.

Monteiro, P., & Nicolini, D. (2014). Recovering materiality in institutional work: Prizes as an assemblage of human of material entities. *Journal of Management Inquiry, 24*(1), 1–21.

Norman, D. (1988). *The psychology of everyday things.* New York: Basic Books.

Norman, D. (1991). Cognitive artifacts. In J. M. Carroll (Ed.), *Designing interaction: Psychology at the human-computer interface* (pp. 17–38). New York: Cambridge University Press.

Ostrom, E. (2005). *Understanding institutional diversity.* Princeton: Princeton University Press.

Ostrom, E. (2007). Institutional rational choice: An assessment of the institutional analysis and development framework. In P. A. Sabatier (Ed.), *Theories of the policy process* (2nd ed., pp. 21–64). Boulder: Westview Press.

Ostrom, E., & Basurto, X. (2011). Crafting analytical tools to study institutional change. *Journal of Institutional Economics, 7*(3), 317–343.

Philips, N., & Lawrence, T. B. (2012). The turn to work in organization and management theory: Some implications for strategic organization. *Strategic Organization, 10*(3), 223–230.

Phillips, N., & Malhotra, N. (2008). Taking social construction seriously: Extending the discursive approach in institutional theory. In R. Greenwood, C. Oliver, K. Sahlin, & R. Suddaby (Eds.), *The SAGE handbook of organizational institutionalism* (pp. 702–720). Thousand Oaks: Sage.

Phillips, N., Lawrence, T. B., & Hardy, C. (2004). Discourse and institutions. *Academy of Management Review, 29,* 635–652.

Pope, C., Smith, A., Goodwin, D., & Mort, M. (2003). Passing on tacit knowledge in anaesthesia: A qualitative study. *Medical Education, 37,* 650–655.

Powell, W. W., & Colyvas, J. A. (2008). Microfoundations of institutional theory. In C. Oliver, K. Sahlin, & R. Suddaby (Eds.), *The Sage handbook of organizational institutionalism* (pp. 276–298). London: Sage.

Rao, H., Monin, P., & Durand, R. (2003). Institutional change in Toqueville: Nouvelle cuisine as an identity movement in French gastronomy. *American Journal of Sociology, 180*(4), 795–843.

Relieu, M. (2006). Remarques sur l'analyse conversationnelle et les technologies médiatisées. *Revue Française de Linguistique Appliquée, XI*(2), 17–32.

Sacks, H. (1984). Notes on methodology. In M. Atkinson & J. Heritage (Eds.), *Structures of social action: Studies in conversation analysis* (pp. 21–27). Cambridge: Cambridge University Press.

Suchman, L. (2009). *Human-machine reconfigurations: Plans and situated actions.* Cambridge: Cambridge University Press.

Suddaby, R., & Greenwood, R. (2009). Methodological issues in researching institutional change. In D. Buchanan & A. Bryman (Eds.), *The Sage handbook of organizational research methods* (pp. 176–195). Los Angeles: Sage.

Zucker, L. G. (1977). The role of institutionalization in cultural persistence. *American Sociological Review, 42*, 726–743.

Zucker, L. G. (1991). Postscript: Microfoundations of institutional thought. In W. W. Powell & P. J. DiMaggio (Eds.), *The new institutionalism in organizational analysis* (pp. 103–107). Chicago: University of Chicago Press.

Part IV

Body and Embodiment

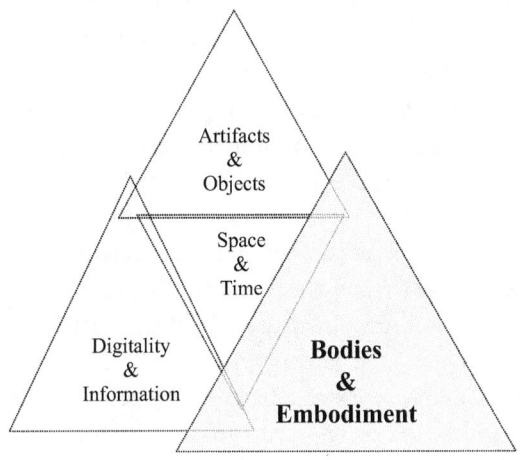

Key Questions

- How do bodies allow for experimentation with institutions?
- How are institutions embodied?
- How do discourse and bodies articulate with one another?

The chapters in this section engage with the relations between bodies and institutions. How institutions become embodied in actors' behaviors and eventually shape human bodies has been debated for a while. Foucault is a frequent reference here but multiple other authors from vastly different traditions (e.g. Bourdieu, Butler, Elias, Goffman to name a few) have pointed to the social mechanisms by which institutions shape behaviors and bodies as well as their consequences. Yet ironically, existing institutional theory has paid little attention to this bodily aspect, focusing primarily on discourse. Whereas some recent institutionalist research has started to engage with this bodily aspect (e.g. Creed et al. 2010), the two chapters in this section explore alternative approaches.

Nørholm Just and Kirkegaard examine how a critical perceptive on the bodily instantiation of an institution can question the institution. Drawing from the field of film analysis, they consider how a documentary on Danish soldiers can question war. War is here considered as an institution. The documentary focuses on the materiality of soldierly bodies and by showing and questioning those bodies, it questions the institution of war that shapes them. Though developing a critical discourse on soldierly bodies, the movie attempts to question and shape social imageries of war. Nørholm Just and Kirkegaard look in particular at moments of 'plasticity', the moment of production (or encoding of meaning), the film as 'meaningful' discourse and the moment of reception (or decoding of meaning). They argue that in those moments, relationship between the soldiers' bodies, the military institution and the social imaginary of war can be revealed, questioned and potentially reconfigured. They suggest that such plasticity may work as a bridge between the material ontology and discursive epistemology of institutional configurations.

De Vaujany's chapter does not entirely focus on bodies. Focusing on legitimacy, a central notion of institutional theory, he suggests a distinction between three ontologies: an ontology of discourse (which would stress the importance of social judgment, rhetoric, discursive structures and their conditions of felicity in the process of legitimation), an 'ontology of sculpture' (which would emphasize the spatial and material dimensions of legitimation but remain partly discursive), and an ontology of bubbles (that would emphasize jointly the importance of bodies, materiality, spatiality and temporality in the legitimation process and would

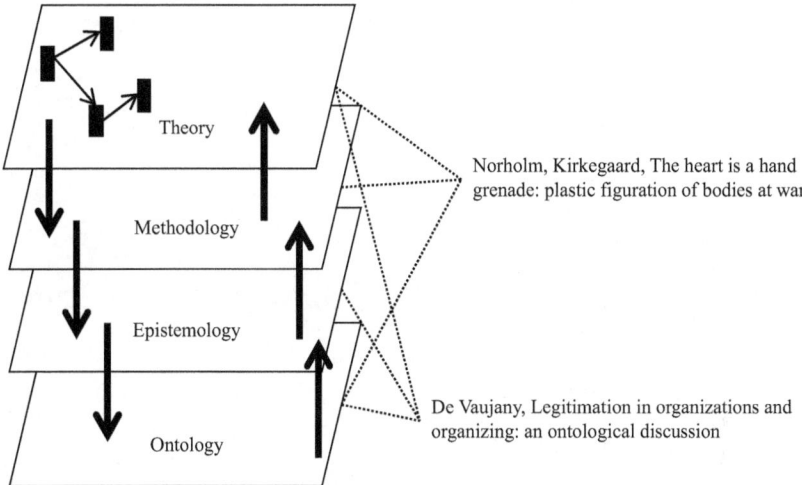

Norholm, Kirkegaard, The heart is a hand grenade: plastic figuration of bodies at war

De Vaujany, Legitimation in organizations and organizing: an ontological discussion

Fig. 1 A reflexive journey on bodies and embodiment through the chapters

move from considering legitimacy in the eyes (and mind) of the beholder, to consider legitimacy in the (moving) bodies of the people involved in a collective movement). He specifies the contribution of these ontologies to knowledge creation and institutional theory.

The two chapters introduce different perspectives into institutional analysis in a broad sense, and both point to the centrality of bodies and embodiment not only from a theoretical but also from ontological, epistemological and methodological stances (Fig. 1).

References

Creed, W. E. D., DeJordy, R., & Lok, J. (2010). Being the change: Resolving institutional contradiction through identity work. *Academy of Management Journal, 53*, 1336–1364.

11

The Heart Is a Hand Grenade: Plastic Figurations of Bodies at War

Sine Nørholm Just and Line Kirkegaard

Introduction: Institutionalized Representations of Bodies at War

War films offer civilians an opportunity to glimpse into 'the heart of darkness'; to become affectively and cognitively involved in acts of war, usually too distant for unaided imagination and interpretation (Koppes and Black 1990). Following this premise, we extend the argument that popular culture should be of interest for organization studies, generally (Rehn 2008; Rhodes and Westwood 2008), to include the study of the organization of the army, more specifically (Godfrey 2009). That is, studies of war films may provide insights into how the institutions of warfare

S. Nørholm Just (✉)
Department of Communication and Arts, Roskilde University, Roskilde, Denmark
e-mail: sinenjust@ruc.dk

L. Kirkegaard
University College Absalon, Næstved, Denmark
e-mail: liki@pha.dk

© The Author(s) 2019   313
F.-X. de Vaujany et al. (eds.), *Materiality in Institutions*, Technology, Work and Globalization, https://doi.org/10.1007/978-3-319-97472-9_11

are filtered through the institutions of popular culture so as to provide the public with frameworks for making sense of historical as well as contemporary acts of war. Such films, then, offer opportunities for researching the social imaginary of war.[1]

This chapter introduces the method of film analysis as a means of exploring the relationship between institutions and their publics. We focus on war films as privileged sites for gauging the public understanding of the institutional field of warfare. Here, an institutional field is defined as the relationship between a set of involved actors that endows them with a purpose (Barley 2010, p. 780), but also as the process of negotiating this purpose (Green et al. 2008, p. 42). *In casu*: what are the military commands, what are the political priorities, what are the public concerns? And, most importantly, how are these configured in relation to each other so as to constitute the institutional field of warfare?

In seeking to answer these questions for our present day and age, we have identified a group of similarly configured and configuring films that seems to have emerged around the coalition forces' involvement in Afghanistan. Notable examples include the American productions *Restrepo* (2010) and *Lone Survivor* (2014), the Danish *Armadillo* (2010) and the British *Kajaki* (2014). Two of these, *Restrepo* and *Armadillo*, are documentaries while *Lone Survivor* and *Kajaki* are feature films based on true stories. The tendency towards documentarism—or, perhaps more accurately, of blending fact and fiction—is a common trait of this group. Another shared feature is that the films are close-up and personal narratives of individual soldiers who remain loyal to the portrayed subjects and do not offer explicit ethical or political evaluations of their characters or actions. The viewing public, then, is provided with opportunities for intense identification with the soldier on the ground, but the films do not enter the strategic war room and, hence, do not explain the broader political and/or social meanings of the portrayed events. If anything, the message one is left with is that the efforts and sacrifices of the soldiers are

---

[1] Here, and in the following, we use the term 'social imaginary' in the sense advocated by Castoriadis: "The imaginary of which I am speaking is not an image *of*. It is the unceasing and essentially *undetermined* (social, historical and psychical) creation of figures/forms/images, on the basis of which alone there can ever be a question *of* 'something'. What we call 'reality' and 'rationality' are its works" (Castoriadis 1987, p. 3; emphasis in original).

meaningless. This, in turn, could be seen as an indirect critique of the military institution; if there is no higher purpose to the 'legitimate use of violence', is it, in fact, legitimate? The films raise this issue, but provide no easy answers, leaving the institutional field of warfare open to (re-) figuration.

In the case of *Armadillo*, which will be the object of close analysis in this chapter, the films' shared features take the specific form of close scrutiny of a group of soldiers as they—literally and figuratively—become other. Other to themselves as they are trained for and enter into combat. Other to society as they enact the military command. Importantly, the act of killing figures as both the final inclusion and the ultimate exclusion. That which makes the soldier, but also sets him (and in *Armadillo* the soldier is a 'him') apart and renders him (an)other. Thus, a duality— rather than dichotomy—of making *and* breaking configures the relationship between the individual soldier, the institution of the army and the country he serves.[2] The image on the promotional material for *Armadillo* indicates what is at stake: it features a heart that is also (or is becoming) a hand grenade. We take our cue—and our title—from this figurative merger of body and weapon as we explore how the merger is enacted in and through the story of the soldiers whose tour in Afghanistan the film documents; how destruction and death meet pleasure and life in one devastatingly excessive (speech) act. It is in exposing this moment of becoming-through-destruction that *Armadillo* both provides the most revealing insights into the private tragedies of war and prompts the most resounding public reactions: if no longer able to ignore the atrocities of war and if unable to perceive their higher purpose, how can the public continue to allow them to be carried out in its name?

This, we will claim, is the question with which *Armadillo* leaves its viewers. Thereby, the film provides the empirical inspiration for our theoretical contribution, which consists of a recalibration of the relationship between materiality and discourse in the study of institutions and institutional change. The relationship between the soldiers' bodies, the

---

[2] Relationships between institutions and society are at stake in other chapters of the book. In Chap. 2, Jourdan explores the ways institutions leave a footprint in society. In Chap. 6, Adrot and Bia-Figueiredo explore the institutional stakes related to the effectiveness of emergency response.

military institution and the social imaginary of war, we argue, may be conceptualized through the notion of plasticity: of giving, taking and blowing up form (Malabou 2007, 2010). Focusing specifically on the materiality of soldierly bodies, we seek to show how even the immediate physicality of these bodies is riddled with discourse—it is both formed by and formative of social expectations and, hence, institutional arrangements.

In order to conceptualize and illustrate the plastic relationships between bodies and discourses, and institutions and social imaginaries, the chapter will unfold the moment of becoming-through-destruction as central to the identity of not only individual soldiers, but to the public configuration of the institutional field of warfare as such. The argument will be presented in three main steps: first, we discuss the relationships between ideas and materiality, generally, and discourse and bodies, specifically. Here, we position our framework within institutional theory and offer the notion of plasticity as an intermediary concept for the analysis of institutional fields as configured by the relationships of materiality and ideas, and bodies and discourse. Second, we suggest how the philosophical concept of plasticity may be operationalized for empirical studies, thereby establishing the methodological framework for the analysis of *Armadillo*. Finally, we conduct the analysis and offer our conclusions.

Theory: Plastic Bodies in Institutional Fields

In focusing on the interrelations of political institutions and popular cultural products, generally, and social imaginaries of war and public exposure to acts of killing, specifically, we are, on the one hand, building on the assumption that ideas drive institutional dynamics (see inter alia Orren 1995; Campbell 1998; Carstensen and Schmidt 2016). On the other hand, however, we seek to qualify assumptions of simple causality by teasing out the dynamic interrelations of ideas and materiality (see inter alia Jones et al. 2013; Lawrence et al. 2013; Hardy and Thomas 2015). Hence, we find that the (re-)introduction of materiality in institutional analysis is both timely and useful, but we caution against ruling out discourse altogether. Our aim is not to (re-)assert the performative power of matter over mind (Butler 1993; Barad 2003). Rather, we advocate an approach that is fully sensitive to the co-productions of material realities and discursive articulations and teases out their performative interrelations (Cederström and Spicer 2014). A materialist ontology with an ideational epistemology, we might say.

How, then, are ideas and materialities co-productive of institutional fields and, more specifically, how do discourses and bodies figure in such fields? Translating this theoretical query to the particular context of war on film, how are specific soldierly bodies configured and configuring in relation to particular films? And how do these specific body-discourse relations, in turn, relate to the broader ideational-material configuration of the institutional field of warfare? Before turning to the methodological issue of how these questions might be answered empirically, let us unpack their conceptual dimension.

The general relationship between ideas and materialities has already been hinted at in the initial definition of institutional fields. While not exactly physical things, institutions are commonly viewed as rather stable entities. North (1991), for instance, defines institutions as "the humanly devised constraints that structure political, economic and social interaction" (p. 97). However, institutions not only form the context of interaction, they are also products of interaction—as emerges from North's acknowledgement that institutional constraints are 'humanly devised'. Institutions condition social construction and are themselves social constructs.

The issue of the social construction of institutions lies at the heart of the strands of neo-institutional literature that expound the institutional roles of rhetoric, logics, discourse or, simply, communication (see inter alia Phillips et al. 2004; Green and Li 2011; Thornton et al. 2012; Cornelissen et al. 2015). The sheer amount of such contributions may testify to their weight, suggesting that institutions are all but thoroughly communicative constructs. However, recent contributions to this literature conceptualize communication as not only related to materiality, but, indeed, itself material. Thus, Ashcraft et al. (2009) argue that "...an organization is both symbolically made *and* materially real: 'It' assumes meaning as agents move on its behalf; and 'it' becomes material as embodied in these very agents" (p. 37, emphasis in original). The organization, then, emerges as "...the *configuration* of human and non-human representatives" (ibid., emphasis in original). This entanglement of ideational and material aspects of organizing may be extended to processes of institutional configuration:

> Thus, institutional work, similar to any form of work, needs to be understood as the result of a distributed effort of humans and materials, not simply as the product of individual intentional action. The same way a mason cannot construct a wall without cement and bricks, no institutions can be created, maintained, or disrupted without materials. (Monteiro and Nicolini 2015, p. 74)

Institutions are the intermittent outcomes of socio-material processes in and through which social and material elements are ordered in relation to each other so as to enable the articulation of certain views (and not others) and the execution of certain acts (and not others).

The assertion of a mutually constitutive relationship between matters and ideas in the formation of institutions provides a general starting point for investigating the more specific link between bodies and discourse; the point being that ideational-material relationships are specified in and as relationships between discourses and objects. Just as "…an object has a socially meaningful existence only insofar as it is rendered intelligible through discourse", so discourses are "embodied in certain material manifestations" (Cederström and Spicer 2014, p. 10). Here, discourses are defined simply as patterns of meaning formation; communicative regularities for rendering social and material realities meaningful. As such, discourses do not talk material objects into being, but we can only understand materiality by way of discourse; for example, a piece of paper may exist independently of what is written on it, but it only becomes available as a technology for writing in and through discursive interventions that, for instance, teach how to write or instruct on what to write (Withagen et al. 2012). Conversely, discourses are not in themselves material entities, but can only be expressed materially; a text only takes shape as text by means of pen and paper—or other technologies for writing and reading (Scollon and Levine 2004).

Although we tend to think of the body as a different kind of object than, say, paper, it can also be shaped by and give shape to discourse.

Hence, the body becomes meaningful in and through the (re-)enactment of social norms and it may in its very corporeality push against and potentially change existing norms:

> As a consequence of being in the mode of becoming, and in always living with the constitutive possibility of becoming otherwise, the body is that which can occupy the norm in myriad ways, exceed the norm, rework the norm, and expose realities to which we thought we were confined as open to transformation. These corporeal realities are actively inhabited, and this "activity" is not fully constrained by the norm. (Butler 2004, p. 217)

The body, then, is shaped by its discursive 'habitat' or social context, but can also shape it:

> ...which bodies "logically" or "naturally" align with tasks is never self-evident; neither is it a matter of economic, institutional, or even cultural destiny. Instead the work-body relation is always up for grabs ... communication is the dynamic mechanism of that struggle; it is how individual and institutional voices vie for the particular combination of materiality and symbolism in which they are invested. (Ashcraft 2011, p. 17)

Existing discourses enable certain bodies (and not others) to take on specific roles and tasks (and not others) in the institutionalized contexts into which these bodies enter, for instance those of work. However, conditions of bodily possibility are never stable, but actively shaped and reshaped by the encounters between bodies and discourses within institutional settings. That is, while some institutionalized materialities may work directly on the bodies of individual actors (say, is that chair uncomfortable?), such purely material relationships only become meaningful when articulated in discourse (No? Then you ought to get a new chair). Further, such articulation is never passive, but will influence the broader socio-material relationships of which it speaks (are the current policies on the physical environment at your workplace sufficient to cater for your ergonomic needs?) (see Table 11.1 for a systematic overview of the interrelations of materialities, bodies, discourses, ideas and institutions).

In seeking tools for studying the discursive-bodily/ideational-material interrelations, we introduce Malabou's notion of plasticity as an intermediary

Table 11.1 Relationships between materialities, bodies, ideas, discourses and institutions

	Materiality-body	Materiality-discourse	Discourse-body	Idea-institution
Relationship	Institutionalized materialities shape our bodies	Who gets to speak, what can be said, and how it can be uttered are materially conditioned	Discourse shapes how we make sense of bodily and other materialities	Discursively articulated ideas maintain/reform institutional configurations
Illustrative example	The furniture supplied in offices (cubicles), classrooms (rows of chairs and tables) and other institutionalized settings influence how we physically twist and turn in the room	The arrangement of furniture directs communication; e.g. impairing conversation (each individual working alone in the cubicle) or inviting monologue or controlled dialogue (in the classroom the teacher talks and students ask—or answer—questions)	What are we to make of the current seating arrangements in institutionalized settings like offices and classrooms? Are they efficient in terms of getting the work done? Healthy for the human body? Conducive of creative encounters? The questions asked and answers given shape our understanding of the current situation	If the current material arrangements do not meet discursively articulated norms (ideational means or ends), they can be changed. If, for instance, dialogue becomes an ideal of interaction, it is possible to alter materialities according to this ideal; e.g. rearrange the furniture in institutional settings (open offices, groups of tables)

concept. Plasticity, we suggest, may work as a bridge between the material ontology and discursive epistemology of institutional configurations. Malabou recovers the notion of plasticity from within the Hegelian *oeuvre* and, in broad terms, uses it to rework relations of sameness and difference, stability and change, placing these relations squarely within the realm of form. Plasticity is an immanent force of figuration: "There is no outside, nor is there any immobility" (Malabou 2010, p. 44). More specifically, "plasticity designates the double aptitude of being able both to receive form (clay is plastic) and to give form (the plastic arts or plastic surgery)" (Malabou 2007, p. 434). Further, we may speak of 'plastic explosives' or explosive plasticity, and introducing this third type of plasticity allows Malabou to establish a spectrum of taking, giving and exploding form: "Plasticity is clearly placed between two polar extremes, with the sensible figure that is the taking shape in form (sculpture or plastic object) on the one side and the destruction of all form (explosion) on the other" (Malabou 2010, p. 87).

The ability to take, give and blow up form, Malabou (2010, p. 45) asserts, is inherent to form itself; plasticity is 'essentially material': form is not just a raw material substance that must be worked, reworked and if necessary destroyed by something else, a transcendent force; form itself gives itself the ability to shape, receive, and blow up forms (Crockett 2010, p. xiii).

Thus, the plastic process, whatever form it takes, does not have recourse to an outside, but works on form from within: "*There is no exceeding of form that does not assume the plasticity of form and hence its convertibility*" (Malabou 2010, p. 46, *emphasis in original*).

In a piece written conjointly with Butler, Malabou investigates what this plasticity of form means for the relationship between mind and body in the thinking of Hegel. Specifically, the two authors explore the notions of lordship and bondage, beginning from an earlier work of Butler's in which:

> She ventriloquizes Hegel by giving speech to the master: "the imperative to the bondsman consists in the following formulation: you be my body for me, but do not let me know that the body you are is my body." Bodily

substitution characterizes both detachment and attachment; detachment, because the master is the "I" who delegates his body (he detaches himself from his own flesh) to the bondsman. The lord's body is then to be found outside itself, in another being or consciousness. (Malabou and Butler 2011, pp. 613–614)

Beginning from this idea that the body only exists in a kind of vexed relationship, as a redoubling or deferral, a simultaneous attachment and detachment, Malabou writes in her response to Butler:

Originally, the self is not identical to itself; the mind and the body are definitely split. This doubling of the self is intolerable and maddening. The "feeling of self" in its immediate form is a "mental derangement." The "body is a foreign being" that contradicts the unity of the self. [...] Self-consciousness always asks somebody else "to be its body in its place," always tries to detach itself from its own incarnation. At the same time, this detachment always comes to fail, revealing the impossibility of a constant, pure, and permanent mastery over things and laboring bodies. (Ibid., p. 624)

The tension of difference and sameness, of being at one with yet other to oneself, means the 'subject is plastic', "both capable of shaping itself (of bestowing form on itself) and of receiving the very shape that it gives to itself as if it came from outside" (Ibid., p. 623). The subject is shaped by and takes shape from its own body—and is shaped by/gives shape to the minds and bodies of others—in a perpetual process that only stops when "the form of the 'I' explodes and dissolves itself" (Ibid., p. 624).

While Malabou (2010, pp. 12–13) offers the notion of plasticity as a 'hermeneutic motor scheme', a concept that may 'drive' interpretative efforts, generally speaking, the ensuing analysis will focus specifically on how it applies to the body. This does not mean that we will avoid broader issues; rather, we will study 'the plasticity of the body' as a synecdoche of institutional figuration. Before the analysis, we will briefly present its methodological practicalities, operationalizing the notion of plasticity and presenting the material to which it is applied.

Method: Moments of Plasticity

In the context of organizational studies of war, focusing on the interrelations of discourse and matter leads to subtle analyses of how socio-cultural interpretations are constituted by *and* constitutive of the individual soldier as well as the military institution (for a recent collection of such work, see Cornish and Saunders 2014). It is to this particular subfield of empirical knowledge that we will contribute with our case study of how the soldier-army relationship is figured in popular culture.

Theoretically and methodologically, however, we move beyond the case to offer concepts and tools for studying the interrelations of institutional arrangements and public understandings, more generally. Thus, the (possibly extreme) case of the institutions of war is illustrative of other institutions as well. The social imaginary of war, we argue, is significantly shaped by cinematic renditions of it: *Deer Hunter* (1978), *Apocalypse Now* (1979), *Platoon* (1986), *Born on the Fourth of July* (1989), *Black Hawk Down* (2001) … the list of iconic films that have shaped generationally and geographically segmented publics understandings of war goes on. The same, however, may be said for other socio-political and economic institutions; even though the public may have more ready access to at least some of these, films make up a significant shaping force of the social imaginary of them. For instance, there are iconic films about mental institutions (say, *One Flew Over the Cuckoo's Nest*, 1975), boarding schools (*Dead Poets Society*, 1989) and the law. The court room drama is, indeed, as established a genre as the war movie, replete with sub-genres, plot structures, set characters and so on. Think of *Kramer vs. Kramer* (1979), *Philadelphia* (1993), *Erin Brockovich* (2000) or, linking the law and the military, *A Few Good Men* (1992). Further, the financial markets have been the subject of major motion pictures: most famously in *Wall Street* (1987), the original story of ruthless greed, and most recently in *The Wolf of Wall Street* (2013) and similar attempts to come to terms with the causes and consequences of the global financial crisis.

Popular culture, then, offers rich resources for studying the social imaginary of organizations and institutions (see e.g. Rehn 2008; Rhodes and Westwood 2008 for the theoretical argument and Boncori 2017; Ewalt and Ohl 2013; Bugos 1996 for relevant case studies). In this context, we contribute a conceptual framework for understanding the plastic relationships between (popular cultural) discourses about and (institutionalized) materialities of the body, as established above, and a specific methodology for movie analysis, as will be presented and applied in what follows.

First, let us explicate the analytical focal points that follow from the application of our theoretical framework on the chosen empirical field: how are the bodies of soldiers given form in and how do they give form to social imaginaries of war? In order to address this issue, we will operationalize the concept of plasticity in relation to the production and reception of social imaginaries, just as we will inquire into the relations between the bodies of soldiers and the popular cultural products (war films) that figure them for the public. Thus, the analysis covers three 'moments of plasticity', that is, three distinct occurrences of the processes of giving, taking and, possibly, exploding form: the moment of production (or encoding of meaning), the film as 'meaningful' discourse and the moment of reception (or decoding of meaning) (Hall 2001; see also Just and Berg 2016; for an overview, see Table 11.2).

We study these three moments in relation to one particular film: the Danish documentary *Armadillo*. Admittedly, this choice incurs a loss in generalizability, but the single case is not only illustrative of our conceptual and methodological points; it is also, as indicated in the introduction, part of an empirical trend in the current public configuration of bodies at war. That said, we would like to emphasize that *Armadillo* is an extreme case (Flyvbjerg 2006, pp. 229–230) in the sense that it incurred more debate and, hence, held more potential to form the social imaginary than any of the other films in the group of real or realistic renditions of the war in Afghanistan. Further, while the film did gain international attention and acclaim—for instance, it won the prestigious Semaine de la Critique-award in Cannes 2010 and an Emmy Award for best editing in 2012—most of the controversy around it was confined to the Danish context.

The analysis, then, is, strictly speaking, an account of the shaping and reshaping of (social imaginaries of) bodies at war in one particular process of encoding and decoding of one specific film. We collected data for

Table 11.2 Moments of plasticity

	Taking form	Giving form	Exploding form
Moment of production	How is the film shaped by the producers' preconceptions of the content (e.g. political stance) with which it deals and the form it is to take (e.g. genre conventions)? How do the ideas materialize in and through the process of shooting and editing the film?	How does the process of making the film shape the producers' understanding of the material and its form? What opportunities for meaning formation arise in and through the obtained material?	Does the film shatter (individual) expectations and/or (social) conventions?
Meaningful discourse	How does the film take form from the reality it represents? How is it shaped by its topic (the institutional context) and the individuals (the bodies) it depicts?	How does the film give form to its topic? How do individuals and/or institutions appear on the screen? How is reality shaped by/ in the film?	Does the film shatter individuals and/or institutions?
Moment of reception	How is the film shaped by its reception? What are critics' and audiences' opinions of it?	How does the film shape its recipients? (How) does it alter their understanding of its topic?	Does the film shatter public opinions and/ or social imaginaries?

this study in three rounds, focusing, first, on the film as meaningful discourse. Here, we conducted a close reading of the film that aimed to identify and explain the relations between the soldiers' bodies and the film-as-discourse. Thus, we asked how the portrayed bodies take form in and give form to the film. Second, we looked back upon the moment of production by means of an interview with Janus Metz, the director of *Armadillo*. We met with Metz in April of 2016 and asked him to reflect upon how his preconceptions of bodies at war shaped the production of the film, how his close encounter with the bodily reality of war in the process of filming reshaped his conceptions, and how both pre- and reconceptions were encoded in the film. Finally, we investigated the reception of the film by means of a content analysis of the controversy it sparked. Here, we may first note *Armadillo's* numerical success with the

Danish public; more than 100,000 people saw it in cinemas across the country, and there were more than one million viewers when it was shown on national television (DFI 2012). The film was also reviewed in all major newspapers and other mainstream media, just as it was the subject of commentaries, features and analyses. We gathered and coded all such contributions, asking how the film was shaped by and gave shape to a prevailing social imaginary about the corporeality of war and, in so doing, contributed to a possible reconfiguration of the institutional field for talk and action concerning Danish involvement in military interventions abroad.

For the analysis, these three sources of data have been rearranged so as to reflect the taking, giving and explosion of form that runs through (or, perhaps more appropriately, cuts across) the film itself as well as its encoding and decoding. Thus, we identify and explain the dynamics that make and break (the social imaginary of) the soldier in *Armadillo*.

Analysis: Making and Breaking (the Social Imaginary of) the Soldier

As mentioned, the analysis shows how *Armadillo* takes form from, gives form to and explodes the form of bodies at war. Further, we seek to understand how these formative processes are experienced by the director at the moment of production, how they appear in the film-as-discourse and how they are received by the Danish public at the moment of reception. Thus, we began the analysis by searching for distinct 'moments of plasticity', but we soon found that these moments could not be as neatly ordered as we had expected. While one might assume that taking form could be linked to the moment of encoding, whereas giving form might be more prevalent at the moment of decoding, the process turned out to be more complex and entangled. We found that at the moments of encoding and decoding as well as in the film itself the dominant plastic relationship is one of duality; of making *and* breaking simultaneously. Here, three patterns recurred: one concerning the training and socialization of the soldiers; another having to do with the soldiers' bodies; the third relating the soldiers to society at large.

In what follows, we trace these three plastic relations across the film-as-discourse as well as its moments of encoding and decoding, detailing the interrelations of making, taking and breaking form that constitute them—materially and discursively. Thus, we will argue, each constitutes a particular articulation of the plastic duality of becoming-through-destruction. This duality, in turn, is the organizing logic of the social imaginary of war as offered by *Armadillo*.

'There and Back Again': The Narrative of the Soldier

In the interview with us, Metz explained how his documentary work relates to cinematic expositions of the experience of war:

> I have a deep interest in trying to understand what war really is. I mean, I have always been deeply fascinated by war films and war as a theme. [...] And war films have always been some of my favourite films and a point of reference in my artistic work, films like *Apocalypse Now* and *The Deerhunter* and *Full Metal Jacket*. I think most people, when they see *Armadillo*, will be able to see that those films exist alongside *Armadillo*. And it's not that I've been inspired by those film – or yes, I have also been inspired, but I could see the themes of those films being totally present and relevant in the conflict in Afghanistan when I went there.[3]

The director's preconception of war was shaped by war films and gave shape to *Armadillo*—thematically and narratively. Thus, the plot structure of *Armadillo* mirrors that of many classical war films. Following the pattern of 'there and back again', the film moves chronologically from the soldiers' preparation for their tour in Afghanistan through the events of the tour and ends with scenes of their homecoming. In sum, *Armadillo* follows the transformation of a platoon of recruits from ordinary young men to seasoned soldiers—and takes its form from this process.

Hence, the film follows the formation of the soldiers, beginning with their socialization into the military institution and its concomitant

---

[3] All material—the film, the interview with Metz and the media coverage—was originally in Danish. The translations are our own.

subject positions. The pattern is well known, including scenes of hard physical training and impeccable discipline, of macho bravado, but also more tender displays of hesitation and doubt. Then the training is over and the soldiers begin their tour at Forward Operating Base Armadillo (from which the film takes its name) in Helmand, Afghanistan; the year is 2009, eight years on from the ejection of the Taleban from its seat of power in Kabul and eight years into the international forces' attempt at stabilizing the country. The bulk of *Armadillo* takes place in the theatre of war, following what happens to the soldiers while there, and the film reaches its conclusion as the soldiers' tour ends. Again, the scenes are reminiscent of those of other renditions of soldiers' return: greetings with banners and flags, commemorative parades, solitary motorcycle rides, moments of silence. The final frame is particularly iconic: one soldier's naked body, alone in the shower, eyes closed as the water pours down.

Metz acknowledges that following a well-known plot structure and drawing on the established imaginary of war films lends a certain shape to reality, but he also finds that *Armadillo* as a documentary is different from both works of fiction and journalistic accounts. Against accusations that documentaries are closer to fiction than reality, he says:

> I don't find that reality lives one place or another [in feature films or journalism]. To the contrary, I'd say there is a lot of journalism that has a particular angle on reality while there are films, which have a freedom because they don't have to account to real people who might want to sue or something; that gives them freedom. And based on research or on experience they are able to get even closer, and maybe also because they are art, they can get closer to a difficult reality.

However, the documentary is also different from the pure work of art, he argues:

> ...we step out of the museum of art into where it's suddenly dangerous. And that is why the discussion of such a film becomes fiercer, also the political discussion about what is reality or not reality.

And:

> The negotiation of reality becomes very intense when we are dealing with documentarism.

Here, Metz touches upon one of the controversies that the film spurred at its reception; many commentators focused on the question of whether or not the film manipulated reality (i.e. formed it unduly) (Funch 2014). Some used the matter of the film's form as a means of dismissing its content (Kornø 2010). Accepting that reality is 'always already manipulated', however, others went on to debate *Armadillo*'s potential to blow up the institutional field of Danish military intervention in Afghanistan. As one reviewer put it:

> *Armadillo* is a film that may change Danish history. It is not certain that it will do so, but it might. It is doubtful whether it will have any direct political influence, but it might. Nor is it certain that it will change the Danes' relationship to the war we are a part of in a poor country far, far away, but it might. (Carlsen 2010)

The film, then, provides the public with a recognizable pattern in and through which to interpret reality. It makes accounts of actual experiences of war available to the Danish public, but these accounts can, potentially, be dismissed as fiction.

In sum, the first duality is one of absence *and* presence. The narrative pattern of 'there and back again' sets the soldiers apart from civilians, but it does so in a familiar way. Thus, the soldiers of *Armadillo* become recognizable as soldiers. The fictionalized account means audiences can both become involved with the reality of war *and* distance themselves from it. We will return to the details of how this involvement-at-a-distance played out in the third analytical round, but first we zoom in on the formation of the soldiers' bodies.

'The Act of Killing': The Body of the Soldier

Couched within the narrative frame of 'there and back again', *Armadillo* zooms in on what happens to the soldiers during their time in Afghanistan.

Three bodily (trans)formations—or figures of the body at war—recur: the bored body, the wounded body and the killing body. The introduction of these figures follows the chronology of the tour loosely: long sequences of waiting in the camp are (finally) replaced by engagement in combat that result in casualties and gradually introduce the killing body, which becomes the dominant motif in a long sequence towards the end of the film. We will focus particularly on this last figure as this is also where the film, ultimately, places its focus. In *Armadillo*, we will seek to show, the act of killing is the key transition, the crystallization of becoming-through-destruction. It is the taking of someone else's life that renders the individual other from the society of civilians and one with the collective of soldiers. Before making this point, however, let us briefly explore how the two other figures are formative of the soldiers' bodies.

Upon arrival, the soldiers are assured that they will see plenty of action in the field, but soon discover that a lot of their time is spent within the confines of the camp. The duties of the soldiers quickly become tedious routines. Shifts in the watchtower are long and enervating. Patrols of the neighbouring fields and villages are like "going to the Tivoli and getting the most boring instead of the most exciting ride", as one of the recruits puts it. Local civilians are generally unwilling to share any information or even to engage in conversation with the Danish soldiers. And when they do talk, they mostly complain. The soldiers are increasingly unable to tell friend from enemy. Briefs and debriefs are tiresome reminders of the importance of compliance with every rule. The soldiers, in consequence, spend much of their time vacillating between boisterous expressions of how they long for hostile engagement and more hesitant articulations of doubts—even fears—as to how they will react when actually facing the enemy. "There is no way of knowing until you've tried", they conclude. The bored body is tense with inertia, stressed from doing nothing. It demands relief.

When action first arrives, it is as unexpected as it has been longed for. The routine of patrolling is suddenly interrupted by gunshots. The exchange of fire is intense, but brief, and soon hostile engagements become part of the routine; monotonous inactivity with patches of hyper-action as markers of time. Thus, engagement in combat only temporarily releases the body from boredom; it quickly subsides and leaves the bored body craving more. A deeper transformation takes more than a little action; it takes a wound. The first wounded soldier in the film is the platoon commander who is transferred to Denmark for medical care, but is set on returning to active service in Afghanistan. And he does come back. Here, the wounded body is a heroic figure; he has made a sacrifice and is justified in his desire to continue to fight.

The next wound, however, is less noble. This time the wounded is a private; he steps on a land mine during what was supposed to be a routine patrol. At a subsequent briefing one of the commanding officers describes his condition as stable, but both legs have been amputated and he has serious damages to his scrotum and abdomen. While this soldier will survive, he will not return to the battlefield. Here, a greater price is paid, but no personal redemption is in sight. In response to such injustice, the rest of the group feels shooting 'the assholes' is warranted. The destruction of one body makes the collective body more destructive. It marks the introduction of the third figure: the killing body.

The appearance of the killing body was one of the aspects that shaped Metz' encoding of the film most definitively. As he described it:

> I found that it was a much darker narrative than I'd thought it would be. I had this heroic image of the soldier who goes to war, maybe because he's carried along by some thoughts about a community and some ideas, but when he realizes the horror, then he gets scared, then he wants to go home, and then he really does not want to kill anybody [...] But I found something much darker, which was the desire to kill. Which was the will to make it about taking a scalp and about doing the ultimate thing. And I experienced that drive to be very, very strong in that group of young people. It was surprising to me that it was that dark.

While Metz found 'the darkness' overwhelming, it was not completely unexpected as it is a stable of the popular cultural representations of war: darkness and cynicism versus idealism and hope as well as the stereotypes of the soldier as either a hero or an executioner. Further, he was interested in war as a rite of passage; an interest that was confirmed in the meeting with the soldiers:

That was also the first thing I experienced the soldiers talking about, that was how much it had changed them, and how much it had meant and what a momentous experience it had been.

What surprised him, then, was not the issues dealt with, but how they were dealt with; that the dichotomies he had expected were subsumed under the deep 'death drive' in the soldiers:

It was a different type of emotion than I had expected. They sought the excitement, they sought the action. [...] Fear came later, and it came for some, but for many it was just like: 'Wow, that was great! One more time!'

In the film, the figure of the killing soldier is introduced almost literally through the eyes of the soldiers, recorded with helmet cameras worn by those directly involved in combat. The recording first shows civilians hurriedly clearing the area, then the first shots ring out and all is chaos—running, shouting, shooting. When the soldiers locate enemy activity coming out of a nearby ditch, they throw in a hand grenade then shoot—and keep shooting. While there are also wounded on the side of the Danish soldiers, what is most remarkable about this scene is that it is the first (and only) time Taleban casualties are shown. These dead bodies appear in the most graphic detail as the soldiers search them for weapons, poking at and rearranging their limbs in the process.

At the debriefing, following return to base, the soldiers are in an array of shorts and T-shirts rather than uniforms. Some are bare-breasted, most sport Taleban weapons and ammunition that were brought back from the battlefield. The commander congratulates everyone on their bravery and good work, then a retelling of the events is carried out: "we find four men in the ditch who are in a pretty bad shape, and we liquidate them in the most humane way possible" [laughter], "we finish them off", "and it's over".

The killing body, it appears, celebrates itself, but soon the grounds for celebration are questioned. The platoon commander gathers his men to inform them that he has been interrogated by the military police because one of them has called his parents and told them that they have liquidated people and laughed about it. "What is on my mind", the commander goes on to say, "is the loyalty thing. I need to know; does anyone think that's what we did?"

This scene sparked much debate at the moment of reception; did Danish soldiers commit crimes of war? Could the film be used as documentation in a trial? Or was the film itself criticizable, perhaps even punishable, for manipulating quotes and sequences? Both positions were advocated and both issues investigated (e.g. Glanowski 2010; Zemanova 2010). In the end, the soldiers were vindicated in an official investigation just as the film was acquitted in the informal court of public opinion.

Through *Armadillo*'s dramatization of the act of killing, the public is confronted with the figure of the soldiers as bodies at war in the fullest sense, and the soldiers face the fact that (the acts of) such bodies might be incomprehensible to "those at home", as one soldier puts it: "I think it's difficult for them to understand how you couldn't care less about taking another person's life", and "I think you have to have tried it in order to understand", two other soldiers ruminate. The act of killing, then, is a condensation of the process of becoming-through-destruction; as he takes another man's life the soldier passes the point of no return; becoming other to his former self and to the society of civilians, which he serves. This is the second duality of the film; the act of killing is simultaneously the point of full identification and of total alienation—and it leads to the third duality of meaninglessness and meaningfulness.

'You Need Me on That Wall': The Institution of the Soldier

Armadillo provides a 'close up and personal' encounter with the soldiers' experience of being at war; it offers the public an opportunity to follow a group of recruits as they are socialized into the military institution and undergo a bodily transformation from civilians to soldiers. The film also depicts the soldiers' journey back, but only briefly and with clear indications that this journey is not an easy one. In fact, the final credits indicate that the majority of the soldiers who appear in *Armadillo* have gone back to active service and that only one of them has left the army. While the film in many respects depicts the meaninglessness of war, the humdrum life of active service has somehow become more meaningful to the soldiers than their civilian lives—and coming home now seems more difficult than going away.

Here, the film points to a decisive split between the experiences of the soldiers and the civilians' ability to comprehend them. The general public cannot understand what it means to be at war, and the social imaginary is based on this very impossibility of understanding. Society needs the soldiers 'out there', but it also needs them to stay away, to keep the experience of war out of ordinary life, distant and incomprehensible. However, in pointing out this fundamental formative principle of the relationship between soldiers and civilians, *Armadillo* also threatens to destroy it. If we realize that our imaginaries are based on ignorance, we are no longer ignorant; and if we find that our beliefs are based upon illusions, we may have to change what we believe. In this sense, the meaninglessness of war may become as meaningful to the public as it is to the soldiers and, hence, as formative of the public's experience of war.

The futility and opacity of the soldier's experience significantly shaped Metz' encoding of the film:

> The big surprise for me was the lack of transparency. That is, it was totally unclear what was going on. Totally obscure to the soldiers. It is actually also obscure to the film, but at least the film can point out that there are some Danish soldiers inside a camp who are creating their own truths about what is going on outside of the camp.

The film, then, took shape from the soldiers' lack of a sense of direction and inability to see the broader context. This, to Metz, became the political message:

> It is brutalizing for us as humans to go to war, because if it is not brutalizing, then we will be way too open to the trauma of war. Therefore, one has to establish a cynical, pragmatical ethic with oneself, or an acceptance that this is something I do for a greater cause. And if I do not distance myself from death and from the horror and from the killing, then I will go crazy, then the trauma kicks in.

This distancing, he finds, is a central figure:

There is a production of distance that recurs on all levels. There is the political level; this is something that is happening far away, it is difficult to understand, the stories are polished. That is why we shouldn't see the ditch, that is why we shouldn't see the wounded and the dead, that is why we shouldn't see the killings, because then we can rewrite it as necessary deeds done for a greater cause. We are free from the horror. Then you might say that distances are also produced in this camp situation where one has to produce distance in order to be able to stand being there. The enemy has to be dehumanized in order to be killed. So, it happens on the top political level, but it also happens for the individual soldier.

In his encoding of *Armadillo*, then, Metz wanted to reveal the distancing that gives form to the soldiers so as to make it impossible for the social imaginary to uphold the distancing it, in turn, is formed by. Or, at least, point out how the distancing works at all levels—individual, institutional, public—by rendering war meaningful in and through its very meaningless-ness. When this formative trick of creating and upholding illusions of difference *and* sameness, distance *and* proximity, is revealed, it becomes difficult to uphold. Thereby, *Armadillo* threatens to explode the social imaginary of war. But, we may ask, did *Armadillo* change individual citizens' view of war? And did it change the institutional field for military intervention?

As might be expected, there are no simple answers: on the one hand, reviews of the film and commentaries on it at the time of its release were brimming with shock and indignation. It is hailed as 'an incredibly brave' and 'incredibly openhearted' "portrait that for ever will change the Danes' picture of not only the war in Afghanistan, but also of the Danish soldiers" (Skotte 2010). On the other hand, we may note how the particular intervention of *Armadillo* soon lost its grip on the public (*Force Weekly* 2012). The fact that the film is no longer immediately present, however, does not necessarily mean that it has not made an impact. One commentator described *Armadillo* as "an earthquake in a nation's self-understanding" (Jensen 2010), highlighting the film's disruptive and destructive potential, but also indicating an opportunity for recovery and reconstruction. This duality, commentators agree, is *Armadillo*'s main strength (Levinsen 2010), but it also means that it is difficult to assess its actual impact.

Armadillo's potential for socio-political disruption stems from its lack of clear answers and easy solutions. The film is not political in the sense that it offers a specific opinion, but because it shows the 'meaningful meaninglessness' of war (Mylenberg 2010). Thus, some argue that seeing the acts of war from the personal angle of the soldiers provides a strong antidote to political accounts, but others focus on the fact that this is also only 'half the truth' and caution us to remember that "the individual soldiers' experience is not relevant to the strategic level and the debate conducted there" (Breitenbauch 2010). This, however, is the very logic that *Armadillo* works against: the individual, the film argues, is as relevant as the institution; the two form each other in a logic of duality. Thus, we may assess the film's impact on the configuration of the institutional field in terms of how the individual soldier is now positioned in this field. Is it possible to separate individual experiences from institutional concerns or do soldiers' lives matter at the political as well as the personal level? If nothing else, *Armadillo* brought this question to public attention.

Looking back on what happened after the release of the film, Metz concludes:

> Time has worked with the film. The fall from grace, which Denmark as a nation maybe was in the middle of and which was really accentuated when *Armadillo* came out because *Armadillo* was the shocking image, which the nation needed – or was ready for.

Before *Armadillo* was released, we should note, one change was already in the making, and by November 2010 Forward Operating Base Armadillo was shot down.

Conclusion: The Heart Is a Hand Grenade

Armadillo, the analysis shows, is an account of how war, generally, and acts of killing, specifically, transform men into soldiers. Soldiers, we have argued, are different from ordinary people exactly because they are able to kill. This is what sets them apart, but also what makes them necessary for society: we, as civilian members of society, need soldiers to be our bodies for us in this particular sense; we need them to kill. Further, soldiers must bear the burden of killing for society. "You be my body for me, but do not let me know that the body you are is my body" (Malabou and Butler 2011, p. 614). This is the organizing principle of the social imaginary of warfare that *Armadillo* reveals and troubles; once society knows what soldiers are actually doing in the service of society, the soldiers' deeds cannot be ignored. Thus, the body at war becomes a main actor in the institutional field of warfare.

Becoming-through-destruction is the organizing logic of this field as it is perceived in and, possibly, altered by *Armadillo*: the soldiers come into life as they take the lives of others and we, as society, become implicated in the act of killing because we can no longer ignore that it is carried out on our behalf. But can society live with and by this logic? Can it accept its own cruelty? It seems that yes, this is indeed possible. After *Armadillo*, there has been no return to blissful ignorance, but no decisive reconfiguration of the institutional field either. It seems the reaction to the discovery of what bodies at war are doing has not caused society to demand a change in the military institution, but rather to rearrange its social imaginary so as to be able to live with what it now knows. Yet this configuration, too, may pass. Just as the soldier's heart is a hand grenade so is the social imagination; it may have hardened into one particular form, but it can still explode.

This, we argue, is also our key theoretical contribution; the potential of institutions to give and take form—*and* to explode. The concept of plasticity offers a theoretical and methodological lens through which to explore the ideational and material configuration of institutional fields. Such studies of how institutions give and take form may focus on the social imaginary of institutions, as in the present case, but they could also deal with institutional formations directly. Tracing the dualities of making and breaking, in this respect, is not restricted to certain types of empirical material or to particular empirical fields. It is, we suggest, a stable of institutional figuration.

References

Ashcraft, K. L. (2011). Knowing work through the communication of difference: A revised agenda for difference studies. In D. K. Mumby (Ed.), *Reframing difference in organizational communication studies. Research, pedagogy, practice* (pp. 3–30). Los Angeles: Sage Publications.

Ashcraft, K. L., Kuhn, T. R., & Cooren, F. (2009). Constitutional amendments: "Materializing" organizational communication. *Academy of Management Annals, 3*(1), 1–64.

Barad, K. (2003). Posthumanist performativity: Toward an understanding of how matter comes to matter. *Signs: Journal of Women in Culture and Society, 28*(3), 801–831.

Barley, S. R. (2010). Building an institutional field to corral a government: A case to set an agenda for *Organization Studies*. *Organization Studies, 31*(6), 777–805.

Boncori, I. (2017). Mission impossible: A reading of the after-death of the heroine. *Culture and Organization, 23*(2), 95–109.

Breitenbauch, H. Ø. (2010). Armadillo fortæller ikke hele sandheden. *Berlingske*. http://www.b.dk/kronikker/armadillo-fortaeller-ikke-hele-sandheden. Accessed 5 May 2018.

Bugos, G. E. (1996). Organizing stories of organizational life: Four films on American business. *Studies in Culture, Organizations and Societies, 2*(1), 111–128.

Butler, J. (1993). *Bodies that matter. On the discursive limits of "sex"*. New York: Routledge.

Butler, J. (2004). *Undoing gender*. New York: Routledge.

Campbell, J. L. (1998). Institutional analysis and the role of ideas in political economy. *Theory & Society, 27*(3), 377–409.

Carlsen, P. J. (2010). Anmeldelse: Sådan er danskere i krig. DR. https://www.dr.dk/nyheder/kultur/anmeldelsesaadan-er-danskere-i-krig. Accessed 23 Aug 2018.

Carstensen, M. B., & Schmidt, V. A. (2016). Power through, over and in ideas: Conceptualizing ideational power in discursive institutionalism. *Journal of European Public Policy, 23*(3), 318–337.

Castoriadis, C. (1987). *The imaginary institution of society*. Cambridge, MA: The MIT Press.

Cederström, C., & Spicer, A. (2014). Discourse of the real kind: A postfoundational approach to organizational discourse analysis. *Organization, 21*(2), 178–205.

Cornelissen, J. P., Durand, R., Fiss, P. C., Lammers, J. C., & Vaara, E. (2015). Putting communication front and center in institutional theory and analysis. *Academy of Management Review, 40*(1), 10–27.

Cornish, P., & Saunders, N. J. (Eds.). (2014). *Bodies in conflict. Corporeality, materiality, and transformation.* London: Routledge.

Crockett, C. (2010). Foreword. In C. Malabou (Ed.), *Plasticity at the dusk of writing* (pp. xi–xxv). New York: Columbia University Press.

DFI. (2012). Armadillo vinder Emmy. https://www.dfi.dk/omdfi/armadillo-vinder-emmy. Accessed 5 May 2018.

Ewalt, J., & Ohl, J. (2013). 'We are still in the desert': Diaspora and the (de) territorialisation of identity in discursive representations of the US soldier. *Culture and Organization, 19*(3), 209–226.

Flyvbjerg, B. (2006). Five misunderstandings about case-study research. *Qualitative Inquiry, 12*(2), 219–245.

Force Weekly. (2012). Arven fra Armadillo: Filmen fylder 2 år. http://force-weekly.com/2012/05/27/arven-fra-armadillo/. Accessed 5 May 2018.

Funch, S. M. (2014). Armadillo i skudlinjen. *Journalisten.* http://journalisten.dk/armadillo-i-skudlinjen. Accessed 5 May 2018.

Glanowski, S. M. (2010). Ekspert frifinder 'Armadillo'. *Politiken.* https://politiken.dk/kultur/filmogtv/art4966383/Ekspert-frifinder-Armadillo. Accessed 5 May 2018.

Godfrey, R. (2009). Military, masculinity and mediated representations: (Con) fusing the real and the reel. *Culture and Organization, 15*(2), 203–220.

Green, S. E., Jr., & Li, Y. (2011). Rhetorical institutionalism: Language, agency, and structure in institutional theory since Alvesson 1993. *Journal of Management Studies, 48*(7), 1662–1697.

Green, S. E., Jr., Babb, M., & Alpaslan, C. M. (2008). Institutional field dynamics and the competition between institutional logics. The role of rhetoric in the evolving control of the modern corporation. *Management Communication Quarterly, 22*(1), 40–73.

Hall, S. (2001). Encoding/decoding. In C. L. Harrington & D. D. Bielby (Eds.), *Popular culture: Production and consumption* (pp. 123–132). Malden: Blackwell Publishers.

Hardy, C., & Thomas, R. (2015). Discourse in a material world. *Journal of Management Studies, 52*(5), 680–696.

Jensen, C. (2010). Velkommen til Armadillo. *Ekko.* http://www.ekkofilm.dk/artikler/velkommen-til-armadillo/. Accessed 5 May 2018.

Jones, C., Boxenbaum, E., & Anthony, C. (2013). The immateriality of material practices in institutional logics. In M. Lounsbury & E. Boxenbaum (Eds.), *Institutional logics in action, part a* (pp. 51–75). Bringley: Emerald Group Publishing Limited.

Just, S. N., & Berg, K. M. (2016). *Disastrous Dialogue*: Plastic productions of agency-meaning relationships. *Rhetoric Society Quarterly, 46*(1), 28–46.

Koppes, C. R., & Black, G. D. (1990). *Hollywood goes to war*. Berkeley: University of California Press.

Kornø, K. (2010). 'Armadillo' er manipuleret. *Ekstra Bladet*. http://ekstrabladet. dk/flash/filmogtv/film/article4257696.ece. Accessed 5 May 2018.

Lawrence, T. B., Leca, B., & Zilber, T. B. (2013). Institutional work: Current research, new directions and overlooked issues. *Organization Studies, 34*(8), 1023–1033.

Levinsen, J. (2010). Armadillo. *Jyllands-Posten*. http://jyllands-posten.dk/kultur/film/ECE4333932/armadillo/. Accessed 5 May 2018.

Malabou, C. (2007). The end of writing? Grammatology and plasticity. *The European Legacy: Toward New Paradigms, 12*(4), 431–441.

Malabou, C. (2010). *Plasticity at the dusk of writing*. New York: Columbia University Press.

Malabou, C., & Butler, J. (2011). You be my body for me: Body, shape, and plasticity in Hegel's *Phenomenology of the Spirit*. In S. Houlgate & M. Baur (Eds.), *A companion to Hegel* (pp. 611–640). Chichester: Blackwell Publishing.

Monteiro, P., & Nicolini, D. (2015). Recovering materiality in institutional work: Prizes as an assemblage of human and material entities. *Journal of Management Inquiry, 24*(1), 61–81.

Mylenberg, T. (2010). Meningsfyldt meningsløshed. *Fyens.dk*. http://www.fyens.dk/Troels-Mylenberg/Meningsfyldt-meningsloeshed/artikel/1606909. Accessed 5 May 2018.

North, D. C. (1991). Institutions. *Journal of Economic Perspectives, 5*, 97–112.

Orren, K. (1995). Ideas and institutions. *Polity, 28*(1), 97–101.

Philips, N., Lawrence, T. B., & Hardy, C. (2004). Discourse and institutions. *Academy of Management Review, 29*(4), 635–652.

Rehn, A. (2008). Pop (culture) goes the organization: On highbrow, lowbrow and hybrids in studying popular culture within organization studies. *Organization, 15*(5), 765–783.

Rhodes, C., & Westwood, R. (2008). *Critical representations of work and organization in popular culture*. Oxon: Routledge.

Scollon, R., & Levine, P. (2004). Multimodal discourse analysis as the confluence of discourse and technology. In R. Scollon & P. Levine (Eds.), *Discourse
and technology. Multimodal discourse analysis* (pp. 1–6). Washington, DC:
Georgetown University Press.

Skotte, K. (2010). Kim Skotte: 'Armadillo' er en forbløffende modig film.
Politiken. http://politiken.dk/kultur/filmogtv/ECE972833/kim-skotte-arma-
dillo-er-en-forbloeffende-modig-film/. Accessed 5 May 2018.

Thornton, P. H., Ocasio, W., & Lounsbury, M. (2012). *The institutional logics
perspective. A new approach to culture, structure, and process*. Oxford: Oxford
University Press.

Withagen, R., de Poel, H. J., Araujo, D., & Pepping, G.-J. (2012). Affordances
can invite behaviour: Reconsidering the relationship between affordances
and agency. *New Ideas in Psychology, 30*(2), 250–258.

Zemanova, C. (2010). 'Armadillo'-instruktør: Soldaterne gjorde ikke noget
galt. *Politiken*. https://politiken.dk/kultur/filmogtv/art4959760/Armadillo-
instruktør-Soldaterne-gjorde-ikke-noget-galt. Accessed 5 May 2018.

12

Legitimation Process in Organizations and Organizing: An Ontological Discussion

François-Xavier de Vaujany

Introduction: Three Ontologies to Describe Legitimation Processes in the MOS Literature?

Current societal and organizational transformations have made legitimacy a key stake (Dowling and Pfeffer 1975; Suchman 1995; de Vaujany and Vaast 2016). More than ever, legitimacy is evolving and questioned. As people are more and more informed, reflexive and involved in digital tools (thus increasing their connectivity but also the disembodiment of sense-making (Hayles 2008)), institutions are questioned for the very

This chapter is based on a keynote delivered at the Asia-Pacific Researchers in Organization Studies (APROS) conference in Sydney (December, 2015) and a further draft presented at the sixth Organizations, Artifacts and Practices (OAP) workshop in Lisbon (June, 2016). I thank participants of both events for their precious questions and feedback about this proposal, in particular Thomas Clark, Candace Jones, Stewart Clegg, Julien Jourdan, Nathalie Mitev, André Spicer, Jeremy Aroles and Ann Morgan-Thomas.

F.-X. de Vaujany (✉)
Université Paris-Dauphine PSL, Paris, France
e-mail: Francois-Xavier.deVAUJANY@dauphine.fr

© The Author(s) 2019
F.-X. de Vaujany et al. (eds.), *Materiality in Institutions,* Technology, Work and Globalization, https://doi.org/10.1007/978-3-319-97472-9_12

reasons which made them institutional (i.e. their age and the tradition(s) to which they correspond) and in that context, legitimacy needs to be put into perspective with space and time. More than ever, it needs to be narrated, maintained, re-created, re-enacted, re-spatialized and performed in different ways. It needs to be seen as a more or less harmonious activity or set of activities involving changing human and non-human entities.

The contemporary search for finance and funding epitomizes these trends.[1] Forty years ago, most attempts to finance a project or a new business venture were focused on strong external stakeholders and how to convince them. A bank, a major investor and a group of stakeholders would be involved in a legitimation process. Today, crowdfunding has deeply changed this process (Allison et al. 2015; Bouncken et al. 2015; Manning and Bejarano 2017). *The inside and the outside, the number of stakeholders, the variety and versatility of preferences and criteria along with the nature of the legitimation process* (with a crowd that is more emotional in its small contributions that a major structured stakeholder in its 'investment') *have made the legitimation process itself both more open, more emotional and more problematic with regard to its own temporalization and spatialization.* More than ever, sense making is decentered (Introna 2018). Key stakeholders are everywhere or nowhere. They can inhabit any temporality. Beyond the example of crowdfunding, the fragmentation and the explosion of the time space of organizing and work practices (Kallinikos 2003; Halford 2005) make it increasingly more difficult to identify a stakeholder or group of stakeholders outside and before investment, with a stable mode of cognition, a centered agency and a pre-defined set of preferences.

The institutional literature, however, remains largely discursive, cognitive, centered and judgemental in its approach to legitimation as a process (see in particular the literature review of Bitektine (2011) and its description of the 'process of legitimacy judgement formation'). Legitimation is rarely described as an (embodied) experience constituting a legitimate space and time for those involved in it (Voronov and Vince 2012; Voronov

---

[1] Several chapters of the book investigate legitimacy as a key stake for diverse sectors. In Chap. 6, Adrot and Bia-Figueiredo explore how the emergency sector adapts to their loss of legitimacy, catalysed by digitization and information access. In Chap. 7, de Vaujany, Winterstorm Varländer and Vaast analyse universities' reliance on space to claim legitimacy. In Chap. 8, Santos focuses on the game industry and examines the role of digital artifacts in digital entrepreneurs' legitimacy claims.

2014; Friedland 2018). As suggested by Friedland (2018, p. 515), 'emotion not only mediates the formation and reproduction of institutions, but is sometimes itself institutional'. Yet, emotions and their 'here and now' are often absent from the theories and concepts used, in particular in the context of the neo-institutional literature (de Vaujany and Vaast 2014; Voronov 2014).

Those are the dimensions and movement that we want to capture here through three ontologies which we see as present or emergent in institutional debates: an 'ontology of discourse' (which stresses the importance of social judgement, rhetoric and discursive structures in the process of legitimation); an 'ontology of sculpture' (which emphasizes the spatial and material dimensions of legitimation but remains partly discursive), and an 'ontology of bubbles' (which departs more radically from a judgemental view of legitimation by including spatial, temporal and pre-reflexive dimensions in the process of legitimation). If for the ontologies of discourse and sculpture, legitimacy remains largely in the eyes of the beholder, the ontology of bubbles locates legitimacy more in the bodies of the beholders. In turn, this implies a more embodied vision of the process of legitimation. For the ontology of bubbles, *there is no inside which would need to be aligned with an outside, or a before which would need to be in line with the present.* Emotional flow (Merleau-Ponty 1945) goes beyond these usual boundaries of academic thinking. Our experience of the world involves a shared and common world that is, by itself, emotionally legitimate or a legitimate emotion (see Table 12.1 below).

The ontologies of sculpture and bubbles both attempt to overcome traditional views of legitimacy and legitimation. While the former is already coherent with most institutional analysis regarding the process of social judgement involved in legitimation (as partly *discursive*), the latter requires some new ontological explorations (around the process and sociomaterial nature of legitimation). Drawing on the work of Merleau-Ponty (1942, 1945, 1964) and related phenomenologies (Heidegger 1962; Schatzki 2010), this chapter sets out to explore further the ontology of bubbles.

First, I will come back to the neo-institutional literature and how it conceptualizes legitimacy and legitimation in the context of the ontology

Table 12.1 Three ontologies about legitimation process in the institutional literature

	Ontology of discourse	Ontology of sculpture	Ontology of bubbles
Key dimensions of the legitimation process	Legitimation is the product of a discourse aligned with social expectations (those of one or several (dominant) stakeholders)	Legitimation is the product of a process that is jointly discursive, material and spatial. Objects, spaces and words are wrapped in legitimacy claims that will (or not) produce a legitimating effect on external stakeholders. Legitimacy is reached once people share a common world, after several loops of justificatory works	Legitimation is neither a process of alignment (between legitimacy claims and social expectations) nor a justificatory work. Legitimation is the emergence of a specific space-time, a narration, a shared 'here and now' by a group of people, places and artifacts. It is an unquestioned here and now, an embodied experience making possible other experiences. Language and narrations are not after or beyond pre-reflexivity. They are another facet of it, an 'expression'
Status of space and time	Space is a context. Time is out there, a linear and objective landmark for legitimacy claims	Materiality and space play an active role in legitimacy claims and justification. *Objects and devices can produce measures and comparisons. Yet, time and embodiment are not really 'part of the story'*	Space and time are co-produced by the legitimation process. They are the shared, common world made of emotions and affects produced by the narration. Legitimation is the experience which makes things emerge self-evidently, or naturally. *The process is constitutive of both the thing and its valuation or presence*
Conceptual focus	Cognition, discourses, social judgements, practices	Practices, common worlds, materiality, justification, space	Emotions and emotional energy, affects, embodiment, space, time, narration
Philosophical underpinnings	Weber (1978), DiMaggio and Powell (1983)	Friedland and Alford (1991), Boltanski and Thévenot (1991), Lefebvre (1991)	Merleau-Ponty (1945, 1964, 2003), Heidegger (1962), Ricoeur (1985)
Examples in the MOS literature	Zimmerman and Zeitz (2002), Bitektine (2011)	Proffitt and Zahn (2006), de Vaujany and Vaast (2014)	Voronov and Vince (2012), Granqvist and Gustafsson (2016), Pittz et al. (2017), Friedland (2018)

of discourse. It appears that legitimation is mainly theorized as a discursive, judgemental and ideational process. Then, I will describe the ontology of sculpture. I will detail the Marxist underpinnings (e.g. Marxist phenomenology) I see behind these dichotomist views of the process of social judgement corresponding to legitimation and the evolution of organizational space. Legitimation appears here as both a discursive and material set of activities (appropriation, re-appropriation and de-appropriation of space). I will illustrate the ontology of sculpture through a case narrative about a former NATO building transformed into a university. Then, I will develop the ontology of bubbles, which departs radically from a discursive and judgemental view of legitimation. This ontology emphasizes jointly the importance of bodies, materiality, spatiality and temporality in the legitimation process. The emotional flow involves both sensations and various material mediations (e.g. gestures, movements, faces, instruments, colours), which produce a specific space-time, a 'here and now'. *The emergence of objects and their legitimation are not separated anymore in space and time (which is still the case in the two other ontologies). There is at best a deeper sedimentation of some practices, more or less exclusively pre-reflexive at some points.* This view will be illustrated through a case narrative about the legitimation of activities in and around a makerspace in Paris. I will conclude this chapter with a systematic comparison and discussion of the two post-discursive ontologies, namely the ontology of sculpture and the ontology of bubbles.

Legitimation as a Discursive and Judgemental Process in the Neo-Institutional Literature

From Legitimacy to Legitimation

Legitimacy is a core philosophical and sociological concept. It is grounded in Max Weber's (1978) work on the legitimacy and sources of authority. The key questions are: what will make people obey other people? What are the deep underpinnings of authority? As reminded by Friedland (2018, p. 517), Weber's thought includes an emotional component: 'Max Weber analysed value rationality as an emotional state. Value rationality has a conceptual affinity to *"affectual" action, action determined by "the actor's specific affects and feeling states"* (...), one of Weber's four types of social action. Each—value and affect—is done *"for its own sake"*, the difference between them located in the former's *"self-conscious formulation"* and its *"planned orientation"* (Weber 1978, p. 25). For Weber, values are not simply valid ideas, but value feelings. In addition, Weber's thought was subtly historical, capturing a major shift towards rationality and rational-thinking, a move towards 'colder' emotions and relationship with the world. Nonetheless, emotions remained more a state and a dimension to explore the sources of legitimacy than a process constitutive of the obviousness of authority (see e.g. Merleau-Ponty 1945; Arnasson 1993).

Beyond Max Weber and the field of sociology, MOS have changed the focus of legitimacy-oriented studies. Organizations, and the products or services they provide, are now part of the scope of legitimacy. Collective activity can be more or less legitimate, in particular its organization and the resources it gathers. How organizations acquire and maintain their legitimacy in complex and changing institutional contexts has been a significant topic in institutional theory (e.g. Meyer and Rowan 1977; DiMaggio and Powell 1983; Elsbach 1994; Scott 1995; Lounsbury and Glynn 2001; Suddaby and Greenwood 2005). Organizational legitimacy thus corresponds to 'a generalized perception or assumption that the actions of an entity are desirable, proper, or appropriate within some socially constructed system of norms, values, beliefs, and definitions' (Suchman 1995, p. 574).

Suchman (1995) has provided a major summary of perspectives about organizational legitimacy, putting forward, among others, a distinction between cognitive, normative/social and pragmatic legitimacy. Legitimacy can thus be the taken for grantedness of a situation (cognitive legitimacy), its unquestionable and compelling power (normative legitimacy), or a necessary instrumental way to act (pragmatic legitimacy). Legitimacy (in particular normative legitimacy) is grounded in a context in which individual behaviours, patterns of collective behaviours and artifacts involved in behaviours are meaningful in a particular way. This context is the broader institutional or organizational field (DiMaggio and Powell 1983). A field is a set of codes, rules and actors defining capital, reputation and prestige. Some behaviours, if adopted by legitimate people (in view of the rules of the field) and in a legitimate manner, will be judged as legitimate by external stakeholders observing them (competitors, customers, etc.). In addition, the field itself will exert normative, mimetic and coercive pressures favouring isomorphism (DiMaggio and Powell 1983). In order to be part of the field and to be potentially identified as 'good', 'dominant', 'innovative' or 'prestigious', individuals and collective entities will have to look somewhat similar and, for instance, adopt partly identical structures and technologies.

In the early nineties, different streams of research suggested to go beyond field-based views of legitimacy to stick more closely to legitimation. Two linguistic fields (American neo-institutionalism and French pragmatism) have thus co-elaborated two different theoretical perspectives on legitimation processes that share numerous communalities: sociology of justification (Boltanski and Thévenot 1991) and institutional logics (Friedland and Alford 1991). If the former is grounded into a form of French pragmatism, the latter still draws on typical assumptions of neo-institutional debates.

For Boltanski and Thévenot (1991), our everyday work of justification is based on a closed set of 'worlds' with their own criteria, principles and metaphors. Justificatory work can borrow from one or several worlds that will have a legitimacy for their inhabitants. Sometimes, the work of justification can wrap different worlds or introduce inhabitants from different worlds that will lead to conflicts and particular modes of resolutions of these conflicts. Interestingly, the sociology of justification remains largely rhetorical (see recent attempts at introducing artifacts, materiality and space into the framework or to come back to material dimensions in the seminal work of Boltanski and Thévenot 1991). Emotions are not really present in the seminal writings that are rather discursive and cognitive. Friedland (2018, p. 519) thus stresses that 'in the conventions of worth approach, Boltanski and Thévenot understand actors' critical capacities to agree about the goodness of common goods, to establish relations of equivalence through "things that count," as a "cognitive ability" or competence'. Nonetheless, material agencies are present in the devices and measures likely to establish order (Gond et al. 2017).

Institutional logics are macro-level belief systems that shape actors' cognitions and actions at the field level (Friedland and Alford 1991; Ocasio 1997; Thornton 2004). They connect institutions to the behaviour of organizations and their members (Thornton 2004). Institutional logics correspond to 'organizing cognitive frameworks that provide social actors with 'rules of the game' (…) and that operate, often implicitly, as practical guides for action' (Jones et al. 2013, p. 52). Empirical research has shown that rather than a single dominant logic, oftentimes several competing logics exist at the field level (Lounsbury 2007; Kraatz and Block 2008; Reay and Hinings 2009; Greenwood et al. 2010; Jarzabkowski et al. 2013), as in the case of higher education (Gumport 2000). Multiple logics may thus reside in parallel over long periods of time leading to competition, tensions and conflict between different forums drawing on different logics.

Making Sense of Materiality, Spatiality and Temporality in Legitimation Processes

It is increasingly acknowledged that logics include cognitive, normative, spatial and material dimensions (Thornton et al. 2012; Boxenbaum et al. 2016). The material dimension of logics has so far mostly been conceptualized as practices or structures rather than actual physical artifacts (Friedland and Alford 1991). Scholars have only very recently acknowledged the need to attend to how materiality plays a role in sustaining or changing logics (Jones et al. 2013); 'At times, it appears as though institutional logics are located at the level of language […] the ideal elements, on the other hand, appear to constitute the institutional logic' (Friedland 2012, p. 589). Furthermore, how materiality is implicated with logics has rarely been explored. In a recent study, Monteiro and Nicolini (2015, p. 63) argue for the importance of including materiality in institutional analyses, suggesting that it will yield 'richer explanations […] that are closer to the reality of social processes'. This processual perspective is likely to make sense jointly of the materiality, spatiality and temporality of legitimation.

Indeed, and before the debates about institutional logics and their dynamics, the idea of looking at legitimation or institutionalization as a process (not a 'state' or an 'entity') is not new (see Della Fave 1986; Oliver 1991; Stryker 2000; Bitektine 2011). But surprisingly, this has led to more longitudinal or historical views of processes (instead of an exploration of philosophies likely to make sense of the embodiment, materiality, movement and temporality at stake in legitimation processes) and discursive postures. Bitektine (2011) thus describes the 'process of legitimacy judgement formation'. Bitektine (2011, p. 159) identifies five stages in the process of legitimation: (1) Perception by an audience; (2) Classification (managerial vs technical legitimacy) and scrutiny (about the legitimacy type: consequential, procedural, structural, personal, linkage); (3) Analytical processing (cognitive judgement or socio-political judgement); (4) Benefit diffusion (inducement); (5) Compliance mechanisms (normative vs regulative legitimacy).

Fundamentally, three core elements are involved in the process of legitimacy judgement formation: 'the evaluating audience's perceptions of an organization or entire class of organizations (1), judgement/evaluation based on these perceptions (2), and behavioural response (acceptance, support, avoidance, sanctions, etc.) based on these judgements (3)' (Bitekine 2011, pp. 159–160). In that context, legitimacy is conceptualized as something that can be told, shared, computed and intellectualized. It remains quite symbolic and discursive. Spatiality and materiality are not relevant by themselves, until they are involved in the judgemental process of a human being: *he/she* judges, beyond sensations and feelings, with a transcendental capability.

In contrast, some scholars have recently emphasized the materiality (Jones et al. 2013), spatiality (Profitt and Zahn 2006) and historicity (de Vaujany and Vaast 2014) of the process of legitimacy, particularly in contexts where organizational members draw on various institutional logics to legitimate their activities (Varländer et al. 2014). They suggest that *it* can judge as much as *he or she* judges, or that the judgement process involving a manager implies a lot of material mediations. Yet, embodiment, emotions and affects as key components of the process of legitimation are still put aside in explicit or implicit ontologies that remain largely discursive, cognitive and judgemental. This is an issue we will try to make more visible in the next section (focused on the ontology of sculptures) before detailing a possible alternative ontology that would depart more radically from discursive perspectives.

The Ontology of Sculptures: Stressing the Material and Spatial Dimensions of Legitimation

A Post-discursive Vision of Legitimation: A Focus on Activities of Appropriation, Re-appropriation and De-appropriation of Space

The relationship between space and legitimation has been recently explored by the institutional literature. At large, various discursive (i.e. story telling) and material (i.e. re-configuration or re-design of space) activities can help to better align organizational space and its connotations to the expectations of key stakeholders (Profitt and Zahn 2006; de Vaujany and Vaast 2014). This can be related to a threefold process. The first process is that of immediate discursive and material evolutions of organizational space through practices of appropriation, re-appropriation and de-appropriation[2] that can be described the following way (see Fig. 12.1):

The second process is the evolution of legitimacy claims grounded into this process. Communication practices can help produce deliberate legitimacy claims that can leverage (or not) the alignment between organizational space (as perceived by external stakeholders) and social expectations. The third and final process is the social judgement described by Bitektine (2011). It is the continuous judgement by specific stakeholders about the social acceptability of an organization, a set of organizational activities or some specific stakeholders of the organization. All three processes can be described the following way (Fig. 12.2):

---

[2] A practice which is close to home-staging activities in the context of the sale of an apartment. Owners are invited to clean the space and remove from it all personal belongings (to favour the projection of visitors into the space).

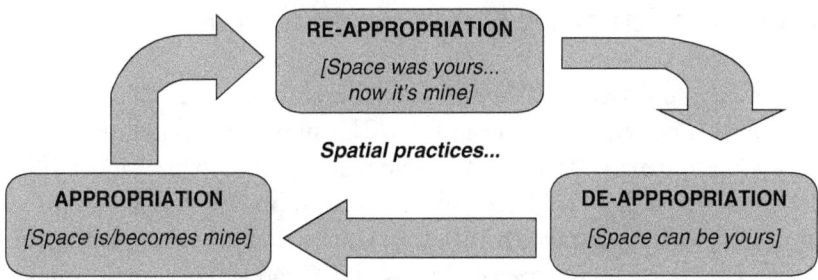

Fig. 12.1 Three key spatial practices (From de Vaujany and Vaast 2014)

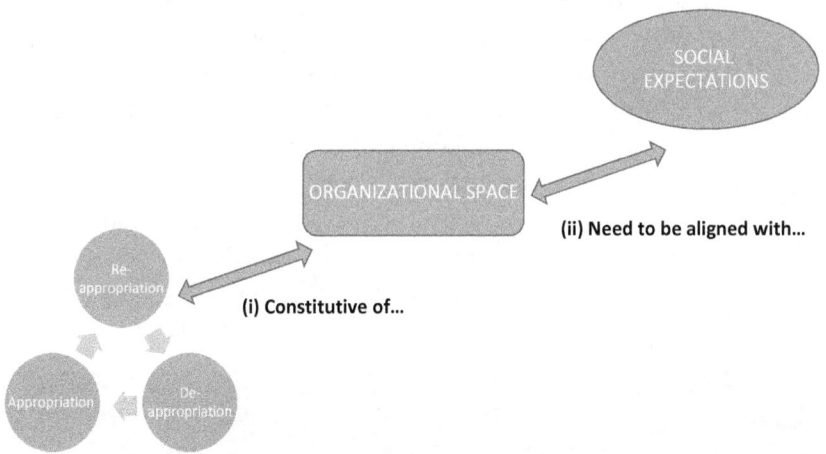

Fig. 12.2 Legitimation as a sculpture of organizational space through practices

The sculpture can be more or less continuous and recursive, depending on the theoretical lens used to describe the spatial practices themselves. In line with Lefebvre's (1991) Marxist phenomenology, spatial practices are at the heart of the 'lived' space, the one experienced by individuals in the space of domination as 'conceived' by some dominant stakeholders and then 'perceived' by its inhabitants. To free themselves, individuals will circumvent some parts of the space, complete 'bricolage' and re-appropriate the space in a way that will produce emancipation. Of course, this can be far from the legitimacy claims produced by dominant stakeholders.

An Illustration of the Ontology of Sculpture

De Vaujany and Vaast (2014) have used this ontology to explain the legitimation of a nascent university in Paris. This university re-used the former
NATO headquarters (from 1959 to 1966) and was set up in October 1968.
In short, the authors have identified two main phases. A first one (of re-
appropriation) during which the space has been largely kept as it is, and
NATO memorabilia has been enacted so as to produce coherent legitimacy
claims through the stars on the entrance grid (shown on the first leaflets),
the NATO maxim (used in the first logo designed in 1971), the first teaching rooms (located in a set of two or three re-shaped offices, which lever-
aged small group teaching and innovative pedagogy), the NATO former
commandment room (re-used for executive and key meetings), and so on
(see Fig. 12.3 below). This connoted a prestigious and international setting
that could be used to persuade bourgeois parents of the 16th arrondisse-
ment of Paris. This was also used to legitimate an expected (for a French
public university) selection of students. Compared to the students of
another nascent university (University of Vincennes in the east of Paris),
students of the University 'entered into Dauphine' (and the former NATO
'fortress'), whereas Vincennes students simply 'went' to Vincennes.

Fig. 12.3 Views of important artifacts of the former NATO headquarters re-used
by Paris-Dauphine University. (Source: Author's own photographs and Université
Paris-Dauphine)

In the 1990s, the university started to renovate itself and gradually removed key NATO artifacts (de-appropriation phase). The ground floor has been completely renovated, a new wing has been added, the former NATO commandment room has been completely redesigned, and recently, the main hall has been completely restructured in a more 'corporate' way. The search for executive students and corporate sponsors is now a key strategic stake. Legitimacy claims grounded into organizational space have thus evolved (de Vaujany and Vaast 2014).

The ontology of sculpture assumes *(dominant) external stakeholders judging the legitimacy of an organization, far from its collective activity.* This view is not always relevant, in particular in the context of today's collaborative and crowd-based economy. Customers and shareholders are more and more included into 'users' experiences' (online experiences of the service, campus or corporate tours, beta-testing, open innovation, open strategies, etc.). Value co-creation processes involve all stakeholders recursively and continuously in the production of services. In some industries, the very distinction between consumers (or users) and producers collapses (Lin and Cornford 2000; de Vaujany 2006). All this makes it difficult to conceptualize an external stakeholder, judging the physical setting, the collective activity and its acceptability from afar ('outside'). This requires a new view of space and legitimacy locating legitimation within collective activity itself, and the embodied reflexivity of individuals' materially and discursively co-producing legitimacy more than they judge it.

The Ontology of Bubbles: A Radical Departure from a Judgemental View of Legitimation

Key Theoretical Dimensions

We develop here a different view of space and legitimacy, one that departs from the Marxist phenomenology developed by Lefebvre (1991) and that engages with an embodied connectivity as a way of moving from legitimacy in the eyes (and mind) of the beholder to legitimacy in the (moving) bodies of the people involved in a collective movement. This shift corresponds to a conception of sociality that is less sculpted by macro forces of logics, hegemonies and so on and ultimately more attuned to a world in which aggregates of micro-spheres border each other, with each sphere being a bubble bouncing off other bubbles constituting the social totality. To describe this ontology and grasp this complex embodied connectivity, we rely on two key authors, mainly Merleau-Ponty (1942, 1945, 1964, 2003), but also Sloterdijk (2011), with whom the notion of bubble is contemporaneously associated. According to Merleau-Ponty (1942, pp. 141–142): 'in a soap bubble, as in an organism, what happens in each point is determined by what happens in all others'. Through this, the interconnectivity of each intra and inter-individual experiences but also of the focus of experience is stressed (in particular in a world constituted by meaning and language). Merleau-Ponty sees structures as an object of perception rather than as constraints on perception. He also insists on the difference between biological, physical and social structures as part of experience. In other words, he often describes the sudden 'explosion' or collapse of perceptions in the contexts of sense-making processes (Merleau-Ponty 1945). Likewise, Sloterdijk (2011) highlights spheres of aerial, bubble-centred experience and shared experience of life, extended and transformed through activities that are ultimately described spatially in an 'archaeology of the intimate' making time something deeply constituted by everyday activities while often 'spatialized' for collective activities because of the reification and spatialization their materializations require.

I set to extend the bubble metaphor to some key aspects of experience as described by Merleau-Ponty. A soap bubble requires energy to exist and expand (and to blow). The bubble and its expansion give visibility to this energy. It is fragile and can easily explode (leaving a fluid and almost invisible trace of its past existence). In contrast to an opaque sphere, it is transparent and open to the world. It can melt into another bubble to constitute a bigger bubble. Most of all, being 'inside' (with a cognitive focus) does not prevent one from seeing what is 'outside'. Beyond the bubble one can always see and perceive other parts of the world and as the bubble bumps into other bubbles that randomly border it, our perceptions order this randomness into continuity, discontinuity, visibility and invisibilities.

To extend still the metaphor in another way, I will distinguish here three interrelated 'bubble units', three 'levels of being' as described by Merleau-Ponty from the self to collective activity[3]:

> There is an entire architecture, a complete "tiering" of phenomena, a complete series of "levels of being", which differentiate themselves through the enrolment of the visible and the universal over some visible where they are strengthened and inscribed (…) The Being is not in front of me, but it surrounds me, and in a way it goes through me. My view of Being does not come from elsewhere, but from the middle of the Being, the so-called facts, spatio-temporal individuals, are weighted through axes, pivots, and the dimensions or generality of my body are already embedded into these joints. (Merleau-Ponty 1964, p. 151).

The first bubble unit will be *being itself* in the world, the second bubble unit, *being in acting with others*, the third *being in being with others*. The move from the first to the third level of being describes a move from an isolated individual to a more socialized and finalized world, bursting with human and non-human agencies constituted through activity. Of course, each level cannot be separated from the others, and gains visibility in activities that include all levels in the same movement.

The first 'bubble unit' is deeply cognitive, lonesome and 'immobile'. It is grounded into the 'corps propre' (proper body) and the 'schéma corporel' (corporeal scheme) described by Merleau-Ponty (1945). People do not perceive external signals produced by artifacts they encounter. They actively constitute their immediate environment through assimilated structures of behaviours quickly (unconsciously) activated and deeply embodied (far from any view of mental thoughts adjusting and transmitting orders to a body). In a way, the body and the feeling of what it is, and how it continuously mediates our relationship with the world (corporeal scheme[4]) constitute a sensorial bubble which is both the inside and

---

[3] This view is also coherent with the spatial and immunologic project proposed by Sloterdijk (2011) that moves from the discovery of the self (bubble) to the exploration of the world (globe) to the poetics of plurality (foam).

[4] 'Likewise, my all body is not for me an assemblage of organs superimposed in space. I see it in an indivisible situation, and I know the position of each of my members through a corporeal schema into which they are folded' (Merleau-Ponty 1945, p. 127). This corporeal scheme is also close to

outside of perception. *This bubble is a continuous present. Indeed, in our perceptions* 'there is no anteriority, there is simultaneity and even delay' (Merleau-Ponty 1964, p. 162).

An individual will not hear all of the surrounding noises, not see everything and not be attentive to all feelings in one's body. One will actively select one's visible and tangible world through one's lived body. Individuals will continuously recreate new bubbles. And should one bubble blow up, another one can immediately replace it, such that there is never 'ontological emptiness' in perception. All this will result in particular relationships with the environment and space. As interpreted by Giddens (1984, p. 65), 'the body, Merleau-Ponty points out, does not "occupy" timespace in exactly the same sense as material objects do. As he puts it, 'the outline of my body is a boundary which ordinary spatial relations do not cross'. This is because the body, and the experience of bodily movement, is the centre of form of action and awareness, which really define its unity. The time-space relations of presence, centred upon the body, are geared not into a 'spatiality of position', in Merleau-Ponty's words, but a 'spatiality of situation'. The 'here' of the body refers not to a determinate series of coordinates but to the situation of the active body towards its tasks.

Depending on emotions and sensations, the bubble will expand or not (to cover a broader space), explode or not (if emotions become too extreme). The bubble will also be constitutive of that invisibility which makes action possible (Merleau-Ponty 1964, 2003), an invisibility that is not the opposite of visibility (Merleau-Ponty 1964). It is simply the inactivated, circumvented and other side of the bubble. While it could be physically possible sometimes to 'see' what is bordering the bubble (as it is transparent), most people will not do it, or will be in a mood in which they do not need to do so.[5] Being in a bubble has a recursive and reflexive legitimacy of its own design. Finally, Merleau-Ponty (1945) provides a

what philosophers or sociologists call agency: '[corporeal scheme is also an agency] (…) my body appears to me as a posture in view of some actual or possible tasks. Indeed, its spatiality is not like those of external objects or that of 'spatial sensations', a spatiality of position, but it is a spatiality of situation' (Ibid.: 129).

[5] Merleau-Ponty (1964) uses the example of walking and seeing the back of someone. Her face is invisible. But our perception extrapolates it. If I think I know the person, I can call her, and expect her face and her voice to occur. Invisibility is not the opposite of visibility, it is more the continuity of it, a condition of possibility of our perception, experience and agency.

phenomenological critique of 'judgment' at the level of being (which will be particularly crucial for our deconstruction of legitimacy). Judgement is not an intellectual move beyond sensations and feelings, and Merleau-Ponty (1945, p. 56) is sceptical about intellectualist theses defending this view:

Judgement is often introduced by what is missing from sensations in order to make possible a perception. A sensation is not supposed to be a real element of consciousness (...) Intellectualism lives from the refutation of empiricism and judgment has often had the function to cancel the possible dispersion of sensations. Reflexive analysis is established by pushing realist and empiricist theses to their end-point, and by showing through absurdity the anti-thesis.

Merleau-Ponty defends a more experiential view of judgement,[6] which is embodied and always interconnected (to things and other people's experience). He states:

Between sensations and judgement, common experience makes a clear distinction. Judgment is for that a stance, it aims at knowing something valuable for my-self at all times of my life and for the other existing or possible spirits; sensation, conversely, is subject to appearance. It is beyond possession and any search for truth. This distinction vanishes in the context of intellectualism, as judgment is everywhere where pure feeling is not, which means everywhere. (Merleau-Ponty 1945, p. 158)

Through individual movement, the bubble will be intertwined in space and time with traces of the bubble, or other individuals' bubbles. The individual decision to leave my office to reach another room for a meeting links me, provisionally and transitionally,[7] to a collective dance I need

---

[6] At the opposite of the scientific construction of facts: 'When I engage my body among the things, they co-exist with me as incarnated subject, and this life in things has nothing in common with the construction of scientific objects. Likewise, I do not understand other people's gestures through an act of intellectual interpretation, the communication of consciousness are not grounded into the common sense of their experiences, but they underpin it anyway (...)' (Merleau-Ponty 1945, p. 226).

[7] We see here a key point of departure with the third level of being, which involves more stabilized and finalized relationships with others I need to coordinate myself with. Here, I simply go through a world I do not need to transform or live with.

to share and adapt to. This corresponds to our second 'bubble unit'. It is related to movement itself (both material and physical), for example the practice of walking.

The last 'bubble unit' or 'level of being' deals more systematically with collective activity and the deep and stable interconnectedness of experience it favours. It is a way to emphasize phenomenologically the duration of collective activity. Time and space are constitutive and constituted by collective activity (Merleau-Ponty 1945, 1964). Present time (a notion Merleau-Ponty sees as necessary jointly collective and individual—it is not possible to live present time 'alone' and for oneself as prolonged experience of solitary confinement discloses) is activity itself, a key juncture of past and future activities that flow individually and collectively around it. Merleau-Ponty (1945, p. 481) argues that 'the surge of a new present does not provoke a collapse of the past and a jolt of the future, but the new present is a passage from a future to a present and from the former present to the past, it is in a single move that from one end to another time starts moving'.

Following Gosden (1994) and Schatzki (2010), we will also consider the 'systems of reference'. Basically, a system of reference is a network of actions conveying their own time and space. This concept is designed to highlight the interconnectedness of actions and events (see also Hernes (2014) on the issue of the relationships between events). Gosden's (1994) discussion emphasizes that time and space are dimensions of action networks; 'Space and time are not … abstract qualities providing the medium of social action, but rather… dimensions created through…systems of references' (Schatzki 2010, p. 40). From the perspective of collective activity, in particular that of a set of individuals and artifacts involved in the production of a service, various collective bubbles are involved (see Fig. 12.4).

Depending on the 'system of references' (Gosden 1994), these bubbles will be completely independent (see bubble 3 in comparison to bubbles 1 and 2), or bordering and overlapping (see bubbles 1 and 2). Overlap will be harmonious or disharmonious, depending on the level of dyschrony (Alter 2000, 2003). Indeed, temporal orientations (e.g. a pres-

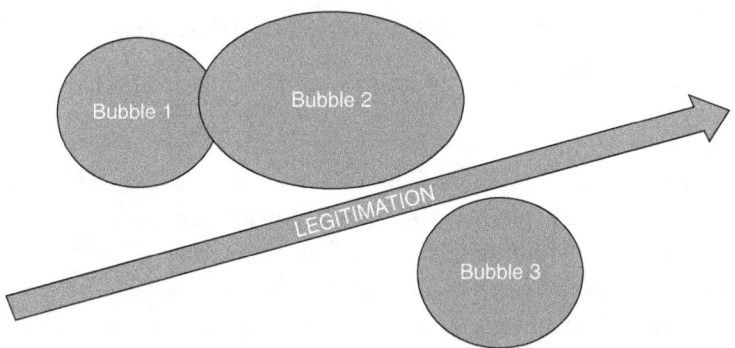

Fig. 12.4 Collective activity as a set of events, time-space bubbles

ent anchored in the past of nostalgia or a present focused on the anticipation of a future driven by anxiety) of the various collective activities at stake can be more or less conflicting. This can result in more or less conflicting, more or less shared perceptions and emotions about ongoing activities.

What about legitimation from the perspective of our three bubble units? We clearly depart here from a discursive and judgemental authority and legitimacy (from one person to another, an external judgement and perception). Judgement becomes here an embodied co-valuation, the emergence of an unquestioned shared world in the flow of collective activity. People feel each other out and legitimation is always a shared feeling. There is no external third party mentally 'judging' a situation (as in the context of the process described by Bitektine (2011)) on the basis of legitimacy claims produced by the organization, whether intentionally or not. Legitimation is ultimately a deeply shared temporality, the ordering of a set of events at the heart of collective activity. It is related to the joint emergence or disappearance of 'institutions' in Merleau-Ponty's (2003) sense. For Merleau-Ponty (2003), an institution is a temporal phenomenon. It corresponds to all particular practices which will contribute to link events felt in the present. It is the broad set of temporal structures ordering the field of our experiences and all passivity activities inside it. Some legitimations processes will be assimilated by this frame. Others will probably accommodate it.

An Illustration of This Post-judgemental View of Legitimation

Collaborative spaces (e.g. co-working spaces, maker spaces, fab lab and hacker spaces) have been blossoming since the early 2000s (Hatch 2014; Lallement 2015). A collaborative space is a place and space structured in such a way that it favours horizontal (between residents) and open collaborations (beyond the immediate involvement in an open space) between entrepreneurs and/or people managing innovative projects.

Whatever their location and configuration, collaborative spaces imply practices whose legitimacy is largely questioned. As any entrepreneurial project and structure (most collaborative spaces in Paris are less than three years old), these places need to demonstrate their acceptability to stakeholders who control resources they need (Lounsbury and Glynn 2001; Zimmerman and Zeitz 2002; Nagy et al. 2012). Their communitarian nature and their inclusive orientation (they host start-up or emergent projects that also need to legitimate themselves) make them a particular organizational setting (Garrett et al. 2014; Lindtner 2015). They need a twofold legitimation process, that is the legitimation of the place and that of the start-up it hosts, with possible synergies between the two.

Basically, collaborative spaces' legitimation is not obvious, both socially (acceptability) and cognitively. One key principle, value co-creation, is rather counter-intuitive. In continuation of digital business models (such as Blablacar or Uber), customers are actively involved in part or the totality of the service provided. In a way, they pay for a service they provide themselves, following the principles of a potluck where everyone brings along the food they wish to eat. The practice is definitely not recent: bars, nightclubs or restaurants involve the co-production of an atmosphere and some features of the service provided. Digital tools make it possible to perpetuate and exploit the community dimension of the process in various ways.

To illustrate these legitimacy stakes and beyond them, the third ontology about legitimation, we will draw from an ethnography of a specific type of collaborative space, a makerspace in Paris which will be called here MS, i.e. Maker Space (see appendix for a summary of data collection).

Collaborative spaces are interesting for the study of legitimacy and legitimation. Ultimately, they are young meta-organizations (Ahrne and Brunnson 2008): young entrepreneurial structures hosting young entrepreneurial structures or individual projects.

MS is a very interesting place and space. It is bounded, iconic and very atypical. The place was set up in the east of Paris (not far from the train station 'Gare de Lyon') after a riot in front of an artistic squat. Dealers fought in front of the squat, and under the pressure of citizens, the mayor decided to take measures and experiment with new places subsidized by the city. MS opened in 2005 in a former power plant (which used to be a squat itself). It accepts professional and non-professional artists, and offers them several floors to practice their art. The ground floor is devoted to fashion designers, actors and co-workers. The second floor is opened to painters and sculptors. The third floor is dedicated to painters and photographers (with an argentic workshop). Finally, the fourth floor is aimed at novelists. MS also includes a fab lab.

Artistic squats are both a model and a counter-model for MS. Part of the structure of squats is reproduced, with an usher (*ouvreur* in French) at the entrance of the place, with a view on the street and of who is coming in and out. The usher is both a controller and a helper. One of the worst fears of the controllers and the manager is to see the place become a squat again. Thus, each resident has a physical member card that is left at the entrance. At the end of each day, there should be no cards in the rail behind the opener. Nobody is allowed to stay overnight. This would be likely to happen, as 60% of the residents are on income support (French RMI, i.e. Revenu Minimum d'Insertion). Some people are thus in highly precarious situations (we heard a phone conversation of a member who did not know where he would spend the coming night).

The place also organizes trainings in management (e.g. a session about business models and another one about accounting). We could say that managers are stuck in the middle of three institutional logics (art, management, social involvement), and the search for horizontality and equality in the treatment of residents is at the heart of it. This is epitomized by the story of the coffee machine. Since the beginning, coffee has been free within the space. It is a filter-based coffee. At some point, several residents asked for a better quality of coffee, in particular for their guests.

They wanted a Nespresso machine. This resulted in intense debates. This coffee (not free anymore) would break the internal logic of the community (equality). It has thus been decided to put this second coffee machine far, at the entrance of the place.

Before detailing the narrative of our three bubbles units, it is important to give details about the body and the situation of the researcher involved in the organizational setting and joining the bubbles he observed. The researcher was mainly seated on the ground floor (in the co-working area). It was a great location to observe the entire floor and to see all the people coming in and out (as he was in front of the only entry point in the building). Sometimes, he went upstairs to work in the kitchen. This was an opportunity for a broader walk and to remain seated and to be at the core of the third bubble unit (lunch).

Let us now move more systematically into the three bubbles units we described in our theory section. Artists are in their individual artistic bubbles. Their schema corporeal is melted with the piece of art they are producing. Most of the time, nothing exists beyond this fragile moment. The activity is completely embodied. People and movement of the outside can or could be seen, as the 'bubble' is transparent. Yet artists remain in the visibility of what they are doing. The level of focus of most artists we crossed was thus amazing. And most bubbles were immobile, outside the time and space of surrounding society. We even saw some artists not leaving to eat during lunchtime, still focusing on what they were doing. Obviously, all this created a lot of invisibilities (Merleau-Ponty 1964): that of the preparation and planning of the piece of art, that of the techniques behind simple gestures, that of the punctual discussions and help between residents. Interestingly, some bubbles were more influential and material than others. The noise of people in the fab lab and the use of some tools by sculptors could be disturbing. The smell of painting and the traces of paint could also disturb the bubble of the others.

The second bubble was a more mobile one. Clearly, walking around was a key exercise. It started with the entrance into the building. The usher at the entrance, the very iconic dress workshop on the ground floor, the familiar people whom one needs to greet… Sometimes, walking was a way to apparently explode the bubble. Someone stopped in front of a painting to comment on it and ask questions. We say 'apparently', as often, between regular artists, this was more a way to make the project and what is going on explicit than to really break the dynamic. Quickly after the conversation, the bubble was re-created. Moving bubbles were clearly a way to bigger collective bubbles. Lunchtime, more or less shared (inside and outside) by residents, is an opportunity to 'join', 'reach' and 'move to' a different bubble. The first mainly individual bubble is left behind. At this point in time, it is provisionally broken. Another time and space, more related to the general shared rhythm of the place and society at large, are joined. Walking makes visible the fact that this time and space have always been there, potentially visible, necessarily made invisible to make the activity of artists possible. Interestingly, movement and co-movements at the level of these evanescent mobile individual bubbles are at the heart of what could be seen as legitimation. In particular, it is in the time and space of this shared movement that legitimacy will be at stake and legitimation will move further or not. A strange scene we witnessed epitomized this. A serigrapher, located on the ground floor, has been living through a tough period for several months. It had become almost impossible for him to sell his cards and posters. One day, we saw three interns from the dressmaker workshop (on the same floor) coming close to him to cut pieces of fabrics. Suddenly, we saw him activating, standing up, moving to his big printers and producing a set of posters. Will he sell them? Probably not. Will he learn or test something through this process? Probably not. But this is obviously not what was at stake. What was at stake for him was to share a legitimate movement, dancing with the others. *Legitimation is an embodied and shared movement. It is not the result of an external social judgement* (as summarized by Bitektine 2011). It is an endogenous process, a co-construction, a co-valuation, a shared feeling between the serigrapher and the three interns. Something they feel together, or rather, the serigrapher feels they share together as the three girls are part of the dance and pursue it.

Interestingly, neighbours and external stakeholders are also part of the more general dance and movement, the moving bubbles. From their perspective, this hermetic building and façade is only a mysterious space into which people come and go out. They do not see or feel the individual bubbles of level 1. They see only a set of successive individual movements. They do not understand why people do not have lunch in their restaurants or share their activities (for associations). The dance is just a force they do not share, an illegitimate music that is not part of the broader music of the area.

The last bubble unit is a way to move to what we see afterward as the 'system of references' (Gosden 1994) of the place, the human activities deeply at stake in it. In relationship with our observations in the context of MS, we observed four main collective bubbles that are part of the shared 'system of references'. They constitute 'events', specific durations (Deroy 2008; Schatzki 2010; Deroy and Clegg 2011; Hernes 2014; Hussenot and Missonier 2016) and expressions (de Vaujany 2017): individual artistic projects (1), floors' collaborations (2), training sessions (3), lunchtime (4).

Individual projects are focused on the 'oeuvre', its space and temporality. Both can overcome the boundaries of MS. Floors' collaborations are episodic and more or less improvised (by chance encounter, immediate questions to a neighbour, etc.). Training sessions take place on the ground floor around circular tables. They last a couple of hours and follow an academic logic. They are clearly bound in time and space and mainly involve external people to the space and its temporal dynamic. Lunchtime is a space and time of convergence, the most communal bubble for the residents of MS. Interestingly, these bubbles clash sometimes, making dyschronies (Alter 2000; de Vaujany et al. 2018a, b) stronger. People in the dressmaking workshop can be disturbed by the noise and movements of those involved in training. Collaboration and its noise can be distracting and break the bubbles of others. And more simply, artistic activities can be harmful (because of the smell, the dirty traces, the noise of some tools, etc.) for immediate neighbours. For the temporal and spatial cohabitation of all human activities, multiple mediations are necessary in particular to build a paradoxical legitimation of these punctual disharmonies. The manager of the place and multiple posters displayed in the space describe rules for the storage of wet paintings and the cleaning of the place. Events (on the ground floor) are a way to know each other better and meet people from other worlds.

In contrast to MS, other research I have been involved in (about collaborative spaces' tours) has been an opportunity to identify much more 'scenarized' and deliberate 'bubbles' centered on a guide (who mainly guided the embodied attention of the group).

Interestingly, the collective movement of people and the narration built around it can be a way to reconcile potentially conflicting institutional logics. In a context of institutional complexity with multiple logics (Friedland and Alford 1991; Kraatz and Block 2008), which impose conflicting demands and pressures on organizations and their members (Greenwood et al. 2010; Jarzabkowski et al. 2013), walking was a way for organizational members to invoke artifacts and narratives to mobilize and emphasize the compliance with particular logics.

Discussion: Back to Our Two Post-discursive Ontologies About Legitimation

In short, we can summarize our two post-discursive ontologies of legitimation in the following way (Table 12.2):

The two ontologies we detailed and illustrated each correspond to different phenomenological stances. The first (Marxist) one is mainly rooted in Lefebvre's (1991) triad and his vision of space as a stage on which domination and emancipation take place. Authority and legitimacy are obviously at

Table 12.2 Two ontologies to make sense of legitimation

	Ontology of sculpture	Ontology of bubbles
Key focus	Communication, justificatory work, legitimacy claims	Shared experience, event, expression, narratives
Relationship with space	Space is there, constituted by previous activities. Place is a location	Time and space are co-constituted through teleological activities
Relationship with time	Linear time explored forward or backward ('spatial legacies')	Multiple times in the same experience, possible dyschronies (shared, non-necessary harmonious events)
Status of legitimacy	A process of social judgement	A shared, decentered, feeling of continuity in the collective dance completed by the people and artifacts involved in the movement
Roots	Marxist phenomenology (Lefebvre 1991)	Phenomenology of Merleau-Ponty (1945, 1964)

stake every time. Organizational space needs to be re-invented continuously to win or balance the play. Most of all, Lefebvre is clearly versed into analytical dichotomies (e.g. between social and material or human vs material agencies). In continuation of a Marxist vision, he sees appropriation as a possible move from Nature, a transformation (resulting in something else). In contrast, the phenomenological vision of the second ontology (in particular from the perspective of Merleau-Ponty) is a way to depart from a priori dichotomies (e.g. between nature and culture, materiality and sociality, humanity and sociality) and develop a post-Marxist view of judgement. Each category needs the other to make sense of itself. Beyond that, it is always the invisibility created by the visibility of a perception the other faces. Most of all, this has very interesting implications for the conceptualization of legitimation. It is an exogenous judgement from the first perspective (someone is judging from the outside), while from the perspective of the second ontology, it is an endogenous process (people and their mediations feel something together).

What about the managerial implications of all this? Clearly, the first ontology, closer to common sense language and managerial practice, seems to have more potential (in particular for teaching activities). With a focus on the three spatial practices (of appropriation, re-appropriation and de-appropriation), one can play with space and its communication (legitimacy claims) to adjust space with social expectations. Nonetheless, it is far from a causalist view, as space is constituted by a large (and unpredictable) set of activities, and the final interpretations by a given actor (and his/her preference) remain impossible to anticipate at a point in time.

The potential added value of the second ontology is beyond something that could be said or thought. It is more at the level of doing and pre-reflexivity. The invitation to managers would be to continuously be part of the movement and be immersed within their customers' or shareholders' experience (on line and off line) and then to elaborate emergent conditions of possibilities. If management is an *ex ante* agency for the ontology of sculpture, it is more a transcendence in immanence (de Vaujany et al. 2018b) for the ontology of bubbles. Actors need to produce contextualized conditions of visibilities and invisibilities, continuities and discontinuities in the flow of their activities and what they feel they do. Actors need to get an intimate sense of what is going on, to be continuously part of it, to be aware of potential ruptures in the collective dance, from the shared-point of view of people and objects dancing.

Lastly, we see several avenues for further research about the material, spatial and temporal dimensions of legitimation. The first would be to use the second ontology in the context of a multi-site, distributed organization (far from the controlled and mono-site context of MS). This is likely to introduce interesting spatial and temporal tensions in the collective dance. The second avenue could be a more systematic analysis of bodily movements inside and outside of buildings, combined with ethnography and semi-structured interviews. This could be a way to grasp both movement and reflexivity at stake in joint legitimation. The third would be the study of movement in historical context (as in the case narrative elaborated by de Vaujany and Vaast 2014). This could be a way to understand how past (in particular institutionalized past through vestiges and ruins) can be involved in a collective dance of legitimation.

Appendix: Data Collected for the Illustration of Our Two Ontologies

Data Collected for the Ethnography of Universitas

Type of data	Description	Period of collection
Participant observations	Five years of observations (formalized in a memo)	2009–2014
Semi-structured interviews	5 interviews (around 1.5 hours each): 3 with senior emeritus professors, 2 with senior administrative staff (who had all known the period of the 70s at universitas)	2010–2011
Archives	Centre d'archives du 20ème siècle (archives about the architect of universitas) Internal archives of the university	2011–2012
On-line resources	Websites, social medias, blogs about the university and what is going on in it	2010–2012
Pictures and movies	Institut National de l'Audiovisuel (INA), videos on YouTube and personal pictures (more than 4000) about internal life	2010–2012

Data Collected for the Ethnography of MS

Type of data	Description	Period of collection
Participant observations	3 half-days of observations of the external environment (cafés, neighbourhood associations); 9 half-days of observations within the maker space (in particular on the first floor) Observations were formalized by means of a memo and an observation guideline	2015 (January–July)
Semi-structured interviews	7 semi-structured interviews (around 1 hour each): 2 with staff members (general manager and PR); 2 with residents; 3 with neighbours: 2 with members with an old local association, very close to MS, and one with a neighbour of MS building	2015 (January–July)
Archives	Internal (status of MS, internal rules, leaflets...) and external (publications in journals and magazines about MS)	2015
Online resources	Netnography (Kozinets 2006) of blogs, social networks, websites, forums about the environment, artistic squats and the place	2015
Pictures and movies	500 internal and external pictures of the place and the area around the place	2015 (January–July)

Data Treatment of Universitas and MS: Questions Asked by the Researchers to Himself in the Context of His Observations and Analysis of Interviews and Documents

Main Focus of Observations and Reconstitutions of Practices in the Case of Universitas (Mainly Inspired by Lefebvre 1991)

a) Questions about key spatial practices to enter into and move in the space of universitas (relationship with practices of appropriation, re-appropriation and de-appropriation as physical, embodied activities)

– *What do people do when they enter into the building? What did they do in the past (NATO/post-NATO period)? What are they expected to do/ What were they expected to do while they entered into the space of universitas?*

– *What do people do while moving from one point of the building to another? What did they do in the past (NATO/post-NATO period)? What are they expected to do/What were they expected to do while moving from one point of the building to another (floors, wings)?*

b) **Questions about work practices (relationship with practices of appropriation, re-appropriation and de-appropriation as physical, embodied activities)**

– *What do people do in the context of classrooms and meeting rooms? What did they do in the past (NATO/post-NATO period)? What are they expected to do/What were they expected to do while working and communicating with each other?*

c) **Question about communications practices, how space or spatial practices are enacted in front of external visitors (relationship with practices of appropriation, re-appropriation and de-appropriation as symbolic, communicative activities)**

– *What do inhabitants do in front of external visitors (prospective students, potential sponsors, visiting scholars)? How is the space enacted and possibly re-invented in leaflets given to them, PPT presentations and trajectories chosen inside the building? How do people appropriate, re-appropriate or de-appropriate space (clean it) to please them?*

Main Focus of Observations and Reconstitutions of Practices in the Case of MS (Mainly Inspired by Merleau-Ponty 1945, 1964)

a) **Questions about the way people feel in the space and time of MS activities, how they create, maintain and sometimes blow out the bubble of their creative activity (bubble 1)**

– *What are the continuities-discontinuities of the artistic or managerial activities within MS? What makes them start or stop?*

- *What are the visibilities-invisibilities of artistic activities within MS? For artists themselves and other artists or visitors looking closely at what they do and judging, commenting on it?*
- *What are the postures, the immobilities and mobilities of artists in their immediate artistic bubbles (e.g. their posture in front of their paintings)?*

b) **Questions about the way people move in and across the space of MS (bubble 2)**

- *How do people move from one part of the building to another (rooms or floors)? Inside or outside the building?*
- *How do people move from their immediate bubble of concentration to that of other people in the space? How do they enter into other people's space?*
- *How do people walk (slow/quick, careful/automatic walk, self-centred/ open to the environment, direct/circumventing expected trajectories…)?*

c) **Questions about the way people outside the time and space of MS (e.g. immediate neighbours) feel and perceive the movement of MS members (e.g. in and out of the building (bubble 2))**

- *How are movements (inside or outside the time and space of MS) perceived by non-artists inside and outside the building?*

d) **Questions about how people move together and share a collective movement with other people and other artifacts inside the time and space of MS activities (bubble 3).**

- *How do people move together, what are the shared collective bubbles, the collective time spaces related to MS? The time spaces in and during which people feel obviously together, share a common space in a meaningful way, and common time. The outside is not really part of the process, nobody is expected to look at and judge the collective activity which is not expected at all to depend on external resources. This time space is self-satisfying.*

NB: the exploration of these four questions led us to identify four key time and space in the embodied activities of MS members, particularly explicit at level 3 of our bubbles.

References

Ahrne, G., & Brunsson, N. (2008). *Meta-organizations.* Cheltenham: Edward Elgar Publishing.

Allison, T. H., Davis, B. C., Short, J. C., & Webb, J. W. (2015). Crowdfunding in a prosocial microlending environment: Examining the role of intrinsic versus extrinsic cues. *Entrepreneurship Theory and Practice, 39*(1), 53–73.

Alter, N. (2000). *La logique de l'innovation ordinaire.* Paris: PUF.

Alter, N. (2003). Mouvement et dyschronies dans les organisations. *L'Année sociologique, 53*(2), 489–514.

Arnason, J. P. (1993). Merleau-Ponty and Max Weber: An unfinished dialogue. *Thesis Eleven, 36*(1), 82–98.

Bitektine, A. (2011). Toward a theory of social judgments of organizations: The case of legitimacy, reputation, and status. *Academy of Management Review, 36*(1), 151–179.

Boltanski, L., & Thévenot, L. (1991). *De la justification: les économies de la grandeur.* Paris: Gallimard.

Bouncken, R. B., Komorek, M., & Kraus, S. (2015). Crowdfunding: The current state of research. *The International Business & Economics Research Journal, 14*(3), 407.

Boxenbaum, E., Huault, I., & Leca, B. (2016). Le tournant matériel dans la théorie néo-institutionnaliste. In F. X. de Vaujany, A. Hussenot, & J. F. Chanlat (Eds.), *Théories des organisations.* Paris: Economica.

de DiMaggio, P., & Powell, W. W. (1983). The iron cage revisited: Collective rationality and institutional isomorphism in organizational fields. *American Sociological Review, 48*(2), 147–160.

de Vaujany, F. X. (2006). Between Eternity and Actualization: the Difficult Co-evolution of the fields of Communication in the Vatican. *Communications of the AIS, 18*, 355–391.

de Vaujany, F. X. (2017). Pour un management paradoxal de nos pratiques de recherche-Invitation à un voyage immobile avec Merleau-Ponty. *Revue Française de Gestion, 43*(268), 11–39.

de Vaujany, F. X., & Vaast, E. (2014). If these walls could talk: The mutual construction of organizational space and legitimacy. *Organization Science, 25*(3), 713–731.

de Vaujany, F. X., & Vaast, E. (2016). Matters of visuality in legitimation practices: Dual iconographies in a meeting room. *Organization, 23*(5), 763–790.

de Vaujany, F. X., Fomin, V., Haefliger, S., & Lyytinen, K. (2018a). Rules, practices and Information Technology (IT): A trifecta of organizational regulation. *Information Systems Research*. https://doi.org/10.1287/isre.2017.0771.

de Vaujany, F. X., Aroles, J., & Laniray, P. (2018b). Towards a political philosophy of management: Performativity & visibility in management practices. *Philosophy of Management*. https://doi.org/10.1007/s40926-018-0091-4.

Della Fave, L. R. (1986). Toward an explication of the legitimation process. *Social Forces, 65*(2), 476–500.

Deroy, X. (2008). L'événement entrepreneurial et le modèle entrepreneurial. *Revue Française de Gestion, 7*, 51–63.

Deroy, X., & Clegg, S. (2011). When events interact with business ethics. *Organization, 18*(5), 637–653.

Dowling, J., & Pfeffer, J. (1975). Organizational legitimacy: Social values and organizational behavior. *Pacific sociological review, 18*, 122–136.

Elsbach, K. D. (1994). Managing organizational legitimacy in the California cattle industry: The construction and effectiveness of verbal accounts. *Administrative Science Quarterly, 39*, 57–88.

Friedland, R. (2012). The institutional logics perspective: A new approach to culture, structure, and process. *M@n@gement, 15*(5), 583–595.

Friedland, R. (2018). Moving institutional logics forward: Emotion and meaningful material practice. *Organization Studies, 39*(4), 515–542.

Friedland, R., & Alford, R. R. (1991). Bringing society back in: Symbols, practices, and institutional contradictions. In W. W. Powell & P. J. DiMaggio (Eds.), *The new institutionalism in organizational analysis* (pp. 232–263). Chicago: University of Chicago Press.

Garrett, L. E., Spreitzer, G. M., & Bacevice, P. (2014). Co-constructing a sense of community at work: The emergence of community in coworking spaces. *Academy of Management Proceedings, 2014*(1), 14004.

Giddens, A. (1984). *The constitution of society: Outline of the theory of structuration*. Berkeley: University of California Press.

Gond, J. P., Demers, C., & Michaud, V. (2017). Managing normative tensions within and across organizations. In W. K. Smith, M. W. Lewis, P. Jarzabkowski, & A. Langley (Eds.), *The Oxford handbook of organizational paradox* (pp. 239–259). Oxford: Oxford University Press.

Gosden, C. (1994). *Time and social being*. Cambridge, NIA: Blackwell publishers.

Granqvist, N., & Gustafsson, R. (2016). Temporal institutional work. *Academy of Management Journal, 59*(3), 1009–1035.

Greenwood, R., Díaz, A. M., Li, S. X., & Lorente, J. C. (2010). The multiplicity of institutional logics and the heterogeneity of organizational responses. *Organization Science, 21*(2), 521–539.

Gumport, P. J. (2000). Academic restructuring: Organizational change and institutional imperatives. *Higher Education, 39*(1), 67–91.

Halford, S. (2005). Hybrid workspace: Re-spatialisations of work, organisation and management. *New Technology, Work and Employment, 20*, 19–33.

Hatch, M. (2014). *The maker movement manifesto*. New York: McGraw-Hill Education.

Hayles, N. K. (2008). *How we became posthuman: Virtual bodies in cybernetics, literature, and informatics*. Chicago: University of Chicago Press.

Heidegger, M. (1927/1962). *Being and time* (J. Macquarrie & E. Robinson, Trans.). New York: Sunny Press.

Hernes, T. (2014). *A process theory of organization*. Oxford: Oxford University Press.

Hussenot, A., & Missonier, S. (2016). Encompassing stability and novelty in organization Studies: An events-based approach. *Organization Studies*. https://doi.org/10.1177/0170840615604497.

Introna, L. D. (2018). On the making of sense in sensemaking: Decentred sensemaking in the meshwork of life. *Organization Studies*. https://doi.org/10.1177/0170840618765579.

Jarzabkowski, P., Smets, M., Bednarek, R., Burke, G., & Spee, P. (2013). Institutional ambidexterity: Leveraging institutional complexity in practice. *Research in the Sociology of Organizations, 39*, 37–61.

Jones, C., Boxenbaum, E., & Anthony, C. (2013). The immateriality of material practices in institutional logics. *Research in the Sociology of Organizations, 39*, 51–75.

Kallinikos, J. (2003). Work, human agency and organizational forms: An anatomy of fragmentation. *Organization Studies, 24*(4), 595–618.

Kozinets, R. V. (2006). Click to connect: Netnography and tribal advertising. *Journal of Advertising Research, 46*(3), 279–288.

Kraatz, M. S., & Block, E. S. (2008). Organizational implications of institutional pluralism. *The Sage Handbook of Organizational Institutionalism, 840*, 243–275.

Lallement, M. (2015). *L'âge du faire: hacking, travail, anarchie*. Paris: Seuil.

Lefebvre, H. (1991). *The production of space* (Vol. 142). Oxford: Blackwell.

Lin, A., & Cornford, T. (2000). *Sociotechnical perspectives on emergence phenomena* (pp. 51–60). London: Springer.

Lindtner, S. (2015). Hacking with Chinese characteristics: The promises of the maker movement against China's manufacturing culture. *Science, Technology, & Human Values, 40*(5), 854–879.

Lounsbury, M. (2007). A tale of two cities: Competing logics and practice variation in the professionalizing of mutual funds. *Academy of Management Journal, 50*(2), 289–307.

Lounsbury, M., & Glynn, M. A. (2001). Cultural entrepreneurship: Stories, legitimacy, and the acquisition of resources. *Strategic Management Journal, 22*(6–7), 545–564.

Manning, S., & Bejarano, T. A. (2017). Convincing the crowd: Entrepreneurial storytelling in crowdfunding campaigns. *Strategic Organization, 15*(2), 194–219.

Merleau-Ponty, M. (1942). *La structure du comportement*. Paris: PUF.

Merleau-Ponty, M. (1945). *Phénoménologie de la perception*. Paris: Gallimard, 2013.

Merleau-Ponty, M. (1964). *Le visible et l'invisible: suivi de notes de travail* (Vol. 36). Paris: Gallimard.

Merleau-Ponty, M. (2003). *L'institution, la passivité*. Paris: Belin.

Meyer, J. W., & Rowan, B. (1977). Institutionalized organizations: Formal structure as myth and ceremony. *American Journal of Sociology, 83*, 340–363.

Monteiro, P., & Nicolini, D. (2015). Recovering materiality in institutional work: Prizes as an assemblage of human and material entities. *Journal of Management Inquiry, 24*(1), 61–81.

Nagy, B. G., Pollack, J. M., Rutherford, M. W., & Lohrke, F. T. (2012). The influence of entrepreneurs' credentials and impression management behaviors on perceptions of new venture legitimacy. *Entrepreneurship Theory and Practice, 36*(5), 941–965.

Ocasio, W. (1997). Towards an attention-based view of the firm. *Psychology, 1*, 403–404.

Oliver, C. (1991). Strategic responses to institutional processes. *Academy of Management Review, 16*(1), 145–179.

Pittz, T. G., Boje, D. M., Intindola, M. L., & Nicholson, S. (2017). 'COPE'ing with institutional pressures: A reintroduction of pragmatism to the study of organisations. *International Journal of Management Concepts and Philosophy, 10*(2), 113–129.

Proffitt, W., & Zahn, G. L. (2006). Design, but align: The role of organizational physical space, architecture and design in communicating organisational legitimacy. In S. R. Clegg & M. Kornberger (Eds.), *Space, organizations and management theory* (pp. 204–220). Copenhagen: Copenhagen Business School Press.

Reay, T., & Hinings, C. R. (2009). Managing the rivalry of competing institutional logics. *Organization Studies, 30*(6), 629–652.

Ricoeur, P. (1985). *Temps et récit. Tome III: Le temps raconté.* Paris: Le Seuil.

Schatzki, T. R. (2010). *The timespace of human activity: On performance, society, and history as indeterminate teleological events.* Lanham: Lexington Books.

Scott, W. R. (1995). *Institutions and organizations* (Vol. 2). Thousand Oaks: Sage.

Sloterdijk, P. (2011). *Bubbles: Spheres, volume I: Microspherology.* Los Angeles: Semiotext.

Stryker, R. (2000). Legitimacy processes as institutional politics: Implications for theory and research in the sociology of organizations. *Research in the Sociology of Organizations, 17,* 179–223.

Suchman, M. C. (1995). Managing legitimacy: Strategic and institutional approaches. *Academy of Management Review, 20*(3), 571–610.

Suddaby, R., & Greenwood, R. (2005). Rhetorical strategies of legitimacy. *Administrative Science Quarterly, 50*(1), 35–67.

Thornton, P. H. (2004). *Markets from culture: Institutional logics and organizational decisions in higher education publishing.* Stanford: Stanford University Press.

Thornton, P. H., Ocasio, W., & Lounsbury, M. (2012). *The institutional logics perspective.* Hoboken: John Wiley & Sons, Inc.

Voronov, M. (2014). Toward a toolkit for emotionalizing institutional theory. In *Emotions and the organizational fabric* (pp. 167–196). Bingley: Emerald Group Publishing Limited.

Voronov, M., & Vince, R. (2012). Integrating emotions into the analysis of institutional work. *Academy of Management Review, 37*(1), 58–81.

Varländer, S., de Vaujany, F. X., & Vaast, E. (2014). Exploring the intersection between space, legitimacy and institutional logics: A study of campus tours. *Workshop "Giving visual and material form to ideas, identity and imagination: Architecture, urbanism and sustainable construction"*, Renate Meyer, Candace Jones, Silviya Svejenova and Eva Boxenbaum, VU, Vienna, Austria, 12th and 13rd May 2014.

Weber, M. (1978). *Economy and society: An outline of interpretive sociology.* Berkeley: University of California Press.

Zimmerman, M. A., & Zeitz, G. J. (2002). Beyond survival: Achieving new venture growth by building legitimacy. *Academy of Management Review, 27*(3), 414–431.

13

Conclusion: Ontological Reflections on the Role of Materiality in Institutional Inquiry

François-Xavier de Vaujany, Anouck Adrot, Eva Boxenbaum, and Bernard Leca

The chapters in this book have illuminated four building blocks of debates about materiality in institutions: objects and artifacts, digitality and information, space and time, bodies and embodiment. Each block has been an opportunity to stress the relationships between theoretical,

F.-X. de Vaujany (✉) • A. Adrot
Université Paris-Dauphine PSL, Paris, France
e-mail: Francois-Xavier.deVAUJANY@Dauphine.fr;
Anouck.adrot@dauphine.fr

E. Boxenbaum
Department of Organization, Copenhagen Business School,
Copenhagen, Denmark

Centre de gestion scientifique (CGS), MINES ParisTech - PSL University, i3
UMR CNRS, Paris, France
e-mail: eb.ioa@cbs.dk

B. Leca
ESSEC Business School, Cergy-Pontoise, France
e-mail: bernard.leca@essec.edu

© The Author(s) 2019   **379**
F.-X. de Vaujany et al. (eds.), *Materiality in Institutions*, Technology, Work and
Globalization, https://doi.org/10.1007/978-3-319-97472-9_13

epistemological, methodological and ontological debates on institutional dynamics. Defining what an institution is or becomes, how it is performed and embodied, also have strong implications for the way it can be theorized and analyzed.

A prominent feature of this book is that materiality matters for legitimation. A bank may legitimate its existence and activities by building an impressive headquarter in the city center with a vast marble hall to welcome customers. This material existence signals to visitors that the bank is both obvious and irreversible. In contrast, other activities need to be materially flexible and regularly re-located to gain legitimacy. The use of digital infrastructures, flex offices, and mobility can materially convey discontinuities, for instance through a light, distributed, invisible materiality, which can imbue temporary or mobile activities with legitimacy.

Another prominent feature is that materiality enables the institutionalization of novel ideas (see e.g., Chap. 2). Materiality facilitates the comprehension and acceptance of novel ideas and enhances their diffusion and durability (see also the post-script). The malleability and flexibility of some material forms can also serve to adapt ideas to specific contexts and purposes, thereby enabling their institutionalization.

This edited volume has not only illuminated material dimensions of specific theoretical components, but has also started a deeper exploration of the ontological underpinnings of materiality in relation to institutional theory.

Some institutional research adopts a dualistic ontology (see Bitektine 2011), which involves a pre-existent entity that may evolve from being illegitimate to legitimate or, in contrast, that loses its legitimacy (see Chap. 6). In contrast, a phenomenological ontology posits that there are no pre-existing entities that can be gradually legitimated (see e.g., Chap. 7). For instance, in a crowdfunding operation, people may like a call, re-tweet it and comment upon it; they jointly explore and constitute an emergent phenomenon that is constantly undergoing change. Since the project does not exist independently of the process that constitutes it, there is no entity to legitimate and no audience to confer legitimacy upon it. In short, materiality may matter to legitimacy and institutionalization, but *how* it matters is not trivial. Ontological positions may span from

Marxist and critical realist perspectives to phenomenological and pragmatist orientations.

From an ontological perspective, the four types of materiality that structure the book (i.e., artifacts and objects, space and time, bodies and embodiment, and digitality and information) are intricately related to each other through their material properties (see e.g., Chap. 9 and the postface). The unbounded nature of materiality opens multiple possibilities for articulating the ontological relationship between their material properties (see Chap. 12). In this light, we encourage ontological reflexivity about the nature of materiality, including its properties and boundaries, and its role in institutional dynamics.

Among the four types of materiality, space and time appear as the heart of ontological discussions. A non-dualistic description of legitimation, institutional logics and institutional work may require an emergent, practice-based, and performative orientation. Scholars may draw inspiration from traditions beyond institutional theory. For instance, Merleau-Ponty's (1954–1955/2015) exploration of institutions and passivity or Deleuze's (1967) analysis of instincts and institutions may illuminate both actual and possible ontologies that could sustain the analysis of materiality in institutional dynamics as much as they stress the embodiment, temporalities and politics at stake in institutions. Materiality such as tools, artifacts, technologies, and buildings may appear as an 'encounter', a consequential matter of everyday activities. From a methodological perspective, ontological reflexivity, in particular on space and time, can be a source of creativity. Such reflexivity can foster the emergence of new methodologies, such as auto-ethnographies and ethnographies, which may gain renewed importance to the extent that they help overcome, or better bridge, levels of analysis or strata of the real (e.g., individual, groups, society, state).

In this edited volume, we have sought to engage authors and readers in reflecting upon the ontological and epistemological assumptions that implicitly guide institutional inquiry. Specifically, we aimed to stimulate the development of methodology and theory that can help integrate materiality coherently into institutionalist inquiry. We hope that readers will join us in this worthwhile quest.

References

Bitektine, A. (2011). Toward a theory of social judgments of organizations: The case of legitimacy, reputation, and status. *Academy of Management Review, 36*(1), 151–179.

Deleuze, G. (1967). *Instincts & institutions*. Paris: Hachette.

Merleau-Ponty, M. (1954–1955/2015). *L'institution, la passivité*. Paris: Belin.

14

Postface: Exploring the Material in Institutional Theory

Candace Jones

This article examines the relationship between materiality and institutional theory in two parts. The first part examines the chapters of the current volume and how these chapters enlighten our understanding of the relationships between materiality and institutional logics, institutional work and legitimation. I focus on empirical chapters because the relationships among materiality and aspects of institutional theory are clearer and more elaborated. The second part explores the material basis of institutions and offers a few thoughts on the gaps in and directions for future research in materiality and institutional theory.[1]

[1] I am grateful to the editors of the volume, François-Xavier de Vaujany, Anouck Adrot, Eva Boxenbaum and Bernard Leca, for their amazing work and inspired ideas that offer insight into materiality and provocations and new directions to explore in institutional theory. A part of this chapter is drawn from the keynote speech that I delivered to OAP at the 2016 Lisbon conference and the chapter that I was developing at that time with colleagues—Renate Meyer, Dennis Janczary and Markus Hollerher. I focused on materiality whereas they focused on the role of visuality in

C. Jones (✉)
University of Edinburgh Business School, Edinburgh, UK
e-mail: Candace.Jones@ed.ac.uk

© The Author(s) 2019
F.-X. de Vaujany et al. (eds.), *Materiality in Institutions*, Technology, Work and Globalization, https://doi.org/10.1007/978-3-319-97472-9_14

Institutions and Materiality: The Volume

The volume editors, François-Xavier de Vaujany, Anouck Adrot, Eva
Boxenbaum and Bernard Leca, explore the interaction between institutions and materiality in their introduction. One insight the editors offer
is the dominant slant of institutional theory toward a cognitive and ideational bias that focuses on discourse as data; they highlight discourse
analysis as the primary method to gain insight into institutional dynamics. This has left an important gap and area of contribution for the "analysis of how objects and artifacts contribute to institutional dynamics". A
second insight is the diversity of approaches that scholars take when uti-
lizing materiality in terms of ontology, epistemology and methodology.
The editors call for greater clarity and reflexivity about how a particular
approach to materiality reveals and hides insights into institutional
dynamics. The empirical articles in the volume offer greater clarity by
illuminating in concrete situations how materiality informs institutional
dynamics.

Institutional theory has tended to engage materiality in a limited way.
It has treated materiality either generically as resources (Thornton et al.
2012) or as carriers of institutions (Scott 2008). By conceptualizing
materiality as either resources or carriers, scholars suggest a relatively passive role of materiality in shaping institutions; they imply that artifacts
are inscribed or encoded with meaning, symbols or beliefs. This stance
shares common assumptions with several approaches in materiality, such
as material culture where artifacts are examined to discern cultural meaning, changes in cultural meaning systems and how artifacts reflect and
capture social dynamics such as status (Hicks and Beaudry 2010; Miller
2010).

Table 14.1 reveals chapters in the volume that are exceptionally clear
in how they treat material objects: either as carriers of institutions or as
performative in institutions. As carriers, material objects are encoded and
decoded by humans, whether MOOCs or classrooms, to represent logics
or enable institutional work of organizational practices, such as virtual

---

institutional theory. The chapter, "The material and visual basis for institutions" has been published
in Greenwood et al. (2017) *Sage Handbook of Organizational Institutionalism*.

Table 14.1 Institutional theory and materiality: some chapters and insights

	Institutional theory		
Materiality	Institutional logics	Institutional work	Legitimacy
Active role: performative	Material practices such as campus tours become the means by which institutional logics are either enacted or reconciled with one another through synecdoches or downplayed through asyndetons (de Vaujany, Winterstorm, Walander & Vaast)	Practices of war, how the military trains humans and their bodies to kill, shifting identities of soldiers to themselves, to society and to each other (Norholm Just & Kirkegaard) How change agents at Oxford engaged in material and discursive assemblages over time to change the organization (Arena & Douai)	Legitimation processes involve spatial, temporal and material practices—how space is appropriated and used to both elicit and render judgments (de Vaujany) Legitimacy of firefighters is revisited and re-established in six spaces— topology, virtuality, objects, self, others and conceptual what ifs —resulting in changes related to digital technology (Adrot & Bia-Figueiredo)
Passive role: carriers	Products as resource imprinting that signal conformity to logics and constrain action (Jourdan) Spaces (digital MOOCs versus a physical campus) as encoded materialization of distinct logics of education (free vs. premium) (Thomas, Abrunhosa, Canales)	Simulations and lifelike virtual mannequins are the material means by which medical institutions are enacted and situated (Felix, Arena & Conein)	Products as resource that audiences can observe and use to assess legitimacy of actions (Jourdan) How websites are material artifacts that instantiate and spread legitimation efforts to audiences (Santos)

simulations. As performative, material objects enact institutional logics, perform institutional work and generate legitimacy from audiences that view those material products, whether websites, digital dashboards or campuses. These articles push our understanding of materiality and how material objects, whether human bodies, or digital forms, shape institutions through either active and performative uses or as repositories of knowledge and logics that are encoded into the material object. The core insight is that cultural products, whether seen as active or passive, require active human agency to imbue them with meaning and ensure their continued relevance across time (Lawrence et al. 2001).

The Material Basis of Institutions: Enhancing Relative Permanence

Institutions are "relative permanence of a distinctly social sort" (Hughes 1936), providing stability and meaning to social life (Scott 2008). Two themes are highlighted in this definition of institutions and have been expanded and emphasized within institutional theory: the focus on human, rather than material, actors and permanence through sedimentation in a sign system. Both human interaction and permanence involve materials; yet, institutional theory has not explored this relationship adequately and its implications for both institutions and institutional theory are discussed next.

Relative Permanence Through Human Action

Human actors create that relative permanence of institutions through their actions. This focus on human actors is also mirrored in material theories of science and technology studies and sociomateriality perspectives, where human use of or interaction with tools, technology and material objects is the focus of attention (e.g., Orlikowski and Scott 2008). In these studies, institutions are captured in role relations and practices, which may shift when a technology changes (Barley 1986) or may reflect distinct power dynamics and interests of social groups in material objects, such as French laws that attempted to ban burkinis at beaches or hijabs in schools (McAuley 2016). These studies highlight how institutions are mutually constituted of things and people. As Durkheim (1897/1951: 313) argued: "it is not true that society is made up only of individuals; it also includes material things, which play an essential role in the common life…[that]…acts upon us from without". It is the relationship between humans and objects that enables human action to become institutions that have relative permanence. Human action and interaction with materials writ large have been examined; how materials influence that interaction is the less explored area that I wish to focus on.

Relative Permanence Through Sedimented Sign Systems

For most institutionalists, relative permanence is socially constructed and achieved through sedimentation in a sign system (Berger and Luckmann 1967; Jones et al. 2017). In this way, institutional theory emphasizes cognition and traces linguistic artifacts (Lawrence and Suddaby 2006; Lawrence et al. 2011; de Vaujany et al. 2018). Although this cognitive privilege is grounded in the work of Max Weber, who provided a "common start" for both North American and Scandinavian institutionalism (Czarniawska-Joerges and Joerges 1990: 3) and likened ideas to "switchmen", determin[ing]"the tracks along which action has been pushed by the dynamic of interest" (Weber 1958: 280), it has a parallel movement in anthropology with Mary Douglas' (1986) focus on institutions as being grounded in analogies with cognitive rather than material foundations. In the institutionalist approach, sign systems are primarily linguistic artifacts that are encoded into and transmitted by materials. For example, Scott (2003: 81) notes in passing that "writing on stone or clay is preserved longer than on papyrus, and the latter outlasts paper, but paper can readily be transported and more widely distributed".

Institutionalists are less likely to recognize the existence of material sign systems which are not primarily linguistic artifacts. An idea or concept, such as nationalism, is materialized and sedimented with colors or sounds through objects, such as flags and national anthems (Cerulo 1995), or embodied into people's actions, such as patriotism means standing with hand over heart rather than kneeling or with clenched fists raised above the head when one's national anthem is played. Moreover, material objects are not simply institutional carriers, but flexibly interpretive boundary objects (Star and Griesemer 1989) that are in relationship with other material objects (Law 2002) and with humans (Latour 1896, 1992). We cannot understand institutions if we do not understand the material artifacts (Pinch 2008). A key insight from material culture and social technical studies is that material artifacts have a duality: they are actors in—even if inert and not active agents—as well as carriers of institutions.

In short, for many institutional theories, the materiality that defines and enables sign systems is taken for granted despite the recognition by foundational sociologists that ideas and beliefs must be made material to signify; that is made exterior and objective (Berger and Luckmann 1967; Durkheim 1897/1951; Friedland 2001, 2013). As Latour argues (1986: 7): "You have to go and to come back with the 'things' if your moves are not to be wasted. But the 'things' have to be able to withstand the return trip without withering away". These moves demand not only relative permanence in the material artifact—otherwise the material object decays or fragments erasing the sign system—but also relative permanence, or a certain stability, in a meaning system because any sign system that is not relatively durable likely means that the sign system becomes open to multiple interpretations, such as McDonnell's (2010) work on AIDs campaign in Ghana shows. The decay of material sign systems influences the relative permanence of meaning systems. When the meaning of the sign systems fluctuates, the material may remain but it becomes uninterpretable to humans and may have limited impact on institutions.

Material artifacts not only underpin and support the sign systems but are also central to the relative permanence of meaning systems that define and direct institutions. In this way, materiality shapes institutions and institutions shape materiality. Materiality alters the durability, transferability and relationality by which meanings and practices are experienced and shared across time and space. In this way, materiality shapes how institutions are demarcated and become relatively permanent and the properties of materials—their durability, transferability and relationality—influence the capacity of materials to aid institutions in becoming relatively permanent. These material properties of durability, transferability and relationality and their influence on institutions are discussed next.

Materiality Underpins Institutions: Durability, Transferability and Relationality

These three aspects of materiality—durability, transferability and relationality—have not been systematically examined within institutional theory and their absence suggests that we do not yet have a fully informed understanding of how relative permanence of institutions is constructed and stabilized because materiality enables durability and transferability of institutions across time and space (Jones et al. 2013, 2017).

Durability is a property of material artifacts, such as strength, flexibility and rates of decay. Durability gives "structure to social institutions… persistence to behavior patterns" (Gieryn 2002: 35). When we perceive material objects or practices as illegitimate or wish to undermine an institution, we strike at and attempt to eradicate the material objects that signify the institution (Jones and Massa 2013). Thus, we burn literary books that are deemed pornographic. We destroy religious icons from rival groups, whether Protestants toward Catholics during the Reformation, or Islamic State of Iraq and the Levant (ISIL)/ Islamic State in Iraq and Syria (ISIS) toward traditional Muslims in current times. Materiality is also critical to how we engender familiarity of innovations to enable comprehension and establish cognitive legitimacy. For example, Edison designed the electric lightbulb to resemble the familiar form of gas lamp (shape of bulb, flickering) and by imitating taken-for-granted material forms (surface features) helped to secure acceptance of electricity. In short, Edison needed to "overcome the institutions—the existing understandings and patterns of action—that had, over the fifty years of the gas industry's existence, accreted around these fundamental physical properties and now maintained the stability of the gas system" (Hargadon and Douglas 2001, p. 493). The durability of material objects may limit or enable change in institutions and cultural products and offers insights for future research. For example, when buildings are constructed to be adaptable, they enable learning by the building and its users and con- structors over time (Brand 1994), such as modern architecture with open floor plans (Jones et al. 2012). In these cases, the temporal patterns and material markers of institutions may leave residues that trace history and interpretations in the buildings themselves, or if buildings are restrictive and non-adaptive, then the material artifact will be either demolished, and its absence becomes an interesting focus of study, or it requires changes in institutions, such as preservation laws, to protect the building and its history encoded into the building (Jones and Svejenova 2018), which also becomes a fruitful way to study institutional processes and change.

Transferability involves the mobility of material artifacts, which influ- ences how easily ideas are shared within groups and translated across dif- ferent groups (Latour 1986). Material artifacts that can travel or that link distinct groups are called boundary objects, which include sketches, pro- totypes or blueprints that coordinate action among diverse groups (Bechky 2003), transfer knowledge (Carlile 2002) and generate locally situated meanings from abstract knowledge (Thurk and Fine 2003). Boundary objects "are both plastic enough to adapt to local needs…yet robust enough to maintain a common identity across sites" (Star and Griesemer 1989: 393). Although the focus has been on how boundary objects are portable and can connect groups, the transferability of mate- rial elements may be their material form, or shape, rather than a specific material object. For example, a spire with a cross is easily recognized worldwide as a Christian church. The tallest material object in a com- munity often signifies what is most worshipped, whether a minaret in Islam, a commercial skyscraper in capitalist societies, or a church spire in early Christian societies. In these cases, the form and meaning of the tall- est building becomes a boundary object that links members to a specific institution and is also translated as it travels across time and space (Sahlin-Anderson 1996). The transferability of material artifacts or material forms enables change, diffusion and translation of institutions. The implication and future direction for research is that the transferability of materials shapes discursive forms of legitimation and institutional work through the speed and transfer of information and how communication is enacted.[2] The communication may be virtual interactions and connections (e.g., email, Facebook, snapchat); the communication and transfer of information may expand or restrict institutional work and legitimation strategies by shaping who can communicate with whom and the depth and quality of interaction (e.g., 140 word tweets).

Relationality emphasizes how the relations among ideas, objects and people shape the relative permanence and meaning of institutions. For example, a religion has a deity and beliefs, worshippers and clergy, a special building and objects. Not only does an object have stable networks of relations (e.g., a functioning ship has oars, sails, crew, water, wind) (Law 2002: 95), but it has a relationality with ideas and people. It is this relationality that enables (in)coherence and (in)stability in practices and meaning systems. For example, the automobile had to establish its reputation and viability by highlighting the similarity between horses and cars. Cars had to demonstrate that they were faster and more reliable than the horse that they were replacing (Rao 1994). This historical knowledge and association of cars with horses was still highlighted 100 years later by Ford in its ads and naming strategies: the Mustang as the sportscar. The ads showed a race horse with jockey sprinting next to a speeding Ford Mustang, imbuing the new car with symbolic meaning—fast, youthful, free, spirited and elite. By imitating material assemblages, social actors can reframe practices and meanings. Another example is how film entrepreneurs gained legitimacy for their emerging industry by imitating the material assemblages of Broadway plays, including narrative forms as the basis of films which were played by actors in lavish theaters rather than scientific films viewed individually in peep houses called kinetoscopes (Jones 2001). This relationality creates polyvocality and "enables different meanings or uses" for material objects (McDonnell 2010: 1806), which shapes an institution's durability over time: how

---

[2] Illustrations of the transferability of materiality and its impacts on information exchanges can be found in Chaps. 6 and 8. In Chap. 6, Adrot and Bia-Figueiredo examine the influence of institutional change on information transmission, partly fostered by the implementation and adoption of a standard collaborative digital platform. In Chap. 8, Santos explains how entrepreneurs in the game industry align their practices to standards within a specific field frame.

actors, objects and meanings can be reinterpreted to adjust to social changes.[3] Prior research has tended to ignore the material and relational basis of institutions and their meaning systems.

Relationality of material objects is another relatively understudied topic within institutional theory. The relationality of material objects, whether technologies or human bodies, is vital to which institutions are enacted, supported, valued and appropriated. For example, the color red became the basis for global trade wars in the sixteenth century as countries sought to identify and then control cochineal, bugs on cacti plants, that produced the most vibrant red Europe had ever seen (Greenfield 2005). Color and the desire for color still shapes our institutions today, such as the fashion industry with the company Pantone setting the color that drives production of fabrics for clothes, household goods and fashion and its semiotic system. A relatively understudied area for institutions is the intersection of how ideas, such as what red represents and why it is valued, and materiality and material practices (which goods are produced and how the core ingredients for a vibrant red are secured). This intersection will illuminate not only institutional processes, such as trade practices, globalization processes and company research and development, but also which material objects are produced. A material relational approach can engender a potential synergy and fruitful dialogue of institutional scholars with distinct disciplines such as material culture (anthropology, architecture, cultural history), semiotics, actor network theory and structural network approaches. By examining these relational networks, we reveal the material basis of institutions and can offer important insights into the foundations of institutions and institutional dynamics (e.g., change and stability).

This short postface has sought to reveal how a material approach to institutions may offer new avenues of research and new insights into institutional processes because materiality influences the relative permanence of institutions and institutional practices. Thus, materiality should be central rather than peripheral to institutional analysis.

---

[3] Chapter 11, by Norholm and Kirkegaard, provides a nice description of a possible assemblage between discourse, bodies and ideas through the investigation of the representation of the killing body's plasticity in the documentary entitled Armadillo.

References

Barley, S. R. (1986). Technology as an occasion for structuring: Evidence from observations of CT scanners and the social order of radiology departments. *Administrative Science Quarterly, 31*, 78–108.

Bechky, B. A. (2003). Sharing meaning across occupational communities: The transformation of understanding on a production floor. *Organization Science, 14*(3), 312–330.

Berger, P. L., & Luckmann, T. (1967). *The social construction of reality: A treatise in the sociology of knowledge*. New York: Anchor Books.

Brand, S. (1994). *How buildings learn: What happens after they are built*. New York: Penguin Books.

Carlile, P. R. (2002). A pragmatic view of knowledge and boundaries: Boundary objects in new product development. *Organization Science, 13*(4), 442–455.

Cerulo, K. (1995). *Identity designs: The sights and sounds of a nation*, The Arnold and Caroline Rose Book Series of the American Sociological Association. New Brunswick: Rutgers University Press.

Czarniawska-Joerges, B., & Joerges, B. (1990). Linguistic artifacts at service of organizational control. In P. Gagliardi (Ed.), *Symbols and artifacts: Views of the corporate landscape* (pp. 339–379). Berlin: de Gruyter.

de Vaujany, X.-F., Adrot, A., Boxenbaum, E., & Leca, B. (2018). Introduction. In F.-X. De Vaujany, A. Adrot, E. Boxenbaum, & B. Leca (Eds.), *Materiality in institutions: Spaces, embodiment and technology in management and organization*. New York: Palgrave Macmillan.

Durkheim, É. (1951). *Suicide: A study in sociology*. Glencoe: The Free Press.

Friedland, R. (2001). Religious nationalism and the problem of collective representation. *Annual Review of Sociology, 27*, 125–152.

Friedland, R. (2013). God, love and other good reasons for practice: Thinking through institutional logics. In M. Lounsbury & E. Boxenbaum (Eds.), *Research in the sociology of organizations*. Oxford: Elsevier Ltd.

Gieryn, T. F. (2002). What buildings do. *Theory and Society, 31*(1), 35–74.

Greenfield, A. B. (2005). *A perfect red*. New York: Harper Perennial Books.

Greenwood, R., Oliver, C., Lawrence, T., & Meyer, R. E. (2017). *Sage handbook of organizational institutionalism* (2nd ed.). London: SAGE Publications.

Hargadon, A. B., & Douglas, Y. (2001). When innovations meet institutions: Edison and the design of the electric light. *Administrative Science Quarterly, 46*(3), 476–501.

Hicks, D., & Beaudry, M. C. (2010). Introduction: Material culture studies: A reactionary view. In M. C. Beaudry & D. Hicks (Eds.), *The Oxford handbook of material culture studies* (pp. 1–21). Oxford: Oxford University Press.

Hughes, E. C. (1936). The ecological aspect of institutions. *American Sociological Review, 1*, 180–189.

Jones, C. (2001). Co-evolution of entrepreneurial careers, institutional rules and competitive dynamics in American film, 1895–1920. *Organization Studies, 22*(6), 911–944.

Jones, C., & Massa, F. (2013). From novel practice to consecrated exemplar: Unity temple as a case of institutional evangelizing. *Organization Studies, 34*(8), 1099–1136.

Jones, C., & Svejenova, S. (2018). The architecture of city identity: A multi-modal study of Barcelona and Boston. *Research in the Sociology of Organizations, 54B*, 203–234.

Jones, C., Boxenbaum, E., & Anthony, C. (2013). The immateriality of material practices in institutional logics. In M. Lounsbury & E. Boxenbaum (Eds.), Institutional logics in action, part A: pp. 51–75. Research in the sociology of organizations, 39. Bingley: Emerald Group.

Jones, C., Maoret, M., Massa, F. G., & Svejenova, S. (2012). Rebels with a cause: The formation, contestation and expansion of the de novo category modern architecture, 1870–1975. *Organization Science, 23*, 1523–1545.

Jones, C., Meyer, R. E., Janczary, D., & Hollerher, M. (2017). The material and visual basis of institutions. In R. Greenwood, C. Oliver, T. Lawrence, & R. E. Meyer (Eds.), *Sage handbook of organizational institutionalism* (2nd ed., pp. 651–678). London: SAGE Publications.

Latour, B. (1986). Visualization and cognition: Thinking with eyes and hands. In H. Kuklick (Ed.), *Knowledge and society: Studies in the sociology of culture: Past and present* (Vol. 6). London: JAI Press.

Latour, B. (1992). Where are the missing masses? The sociology of a few mundane artifacts. In W. E. Bijker & J. Law (Eds.), *Shaping technology/building society: Studies in sociotechnical change* (pp. 225–258). Cambridge, MA: MIT Press.

Law, J. (2002). Objects and spaces. *Theory, Culture & Society, 19*(5–6), 91–105.

Lawrence, T. B., & Suddaby, R. (2006). Institutions and institutional work. In S. R. Clegg, C. Hardy, T. B. Lawrence, & W. R. Nord (Eds.), *The Sage handbook of organization studies* (2nd ed., pp. 215–254). London: SAGE Publications.

Lawrence, T. B., Suddaby, R., & Leca, B. (2011). Institutional work: Refocusing studies of organization. *Journal of Management Inquiry, 20*, 52–58.

Lawrence, T. B., Winn, M. I., & Jennings, P. D. (2001). The temporal dynamics of institutionalization. *Academy of Management Review, 26*, 624–644.

McAuley, J. (2016). France's burkini debate: About a bathing suit and a country's peculiar secularism. See www.washingtonpost.com/world/europe/frances-burkini-debate-about-a-bathing-suit-and-a-countrys-peculiar-secularism/2016/08/26/48ec273e-6bad-11e6-91cb-ecb5418830e9_story.html?noredirect=on&utm_term=.4480a60752f3. Downloaded 9 May 2018.

McDonnell, T. E. (2010). Cultural objects as objects: Materiality, urban space, and the interpretation of AIDS campaigns in Accra, Ghana. *American Journal of Sociology, 115*, 1800–1852.

Miller, D. (2010). *Stuff*. Cambridge: Polity Press.

Orlikowski, W. J., & Scott, S. V. (2008). Sociomateriality: Challenging the separation of technology, work and organization. *Academy of Management Annals, 2*, 433–474.

Pinch, T. (2008). Technology and institutions: Living in a material world. *Theory and Society, 37*(5), 461–483.

Rao, H. (1994). The social construction of reputation: Certification contests, legitimation, and the survival of organizations in the American automobile industry: 1895–1912. *Strategic Management Journal, 15*(S1), 29–44.

Sahlin-Andersson, K. (1996). Imitating by editing success: The construction of organizational fields. In B. Czarniawska & G. Sevón (Eds.), *Translating organizational change* (pp. 69–92). Berlin: de Gruyter.

Scott, W. R. (2003). Institutional carriers: Reviewing modes of transporting ideas over time and space and considering their consequences. *Industrial and Corporate Change, 12*, 879–894.

Scott, W. R. (2008). *Institutions and organizations: Ideas and interests* (3rd ed.). Thousand Oaks: Sage.

Star, S. L., & Griesemer, J. R. (1989). Institutional ecology, 'translations' and boundary objects: Amateurs and professionals in Berkeley's Museum of Vertebrate Zoology. *Social Studies of Science, 19*(3), 387–420.

Thornton, P. H., Ocasio, W., & Lounsbury, M. (2012). *The institutional logics perspective: A new approach to culture, structure and process*. Oxford: Oxford University Press.

Thurk, J., & Fine, G. A. (2003). The problem of tools: Technology and the sharing of knowledge. *Acta Sociologica, 46*(2), 107–117.

Weber, M. (1958 [1946]). Essays in sociology. In M. Weber, H. Gerth, & C. W. Mills (Eds.), *From Max Weber*. New York: Oxford University Press.

Index

© The Author(s) 2019
F.-X. de Vaujany et al. (eds.), *Materiality in Institutions*, Technology, Work and
Globalization, https://doi.org/10.1007/978-3-319-97472-9